Genders and Sexualities in History

Series Editors

John Arnold
University of London
Birkbeck College
London, UK

Sean Brady
University of London
Birkbeck College
London, UK

Joanna Bourke
University of London
Birkbeck College
London, UK

Aim of the Series

Palgrave Macmillan's series, Genders and Sexualities in History, accommodates and fosters new approaches to historical research in the fields of genders and sexualities. The series promotes world-class scholarship, which concentrates upon the interconnected themes of genders, sexualities, religions/religiosity, civil society, politics and war. Historical studies of gender and sexuality have, until recently, been more or less disconnected fields. In recent years, historical analyses of genders and sexualities have synthesised, creating new departures in historiography. The additional connectedness of genders and sexualities with questions of religion, religiosity, development of civil societies, politics and the contexts of war and conflict is reflective of the movements in scholarship away from narrow history of science and scientific thought, and history of legal processes approaches, that have dominated these paradigms until recently. The series brings together scholarship from Contemporary, Modern, Early Modern, Medieval, Classical and Non-Western History. The series provides a diachronic forum for scholarship that incorporates new approaches to genders and sexualities in history.

More information about this series at
http://www.springer.com/series/15000

Aidan Beatty

Masculinity and Power in Irish Nationalism, 1884–1938

palgrave
macmillan

Aidan Beatty
Azrieli Institute of Israel Studies
& School of Canadian Irish Studies
Concordia University
Montreal, QC, Canada

Genders and Sexualities in History
ISBN 978-1-137-44099-0 (hardcover)   ISBN 978-1-137-44101-0 (eBook)
ISBN 978-1-349-68416-8 (softcover)
DOI 10.1057/978-1-137-44101-0

Library of Congress Control Number: 2016953140

© The Editor(s) (if applicable) and The Author(s) 2016, First softcover printing 2018
The author(s) has/have asserted their right(s) to be identified as the author(s) of this work in accordance with the Copyright, Designs and Patents Act 1988.

This work is subject to copyright. All rights are solely and exclusively licensed by the Publisher, whether the whole or part of the material is concerned, specifically the rights of translation, reprinting, reuse of illustrations, recitation, broadcasting, reproduction on microfilms or in any other physical way, and transmission or information storage and retrieval, electronic adaptation, computer software, or by similar or dissimilar methodology now known or hereafter developed.
The use of general descriptive names, registered names, trademarks, service marks, etc. in this publication does not imply, even in the absence of a specific statement, that such names are exempt from the relevant protective laws and regulations and therefore free for general use. The publisher, the authors and the editors are safe to assume that the advice and information in this book are believed to be true and accurate at the date of publication. Neither the publisher nor the authors or the editors give a warranty, express or implied, with respect to the material contained herein or for any errors or omissions that may have been made.

Printed on acid-free paper

This Palgrave Macmillan imprint is published by Springer Nature
The registered company is Macmillan Publishers Ltd. London

For Leslie

Series Editors' Preface

Masculinity and Power in Irish Nationalism is a groundbreaking study of the development of a distinctly Irish nationalism that had at its core an imagined, vigorous and agrarian masculinity. In this fascinating and highly original book, Aidan Beatty explores how Irish nationalists conflated ideas of national sovereignty with masculine strength – and submissive, pious femininity – in ideas of Irish independence and national destiny. Beginning in the 1880s, the trajectories of these notions of masculinity and power in Irish political and cultural life are traced, culminating in Éamon de Valera's sclerotic vision of the ideal Irish agrarian homeland in the 1930s.

Ideologies and practices of distinctly Irish concepts of masculinity, power and nation are compared resonantly with concepts of masculinity in Jewish Zionism in this period. Through this comparative lens, Beatty opens new fields of analysis in European postcolonialism, and the development of normative, culturally specific and nationalistic masculinities at Europe's fringes. In common with all volumes in the Genders and Sexualities in History series, *Masculinity and Power in Irish Nationalism* presents a multifaceted and meticulously researched scholarly study, and is a sophisticated contribution to our understanding of the past.

John H. Arnold, Joanna Bourke and Sean Brady

Acknowledgements

This work began as a dissertation at the University of Chicago. During my time at Chicago, I benefited greatly from the support and advice of my doctoral committee: Leora Auslander and Maud Ellmann (who chaired my committee), Alison Winter and Fredrik Albritton Jonsson. Similarly, Declan Kiberd at the University of Notre Dame has been an invaluable source of advice and assistance since I first invited myself to his office in South Bend.

Profs. Susan Gal, David Nirenberg and Bernard Wasserstein discussed specific aspects of this project with me and gave me much useful advice. I am also grateful to the participants in the University of Chicago's Transnational Approaches to Modern Europe workshop and the Gender and Sexuality Studies Working Group, where I presented early versions of two chapters.

I wish to thank all the staff members of the 13 different archives that I consulted for this work. I gratefully acknowledge the help of the National Archives of Ireland and their Director, who granted permission to reproduce material from their files. A year of research at archives in Ireland and a shorter visit to Israeli archives was funded with grants from the Nicholson Center for British Studies, the Chicago Center for Jewish Studies and various grants from the University of Chicago's History Department. I also received a writing fellowship from the Mellon Foundation and the University of Chicago/Division of the Social Sciences. I am grateful to all the staff at the University of Chicago History Department, particularly David Goodwine and Sonja Rusnak, for their assistance. The process of converting my dissertation into a book was carried out at Concordia University and I am grateful to all my colleagues at the Azrieli Institute of Israel Studies and the School of Canadian Irish Studies.

I have presented various versions of this research at conferences in the USA, Canada, Ireland, the UK and Israel, and am very appreciative of the comments and advice I received. At various stages, I have discussed this project with Prof. Sikata Banerjee (University of Victoria), Prof. Guy Beiner (Ben-Gurion University), Prof. David Biale (UC-Davis), Dr. Michael Feige, z"l (Ben-Gurion Research Institute), Prof. David Fitzpatrick (TCD), Prof. Dermot Keogh (UCC), Prof. Maria Luddy (Warwick), Prof. Timothy McMahon (Marquette), Dr. Ríona Nic Congáil (St Patrick's College, Dublin), Prof. Brian Ó Conchubhair (Notre Dame), Prof. Derek Penslar (Oxford), Oriol Poveda (Uppsala University), Dr. Susannah Riordan (UCD), Dr. Elaine Sisson (DLIADT), and Prof. Ghil'ad Zuckermann (University of Adelaide) and am grateful for the thoughtful advice they offered about archives, arguments and my potential mistakes.

I am grateful to Matan Boord (Tel-Aviv University) for discussing his own research on masculinity and Zionism with me, as well as for helping me clean up my Hebrew translations.

My good friends Peter Hession, Susanna Klosko and Adam Larragy all read drafts of this book and thankfully helped me identify some early problems.

I am grateful to Cathal Brennan and John Dorney for their invitation to publish an early snippet of this research through their *Irish Story* website. My thanks to Mike O'Toole for his assistance with preparing images for publication.

On my many trips back home, my parents, Jane and TJ, and my sisters, Sheila and Claire, were a great source for free accommodation, advice on Irish-language translations, involuntary archival assistants, as well as so much else besides. I owe a similarly large debt to my adopted American family: Bill and Ruthe, Leah and Dean, and Lowell and Henrik.

Most of all I am endlessly grateful to my wife, Leslie Petrovich, for her support, patience and love. This book is dedicated to her.

Glossary of Irish Terms

Árd Fheis
'High Festival', the term used by most Irish political parties to describe their annual general meeting.

Cumann na mBan
'The Women's Organisation', a female militia linked to the Volunteers and, later, the IRA.

Cumann na nGaedheal
'Organisation of the Irish', conservative party founded by the pro-treaty elements of Sinn Féin, and which dominated politics in 1920s Ireland.

Dáil Éireann
'Assembly of Ireland', name used for the parliament of the provisional government of the Irish Republic during the War of Independence, and by that of the Irish Free State. A member of the Dáil is a Teachta Dála (TD), Representative of the Dáil.

Fianna Éireann
'Soldiers of Ireland', boys' militia founded in 1909 and modelled on the Boy Scouts. It was later formally linked to the IRA.

Fianna Fáil
'Soldiers of Irish Destiny', populist Republican party founded in 1926 by Eamon de Valera and his supporters within Sinn Féin.

Fine Gael
'Tribe of the Irish', conservative party formed in 1932 from the merging of *Cumann na nGaedheal*, the smaller Centre Party, and the fascist-inclined Blueshirts.

Gaeltacht
'Irishness', the Irish-speaking parts of Ireland. The Gaeltacht is often contrasted with the Galltacht, 'foreignness', the Anglophone parts of Ireland.

An Garda Síochána
'The Guardians of the Peace', the post-1922 Irish police force. A single member is a Garda (pl.Gardaí).

Óglaigh na hÉireann
'Irish Young Warriors', term used as the Irish title of the Irish Volunteers, the Irish Republican Army, and the national army of the post-1922 state.

Seoinín	'Little John', pejorative term for a sycophantic Irish person who apes English customs and manners (pl. Seoiníní).
Sinn Féin	'Ourselves Alone', name used for various nationalist parties since the early twentieth century. The name is intended to suggest an ethos of nationalist self-reliance.

Contents

1 Introduction — 1

2 Time, Gender and the Politics of National Liberation, 1916–1923 — 21

3 Organised Manhood — 57

4 The Genders of Nationalist Space — 91

5 National Sovereignty, Male Power and the Irish Language — 121

6 Fianna Fáil, Masculinity and the Economics of National Salvation — 153

7 Regulating Sex, Gender and Leisure in the Irish Free State — 187

8 Conclusions — 225

Bibliography — 235

Government Publications 237

Newspapers 239

Published Primary Sources 241

Index 257

List of Figures

Fig. 2.1	*De Valera as Ancient Irish Woman*, Election Poster, 1917	25
Fig. 2.2	*Free State Freaks and Cowardly Truceleers*, Civil War Posters, c.1922	41
Fig. 3.1	*Jew Regard for the Law*, Garda Cartoon, 1924	58
Fig. 3.2	*The Man of the Future*, GAA Advertisement, 1912	63
Fig. 3.3	*A Study in "Still" Life*, Garda Cartoon, 1924	72
Fig. 5.1	*On Which Side Are You?*, Gaelic League poster, 1913	129
Fig. 6.1	*The Economic History of the Land of Erin*, Fianna Fáil pamphlet, 1932	154
Fig. 6.2	*To The Galilee!*, Poster for the Jewish National Fund (JNF), 1938	158
Fig. 7.1	*Gendering the Memory of the Rising*, Postcards, c. 1917	189
Fig. 8.1	*Dressing Up As Ancient Irish Men*, Tailteann Games, 1924	226

CHAPTER 1

Introduction

> The ideal Ireland that we would have, the Ireland that we dreamed of, would be the home of a people who valued material wealth only as a basis for right living, of a people who, satisfied with frugal comfort, devoted their leisure to the things of the spirit—a land whose countryside would be bright with cosy homesteads, whose fields and villages would be joyous with the sounds of industry, with the romping of sturdy children, the contest of athletic youths and the laughter of happy maidens, whose firesides would be forums for the wisdom of serene old age. The home, in short, of a people living the life that God desires that men should live.[1]

Thus spoke de Valera, in his famous 1943 St Patrick's Day speech, laying out his vision of the ideal homeland that Irish men might soon be called upon to protect from a possible German or Allied invasion.[2] This was nothing short of an elegy to an imaginary, ever-agrarian Ireland, with harmonious ideals of vigorous masculinity and submissive femininity at the centre. Long before de Valera's speech, however, Irish nationalists had already been conflating national sovereignty and masculine strength. National power was conceived of as male potency and the recovery of one would supposedly parallel the recovery of the other. This book is a history of how these notions of power and masculinity came to predominance in Irish nationalism, of the forces that fed into them, and of the ideological work that masculinity and power did for

Irish nationalism. This work traces these ideas back to the 1880s and shows how they continued to have resonance into the 1930s. There is an especial focus, however, on the years between 1912 and 1923.

An Irish Revolution?

Between 1912 and 1914, the British Liberal Party, then ruling in a minority government reliant on the support of the Irish Parliamentary Party (IPP), oversaw the passage through Westminster of the Third Home Rule Bill. It looked as if Irish Home Rule, a contentious issue for much of the previous century, was finally about to be achieved. An independent parliament would rule over Ireland for the first time since 1800. In response to this dread scenario, unionists in the northern counties of Ireland, spurred on by a British Conservative party eager to score political points against their Liberal opponents, formed an Ulster Volunteer Force and promised to resist the imposition of Home Rule. Nationalists reciprocated with their own volunteer force, the Irish Volunteers. British troops stationed at the Curragh, not far from Dublin, had already threatened mutiny rather than impose Home Rule. As violence came more to the surface in Ireland, the Liberal government began to have serious doubts about their bill. The international crisis of 1914 thus provided a convenient extrication, allowing the Liberals to postpone full enactment of Home Rule until the ceasing of hostilities on the continent. The IPP's leader, John Redmond, desiring to take control of the Irish Volunteers, promised Lloyd George that this citizens' militia, by then numbering more than 100,000 men, would support the British war effort. Redmond's machinations split the Volunteers along pro- and anti-Imperial lines.

In 1916, a small group of impatient radicals from the anti-Imperial faction staged a rebellion in Dublin, the Easter Rising, hoping to force through Irish independence. The Rising itself was a military failure, but the harsh British response, ranging from the shelling of central Dublin to mass arrests and the execution of the Rising's leaders, helped to create a *post facto* legitimisation. Before the end of the First World War, the more radical Irish nationalists had regrouped under the banner of Sinn Féin, despite this party's not having been directly involved in the rebellion itself. In late 1918 Sinn Féin won a majority of Irish seats in the Westminster general election. Refusing to take their places in the British parliament, they instead formed an Irish assembly and claimed it as the heir of the 'Republic' that had been abortively declared in Easter Week.

In parallel to this high politics, a low-level guerrilla war began in pockets across the country, mainly involving the Volunteers, soon to be renamed the Irish Republican Army. Slowly, Britain lost control of large swathes of the country and an embryonic republic began to emerge. Repressive responses on the part of the British government exacerbated Irish nationalist sympathies.

Not for the last time in the twentieth century, the British constitution collapsed under the weight of Irish politics.[3] By the summer of 1921 the situation had become serious enough for the British government to begin treaty negotiations to end the violence. Nonetheless, the situation was not grave enough to force the British government to make too many concessions. Rather than a fully sovereign republic, the Anglo-Irish Treaty of 1921 offered a limited sovereignty within the Empire, a parliament that would swear loyalty to the Crown, and partition of the north east corner of the island.[4] The Treaty led to the founding of the Irish Free State, but its terms were odious enough for its opponents and supporters to first wage civil war against each other.

The period between 1912 and 1923 is the most heavily privileged in modern Irish history and is conventionally seen as the Irish Revolution.[5] This period provides the central temporal focus of this book. Unlike other accounts, however, I am wary of using the term 'revolution'. As an analytical tool, the word 'revolution' can be fraught with problems. As Immanuel Wallerstein notes, it is a term that connotes 'sudden, dramatic, and extensive change. It emphasizes discontinuity.' Yet, when many scholars come to study 'revolutions', what they usually end up studying are the much slower long-term social changes that feed into ostensibly sudden ruptures with the past.[6] Therefore, this book suggests that rather than identifying a sudden rupture in Irish life in the second decade of the twentieth century, as many Irish historians have done, it is more profitable to trace a long arc of development from the latter nineteenth century well into the twentieth. In addition to studying the aetiology and ideological work of Irish nationalist ideals of masculinity, a secondary aim of this work is to question the historiographical utility of a term like 'revolution' for understanding the events of 1916 or 1922.

Taking a cue from Frank Mort's recent discussion of how 'Victorianism', an ideology of public respectability, outlasted Victoria's reign by at least a half-century, I argue that much that has come to be associated with the 'Irish Revolution' (meritocracy, violence, the excitement of acquiring national power) not only predated 1916 by several decades but also lasted well into the twentieth century.[7] There was perhaps as much continuity as there was rupture and change and this book offers an argument not all that different from Patrick Maume's notion of a 'long gestation'[8] in Irish politics and culture. Additionally, it is impossible to understand Irish nationalist culture outside of a British imperial context. The form and content of Irish nationalism, how it conceived of the state and of the economy, as well its tropes of muscular men and subtly expressed anxieties about racial purity, were not only a reaction against British rule but also at the same time, paradoxically, strongly influenced by contemporary British politics.

Michael de Nie argues that in Victorian Britain, the Irish were seen as inferior on grounds of race, religion and class: 'In British eyes, the eternal Paddy was forever a Celt, a Catholic, and a peasant.'[9] Victorian cartoons and caricatures often focused on the supposed physical deformities of Irish men and provide a useful insight into racial attitudes. Irish men were depicted as 'dark, heavy-jawed criminals, semibestial ape-men, or even outright inhuman monsters', and thus, 'these Irish subjects inhabited a lower branch on the human family tree.'[10] Alison Winter similarly observes the harshly negative perceptions that Irish immigrants to Victorian cities faced: 'The English saw the Irish poor as the lowest of the low. By their reckoning the Irish were purveyors of physical and social disease, threatening the health of the social body by their very presence in the urban centers.'[11] And Theodore Allen, in his polemical study of *The Invention of the White Race*, notes the similarities between English perceptions of the Irish 'race', and anti-black racism in Anglo-America.[12] Put plainly, the Irish were seen as an inferior race and this work argues that these British racial accusations had a determining impact on Irish nationalists. Irish nationalism was a concerted effort to disprove such stereotypes and create a more prideful self-image of a 'white' nation. Crafting an image of strong and racially redeemed Irish men was a key part of this.

In fact, a large corpus of literary scholarship has argued that Irish culture should be understood as a postcolonial culture, in the manner in which it strove to refute negative anti-Irish stereotypes.[13] Whether or not Ireland was a 'colony' in any conventional sense remains open to question. In terms of economics, for example, there is a large dose of fuzziness as to whether Ireland was a colony of Britain or merely an impoverished, mostly rural, periphery. It is quite debatable if nineteenth-century Ireland was more akin to the Raj or to rural Cornwall.[14] In addition, while coercive social engineering is often a hallmark of postcolonial state-building, the coercive masculinist project of Irish nationalism cannot be reduced solely to colonial forces. George Mosse, for example, notes how nationalism in Europe often emerged alongside coercive ideals of respectable masculine and feminine behaviour. The modern man, Mosse argued, was (re)made as disciplined, orderly, restrained.[15] The complicated nature of Irish nationalism is that it was part of this general European trend but simultaneously was a project which aimed to conclusively prove that the Irish were indeed European and white. Sikata Banerjee sums this up succinctly in her comparative study of gender and violence in Irish and Indian nationalisms. The Irish, she says, were situated 'on the border between "this" and "the Other", occupying the borderlands of imperial power.'[16] Which is to say, the Irish were constructed as neither 'white' colonisers nor 'black' colonised, but were instead imagined to inhabit a discomfiting zone of racial indeterminacy.[17] Indeed, Charles Kingsley, one of the most prominent public intellectuals of mid-Victorian Britain described his travels through Ireland in 1860 thusly: 'I am haunted by the human chimpanzees I saw ... to see white chimpanzees is dreadful; if they were black, one would not feel it so much, but their skins, except where tanned by exposure, are as white as ours.'[18] This idea of racial indeterminacy, of being neither white nor black, which Kingsley's quote highlights so frankly, had an important impact on Irish identity-formation. It was a major cause of the push by Irish nationalists to create a more idealised and stable self-image. This self-image of newly powerful men would be a symbolic means of escaping the nation's weak quasi-colonial status.[19]

A Zionist Mirror

In its complicated mix of Europeanness and 'quasi-colonialism', Irish nationalism bore a strong resemblance to Zionism. The primary methodological approach of this work is to study Irish nationalist concerns about masculinity in comparison with Zionist attitudes to masculinity. Both Jewish and Irish cultures were greatly affected by their weakness vis-à-vis the stronger majority, and Jewish and Irish men faced some conceptually similar stereotypes about their supposed deficiencies. Zionism, like Irish nationalism, was also a concerted effort to refute popular racial stereotypes and create a more prideful image of Jewish strength and power; this book seeks to understand Irish nationalist self-fashioning by comparing it to Zionism's similar goals.

Derek Penslar points out that the 'Jewish Question' (or 'Jewish Problem') of nineteenth-century Europe shared a similar 'taxonomy of dysfunction' with British society's contemporary 'Irish Question'. As Penslar observes, 'a hegemonic or dominant majority group that discriminated against a subaltern or minority group called the latter a "problem", suggesting that the members of the group *were themselves mainly responsible for its disabilities.*'[20] George Bornstein similarly discusses the striking similarities between anti-Irish, anti-black, and anti-Jewish stereotypes in nineteenth-century America, which drew heavily from contemporary European ideas of racial inferiority.[21] Jews were certainly seen as being somehow not fully 'white', and this is one of the central justifications for the comparative analysis engaged in here. Jews, as Homi Bhabha felicitously phrases it, inhabited an uncomfortable racial status that was 'not white and not quite'[22] or were perceived, as 'an off-white race', in Karen Brodkin's blunt phrasing.[23] Eric Goldstein notes that Jews posed a 'racial conundrum' for white America, since they were neither 'stable outsiders' nor 'stable members of white society'.[24] While questions of 'whiteness' may have appeared more pronounced in American contexts, they were not absent in nineteenth- and twentieth-century Europe.

David Myers, in his provocative book *Re-Inventing the Jewish Past*, contends that a complex paradox resided at the heart of the Zionist project. He argues that to understand Jewish nationalism we have to recognise that it is similar to other European national movements. Yet, Myers suggests, Zionism's attempts to disprove racist stereotypes also bears a close similarity to non-European, anti-colonial nationalism.[25] Myers says that this is something unique to Zionism but, as this book argues, it was in fact something Zionism shared with Irish nationalism. The perceived racial indeterminacy of the Jews and the Irish had a distinct political register. European Jews were regularly seen as an unsettled and wandering people incapable of loyalty to a state or normative private property ownership and unable to perform productive labour or creative acts. The Irish, seen as violent, incapable of sobriety, unhygienic and primitive, were also perceived to be incapable of exercising national sovereignty. The form of these racist stereotypes may have differed drastically, but the political lessons one was supposed to draw from them were remarkably similar. In both cases, the Irish and the Jews were said to be incapable of self-rule. Therefore, Irish nationalism's desire to create a more honourable self-image was part of a broader project that would prove the Irish were capable of national sovereignty. Similarly, disproving antisemitic stereotypes was at the heart of the Zionist project to create a stable, productive, European-style nation, one that would quickly result in a European-style nation-state.[26]

Myers links the movement for a redeemed Jewish nation to the popular Zionist desire for a 'muscle Jewry', a more physically powerful image of Jewish masculinity. Indeed, many of the prevalent anti-Jewish stereotypes in nineteenth-century Europe focused on the purportedly defective bodies of Jewish men.[27] And much of the scholarship on the interplay of masculinity and modern Jewish identity places a large emphasis on the power of these bodily stereotypes and the degree to which much of modern Jewish politics, Zionism included, was an organised attempt to disprove them.[28] Some of these scholars, such as Breines or Gilman, perhaps oversubscribe to the importance of external forces, in an approach that elides a fuller understanding of internal developments. Nevertheless, taken collectively, these historians provide an important body of work for understanding European minority nationalist masculinity. Their findings are especially relevant for studying other European minority nationalisms in quasi-colonialist contexts. The major methodological tack of this work is to use these studies of modern Jewish masculinity as a comparative framework for understanding modern Irish identity and masculinity.

Additionally, Irish nationalism and Zionism have shared a number of noticeable links and parallels in the nineteenth and twentieth centuries. Noting that the two situations of Ireland and Israel-Palestine are 'increasingly associated', Joe Cleary highlights a number of important points of comparison here: their contemporaneous peace processes; the centrality of diasporas to Irish, Israeli and Palestinian nationalisms; the role of major traumas (the Famine, the Holocaust, the *Nakba*) in these identities; the political weight of Irish and Jewish communities in America; their tortuous relationship with the British Empire; and 'possibly the most significant structural parallel is the virtual collapse of the original partition settlements in both Ireland and Palestine since the end of the 1960s.'[29] Furthermore, both Zionists and Irish nationalists sought to revive ancient languages as part of their drive to create a respectable national identity. Both viewed agrarian labour and militaries as key means for national redemption. And more anecdotally, leading figures of both movements (such as Michael Davitt, Arthur Griffith and Eamon de Valera, and Ze'ev Jabotinsky and Avraham Stern) had an active interest in the successes and failures of the other. Zionism, John Maher observes, is 'classical in terms of its European focus on land, language and people' and goes on to suggest that 'unpopular as the idea may be in many quarters, Israeli nationalism/Zionism has much in common with traditional southern Irish nationalism'.[30]

Unsurprisingly, there is a growing body of work that compares these two national movements. Along with the work of George Bornstein, Joe Cleary and John Maher, both Matthew Frye Jacobsen and Dan Lainer-Vos have identified some remarkable parallels between the political activities and nostalgia for home of Irish- and Jewish-Americans.[31] Of more specific relevance here, Daniel Boyarin's study of Jewish masculinity has made much of Donald Hall's suggestion that in the nineteenth century, 'the caricatured bodies of lower-class, Irish, and non-European men provided remarkably similar sites [to the bodies of women and gay men] for the play of classist, racist, and imperialist beliefs.'[32] In the same vein, Jay Geller demonstrates how the 'Street-Jews' and the 'Street-Irish' filled a similar niche at the very bottom of the Victorian economy, as famously discussed in Engels' *Condition of the English Working Class* (1845). Pushing this comparison to its outer linguistic limits, Geller shows how both Engels and Marx used the words *Lump* and *Lumpen* in their German-language texts to describe both peoples; the Irish wore *Lumpen* [rags] and ate *Lumpenkartoffeln* [rotten potatoes] and the word *Lump*, meaning rag, rotten, rascal or rogue, was also used not just to describe Jews, but to place them outside of the conceptual boundaries of respectable German society.[33] Mikhal Dekel has persuasively discussed how *Altneuland*, Theodor Herzl's 1902 Zionist utopian novel, can be usefully compared to *Dracula* (first published in 1897), in the manner in which both depict gender, modernity and their central character's sense of Europeanness as he travels through an exotic non-European space. Dekel presents both works as extended fantasies about a future Europeanised and hyper-masculine Jewish or Irish society. Herzl and Bram Stoker, two 'fin-de-siècle minority European writers,' were both, Dekel suggests, using their novels' exotic locales as means to project fantasies about their future ideal societies. Their novel's locations are removed from the heart of Europe and yet, paradoxically, they also represent a return to Europeanness and whiteness.[34]

This book seeks to add to that growing debate. Not unlike Theodore Allen, who took 'a long look into an Irish mirror'[35] so as to better understand the African-American experience of racism, this work seeks to look at Irish history via a Jewish mirror, thus to better understand the development of Irish nationalism on the fringes of Europe. Declan Kiberd has suggested that bringing Irish studies into conversation with postcolonial studies would serve to 'complicate, extend and in some cases expose the limits of current models of postcoloniality.'[36] This work has a similar aim: to complicate the scholarly study of Irish nationalism through a comparison with Zionism, two fields of history which have often eschewed comparative analyses.[37]

Masculinity Studies and the Irish *Sonderweg*

R.M. Douglas has accused Irish historians, with some due cause, of being 'strongly resistant to placing the experience of the independent Irish state and society into any kind of comparative framework.' Irish history-writing has certainly tended to avoid the kind of comparative analyses in which this book engages. Rather, in a formulation as barbed as it was judicious, Douglas says that most Irish historians 'have retreated into the comfort of an unarticulated *Sonderweg* thesis for modern Ireland, reassuring themselves that nothing that happened on the European continent need disturb the tranquillity of their scholarly lives.'[38]

For sure, some important comparative and transnational work has recently been done in Irish history. Nonetheless, studies of Irish nationalism still suffer greatly from the specific problem of this Irish *Sonderweg* and, in many respects, masculinity remains the elephant-in-the-room in the study of Irish nationalism; it is a prominent element in Irish nationalism yet, in many of the cases where this has been noted, it has been treated in a disappointingly slight manner. An informative example is Fearghal McGarry's biography of Eoin O'Duffy, IRA commander and founder of the Garda Síochána (the Irish Free State's police) in the 1920s and a pro-Franco fascist in the next decade. McGarry picks up on the General's obsessions with male virility and its relations to national virility, yet no proper attempt is made to explain these anxieties, other than to engage in ultimately unsatisfying (perhaps even pointless) speculations on O'Duffy's possible homosexuality.[39] Similarly, Joost Augusteijn's recent biography of Patrick Pearse addresses the rumours of homosexuality and paedophilia that have often dogged this much-idealised Irish nationalist. These rumours are primarily based on the overt homoeroticism of Pearse's 1909 poem 'Little Lad of the Tricks'. Augusteijn's highly speculative conclusion is that Pearse suffered from 'a kind of stunted sexual development' and 'it seems most probable that he was sexually inclined this way' (i.e., was a paedophile).[40] In this, Augusteijn, despite his other criticisms of Ruth Dudley Edwards' 1977 revisionist study of Pearse, the provocative and selective *The Triumph of Failure*, continues in the same vein as Dudley Edwards, who declared: 'there can be little doubt about his [Pearse's] unconscious inclinations.'[41] And all three historians seem to conflate homosexuality and homoeroticism with paedophilia.

All three of these historical biographies are hampered by a voyeuristic attempt to 'out' both men as gay rather than a more rewarding investigation that would present gender and sexuality in general, and masculinity in particular, as historically dynamic ideas reflecting the societies in which they are produced and ever susceptible to change, rather than being static concepts.[42] None of them see fit to compare Pearse or O'Duffy to any of their European contemporaries, or to place their concerns about masculinity in the context of other early twentieth-century European or anti-colonial nationalists who not only displayed similar anxieties about dangers to masculine virility but also expressed them in ways that twenty-first-century audiences might easily misinterpret as intentionally homoerotic or homosexual.[43]

By comparing Irish nationalism to Zionism, and the study of modern notions of normative masculinity more generally,[44] the problems of an Irish *Sonderweg* will hopefully be avoided. Also, the problematic binary of a singular Western sexuality versus postcolonial notions of gender will be destabilised. George Mosse, for example, presents European notions of sexuality in broadly singular terms.[45] A more blatant example is Joseph Massad, who rightly criticises simplistic perceptions of Arab sexuality and masculinity whilst also presenting Western ideas of gender in singular and monolithic terms.[46] As the Irish and Jewish examples show, not only is European sexuality layered and multifaceted, it is even possible to speak of a *European* postcolonialism and of European ideals of normative gender that operate according to markedly postcolonial dynamics.

The small number of works that have directly studied Irish nationalist masculinity have all worked within such a postcolonialist paradigm. The recent work of Joseph Valente, for instance, identifies Irish nationalism as a 'metrocolonial' ideology, a product of Irish people's ambiguous status as both colonised and coloniser.[47] Much of Valente's analysis is built on what he calls 'the double bind of Irish masculinity'[48]; Irish passivity in the face of British intrusion only reinforced colonialist notions about the inherent passive femininity of Irish men, whilst violent resistance was decried as irrationality, a prominent sign that childish Irish men still needed paternal British supervision. Representations of masculinity in Irish culture and politics were, according to Valente, an attempt to break free of this bind and disprove these negative tropes of Irish men's passive femininity or violent irrationality. Aside from an intriguing chapter on representations of Parnell, however, Valente's work focuses predominantly on high culture and the ways in which masculinity was a major theme in the work of writers such as Joyce and Yeats. Sikata Banerjee's comparative work, briefly mentioned above, also has much to commend it. Her focus, however, is on a small cross-section of the Irish nationalist movement, and she does not address issues of language, economics, or nationalist conceptions of space (all themes which this book explores). Elaine Sisson's *Pearse's Patriots* also places her subject within an ambiguous framework;[49] recognising that the two cannot be separated, Sisson places Patrick Pearse's anxieties about youthful masculinity in both a European modernist context,[50] and in the context of the quasi-colonialism that characterised British rule in nineteenth-century Ireland. As the title suggests, however, its focus is strictly limited to the educational work of Patrick Pearse.

Furthermore, Irish gender historians, such as Louise Ryan and Maria Luddy, have produced important works on the gender biases of both Irish nationalism and its attendant state-building project and this book draws on their research.[51] 'Gender' in Irish gender history, though, has tended to remain a synonym for 'femininity', rather than a dialectical term that recognises how 'masculinity' and 'femininity' are coterminous and each implicated in the other. This work seeks to address this lacuna and to show how masculinity was just as constructed as femininity in late-nineteenth- and early-twentieth-century Ireland.

Structure and Sources

Foregrounding the role of masculinity throughout, all of this book's chapters focus on seminal moments, themes, and texts in Irish nationalism. The argument that Ireland underwent a gradual modernist evolution, rather than the sudden rupture of a 'revolution', is reflected in the sequencing of the book's six chapters.

Chapter 2 focuses on the events from 1916 to 1923, the dates most heavily privileged in the conventional historiography of modern Ireland. This chapter studies the separate but inter-locking perceptions of time, martyrdom, and Irish 'self-hatred' within Irish nationalist thought in this period. This is the central chapter of the book and forms a linchpin for all five subsequent chapters. Therefore, it seeks to provide a review of masculinity during the period from the Easter Rising to the Civil War, but rather than a conventional chronological narrative of high politics or military history it engages in a more impressionistic account of nationalist thought and praxis. The intention is to highlight the gendered nature of nationalist politics during these years. Rather than seeing this period as a revolution, the next five chapters seek to show how the masculinist ideals that played so strong a role in the politics of 1916 to 1923 had a much longer history in Ireland; they were already popular long before 1916 and they continued to have currency long afterwards. Chapters 3, 4 and 5 all examine, in differing ways, how notions of masculinity and power, which were defining elements in Irish nationalist discourse during this 'revolution', had actually been at the fore of Irish public life long before 1916. Conversely, Chaps. 6 and 7 seek to show how this gendered conception of national power continued to have a determining impact on Irish politics after 1922.

Chapter 3 studies the prevalence of muscular ideals of Irish masculinity between the 1880s and the 1930s. It examines the regenerative body politics of the Irish Volunteers as well the *Garda Síochána*, the post-1922 Irish police force. I also compare both of these groups to one of the most successful mass movements in modern Ireland, the Gaelic Athletic Association, a sporting organisation founded in 1884 and heavily invested in a muscular vision of Ireland.

Chapter 4 ranges from the late nineteenth century to the early 1920s and looks at how Irish nationalists strove to create sanitised, male-dominated public spaces. This was a major theme in how Irish nationalists constructed idealised memories of the Rising. As this chapter points out, these issues of space, power and masculinity also featured in the 1915 funeral of Jeremiah O'Donovan Rossa (often seen as a precursor to the Rising) and in various propaganda publications issued during the War of Independence and Civil War. This chapter also examines the role of gender, space and power in the work of the Gaelic League, an Irish-language organisation founded in 1893.

Chapter 5 continues on from the previous chapter in its focus on the Gaelic League; the arguments of both chapters should be understood in tandem. The Gaelic League sought to express their power over the *Gaeltacht* (Irish-speaking) regions but as Chap. 5 shows, the perception that the Irish language intersected with a gendered power was another central element in the League's ideology. Chapter 5 focuses on Gaelic League anxieties that the Irish nation, by oscillating between English, Irish and a hybrid mix of the two called *Béarlachais*, had lost its singular racial identity. The Gaelic League also valorised the Irish language as a means of communing with a heroic ancient Irish (and Irish-speaking) masculinity. Thus, this chapter investigates the movement to revive the Irish language as part of a broader project of racial reform, of undoing the emasculating effects of British rule, and of returning to a racially pure and glorious heroic age of Irish male power and national sovereignty.

Where Chap. 4 focuses on the control of space at a national level, Chap. 6 is about the possession of land at an individual level. This chapter examines the popular view that the Irish nation had been emasculated by the economics of British rule. Irish men, rather than being able to pursue a stable economic life rooted in the soil of their homeland, instead suffered a precarious existence subject to the whims of British market forces. This chapter studies how a specific activity (agriculture on privately owned farms) came to be seen as a curative act for Irish men. The temporal focus here is on Fianna Fáil economic policy during the 1930s.

John Regan argues that there was a strongly anti-democratic element in the politics of the Irish Free State.[52] In this vein, Chap. 7 investigates how, after 1922, the new state sought to coercively force Irish citizens to fit with strict ideals of male and female behaviour. Where Regan, however, suggests that the politics of post-1922 Ireland were a contingent product of partition and British coercion and represented a 'Counter-Revolution', this chapter argues that they also cannot be understood outside of the larger context of a coercive state-building project whose roots went back into the late nineteenth century.

As outlined earlier, Irish nationalism operated according to a similar rationale as Zionism and each chapter pursues this comparison. Zionism also utilised gendered notions of martyrdom, nationalist time, physical culture, and spatial sovereignty. And many Zionists saw language revival, agrarianism and social legislation as key means for achieving national revival. As the following chapters will show, this was due to a similar European/quasi-colonial bifurcation shared by Zionism and Irish nationalism, though there were also important points on which the two national ideologies drastically differed.

The sources used for this book range from the personal papers of leading nationalists to pamphlets, handbills and posters. Above all, the vast collections of surviving ephemera at the National Library of Ireland, the Bureau of Military History and the National University of Ireland-Galway, as well as ephemeral material scattered across various other collections, have been given a central position. A small amount of archival research was also carried out in Jerusalem, at the National Library of Israel, the Central Zionist Archives and the Central Archives for the History of the Jewish People.

Ernest Renan famously spoke of the nation as 'a daily plebiscite'.[53] The goal of this book, in focusing on political ephemera, was to gain a flavour of the dynamic nature of nationalism as a daily lived experience.

Political and individual power were perceived in Irish nationalist thought as privileges that had been cruelly denied to Irish men (and sometimes also to women). A research method focusing on nationalist ephemera will allow us to see how certain gendered ideas and specific words and themes had a determining role within the project of Irish nationalism; words like revival, freedom and slavery, and ideas that expressed notions of national and masculine rebirth. At times, these ideas of masculine national revival were openly and frankly expressed and at other times they were subtle and implicit. But always, I would argue, these words, ideas, and themes operated and found their full meaning within a broader nationalist discourse. It is perhaps only from a bird's-eye perspective, one that analyses a *longue durée* of fifty or so years of Irish nationalism, that we can begin to grasp the scope and content of this masculinist discourse.

Notes

1. 'On Language and the Irish Nation' in E. de Valera, M. Moynihan, ed. (1980) *Speeches and Statements by Eamon De Valera: 1917–73* (Dublin: Gill & Macmillan) p. 466.
2. For background, see: C. Wills (2008) *That Neutral Island: A Cultural History of Ireland During World War II* (London: Faber & Faber) *passim*.
3. J. Regan (2013) *Myth and the Irish State* (Dublin: Irish Academic Press) pp. 67–68.
4. Partition had already been in place since the previous year, under the terms of the Government of Ireland Act.
5. D. Fitzpatrick (1998) *Politics and Irish Life, 1913–1921: Provincial Experience of War and Revolution*, 2nd edn (Dublin: Gill and Macmillan); S. Pašeta (1999) *Before the Revolution: Nationalism, Social Change and Ireland's Catholic Elite, 1879–1922* (Cork: Cork University Press); C. Kostick (2009) *Revolution in Ireland: Popular Militancy, 1917–1923* (Cork: Cork University Press). Fitzpatrick dates the revolution as 1912–23, Pašeta dates it as 1916–22 and Kostick dates it as 1917–23. The dates 1916–22 are increasingly the most popular.
6. I. Wallerstein (2011) *The Modern World-System III: The Second Era of Great Expansion of the Capitalist World-Economy, 1730s–1840s*, 2nd edn (Berkeley, CA: University of California Press, 2011) p. 3 and *passim*.
7. F. Mort (2010) *Capital Affairs: London and the Making of the Permissive Society* (New Haven, CT: Yale University Press) *passim*. Peter Hart says 'One of the things that made the Irish revolution revolutionary was its violence'. P. Hart (2008) 'On the Necessity of Violence in the Irish Revolution' in D. Farquharson and S. Farrell, eds. *Shadows of the Gunmen:*

Violence and Culture in Modern Ireland (Cork: Cork University Press) pp. 14–37. Fearghal McGarry talks of the revolution as 'this rapid period of exciting meritocratic flux.' F. McGarry (2005) *Eoin O'Duffy: A Self-Made Man* (Oxford: Oxford University Press) p. 75.
8. P. Maume (1999) *The Long Gestation: Irish Nationalist Life, 1891–1918* (New York: St. Martin's Press) *passim*.
9. M. De Nie (2004) *The Eternal Paddy: Irish Identity and the British Press, 1798–1882* (Madison, WI: University of Wisconsin Press) pp. 4–5.
10. Ibid., p. 10.
11. A. Winter (1998) *Mesmerized: Powers of Mind in Victorian Britain* (Chicago: University of Chicago Press) pp. 61–62.
12. T. Allen (2012) *The Invention of the White Race, Volume One: Racial Oppression and Social Control*, 2nd edn (London: Verso) p. 29 and *passim*. Pointing to the transnational range of these stereotypes, David Roediger has noted that in antebellum America, 'the Irish were frequently conflated with Blacks' and 'rowdy undisciplined behaviour in the 1830s was sometimes called "acting Irish".' D. Roediger (1991) *The Wages of Whiteness: Race and the Making of the American Working Class* (London: Verso) p. 107.
13. D. Kiberd (1996) *Inventing Ireland: The Literature of the Modern Nation* (Cambridge, MA: Harvard University Press); S. Deane (1983) *Civilians and Barbarians* (Belfast: Field Day); D. Lloyd (1993) *Anomalous States: Irish Writing and the Post-Colonial Moment* (Durham, NC: Duke University Press).
14. Though perhaps these are not such contradictory forms of British rule. Eugen Weber, for example, has argued that Paris, in the late nineteenth century, colonized the rest of France in a vast civilising mission. E. Weber (1976) *Peasants into Frenchmen: The Modernization of Rural France, 1870–1914* (Stanford University Press) pp. 485–496 and *passim*. This, indeed, could be a useful comparative model for understanding not just British colonial rule in Ireland, but also Irish internal-colonial rule in Ireland. Tellingly, not only did nineteenth-century French officials compare their subjects in the rural interior to Arabs and Africans, but one commentator, writing in the *Revue des seux mondes* in June 1864, compared Savoy to Ireland! Ibid., p. 489. See also, T. Mitchell (1998) *Colonising Egypt* (Berkeley, CA: University of California Press), which raises similar questions about centres colonising peripheries.
15. G. Mosse (1996) *The Image of Man: The Creation of Modern Masculinity* (Oxford: Oxford University Press) pp. 3–39 and *passim*; G. Mosse (1985) *Nationalism and Sexuality: Respectability and Abnormal Sexuality in Modern Europe* (New York: Howard Fertig).
16. S. Banerjee (2012) *Muscular Nationalism: Gender, Violence and Empire in India and Ireland* (New York: NYU Press) pp. 37–39.

17. Reinforcing this, Banerjee also observes that 'Although the patient and suffering nation as woman, India and Hibernia, requiring rescue from the violent Paddy or the ape-like effete babu, is an important theme, it must be noted that, in all the research conducted for this book, I did not come across the trope of the fragile Englishwoman being in danger from the simianized Celt.' Banerjee explains this as a result of Irish 'whiteness' and the idea that the Irish were seen as different and dangerous but never as different or dangerous as Nigerian, Egyptian or Indian men. Ibid., p. 42.
18. M. De Nie (2004) *Eternal Paddy*, p. 11.
19. As Banerjee notes: 'in both the Indian and the Irish cases, the retrieval of the warrior model of manhood—imagined in different ways—that has been lost under the yoke of centuries of imperial rule is a major theme.' S. Banerjee (2012) *Muscular Nationalism*, p. 7.
20. D. Penslar (2001) *Shylock's Children: Economics and Jewish Identity in Modern Europe* (Berkeley, CA: University of California Press) p. 9. Emphases added.
21. G. Bornstein (2011) *The Colors of Zion: Blacks, Jews, and Irish from 1845 to 1945* (Cambridge, MA: Harvard University Press). For further discussion of this Black–Jewish comparison, see: A. Memmi (1991) *The Colonizer and the Colonized* (Boston: Beacon Press) p. 122; G. Mosse (1978) *Toward the Final Solution: A History of European Racism* (New York: Harper & Row) p. 236.
22. H. Bhabha (2004) *The Location of Culture* (New York: Routledge) p. 89. Quoted in D. Boyarin (1997) *Unheroic Conduct: The Rise of Heterosexuality and the Invention of the Jewish Man* (Berkeley, CA: University of California Press) p. 262.
23. K. Brodkin (1994) *How Jews Became White Folks And What That Says About Race in America* (New Brunswick, NJ: Rutgers University Press) p. 1. Brodkin's even-tempered work provides an interesting counterpoint to the more polemical work of Noel Ignatiev (2008) *How The Irish Became White* (New York: Routledge).
24. E. Goldstein (2006) *The Price of Whiteness: Jews, Race and American Identity* (Princeton, NJ: Princeton University Press) pp. 2–3. Goldstein goes on to say that 'Irish immigrants, who were vilified as a "simian race" and frequently compared to blacks before the Civil War because of the menial work they performed, had to aggressively defend their status as white. Jews, however, faced fewer challenges than the Irish in establishing their racial credentials in antebellum America … They [Jews] almost never suffered the kind of racial stigmatization meted out to African Americans, and also met with consistently better treatment than the Irish, whose whiteness was questioned for much of the century.' Ibid., p. 5.
25. D. Myers (1995) *Re-Inventing the Jewish Past: European Jewish Intellectuals and the Zionist Return to History* (Oxford: Oxford University Press) pp. 3–4.

26. This is discussed, with varying degrees of sympathy, in G. Piterberg (2008) *The Returns of Zionism: Myths, Politics and Scholarship in Israel* (London: Verso) and A. Shapira (1999) *Land and Power: The Zionist Resort to Force, 1881–1948* (Stanford, CA: Stanford University Press).
27. S. Gilman (1991) *The Jew's Body* (New York: Routledge) p. 243. 'Bodies', Gilman says, 'have a way of being seen again and again in the past, and identity—whether that of Jews or blacks or Hispanics or women—always has to perform a perilous balancing act between self and Other.'
28. For representative examples, see: S. Gilman (1991) 'The Jew's Body'; D. Boyarin (1997) *Unheroic Conduct*; P. Breines (1990) *Tough Jews: Political Fantasies and the Moral Dilemma of American Jewry* (New York: Basic Books); O. Almog (2000) *The Sabra: The Creation of the New Jew* (Berkeley, CA: University of California Press); T.S. Presner (2007) *Muscular Judaism: The Jewish Body and the Politics of Regeneration* (London: Routledge); M. Gluzman (2007) *HaGuf HaTzioni: Le'umiyut, Migdar u-Miniyut ba-Sifrut ha-Ivrit ha-Chadashah* [The Zionist Body: Nationalism, Gender and Sexuality in Modern Hebrew Literature] (Tel Aviv: Ha-Kibbutz Ha-Meuchad).
29. J. Cleary (2002) *Literature, Partition and the Nation State: Culture and Conflict in Ireland, Israel and Palestine* (Cambridge: Cambridge University Press) pp. 5–8.
30. J. Maher (2012) *Slouching Towards Jerusalem: Reactive Nationalism in the Irish, Israeli and Palestinian Novel, 1985–2005* (Dublin: Irish Academic Press) p. 8.
31. M. Frye Jacobsen (1995) *Special Sorrows: The Diasporic Imagination of Irish, Polish, and Jewish Immigrants* (Cambridge MA: Harvard University Press); D. Lainer-Vos (2013) *Sinews of the Nation: Constructing Irish and Zionist Bonds in the United States* (Cambridge: Polity Press).
32. D. Hall (1994) 'Muscular Christianity: Reading and Writing the Male Social Body' in Donald E. Hall, ed. *Muscular Christianity: Embodying the Victorian Age* (Cambridge: Cambridge University Press) pp. 5–6. Quoted in D. Boyarin (1997) *Unheroic Conduct*, p. 19.
33. J. Geller (2011) *The Other Jewish Question: Identifying The Jew and Making Sense of Modernity* (New York: Fordham University Press) p. 181.
34. M. Dekel. *The Universal Jew: Masculinity, Modernity, and the Zionist Moment* (Evanston, IL: Northwestern University Press) pp. 95–129.
35. T. Allen (2012) *Invention*, p. 22.
36. D. Kiberd (1996) *Inventing Ireland*, p. 5.
37. Echoing the solipsistic nature of a lot of Irish history-writing, Ben-Israel Kidron notes that 'It was only recently that the question was raised whether Zionism was like or unlike other national movements', having previously been overwhelmingly understood within the strict confines of

Jewish history. H. Ben-Israel Kidron (2003) 'Zionism and European Nationalisms: Comparative Aspects.' *Israel Studies*, Vol. 8, No. 1, 91.
38. R.M. Douglas (2011) 'Not So Different After All: Political antisemitism in Independent Ireland and Continental Europe in Comparative Perspective.' Paper presented at a conference on *Irish and Jewish Identities: Links and Parallels*, University of Chicago, 22 February 2011.
39. F. McGarry (2005) *O'Duffy*, pp. 141–169.
40. J. Augusteijn (2010) *Patrick Pearse: The Making of a Revolutionary* (London: Palgrave MacMillan) p. 62. That said, these works of Augesteijn and McGarry are, in almost all other ways, quite astute and useful.
41. R. Dudley Edwards (2006) *Patrick Pearse: The Triumph of Failure*, 2nd Edn (Dublin: Irish Acadamic Press) p. 127.
42. Commenting on the micro-histories favoured by Irish historians, John Regan has charged that 'In these approaches—local, personal, intimate—the greater political forces at play—abstract, impersonal, universal—too easily can go overlooked… Rather than liberating us this approach may be limiting, even voyeuristic … It also marginalises ideology as a motivational factor'. J. Regan (2013) *Myth*, pp. 210–211.
43. See, for example, the frontispiece for a 1904 edition of the German Zionist journal *Altneuland*, reproduced in T.S. Presner (2007) *Muscular Judaism*, p. 5, in which two muscular, naked men, one middle-aged and one teen-aged, are depicted marching together to Palestine.
44. G. Mosse (1985) *Nationalism and Sexuality*; G. Mosse (1996) *Image of Man*; A. Najmabadi (2005) *Women with Mustaches and Men without Beards: Gender and Sexual Anxieties of Iranian Modernity* (Berkeley CA: California University Press).
45. G. Mosse (1985) *Nationalism and Sexuality*; G. Mosse (1996) *Image of Man*.
46. J. Massad (2007) *Desiring Arabs* (Chicago: University of Chicago Press) pp. 44–47.
47. J. Valente (2011) *The Myth of Manliness in Irish National Culture, 1882–1922* (Urbana IL: University of Illinois Press) p. 11.
48. Ibid., pp. 1–25 and *passim*.
49. E. Sisson (2004) *Pearse's Patriots: St. Enda's and the Cult of Boyhood* (Cork: Cork University Press) pp. 22–39 and *passim*. As far as I know Banerjee, Sisson and Valente are the only scholars to have produced monographs dedicated to the role of masculinity in Irish nationalism. An important companion work, though, is Jane McGaughey's intelligent study of Ulster unionist masculinity. J. McGaughey (2012) *Ulster's Men: Protestant Unionist Masculinities and Militarization in the North of Ireland, 1912–1923* (Montreal: McGill-Queen's University Press). As Diarmaid Ferriter has boldly and accurately stated, 'the history of Irish masculinity has yet to

be written.' D. Ferriter (2009) *Occasions of Sin: Sex and Society in Modern Ireland* (London: Profile Books) p. 242.
50. Indeed, anxieties about boyhood were a common theme throughout Britain. There seemed to be perennial fears that overly pampered British boys would not grow up to be real imperial men. See, for example, J. Bristow (1991) *Empire Boys: Adventures in a Man's World* (London: Harper Collins) pp. 225–226.
51. M. Luddy (2007) *Prostitution and Irish Society, 1800–1940* (Cambridge: Cambridge University Press); L. Ryan (2002) *Gender, Identity and the Irish Press, 1922–1937: Embodying the Nation* (New York: Edwin Mellen). See also, M. Ward (1983) *Unmanageable Revolutionaries: Women and Irish Nationalism* (London: Pluto Press).
52. J. Regan (1999) *The Irish Counter-Revolution, 1921–1936: Treatyite Politics and Settlement in Independent Ireland* (Dublin: Gill and Macmillan). See also his development of these ideas in his recent collection of essays, J. Regan (2013) *Myth*. R.M. Douglas has also drawn on Regan's idea in his case study of the fascist organisation *Ailtirí na hAiséirghe*. R.M. Douglas (2009) *Architects of the Resurrection: Ailtirí na hAiséirghe and the Fascist 'New Order' in Ireland* (Manchester: Manchester University Press).
53. E. Hobsbawm (1991) *Nations and Nationalism Since 1780: Programme, Myth, Reality* (Cambridge: Canto/Cambridge University Press) p. 7.

CHAPTER 2

Time, Gender and the Politics of National Liberation, 1916–1923

Every period has its great men, and if these are lacking, it invents them.[1]

THE MASCULINE PAST-AS-IT-WILL-BE

On 21 January 1919, the same day that Sinn Féin established an independent Irish parliament, Dáil Éireann, a small group of local nationalists acting on their own initiative, attacked and killed two Royal Irish Constabulary (RIC) constables escorting workmen and dynamite at a quarry in Soloheadbeg in South Tipperary. The ambush at Soloheadbeg has often been seen as the starting point of the Irish War of Independence.[2] In his memoirs of his experiences during this war, Dan Breen offered a lively account of his role as one of the leaders at Soloheadbeg. As well as weaving a romanticised account of an Irish rebel and his adventures on the run from British forces, Breen makes another, slightly more subtle point. Discussing the ambush, Breen is keen to point out that here at Soloheadbeg, 'Brian Boru and his brother Mahon fought their first great battle with the Danes in 968, when Brian with his gallant army of Tipperary men and Clare men routed the invaders'.[3] Dan Breen and his comrades are clearly only the latest in a long line of 'gallant' Irish men fighting unwelcome invaders in this part of the country. Fleeing from Soloheadbeg, Breen and his comrades hid in the Galtee Mountains that 'have ever been the refuge of the Tipperary

© The Editor(s) (if applicable) and The Author(s) 2016
A. Beatty, *Masculinity and Power in Irish Nationalism, 1884–1938*, Genders and Sexualities in History,
DOI 10.1057/978-1-137-44101-0_2

"felon"'.⁴ Indeed, when the violence of the ambush was condemned by mainstream opinion 'our only consoling thought was that the men of [17]98, the Fenians of [18]67 and the men of 1916 were condemned in their day.'⁵ On a later raid, to rescue a captured comrade, Seán Hogan, Breen talked of how they passed 'on the very same road by which Patrick Sarsfield rode on that moonlit night two hundred years before when his sabre brought terror to Dutch William's troops.' Belabouring his point, Breen even suggested that Hogan was descended from Galloping Hogan, 'another Tipperary Outlaw.' Breen claimed it was Seán Treacy, his closest friend in the raiding party, who 'loved his Irish history', that reminded them of this glorious episode.⁶

A bestseller on its initial release in 1924,⁷ Breen's book remains one of the most popular examples of what John Regan tartly calls the 'with-my-comrades-behind-the-ditch-in-the-fight-for-Irish-freedom literary genre.'⁸ Discussing a similar Zionist genre, the Israeli historian Oz Almog notes that 'The social importance of the works of these writers and poets was much greater than their artistic importance.'⁹ One important aspect of Breen's book was its contribution to the creation of a specifically masculine sense of Irish historical-national time. Whether or not Dan Breen or Seán Treacy actually stopped to think of canonical moments and canonical male figures in Irish nationalist history as they carried out violent assaults on British police and troops is, of course, highly debatable.¹⁰ *My Fight for Irish Freedom*, however, is not reality. It is an ideological representation of reality. Breen's collapsing of historical time served to create a highly ideological, atemporal zone wherein all true Irish nationalist men exist together. A zone wherein nationalist men like Breen believe (or at least wish their readers to believe) that their actions are guided and watched over joyfully by past generations of patriotic Irish men. This collapsing of time was a common move in contemporary Irish nationalist propaganda and was an important means of self-legitimisation.¹¹ It was a regular tactic in de Valera's successful by-election in East Clare in 1917, for instance, one of the first of many electoral defeats for the regnant Irish Parliamentary Party.

In at least two of his electoral handbills, de Valera addressed potential voters as 'Dalcassians', a romantic term for the ancient Irish nation, and asked 'Do you want a Hero to Represent you?'¹² De Valera portrayed himself as a true Irish man, rooted in the national past, and by voting for him, other Irish men could also feel rooted in that heroic past.¹³ Conversely, his opponent, Patrick Lynch, was placed outside Irish national time: '*Sé de Bhaléra Fear na nGaedheal*[14] [De Valera is a Man of the Gaels] and *'Sé de Bhaléra Fear na hÉireann'* [De Valera is an Irish Man] whilst *'Sé an Loinnseach Fear an Caisleáin'* [Lynch is a man of Dublin Castle], the seat of British power in Ireland.[15] The reimagining of time and the claim that 'we' are the heirs of a glorious past are, in fact, quite conventional nationalist tropes, particularly in minority and postcolonial situations. The Zionist *chalutzim* [pioneer settlers], for example, saw their kibbutzim as being not just a means of restoring Jews to useful manly labour, but also as 'reincarnations of the agrarian society of the Bible.'[16] Indian nationalist historiography has often operated along similar lines with the obvious lesson that 'we' should become more like our proud forebears and thus build a perfected future as a means of escaping a degraded present.[17]

In 1918, in the run-up to a by-election in Armagh, de Valera wrote an open letter to the constituency's voters that reiterated the idea of politics as a communion with male heroes from the national past. De Valera beseeched voters to find inspiration from 'the blood of our martyrs through the centuries' as well as, closer to home, from 'the bones of Brian of Clontarf [Brian Boru] reposing in your midst'.[18] In another Sinn Féin by-election victory that year, W.T. Cosgrave urged voters to 'Come, show your pride in the men who died, For the cause of Granuaile' (Granuaile, also known as Gráinne Ní Mháille or Grace O'Malley, was a sixteenth-century female pirate, who posthumously became a folkloric symbol for the Irish nation). The same pamphlet ended with the exhortation 'Men of Kilkenny Vote for Cosgrave and Granuaile',[19] thus presenting the nation as a timeless abstract woman (Granuaile) alongside the non-abstract male political actor (Cosgrave).

This rhetoric of time and gender continued to be used in the 1918 general election. A handbill for the general election began by asking voters 'Do you stand by Wolfe Tone', the leader of the 1798 rebellion, before proceeding to point to an obvious paradox in the IPP's public image. The handbill included a reproduction of the membership card of the United Irish League, a grassroots organisation linked to the IPP. The card featured a picture of the eighteenth-century nationalist Theobald Wolfe Tone and the legend 'Who Fears to Speak of '98'. Wolfe Tone's famous statement that 'To break the connection with England and to assert the Independence of my country—these were my objects' was compared with a statement made by the IPP's John Dillon on 25 June 1918: 'What I should like to see in the course of coming [*sic*] autumn is a National Convention … to definitely forswear an Irish Republic.' The handbill asserted that 'Wolfe Tone is good enough for Window Dressing for John Dillon but he would exclude Wolfe Tone and Emmet and Lord Edward and Mitchel [all eighteenth- and nineteenth-century nationalists] from his Irish Convention.' Adding salt to the wound, the handbill asked 'Is this Parnell's policy?' and quickly answered: 'No. Parnell said: "No man has a right to fix the boundary to the March of a Nation." Sinn Fein sets no Bounds to the March of the Irish Nation.'[20] Another Sinn Féin handbill quoted a one-time radical statement from John Redmond, leader of the IPP, made 'When He Was an Irishman'.[21] In other words, a statement he made when he still resided within Irish nationalist time, before he became a traitorous, unmanly, and denationalised puppet of Westminster.

Claiming to be the heirs of radical Irish nationalists had long been a tactic of the IPP.[22] This, though, was a dangerous political game. Like Sinclair Lewis' quip about the similarly conservative Daughters of the American Revolution, politicians like Dillon and Redmond spent 'one half their waking hours boasting of being descended' from seditious nationalists 'and the other and more ardent half in attacking all contemporaries who believe in precisely the principles for which those ancestors struggled.'[23] It was almost inevitable that Sinn Féin would capitalise on so obvious a political contradiction. Conversely, Sinn Féin's ability to portray themselves as the new heirs to male nationalist icons from a heroic past would greatly aid their taking of power.

At times, though, the Irish nationalist playing with time could have curious results, such as the 1917 poster (see Fig. 2.1) in which, opposite a pathetic and deformed approximation of Patrick Lynch, stood a de Valera in drag, as this otherwise austere figure was reimagined as a proud, ancient Irish woman. Here, de Valera was imagined as a woman from the Irish past who showed the way to a glorious future, all of which is contrasted with the decrepit present tense of Patrick Lynch.

This poster again points to some comparable tendencies in other national movements, where the 'nation' is often imagined as a timeless woman in need of 'her' sons' masculine protection. This inclusion of a female figure within national historical time might seem to disprove the notion that this was an exclusionary, masculine phenomenon. Afsaneh Najmabadi, however, in her analysis of gender in Iranian nationalism, has shown that such an inclusion of women in the abstract can often serve to exclude them in reality.[24] Furthermore, imagining the nation as a woman can help to reinforce a highly restrictive notion of female passivity while it simultaneously buttresses an idealised vision of active masculinity.[25] As will

Fig. 2.1 *De Valera as Ancient Irish Woman*, Election Poster, 1917
Source: NLI LO P116

be discussed in Chap. 4, Zionism engaged in a similar strategy, coding the Land of Israel as a feminine entity in need of 'her' male (Jewish) protectors. That Sinn Féin activists could depict de Valera as a woman highlights the malleability of these constructed images of masculinity, even if it is still unclear why exactly they would chose to do this in the midst of this important 1917 by-election.[26]

Zionism also promised a return to history as part of its return to masculine sovereignty; the future Jewish sovereignty in the Land of Israel was imagined as a recreation of a lost, pre-Diasporic sovereignty. Zionism, like Irish nationalism, was invested in creating what Partha Chatterjee labels 'the past-as-it-will-be'.[27] In the case of Zionism, however, the idealised men of the national past had a remarkable tendency to be self-sacrificial martyrs. The cultural historian David Biale was only slightly exaggerating when he argued that suicide became 'almost a cult' in Zionism, 'the most desperate statement of one's commitment to unattainable ideals'.[28] Indeed, Zionists actively mined the Jewish past for ideals of martyrdom. The martyrs of Masada in 70 CE, for instance, were held up as prideful ideals to which the modern Jewish nation should return, notwithstanding the fact that, in Rabbinical Judaism, these martyrs had long been seen as bordering on the fanatical.[29] Max Nordau, a prominent *fin-de-siècle* intellectual and early Zionist leader, praised the martyrdom of Simon Bar Kochba, leader of a first-century revolt against Rome, and held him up as an ideal to which the Jewish nation should return: 'Bar Kochba was not just a brave military hero or a politician who grasped the importance of fighting for the land of Israel against the Roman occupiers; he was a Jewish soldier who, when victory was denied him, "knew how to die"'. The 'New Jew', a much promoted Zionist archetype from the 1900s onward, would be a return to Bar Kochba and other 'noble Jewish heroes of antiquity'. These muscular martyrs would be defined not by their faith in God but as the personification of a militarised and self-sacrificial Jewish honour.[30] They were a convenient means of refuting widespread stereotypes of Jewish male weakness or cowardice and were part of an idealised mythology of heroic and self-sacrificing men from a long-past golden age, all of which would be recreated in the future as a means of escaping a weak and degraded present. Irish nationalism too had its martyrs, but they tended to be found in the more recent past.

MEN, MARTYRDOM AND MARTYROLOGIES

Accounts of martyrdom can never be written by the martyrs themselves. As Jeremy Cohen has pointed out, martyrs are always constructed as martyrs after the fact. Martyrologies, by definition, can only be written by the survivors of those events that later come to be designated as acts of martyrdom. And like any texts, martyrologies represent the politics, culture, anxieties and interests of the society in which they were produced, much more than they do those of the 'martyrdoms' they claim to represent.[31] The prominent historian Roy Foster has said that the Easter Rising was an intentional 'blood sacrifice ritual' and a 'willed loss of life'.[32] While this view has become popular both in academia and elsewhere, it ignores how these images of heroic men, sacrificing themselves for the nation, were constructed (and reconstructed) after 1916. Whether or not Patrick

Pearse, or any other leader of the Rising, went willingly to his death is impossible to know. What is knowable is the ideological work these images of men willing to give their lives for the nation did for an emerging Irish state. These are important considerations for understanding the martyrs of 1916 and the gendered narratives quickly constructed around them, narratives which are far more about the politics of '1917', of the aftermath of the Rising, than of the actual Rising itself.[33]

An instructive example of this construction of male martyrdom can be seen in the series of handbills that appeared after the death of Thomas MacDonagh, one of the first of the leaders of the Rising to be executed. Bearing such evocative titles as 'Last and Inspiring Address of Thomas MacDonagh', these handbills assert MacDonagh's steely resilience in the face of the British state, his pride and his willingness to die for the higher cause of Irish freedom. They are worth quoting at length:

> I chose to think you have but done your duty according to your lights in sentencing me to death. I thank you for your courtesy. It would not be seemly for me to go to my doom without trying to express, however inadequately, my sense of the high honour I enjoy in being one of these predestined to die in this generation for the cause of Irish Freedom ... Gentlemen, you have sentenced me to death, and I accept your sentence with joy and pride, since it is for Ireland I am to die. I go to join the goodly company of the men who died for Ireland, the least of whom was worthier far than I could claim to be. And that noble band are themselves but a small section of the great unnumbered army of Martyrs, whose Captain is Christ who died in Calvary. Of every white-robed knight in all that goodly company we are the spiritual kin ... Take me away, and let my blood bedew the sacred soil of Ireland. I will die in the certainty that once more the seed will fructify.[34]

The speech presents MacDonagh as a strong and heroic figure and places him in the same space-time as other nationalist martyrs. As stirring as this speech may have been, however, it never happened. In fact, his court martial trial was largely uneventful, with little in the way of such boastful nationalist rhetoric.[35] These handbills were forgeries, but they were also one of the most blatant examples of an important development in post-1916 Irish cultural and political history: the construction of a smooth narrative of noble Irish men willing to give their lives for the nation. Rather than taking such accounts of martyrdom at face value, it is more profitable to view these handbills, Easter Rising martyrology, and Irish nationalist culture in general, as part of a diffuse discursive field that put a strong emphasis on heroic ideals of masculinity and service to the nation-state. The deaths of the Easter Rising martyrs would, ultimately, be forcefully (re-)interpreted via this same gendered discourse. Indeed, as early as June 1916, the leading Home Ruler T.P. O'Connor had warned David Lloyd George that the executed leaders of the Rising 'were already passing into legend as sober and pious martyrs.'[36]

The martyrs were quickly moved from conventional linear time into the collapsed time of the nationalist pantheon. That the sexuality of one martyr, Roger Casement, executed in Pentonville Prison in North London in August 1916, was called into question was perceived as an assault on this mythmaking. In 1930, Denis Gwynn, Casement's first biographer, accepted that Casement knew he would be 'execrated' as a traitor. 'But a much more detestable form of obloquy was to be deliberately associated with his name, when he had no means of contradicting it. Not until long after his death was the imputation against his moral character openly formulated ... a deliberate campaign to discredit him on moral grounds was undertaken by some mysterious agency in Scotland Yard.' As if to demonstrate the danger that accusations about Casement's sexuality posed to his image as a heroic martyr, Gwynn concluded that 'it is impossible to leave the accusations unnoticed.'[37] By 1936, however, Gwynn was privately conceding that that he had omitted certain evidence from his book, for fear that readers would find it 'conclusive' and hinted that he knew that the accusations about Casement's homosexuality were genuine.[38] For Gwynn, as for post-1916 Irish nationalists in general, printing the legend was more important than the truth.[39]

Perhaps the most important example of such a carefully constructed narrative of heroic martyrdom, other than that of the Easter Rising, was the death of Terence MacSwiney. A veteran of nationalist politics in Cork and recently elected mayor of that city, MacSwiney was arrested on charges of sedition on 12 August 1920 and incarcerated in Brixton Prison in London. Disputing the legitimacy of not only his arrest, but of British rule in Ireland in general, MacSwiney refused prison food and embarked on a hunger strike that would last 74 days and culminate in his death on 25 October 1920. MacSwiney's death 'gained worldwide sympathy for Sinn Féin, and was a pivotal moment in the war of independence.'[40] It was practically inevitable that he would come to be seen as a martyr. The nationalist poet Brian O'Higgins contemporaneously declared:

> Raise we no *caoine* [lament] for you, Terence MacSwiney,
> High is our pride in your name and your deed;
> Humble our prayer to the great God of Battles,
> That we too be strong in the dark hour of need.
>
> Joy for your love and your faith and your courage.
> Glowing and glad to the last anguished breath!
> Thanks be to God for you, Terence MacSwiney
> Thanks be to God for your life and your death![41]

Another, even more muscular, poet pronounced that:

> The tyrants may think that his spirit will shrink,
> (As forecasted an eminent speaker)
> But they'ill [*sic*] find out at length, not an ounce of its strenth [*sic*]
> Will depart, though the flesh becomes weaker
> For the manhood of old of our forefathers bold
> In spirit will join us and pray,
> While a blessing it gives, that the spirit still lives
> In the heart of McSweeney [*sic*] to-day.[42]

Works such as this contributed to a rapidly forming and highly idealised image of MacSwiney. O'Higgins presented this death as a form of self-sacrifice to the nation, a source of great pride, and a lesson that 'we too [should] be strong'. The second poem links MacSwiney's actions to a return of an ancient masculinity ('the manhood of old ...') and not only will this be a source of national pride, it will be a much needed riposte to the 'tyrants' currently ruling Ireland.

The rumour circulating prior to his death, that MacSwiney had voluntarily broken his hunger strike, cut across this emergent image of a resilient man stoically facing his own death.[43] It particularly irritated his sister, Mary MacSwiney. In an open letter to the British Home Secretary, Edward Shortt, she called the accusation 'another lie told for the purpose of discrediting my brother's position among Foreign Nations, who are watching his struggle with sympathy and interest.' Moreover, Shortt was told that his claims were 'vile' and 'We have ceased to hope for any sign of honour or fair play from any member of the English Government, but you will not succeed in discrediting us or the cause for which we stand— Ireland's independence among the *civilised* Nations of the World.'[44] Mary MacSwiney also attacked those who claimed her brother's actions constituted suicide, and thus went against Catholic teachings. This was not 'self-murder', she declared, but a 'heroic' attempt to 'deliver his Motherland from the oppressor, to give an emphatic denial to an Alien's claim to make laws or to bind him or his people ... To die for a great principle is a noble death, and not even this material age has dared to decry it.'[45] Mary MacSwiney's views covered much of the same ground as the poems just mentioned; this death was a heroic and manly act and one in which Irish people should take great pride.

Terence MacSwiney himself was also complicit in his canonisation as a nationalist martyr. In an open letter to fellow hunger strikers in Cork Gaol, MacSwiney depicted his death as a sacrifice for God and for Ireland: 'I offer everything Thou askest me for Ireland's resurrection; it is Thy Will. Accept our willing sacrifice for our people.' He also referenced the propagandistic benefits that would accrue to Ireland, in the event of their death. 'Comrades! if we twelve go in glorious succession to the grave, the name of Ireland will flash in a tongue of flames through the world, and be a sign of hope for all time to every people struggling to be free. Let that thought inspire us ...'[46] The famous quote ascribed to MacSwiney, 'it is not to those who can inflict most, but to those who can endure most that the victory is certain', was also widely publicised after his death.[47] In fact, MacSwiney had long flirted with the rhetoric of heroic self-sacrifice for the cause of the nation. In his poem 'Ode to a Bullet' he declared: 'Swift Messenger of Death, your kiss of pain / Lay on my brow, before dishonour base / Shall once again drag low our ancient race.'[48] And in 'Teach Us How to Die', a poem he supposedly wrote whilst on hunger strike, he beseeched divine aid for his actions.[49]

The idea that MacSwiney was a selfless and heroic martyr was reinforced by the events following his death. The initial plan had been for his body to be transported back to Ireland via Dublin for maximum political impact. This was prevented, though, when his coffin was seized by Crown forces and sent directly to Cork.[50] Nonetheless, posters were produced to give details for his funeral and of the guard that would accompany him, asserting that his final words were 'God Save Ireland, Fight On! Fight On!'[51] The public display of his body and the spectacle of his open-casket lying-in-state added to this image of a heroic martyr.[52] Indeed, when he saw the corpse, P.S. O'Hegarty, a leading nationalist journalist and MacSwiney's first biographer, felt MacSwiney's body displayed what was 'essentially a warrior face ... this man was fundamentally a warrior, a warrior of the highest caste known to mankind. As one looked at the face, stern and set, one's mind instinctively leaped to the word "Samurai" ... Unflinching courage, unflinching resolution, unflinching self-sacrifice on the altar of duty. That was Terry.'[53] Similarly, the priest who attended MacSwiney at the end of his life mixed together the militarism, Catholicism, self-sacrifice, collapsed time and homosociality central to Irish nationalist ideology:

> I joined him in Brixton Jail, as a friend, as his chaplain. But it was as a brother, a fellow child of St. Francis of Assisi, I bade him farewell and sent him to meet Tomas [Tomás MacCurtain, MacSwiney's predecessor as Lord Mayor of Cork] and Eoghan Roe [a seventeenth century Irish leader] and Joan of Arc in the company of the soldier and gentle patriot of Italy, St. Francis. When the acting President of the Republic over the grave of Terence MacSwiney said, 'St. Joan of Arc welcomes a comrade in Heaven'; he could have added, 'and a brother and fellow-soldier too.'[54]

MacSwiney's case points to the strongly Catholic elements of these narratives of martyrdom. Patrick Pearse had long had a fascination with Christ, martyrdom, and themes of personal and national resurrection, as evidenced in earlier prose works such as 'Íosagán' [Little Jesus] and 'Na Bóithre' [The Roads].[55] In 'A Mother Speaks', a poem written on the eve of his execution and widely published after his death, Pearse directly compared his situation with that of Christ. Written from the point of view of his mother, it declares 'Dear Mary, that didst see thy first-born Son / Go forth to die amid the scorn of men for whom He died / Receive my first-born son into thy arms / Who also had gone forth to die for men'.[56] A poem supposedly written by Thomas Ashe during his imprisonment in Lewes Jail near Brighton similarly asked 'Let me carry your Cross for Ireland, Lord!'[57] Pushing this to its outer reaches, George Plunkett, the father of Easter Rising martyr Joseph Plunkett, was described in God-like terms as 'the man who sacrificed his three [*sic*] sons in order that your son, and every Irish father's son, should be saved from the sacrifice.'[58] These ostensibly Catholic ideals of martyrdom did important propagandistic and political work for Irish nationalism, helping to legitimise a popular ideal of male service to the nation to which all could supposedly aspire.

The events of the Great War reinforced the perception that violence was a legitimate form of service of the nation. George Mosse in his study of the construction of memories of war in twentieth-century Europe, argues that the horrific realities of war were replaced with a quasi-religious 'Myth of the War Experience': 'The memory of the war was refashioned into a sacred experience which provided the nation with a new depth of religious feeling, putting at its disposal ever-present saints and martyrs, places of worship, and a heritage to emulate ... The cult of the fallen soldier became a centerpiece of the religion of nationalism'.[59] A similar process was underway in post-1916 Ireland, as the emerging independent state grasped for legitimation. If the Great War had proven that violence and an ability to compel male self-sacrifice were the hallmarks of a true nation-state, then contemporary Irish men's willingness to die for Ireland had proven that their nation was also capable of exercising sovereignty.

Elsewhere, though, Mosse hints at some other concerns that could underpin how war and violence are remembered and why martyrs are constructed. In a 1990 interview with the Israeli historian Tom Segev, Mosse discussed how Zionist public memorials 'represent primeval masculinity and national strength' [*mesamelim gavriut kama'it ve-otzmah le'umit*].[60] Zionism and Irish nationalism both put a strong emphasis on the recovery of a lost ancient masculine strength, as well as on disproving accusations of national weakness. Both strove to create images of physically and emotionally strong men, ready to sacrifice all for the good of the nation. This can be seen in the life, and, more importantly, the iconic death of Joseph Trumpeldor, 'Zionism's most revered martyr'.[61]

Trumpeldor was a veteran of both the Czarist Russian Army and of the Zion Mule Corps, the Jewish unit of the British Army during the First World War. In 1919, he and a number of other Zionists became involved in a fracas with local Arabs at the ironically named Tel Chai [Hill of Life], in northern Palestine. In the midst of this, Trumpeldor and seven other Zionists were shot. There was to be much mythmaking over this incident, later named the 'Battle of Tel Chai'. Much of the mythology focused on Trumpeldor's supposed last words, '*tov lamot be'ad eretzeinu*' ['It is good to die for our country'],[62] a Hebrew translation of the classically European sentiment *Dolce et Decorum Est Pro Patria Mori*. Much like MacDonagh's supposed last speech, the authenticity of this statement has been much debated, not least because Trumpeldor had only a rudimentary knowledge of Hebrew.[63] The cultural representation of Trumpeldor's death, though, had another, deeper similarity with the martyrs of Irish nationalism.

Where Irish nationalism reworked Catholic ideals of a Christ-like sacrifice that would redeem humanity, Zionism took the ideal of *kiddush ha-shem*, a Jewish martyrdom that would sanctify God's name, and partially secularised it into an ideal of martyrdom for the nation. Despite their religious rhetoric, these Irish and Jewish martyrs were not motivated by 'willingness to die to sanctify God's name' but by 'willingness to die to sanctify the homeland'.⁶⁴ Which is to say, they were not motivated by orthodox ideals of Catholicism or Judaism, but by modern, secularised and perhaps even (from a religious perspective) idolatrous versions of martyrdom. Their actions and the mythologies that grew up around them were didactic ideals to which all could metaphorically aspire: ideals of heroic men's service for the nation. 'Faith in the Zionist destiny granted meaning to random and cruel death in battle. The soldiers died in the name of Zionist ideals, and at the same time the ideal endowed death with moral value.'⁶⁵

Both sets of martyrs became paragons of a new, yet also old, masculine ideal. Oz Almog observes that 'The myth of Tel Chai encoded a symbolic element of great importance to Zionism—reinstating the Jewish people's lost honor. By the very act of fighting[,] the Tel Chai martyrs became a symbol of what distinguished Zionism from the Diaspora Jewish tradition of bowing one's head before the Gentile.'⁶⁶ They 'were viewed as new incarnations of great figures of the past'.⁶⁷ There was an explicit vision of redeemed masculinity at work here. Yet, that also means there was an implicit assumption that some elements of Irish and Jewish masculinity were degraded and thus in need of redemption. That Irish nationalists and Zionists felt the need to construct such visions of both redeemed *and* degraded masculinity points to an obvious issue at the heart of both ideologies: both Zionists and Irish nationalists implicitly accepted antisemitic or anti-Irish stereotypes. Both exhibited traits of national self-hatred.

Republicanism, Separatism and Other Forms of National Self-Hatred

The term 'self-hatred', popularised in Theodor Lessing's 1930 work *Der Jüdische Selbsthass* [*Jewish Self-Hatred*], is one of the most loaded epithets in modern Jewish politics.⁶⁸ It has been used to describe everything from the suicidal Austrian thinker Otto Weininger,⁶⁹ who, despite being of Jewish background, saw Jews as an inherently neurotic and effeminate people, to, more recently, Jewish critics of the State of Israel.⁷⁰ While there is often a strong dose of tendentiousness with which this accusation is thrown around, a large body of serious work argues that many modern Jewish thinkers and political movements held views of Jewish culture, society, and tradition which were remarkably similar to contemporary antisemitism.⁷¹ Often in conversation with each other, and often drawing on a postcolonialist understanding of Jewish identity, this literature advances the argument that Jews, on the receiving end of a powerful complex of antisemitic stereotypes, in turn often internalised these stereotypes. As Sander Gilman says, 'Self-hatred arises when the mirages of stereotypes are confused with realities within the world, when the desire for acceptance forces the acknowledgement of one's difference.'[72] A movement like Zionism was, thus, not just a straightforward movement for national liberation, but was also a movement to 'liberate' Jews from those aspects of Jewish culture that were so regularly decried by a powerful, antisemitic mainstream. A high level of national self-criticism, as well the attempt to craft idealised images of a 'new man' as a kind of national palliative, were the direct results of this 'self-hatred'. A central claim of this entire work is that a similar phenomenon existed in an Irish context, as Irish nationalists accepted many contemporary anti-Irish stereotypes.

'Self-hatred', though, is by no means an exclusively postcolonial phenomenon. In his innovative study of race and constructions of 'normality', Julian Carter notes that such harsh self-critique and idealised self-fashioning can also occur in decidedly non-colonial and non-minority settings. Carter identifies a powerful paradox, one that he labels the 'construction of whiteness as weakness', whereby those at the apex of perceived racial hierarchies claim to recognise their own innate racial inferiority. Doing so, 'allowed activism on behalf of white dominance' and reinforced the idea that 'whites', racially powerful enough to recognise their own flaws and properly reform themselves, are still racially superior.[73] Both Zionists and Irish nationalists seemed to readily admit that their nations exhibited major defects, particularly in the case of Irish and Jewish masculinity. This legitimised their (curative) control over those respective nations, but it is not always clear if they fully accepted these stereotypes or if they took them on strategically as a means of attacking the British rule or scattered Diaspora that they claimed had caused national degeneration.

Compare, for instance, the similarities in form and content of Leo Pinsker's *Auto-Emancipation*, one of Zionism's founding texts, with Terence MacSwiney's *Principles of Freedom*:

> With the loss of their fatherland, the Jewish people lost their independence, and fell into a decay which is not compatible with the existence of a whole and vital organism ... But after the Jewish people had yielded up its existence as an actual state, as a political entity, it could nevertheless not submit to total destruction—it did not cease to exist as a spiritual nation. Thus, the

world saw in this people the frightening form of one of the dead walking among the living. This ghostlike apparition of a people without unity or organization, without land or other bond of union, no longer alive, and yet walking among the living—this eerie form scarcely paralleled in history, unlike anything that preceded or followed it, could not fail to make a strange and peculiar impression upon the imagination of the nations. And if the fear of ghosts is something inborn, and has a certain justification in the psychic life of humanity, is it any wonder that it asserted itself powerfully at the sight of this dead but still living nation.[74]

And in the words of MacSwiney, in comparison:

the moral plague that eats up a people whose independence is lost is more calamitous than any physical rending of limb from body. The body is a passing phase; the spirit is immortal; and the degradation of that immortal part of man is the great tragedy of life. Consider all the mean things that wither up a people in a state of slavery… the aspect of that land and the soul of that people become spectacles of disgust, revolting and terrible, terrible for the high things degraded and the great destinies imperilled.[75]

Pinsker, for all his innovations, was still operating within a deep history of Jewish tradition. As David Biale reminds us, the vast majority of post-dispersion Jewish thinkers 'recognized the condition of *galut* (exile) as fundamentally abnormal and humiliating. In contrast to the memory (if not the reality) of a golden age of ancient sovereignty and the expectation of a messianic restoration, the *galut* was viewed as a period of abject powerlessness.'[76] Whether it was done intentionally or not, *Auto-Emancipation* echoes Deuteronomy 28:25: 'The Lord will cause you to be struck down before your enemies…. and you will be a cause of terror to all the kingdoms of the earth.' Additionally, the idea that Jews were a people who existed outside of history has a long pedigree; it informed Christian theology and eschatology from late antiquity onwards.[77] Zionists like Pinsker, in battling such notions, were taking on an idea that had far deeper roots within European thought than anti-Irish racism. Nonetheless, by the nineteenth century, some conceptually similar ideas about the Irish nation's place within historical time had emerged.

Lord Acton, a Catholic historian and Liberal MP for Carlow, claimed that Celts tended towards the 'stationary' or the 'regressive' and needed 'foreign influence', presumably that of the English, to set them in motion within history. Benjamin Disraeli, writing to the *Times* in 1836, expressed similar views, naming the Irish specifically, who, he said, 'hate our free and fertile isle'. Leaving little room for hope, he talked of the Irish as a primitive and irredeemable people: 'This wild, reckless, indolent, uncertain and superstitious race has no sympathy with the English character.' And in terms of time, 'Their history describes an unbroken circle of bigotry and blood.'[78] Additionally, the overtly simian images of Irish men in Victorian caricatures, which Michael de Nie has exhaustively studied, had a distinctly temporal register.[79] These caricatures suggested that the Irish were less evolved than their English neighbours, less advanced along a set path of historical development. While such perceptions may not have outlived the nineteenth century, they would cast a long shadow over Irish nationalist thought.

MacSwiney shares with Pinsker the idea that a lack of state sovereignty, the normative form of national existence in modern Europe, has placed their respective peoples outside of history and thus made them deformed and degraded.[80] And unlike antisemitic or anti-Irish stereotyping, which tended towards the claim that the Jews or the Irish were incapable of redemption, both Pinsker and MacSwiney hold out the possibility of reform via political sovereignty. Moreover, the title of *Auto-Emancipation* points to a similar politics of social reform as the name *Sinn Féin*. Both carry suggestions that in the process of national liberation 'we ourselves' will also be emancipated, reformed, and taught to be self-reliant (suggesting, of course, that 'we ourselves' are very much in need of such reform). Notwithstanding its more recent origins than in Jewish identity, 'self-hating' rhetoric was certainly a recurring and important feature of Irish nationalism during this period.[81]

Bulmer Hobson, a key figure in the pre-1916 Volunteers, claimed that 'Ireland[,] like every abnormal and unhealthy country[,] is beset with difficulties unknown to free and healthy communities.'[82] In a later pamphlet, Hobson spoke of 'The Flowing Tide' of Ireland, the 'periodic swing and return to life', through which the nation oscillated between heroic glory and weak and abject cowardice.[83] Writing in 1914, Liam de Roiste, who would later rise to prominence as a Sinn Féin and Cumann na nGaedheal politician, said the Irish were a 'childlike' people, and while he displayed a certain ambiguity about this, he also felt it would be preferable if the Irish could instead 'realise the dignity of manhood … It is high time some of us in Ireland grew up, high time that the little mean slave-mind were crushed'.[84] Decades later, the IRA belligerent Tom Barry recalled an operation during the War of Independence that brought him into anglicised Skibbereen, a town where even the great Fenian leader Jeremiah O'Donovan Rossa had 'failed to make the male population ... stand upright.' 'Its inhabitants were a race apart from the sturdy peoples of West Cork. They were different and, with a few exceptions, were spineless, slouching through life meek and tame, prepared to accept ruling and domination from any clique or country'.[85] Reflecting the widespread purchase of Irish self-hatred, a 1906 medical pamphlet claimed the Irish were racially and historically prone to bouts of insanity and said that the 'history of our country is one unbroken record of stress from within and without. It is impossible, in estimating the mental stature of the people to-day, to shut out that history.'[86]

That the Irish were incapable of self-rule, or were a child-like people in need of British parental supervision, had, of course, long been a claim of anti-Irish racism.[87] But it was also a theme prevalent within Irish nationalism itself and was clearly underpinned by an anxiety about the Irish nation's racial status.[88] Arthur Griffith, writing at the outset of the First World War, accused his 'emasculated' compatriots of having a 'slave mind'. This, he held, was the root cause of the 'lack of self-reliance' in contemporary Ireland, something 'which has reduced the stateliest race in Europe—the Gaels—to what they are today.' More than that, 'It is a tacit denial that the Irish are the peers of other white men—a tacit admission that England is right in her treatment of us.'[89] This metaphor of 'slavery', much beloved of Griffith and others, can be placed within a broader Anglo-Saxon political tradition that often contrasted abstract notions of freedom with equally abstract notions of slavery.[90] In a British imperial context, however, this should also be placed in a more specific context of an emerging 'white' identity that compared and contrasted (white) wage labour to (black) slavery. The lack of state sovereignty against which Griffith railed, was regularly equated with 'blackness'[91] and the Irish were thus seen as a not-fully-white nation.

Griffith was obviously offended by English accusations that 'The Irish are a people in a low stage of mental and moral development, turbulent, idle, improvident and intractable; naturally vicious, and incapable of any kind of ordered existence, except under a strong hand.'[92] Similarly, writing during the War of Independence, the popular nationalist historian Alice Stopford-Green, claimed the bulk of the English population rely for their perceptions of the Irish on 'the tradition of Punch caricatures.' These representations sat comfortably, she felt, with 'the pleasant English notion of an incompetent race which Providence has manifestly destined to conquest by a superior people.' While not totally disputing the veracity of these stereotypes, Stopford-Green did suggest the national struggle had created a different Irish racial type: 'A race of keen intelligence, of singular physical endurance, with a long and distinguished tradition in history, has become conscious of its true dignity. They have recovered their old idealism.'[93] Ernie O'Malley, a medical student turned IRA soldier, later remembered that one positive effect of the war was that 'The familiar stage Irishman had disappeared', replaced by the confident, armed men of the IRA.[94]

'Self-hatred', however, was as much a conscious strategy as it was the internalisation of powerful colonial stereotyping. Though Irish nationalists agreed that the Irish were degraded, they also saw social and political means of dealing with their degradation. Chief among these was to support Sinn Féin's project of self-reliant state-building. Where earlier radical nationalist propaganda had accused vast swathes of the Irish population of being slaves or naïve children, by the time of the 1918 elections, Sinn Féin took aim at a far narrower section of the population: the leaders of the Irish Parliamentary Party. Herbert Moore Pim, an odd figure who briefly came to the fore in Sinn Féin before turning to loyalism (and later, fascism),[95] called the IPP 'oily, red-faced, false-eyed, cunning, half-washed, peering creatures … national degenerates.' In contrast, Sinn Féiners were 'clean, clever, hard-headed, sensible, shrewd, monied people … keen business men, who regard the independence of Ireland as a business proposition.'[96] A poster for Sinn Féin's Patrick McCartan during the South Armagh by-election of 1918 depicted McCartan as a muscular, hardworking man in the stokehold of an Irish ship (the ship of state?),who declared: 'Well, even if its hard work and no pay—still its [sic] for my country.' In contrast, his opponent T.P. O'Connor, flabby and out of shape, was shown luxuriating on the deck of a British liner.[97] Not only did this depiction reference a well-publicised recent incident in which O'Connor had travelled to the United States on a first-class ticket, but his decadent male body also called to mind the flabby and out-of-shape condition of the IPP itself. In a Sinn Féin pamphlet from the same year, Michael O'Flanagan, a priest who later became a staunchly anti-Treaty republican, said Sinn Féin espoused a 'manly, straightforward, fearless policy' which would easily defeat 'the servile[,] slavish and futile' politics of the IPP.[98] During the 1918 general election, voters were urged to 'Be Men and Vote for Freedom!'[99] and 'If you make yourself a door-mat for England, John Bull will wipe his feet in [sic] you. And serve you right!' Instead 'Vote for the Manly Independent Policy' of Sinn Féin.'[100] Unlike these strong and self-reliant Sinn Féiners,

Home Rulers were accused of continuously 'whining to England.'[101] De Valera's electoral campaign had already claimed 'Home Rule has been kept for many years dangling before Mr. Redmond's nose like the carrot before the donkey'. Instead of a 'Donkey M.P. for East Clare' the Irish should 'Vote for de Valera!'[102] De Valera partisans supported 'a true patriot hero' and his 'gallant comrades' against 'renegade Irishmen' and 'evil nation-killing influences.'[103] More obliquely, voters in Roscommon were urged to support George Plunkett in 1917, because 'he is a consistent Irishman'.[104] What this kind of consistency represented can clearly be seen in a contemporary song about Plunkett:

Roscommon men ye hold the pass, And Eire looks to see, Your manhood strong with Plunkett throng To win her liberty. Then tell the knaves, who'd keep ye slaves. That Plunkett's name you'll write, By word and deed and vote to lead Him victor through the fight…	Roscommon men awake and tell The cowards that they lie When they proclaim your manhood tame Let this be your reply: 'Count Plunkett speaks for us to-day: Roscommon proudly hails The man exiled, by snobs reviled, Our prince of Irish Gaels.'[105]

Not only does the song bluntly promise that Plunkett will strengthen tame Irish manhood, but the threat is also held out that if the men of Roscommon do not vote for him, and instead choose the 'knaves' of the IPP, the nation will be kept in a status of degraded slavery; the proud freedom of non-enslaved (i.e. sovereign and white) men can only be guaranteed by voting for George Plunkett.

The immediate context of post-war Europe brought another important aspect of this to the fore. Sinn Féin's promise to restore dignity to a humiliated and degraded nation was also a promise to return Ireland to Europe, to secure Irish national sovereignty in the new post-1918 world. In the transnational 'Wilsonian Moment' after the First World War, various sub-state nationalisms, both in Europe and the colonial world, latched on to the vaguely defined idea of 'self-determination' with the hope that this would lead easily to statehood.[106] Already in 1917, in one of the earliest first-hand accounts of the Easter Rising, the Cumann na mBan activist Margaret Skinnider had said the insurrection had partly been motivated by a desire for international respect.[107] In the heady elections of 1917 and 1918, the promise of a return to Europe took centre stage. One Sinn Féin electoral leaflet pronounced that 'Ireland is your country. Don't be ashamed to advocate for it what the world is advocating for every other Small Nation.' As such, voters were urged 'Be a man for Ireland's sake. For your own sake. Think of the blessedness of Freedom.'[108] To do otherwise would be an implicit admission of Irish national inferiority: 'Does not England defame Ireland sufficiently in the eyes of the world? Why should you do it too? By voting against Absolute Independence you will tell the world that the Irish are the one race who cannot manage their own affairs without supervision by some other race.'[109] Fearing that the Irish might be left behind by this global shift, Sinn Féin also noted that 'The Czecho-Slovaks are Demanding Independence' before sarcastically observing that 'Nobody is quite sure who the Czecho-Slovaks are. But the Whole World knows who the Irish are and would wonder if that ancient race did not demand independence.' Beseeching voters, Sinn Féin asked 'Cannot you be as true to Ireland as the Czecho-Slovaks are to Czecho-Slovakia?'[110]

On to Civil War

The claim to be returning to a lost Irish sovereignty, the assumption that martyrdom could prove national masculinity, the belief that racial degradation and national humiliation were now at an end; these were all defining features of Irish politics in the years immediately after 1916. Yet they also drew on deep veins of nationalist thought. Additionally, Sinn Féin's promise of an end to national humiliation was strongly bolstered by the effectiveness of the emerging state, with its army and police, its courts, and its systems of public information. As this state itself came under attack during the Civil War, both the pro-Treaty and anti-Treaty sides turned their symbolic (and real) weapons on each other. Pointing to the depths to which 'Irish self-hatred' had sunk, both sides accused the other of being, in some way, defective or degraded men. A salient example is *The Victory of Sinn Féin*, P.S. O'Hegarty's semi-official Treatyite history of the War of Independence and Civil War, first published in 1924. In a chapter entitled 'The Moral Collapse', O'Hegarty spoke with nostalgia about a lost time when Sinn Féin was 'ascetic and clean, and its personnel corresponded to its ideals.' As it became a mass movement after 1916, however, there was recruited into the party 'a great deal of bad material, drunkards and crooks and morally unsuitable people of all sorts.' These people, he alleged, lowered the standards of Sinn Féin and the Irish 'became a mob, and a mob we remained.'[111] O'Hegarty also argued that the anti-Treaty Republicans were dominated by irrational women (discussed further in Chap. 7).

It was one of these women, Constance Markievicz, who produced one of the most illustrative examples of anti-Treaty propaganda: a series of caricatures of leading Treatyite politicians, now termed, simply, 'Free State Freaks'. W.T. Cosgrave, the President of the Executive Council, was portrayed as a Union-Jack-waving 'Jester in Chief to the Freak State'. Richard Mulcahy was a ghoulish Macbeth-like Minister for Defence, haunted by the dreams of the Irish men he had executed. The Minister for Posts and Telegraphs, J.J. Walsh, was a dissolute figure whilst Minister for External Affairs Desmond Fitzgerald was presented as a preening liar of seemingly indeterminate gender, and a functionary of the 'slave state' (see Fig. 2.2).[112] These were common slurs. At various points, Free State supporters were described as 'Seoinins',[113] 'Spineless worms',[114] 'Slave Staters',[115] 'recreant Irishmen',[116] and 'Unnatural enemies'.[117] In general, the Free State represented 'Rotten Means and Men'.[118] The Treaty was a sacrifice of national honour,[119] which could only deliver 'A Craven State'. The Treaty could not be a palliative to a nation degraded by a lack of

Fig. 2.2 *Free State Freaks* and *Cowardly Truceleers*, Civil War Posters, c. 1922
Source: NLI PD 3061 TX and NLI EPH B6

sovereignty. Anti-Treaty Sinn Féin instead promised 'All Ireland for the Irish, A self-reliant nation … A Fearless nation.'[120]

Conversely, the anti-Treaty side were portrayed by their opponents as people unable to take control of the freedom now presenting itself,[121] as unable to take responsibility for their actions.[122] Anti-Treatyites were often dismissed as 'truceleers' (see Fig. 2.2), dastardly men too cowardly to fight the English in the War of Independence, but who now attacked their fellow Irishmen and adhered to an irrational (for which, read 'hysterical and feminised'?) republicanism. Batt O'Connor, soon to be a member of Cumann na nGaedheal, remarked just before the split:

> the strangest thing of all is the number of weaklings who now are talking big, but who were very mute and done [sic] damn little when the reign of terror was sweeping over the land … I know men who resigned even from our local Sinn Féin club through sheer cowardice of the Black and Tans and now they say they stand for a Republic and 'will not let down de Valera'[.] These same fellows did not visit my house for 9 months when I could not sleep at home fearing they would be marked men if they were seen friendly with O'Connor or visiting his house.[123]

Kevin O'Higgins, rapidly emerging as a dominant Treatyite figure, was aghast at the changes he even saw in de Valera, accusing him of becoming a deeply irrational 'fury-ridden partisan of the wild words and bitter taunts, the leader of men whose methods are rapidly degenerating into emulation of the "Black-and-Tans"'.[124] More broadly, O'Higgins believed that centuries of English rule had left the Irish without 'political faculties' and with little in the way of 'civic sense.' Thus, anti-Treatyite republicans were ignorant that 'man is a social being and not a wild animal.'[125]

Imaginary nationalist time also recurred as a common theme during the Civil War. Anti-Treaty propaganda compared Free Staters to Dermot MacMurrough, the medieval king who had first invited the Anglo-Normans to Ireland, or to Robert Emmet's executioner.[126] Free State soldiers were termed 'Unnatural Irishmen' who had 'violated' the 'holy places' of the homes of Pearse, MacSwiney, and other 'martyrs'.[127] Indeed, an open letter to members of the Free State army had some pointed questions about where the pro-Treaty side fitted into the schema of nationalist time:

> Have you ever read Irish History? If you have. Pause! Think! Let your conscience answer. Why are you fighting for England? Who are your Historical Comrades in the centuries old persecution of Ireland? The Priest-Hunters

of the penal days. The Yeoman Pitch-Cap Brigade of '98. The Proselytisers and Soup Providers of the Famine Days. The Police and Militia of '67. The R.I.C. and the Black and Tans of 1916–'21. England equipped and armed these degraded allies in all her needs, and sent them to do her dirty work. To torture, maim and murder the true men whom Ireland honours … Do not carry on a war for England that will make your kinsmen in the present and your posterity in the future generations hang their heads with shame. Come over while ye may to the side of Ireland—your motherland. Let England find others degraded enough to do the devilish work. Line up with Tone, Emmet, Mitchell, Pearse, Connolly, MacSwiney, and Brugha.[128]

Anti-Treatyite publications regularly bore such legends as, in 1922, 'seventh year of the Republic', as if their loyal readers still inhabited an unspoiled space-time, free from the stain of political compromise.[129]

Nor was this the sole preserve of the anti-Treaty side. With religious zeal, *An t-Óglách* [The Youthful Warrior], the Free State army's newspaper, accused the anti-Treaty Irregulars of 'Taking Tone's Name in Vain.' Where Wolfe Tone sought 'To break the connection, and for this end to unite the people of Ireland', the Irregulars were accused of seeking 'To bring back the Army of England; and for this end to break the people of Ireland.' Obviously, anti-Treatyites could not claim to be occupying the same political space-time as Wolfe Tone. If this was not clear, *An t-Óglách*, in reference to the British-born Erskine Childers' senior position in the anti-Treaty IRA, spoke of him as 'An Englishman leading the destroying bands in their ruthless attacks on Irish property; an Englishman glorying in the shedding of Irish blood; an Englishman vilifying the chosen leaders of the Irish people—the Irregulars may have been wise in their generation to employ him so far; but they should have kept his hands from tampering with the text of Tone.'[130] A contemporary Treatyite handbill ploughed a similar furrow, taking issue with claims that the Irregulars were the heirs of the legacy of Pearse and the Rising. While 'The men of 1916 were organised from the cream of the Irish-Ireland movement', it was conversely claimed that the Irregulars were recruited from 'the irresponsible elements of the community—largely truceleers—men who have never been in any National movement in their lives—the disappointed, the discontented, and the demoralized.' The document was signed simply 'Republican', as if to reinforce the argument that whoever had the right to control memories of the past had also the sole right to ideological legitimacy.[131]

For these writers, to be placed outside of nationalist time was to be a degraded man. There also seems to have been a price to pay to enter this atemporal zone of manly Irish nationalism, and this had a clear didactic element. For both pro- and anti-Treatyites, a man could only consider himself a resident of this atemporal zone if he adhered to the 'correct' politics. This was a useful tool in the process of Irish state-building, as it allowed for an emerging elite to denounce the 'wrong' politics for interfering with their idealised vision of the past. Much of this, of course, was the kind of demonisation and denunciation common to any civil war. But it also drew on a longer and more profound history, of Irish nationalists internalising and strategically using negative anti-Irish stereotypes, in a similar manner to Zionists and antisemitic stereotypes. Indeed, a similar tactic was regularly utilised in Zionism which, 'Like every other religion … condemned those who deviated from its precepts and castigated schismatics and heretics.' Chief among Zionism's heretics were Jews who remained in the Diaspora and who were denounced 'as the diametric opposite of the pioneer[s] of the Land of Israel'. Non-Zionist Jews, echoing common antisemitic stereotypes, were accused of being perennially fearful, unhygienic and aesthetically degenerated.[132]

Moreover, not only did ideas that the Irish were a defective people in need of reform predate the events of 1912–23,[133] they also lasted well into the 1920s, as will be discussed in Chaps. 6 and 7. And if the Irish were a defective nation, voting for Sinn Féin alone would not cure them. A parallel cure, as this chapter has argued, was to engage in almost super-human acts of heroic self-sacrifice, which, much like voting for Sinn Féin, both disproved national weakness and acted as a legitimating glue between citizens and the newly emerging state. And where such acts of self-sacrifice may not have existed, they could always be invented.

As the following chapters will seek to show, in a world in which only the right kind of men were seen as capable of exercising sovereignty, inventing idealised images of heroic masculinity had long been central to the Irish nationalist project. Not least, it featured in debates about sport and militaries.

Notes

1. Quote ascribed to Claude Adrien Helvétius in L. Trotsky (1970) *My Life: An Attempt at an Autobiography* (New York: Pathfinder Press) p. 506.
2. Soloheadbeg 'came to be seen in retrospect as the opening round in the Anglo-Irish War … The reality was less simple and less neatly symbolic; for nearly two years Ireland had experienced a steady increase in violence,

and the country was not plunged overnight from peace into war by the ambush at Soloheadbeg.' M. Laffan (1999) *The Resurrection of Ireland: The Sinn Féin Party, 1916–1923* (Cambridge: Cambridge University Press) p. 266.
3. D. Breen (1924) *My Fight for Irish Freedom* (Dublin: Talbot Press) p. 35. Brian Boru was a late tenth century and early eleventh century Irish king. Traditionally, Breen and Brian are homonyms, reinforcing the comparison between the two.
4. D. Breen (1964) *My Fight for Irish Freedom* (Tralee: Anvil Books) p. 43. This statement is not in the first edition.
5. D. Breen (1924) *My Fight*, p. 51.
6. D. Breen (1964) *My Fight*, p. 62.
7. In his unpublished history of the Talbot Press, John J. Dunne recalls that Breen's book was one of their two best-ever sellers, the other being their ever-popular guide to beekeeping. NLI MS 35134 (4), *The Talbot Press: Sixty Golden Years of Irish Publishing*, 1973.
8. J. Regan (1999) *The Irish Counter-Revolution, 1921–1936: Treatyite Politics and Settlement in Independent Ireland* (Dublin: Gill & Macmillan) p. xv.
9. O. Almog (2000) *The Sabra: The Creation of the New Jew* (Berkeley, CA: University of California Press), p. 15.
10. In his posthumously published account of the Civil War, Ernie O'Malley claimed that during the fighting at the Four Courts during the Civil War, 'I suddenly thought of the dead. Had we maintained the tradition? What would our dead comrades of the Tan war, the men of 1916, the Fenians and the others think?' E. O'Malley (1978) *The Singing Flame* (Dublin: Anvil Books) p. 119. That O'Malley, who did not fight in 1916, and had no personal or familial links to the Fenian Rising of 1867, spoke as if he personally knew these men, is quite telling.
11. See, for instance, Thomas MacDonagh's play *When the Dawn is Come*, first performed in 1908. It is set 50 years in the future, but with characters based on eighteenth-century archetypes who speak in an incongruously archaic language, as if Irish nationalism had a reassuringly timeless essence. In J. Moran, ed. (2007) *Four Irish Rebel Plays* (Dublin: Irish Academic Press). In a more brazen example, the moderately nationalist Irish-American John Quinn recalled Roger Casement telling him: 'I am Wolfe Tone. I am the reincarnation of Wolfe Tone.' Quinn felt Casement had become unbalanced as a result of the First World War. NLI MS 18436, Xerox copies of material formerly in the papers of John Quinn, Memorandum by Quinn on Casement and the Irish situation in the US, 2 June 1916.
12. NLI LO P116, *Dalcassians*, de Valera handbill, n.d. (1917?); NLI LO P116, *A Bit of Dalcassian History*, de Valera handbill, n.d. (1917?).

13. It is worth remembering that at the time of this election, only men of a certain income could vote.
14. Military Archives, BMH CD 227/7/B1 (R), *Ní Fheadar Ca Dédarfadh* [*sic, Déarfadh*] *Seán Buide* [I do not know what John Bull will say], de Valera handbill, n.d. (1917).
15. Military Archives, BMH CD 227/7/B1 (Q), *Dá mBristí an Caisleán Mór* [If Dublin Castle was smashed], de Valera Handbill, n.d. (1917).
16. D. Biale (1987) *Power and Powerlessness in Jewish History* (New York: Schocken Books) p. 148.
17. P. Chatterjee (1993) *The Nation and Its Fragments: Colonial and Postcolonial Histories* (Princeton NJ: Princeton University Press) p. 97.
18. NLI Uncatalogued Election Ephemera, *To the Voters of Armagh*, Patrick McCartan handbill/Open letter from de Valera, 22 January 1918.
19. NLI LO P116, *Up Kilkenny*, W.T. Cosgrave Handbill, n.d. (1917?).
20. Military Archives, BMH CD 264/2/4, *Do You Stand By Wolfe Tone?*, Sinn Féin handbill, n.d. (1918).
21. Military Archives, BMH CD 227/7/B1 (L), *What John Redmond Said When He Was An Irishman*, Sinn Féin handbill, n.d. (1917?).
22. Fitzpatrick observes that in 1913 the Home Rule Party in Clare had spoken quite approvingly of the so-called Manchester Martyrs, three members of the Irish Republican Brotherhood executed in 1867 for the murder of a policeman. D. Fitzpatrick (1998) *Politics and Irish Life, 1913–1921: Provincial Experience of War and Revolution*, 2nd edn (Dublin: Gill and Macmillan, 1998) p. 78.
23. S. Lewis (1935) *It Can't Happen Here* (New York: The Sun Dial Press) p. 5. James O'Kelly, the previous holder of the North Roscommon Westminster seat before Count Plunkett, claimed to have been a member of the IRB during the 1867 rising. As Laffan observes, he 'followed a path familiar to Irish nationalists as he drifted from physical force to constitutional politics.' That he continued to trade on his radical past, and that this was presumably a popular tactic, says a lot about Irish nationalist politics. M. Laffan (1999) *Resurrection of Ireland*, pp. 77–78.
24. A. Najmabadi (2005) *Women with Mustaches and Men without Beards: Gender and Sexual Anxieties of Iranian Modernity* (Berkeley CA: California University Press), pp. 207–231. For a specific discussion of how this happened in Irish nationalism, see: J. Steel, '"And behind him a wicked hag did stalk": From Maiden to Mother, Ireland as Woman Through the Male Psyche' in L. Ryan, M. Ward, eds. *Irish Women and Nationalism: Soldiers, New Women and Wicked Hags* (Dublin: Irish Academic Press) pp. 96–113.
25. As Sikata Banerjee points out, 'the social construction of muscular nationalism … was rooted in a foundational duality of male warriors who

protected a nation symbolized by the chastity of female bodies.' S. Banerjee (2012) *Muscular Nationalism: Gender, Violence and Empire in India and Ireland* (New York: NYU Press), p. 105.

26. Without more detailed information as to who designed this poster, which does not appear to have survived, it is impossible to offer anything other than educated guesses as to the intention of this image. An advanced feminist who inhabited what Banerjee calls the 'borderlands between armed masculinity and chaste femininity' and who wished to challenge the strictures of Irish 'muscular nationalism' may have designed the poster. Ibid., 77. Alternatively, given that the poster was for a by-election in a rural and relatively isolated constituency, its gender-bending themes may point to the survival of some pre-existing and less restrictive gender norms, which had not yet been expurgated by the slow process of Irish modernity.
27. P. Chatterjee (1993) *Nation and Its Fragments*, p. 54.
28. D. Biale (1997) *Eros and the Jews: From Biblical Israel to Contemporary America* (Berkeley CA: University of California Press) p. 198.
29. Y. Zerubavel (1995) *Recovered Roots: Collective Memory and the Making of Israeli National Tradition* (Chicago: University of Chicago Press) pp. 200–203.
30. M. Stanislawski (2001) *Zionism and the Fin de Siècle: Cosmopolitanism and Nationalism from Nordau to Jabotinsky* (Berkeley CA: Univeristy of California Press) pp. 95–96. That contemporary Zionist heroes marked the rebirth of an ancient masculinity was overtly suggested by the name used by Jabotinsky's youth movement, Betar. As well as being the name of the town that Bar Kochba died defending, it was also a Hebrew abbreviation of *Brit Trumpeldor* [The Covenant of Trumpeldor], thus uniting selfless martyrs from the biblical past and Zionist present.
31. J. Cohen (2006) *Sanctifying the Name of God: Jewish Martyrs and Jewish Memories of the First Crusade* (Philadelphia, PA: University of Pennsylvania Press) pp. 1–9 and *passim*.
32. R.F. Foster (1989) *Modern Ireland: 1600–1972* (London: Penguin) pp. 477–484. Contrary to such analyses, Conor Kostick argues that the mentality of those who took part in the Rising should be seen as follows: 'they were committed to a serious attempt to defeat the British army in Ireland rather than seeing themselves as engaging in a sacrifice or a piece of street theatre. In the aftermath of a relatively small mobilization the idea that Britain could have been ousted by such an action seems far-fetched, but at the time the prospects for successful rebellion seemed promising. The IRB had intended to mobilise the bulk of the Irish Volunteers (16,000) right across the country, while the British army had just 6,000 combat troops in Ireland, supported by 9,500 members of the Royal Irish

Constabulary.' C. Kostick (2009) *Revolution in Ireland: Popular Militancy, 1917–1923*, 2nd edn (Cork: Cork University Press), p. 25.

33. Benedict Anderson makes a similar point about nationalist ideology in general: 'the silence of the dead was no obstacle to the exhumation of their deepest desires' as nationalists 'learned to speak "for" dead people with whom it was impossible or undesirable to establish a linguistic connection' in an example of what Anderson sardonically calls 'reverse ventriloquism'. B. Anderson (2006) *Imagined Communities: Reflections on the Origin and Spread of Nationalism* 2nd edn (London: Verso) p. 198.

34. NLI ILB 300 P6, Item 16, *Irish Insurrection. 1916. MacDonaghs [sic] Last Words: Last and inspiring address of Commandant Thomas MacDonagh, M.A., of the Irish Republican Army, given before a Court Martial, after sentence of death had been pronounced upon him for having fought in the recent struggle for Irish Freedom*, handbill, n.d. The title, particularly the use of the term 'Irish Republican Army' suggests this was printed sometime after 1919. See also NLI ILB 300 P6, Item 17, *Last Address of Thomas MacDonagh*, and Item 18, *Last and Inspiring Address of Thomas MacDonaghs*, handbill, n.d., upon which someone has handwritten 'This was not authentic T.W.L. August 21, 1916.' It should be noted, though, that MacDonagh's will did declare 'I am ready to die and thank God that I am to die in so holy a cause, my Country will reward my deed richly'. NLI MS 20644/7, Thomas MacDonagh Family Papers, *The Will of Thomas MacDonagh Esq.*, 2 May 1916.

35. B. Barton, ed. (2002) *From Behind a Closed Door: Secret Court Martial Records of the 1916 Easter Rising* (Belfast: Blackstaff Press) pp. 131–132. It also seems that some of MacDonagh's family were taken in by this. In 1932 a gramophone recording of MacDonagh's supposed speech, read by actor Paul Farrell, was released. Press cuttings related to this record are included in the MacDonagh family papers, one of which has a handwritten note on it that this was 'Tom's Speech', suggesting even whoever wrote this (a family member or close friend?) had come to believe that this was a real speech of MacDonagh's.

36. M. Laffan (1999) '*Resurrection of Ireland*', p. 53. Moreover, 'At least some of the female students in University College, Dublin professed a romantic interest only in those male colleagues who had been imprisoned after the rising.' Ibid., p. 54.

37. D. Gwynn (1930) *The Life and Death of Roger Casement* (London: J. Cape) p. 16.

38. NLI, Bulmer Hobson Papers, MS 17604 (5), Letter from Denis Gwynn to Bulmer Hobson, 30 October 1936.

39. The manner in which Casement was constructed as a heroic figure has been discussed by W.J. McCormack (2003) *Roger Casement in Death: Or, Haunting the Free State* (Dublin: UCD Press). See also M. Hay

(2009) *Bulmer Hobson and the Nationalist Movement in Twentieth-Century Ireland* (Manchester: Manchester University Press), for a discussion of the conspiratorially-minded W.J. Maloney and his 1937 work *The Forged Casement Diaries*. Since this case has been ably analysed by Hay and McCormack, and since it primarily concerns works published well after the period 1916–23, it is not further discussed here.
40. 'MacSwiney, Terence James' (2009) *Dictionary of Irish Biography* (Cambridge: Cambridge University Press).
41. UCDA, Terence MacSwiney Papers, P48B/457, Untitled poem/Handbill about Terence MacSwiney by Brian O'Higgins.
42. UCDA, Terence MacSwiney Papers, P48B/462 (2), *Let Him Die*, Poem by G. O'Driscoll. According to the description in UCDA P48B/462 (1), this poem was written after an MP had suggested the government should let MacSwiney die: 'The acrimony of those callous words aimed at a dying martyr, could only be equalled in its severity, by the words of another class of murderers who once said "Let Him Be Crucified."'
43. This point is made in P.S. O'Hegarty's account of MacSwiney, written in late 1920 but not published until 1922. P.S. O'Hegarty (1922) *A Short Memoir of Terence MacSwiney* (Dublin: Talbot Press) p. 93.
44. UCDA, Terence MacSwiney Papers, P48B/433, Letter from Mary MacSwiney to Edward Shortt, Home Secretary, 22 October 1920. Marked "For Publication." Emphases added. Mary MacSwiney had earlier taken a strong exception to the suggestion that she had requested a reprieve for her brother, from Lloyd George. She called this a 'malicious' lie. UCDA, Mary MacSwiney Papers, P48A/110, Letter from Mary MacSwiney to David Lloyd George, n.d.
45. UCDA, Terence MacSwiney Papers, P48B/436, *Is Self Sacrifice a Crime?*, A reply by Miss Mary MacSwiney to Fr. Bernard Vaughan's Statement about giving the Sacraments to Hunger Strikers, n.d.
46. UCDA, Terence MacSwiney Papers, P48B/437, *A Message from the Lord Mayor of Cork to Irish Prisoners on Hunger-Strike in Cork Gaol*, n.d.
47. It is featured, for instance, on the Catholic memorial card for MacSwiney, on which it is also stated that he 'died for his country in Brixton Prison, England, 26th October, 1920. (4th Year of the Irish Republic)'. CCCA U71/2, Terence MacSwiney Papers, *Terence McSwiney Memorial Card*, n.d.
48. Terence J. MacSwiney. 'Ode to a Bullet.' *Fianna Fáil/The Irish Army. A Journal for Militant Ireland*, Vol. 1, No. 4 (17 October 1914).
49. NLI ILB 300 P6, Item 34, *Before the Last Battle: Poem Written By Terence MacSwiney, now facing death for Ireland in Brixton Jail*, n.d. (1920?).
50. 'MacSwiney, Terence' (2009) in *Dictionary of Irish Biography*.

51. CCCA SM645, Terence MacSwiney Papers, *Terence MacSwiney Funeral Poster*, n.d. (October, 1920?).
52. Paige Reynolds has engaged in a thorough discussion of 'scripting the death' of Terence MacSwiney. P. Reynolds (2007) *Modernism, Drama, and the Audience for Irish Spectacle* (Cambridge: Cambridge University Press) pp. 116–155.
53. P.S. O'Hegarty (1922) *MacSwiney*, p. 97.
54. Ibid., p. 95. As this quote highlights, women, in this case Joan of Arc, did sometimes appear in these narratives of heroic self-sacrifice. There were regular challenges to the idea that self-sacrifice for the honour of the nation was the preserve of warrior-men. The notion of 'women warriors', however, posed a difficult question for a male-dominated national movement. 'Whom did women warriors protect? Theoretically, the answer to this question was quite simple. It was just as possible to envision a band of women warriors united by the bonds of sisterhood, sacrificing their lives to protect Mother Ireland … as to imagine a similar group of male warriors.' S. Banerjee (2012) *Muscular Nationalism*, p. 105.
55. P.H. Pearse (1917) *Collected Works of P.H. Pearse* (Dublin: Phoenix). See also the playbill for the 1915 public performance of *Íosagán*, which include notes by Pearse elaborating on this theme. NUIG, Stephen Barrett Papers, G3/1056, *Íosagán Play-Bill*, The Irish Theatre, Hardwicke Street, May 1915.
56. NLI MS 44337/6, Thomas MacDonagh Family Papers, *A Mother Speaks*, Postcard of Pearse's Last Poem; See also NLI ILB 300 P3, Item 51. During the Civil War one republican handbill drew on rich veins of nationalism, Catholicism and antisemitism. It quoted Matthew 27:22–25, wherein the Jews call for Christ's crucifixion, Pilate washes his hands and the crowd cry out 'His blood be upon us and upon our children.' A republican note of exegesis at the end notes merely 'And "the will of the people" prevailed.' Thus it suggests that the Treatyites were guilty of deicide in their attacks on anti-Treatyite men. Military Archives, BMH CD, 6/42, Undated Civil War Anti-Treaty handbill.
57. Military Archives, BMH CD 264/45/7, *Let Me Carry Your Cross for Ireland, Lord*, Poem/Handbill by Thomas Ashe, n.d. (1917).
58. NLI LO P116, *Why You Should Support Count Plunkett*, George Plunkett handbill, n.d. (1917?).
59. G. Mosse (1990) *Fallen Soldiers: Reshaping the Memory of the World Wars* (Oxford: Oxford University Press) p. 7. See also: J. Bourke (1996) *Dismembering the Male: Men's Bodies, Britain and the Great War* (Chicago: University of Chicago Press) pp. 212–232 and *passim*.
60. T. Segev (27 April 1990) '*Ma Osot HaAndarta' ot Be-Leylot: Doach Masa*'. [What the Statues do at Night: A Travel Report] *Ha-Aretz*. I am grateful

to Dr. Michael Feige, z"l, for first bringing this article to my attention, and to Tom Segev for his help in tracking it down.
61. O. Almog (2000) *The Sabra*, p. 49.
62. This phrase was printed on a large number of postcards and posters of Trumpeldor, which circulated in Jewish Palestine. See, for example, CZA Arieh Rafaeli (Tsentsiper) Collection, PHZPR\1253351, undated photograph of Trumpeldor. Tellingly, the exact wording of the phrase was subject to change. CZA, General Collection, PHG\1102307, undated postcard, for example, gives the phrase as '*eyn davar, kedai lamot be'ad eretz ha-moledet*' [It is nothing, in order to die for the homeland], which it describes as the last words of *ha-gibor* which, in a gendered pun that was commonly used in Zionist propaganda, is a word that can mean both 'the hero' and 'the man'.
63. Y. Zerubavel (1995) *Recovered Roots*, pp. 157–160.
64. O. Almog (2000) *The Sabra*, p. 38.
65. Ibid., p. 72.
66. Ibid, p. 38.
67. Ibid., p. 40.
68. For some of the aetiology of this term, see S. Gilman (1986) *Jewish Self-Hatred: Antisemitism and the Secret Language of the Jews* (Baltimore, MD: Johns Hopkins University Press) pp. 286–308.
69. J.M. Hoberman. 'Otto Weininger and the Critique of Jewish Masculinity' (1994) in N. Harrowitz, B. Hyam, eds. *Jews and Gender: Responses to Otto Weininger* (Philadelphia, PA: Temple University Press) pp. 141–153. Pointing to the potential pitfalls of the term *self-hatred*, Chandak Sengoopta has pointed out, in a work focusing on his private papers, that Weininger does not seem to have been particularly conscious of his own Jewish background, nor was it an overt motivating factor in his work. C. Sengoopta (2000) *Otto Weininger: Sex, Sciences and Self in Imperial Vienna* (Chicago: University of Chicago Press).
70. See, for example, the sophistic accusations made by Alan Dershowitz that 'There has always been a small element within the Jewish community that for largely inexplicable reasons has been hypercritical of everything associated with Judaism, Jews or the Jewish states [*sic*]. Karl Marx, Noam Chomsky and Norman Finkelstein come easily to mind ... I do not mean to suggest by this observation that all anti-Zionists and Israel-bashers are self-hating Jews. People can be wrong on the merits without requiring any psychological explanation. But the reality is that there are some Jews who despise anything Jewish, ranging from their religion, to the Jewish state, to individuals who are "too Jewish."' A. Dershowitz (2003) *The Case for Israel* (New York: John Wiley & Sons) p. 220.
71. Other than S. Gilman (1986) *Self-Hatred*, which has already been mentioned, this argument features, in one way or another, in the following

important works: M. Gluzman (2007) *HaGuf HaTzioni: Le'umiyut, Migdar u-Miniyut ba-Sifrut ha-Ivrit ha-Chadashah* (The Zionist Body: Nationalism, Gender and Sexuality in Modern Hebrew Literature) (Tel Aviv: Ha-Kibbutz Ha-Meuchad); O. Almog (2000) *The Sabra*; D. Boyarin (1997) *Unheroic Conduct: The Rise of Heterosexuality and the Invention of the Jewish Man* (Berkeley CA: University of California Press, 1997); D. Penslar (2001) *Shylock's Children: Economics and Jewish Identity in Modern Europe* (Berkeley CA: University of California Press); D. N. Myers (1995) *Re-Inventing the Jewish Past: European Jewish Intellectuals and the Zionist Return to History* (Oxford: Oxford University Press, 1995).

72. S. Gilman (1986) *Self-Hatred*, p. 4.
73. J.B. Carter (2007) *The Heart of Whiteness: Normal Sexuality and Race in America, 1880-1940* (Durham NC: Duke University Press, 2007), pp. 42–74.
74. L. Pinsker 'Auto-Emancipation: An Appeal to his People by a Russian Jew' (1882/1973) in A. Hertzberg, ed. *The Zionist Idea: A Historical Analysis and Reader* (New York: Atheneum) p. 184.
75. T. MacSwiney (1921) *Principles of Freedom* (New York: E.P Dutton). This collection was first published in book form in 1921, having initially been published serially in *Irish Freedom* between March 1911 and December 1912.
76. D. Biale (1987) *Power and Powerlessness*, p. 34.
77. J. Cohen (1999) *Living Letters of the Law: Ideas of the Jew in Medieval Christianity* (Berkeley, CA: University of California Press) pp. 23–65.
78. Both quoted in S. Banerjee (2012) *Muscular Nationalism*, p. 35.
79. M. De Nie (2004) *The Eternal Paddy: Irish Identity and the British Press, 1798–1882* (Madison, WI: University of Wisconsin Press), *op cit*.
80. As de Valera observed, in 1920, comparing Ireland to India: 'All people are necessarily backward when you deliberately debar them from progress … They are necessarily unable to rule themselves when you deprive them of all opportunity for trying. One cannot swim if the water to swim in, or the opportunity to enter it, is denied.' E. de Valera (1920) *India and Ireland* (New York: Friends of Freedom for India). For a copy of this pamphlet, see UCDA, de Valera Papers, P150/1053.
81. One issue not explored in this chapter, but important to bear in mind, is that such 'self-hating' attacks on the Irish nation should be seen alongside the similarly vitriolic attacks on a supposedly immoral English nation, which were also recurring features in contemporary nationalist propaganda. Such a degraded nation was ostensibly the antithesis of the more heroic Irish, as has been studied by B. Novick (2001) *Conceiving Revolution: Nationalist Propaganda During The First World War* (Dublin: Four Courts Press) pp. 132–169.

82. B. Hobson (1909) *Defensive Warfare: A Handbook for Irish Nationalists* (Belfast: The West Belfast Branch of Sinn Féin).
83. B. Hobson (n.d.) *The Flowing Tide* (Belfast: Freedom Club Leaflets No. 1).
84. Liam de Roiste (10 October, 1914) 'Children and Men.' *Fianna Fáil/The Irish Army: A Journal for Militant Ireland*, Vol. 1, No. 3.
85. T. Barry (1949) *Guerrilla Days in Ireland* (Dublin: Irish Press) pp. 89–90.
86. M.J. Nolan (1906) *The Increase in Insanity in Ireland and Its Causes* (Dublin: Fannin & Co). Nolan was Resident Medical Superintendent for Down District Asylum and had previously served in similar capacities in Dublin and Limerick. This article was written at the behest of *Medical Press and Circular* and was reprinted from that publication.
87. M. de Nie (2004) *Eternal Paddy*, pp. 222–223.
88. 'We had from centuries of oppression the faults of slaves, seldom their vices, and when one met men who were born free one thanked God for it.' E. O'Malley (2011) *Raids and Rallies* (Cork: Mercier) p. 11.
89. A. Griffith (n.d.) *How Ireland Has 'Prospered' Under English Rule, and The Slave Mind* (New York: Irish Progressive League. The National Library of Ireland catalogue suggests this may have been published in 1911, but since it talks of England 'fighting for her life', it was presumably written after the outbreak of the War, but before the Easter Rising (a monumental event of which it makes no mention).
90. D. Losurdo (2011) *Liberalism: A Counter-History* (London: Verso) pp. 35–65.
91. D.R. Roediger (1991 *The Wages of Whiteness: Race and the Making of the American Working Class* (London: Verso) pp. 27–31.
92. A. Griffith (n.d.) *How Ireland Has 'Prospered'*.
93. A. Stopford Green (n.d.) *The Irish Republican Army* (American Association for the Recognition of the Irish Republic). *Punch* magazine was a British satirical publication notorious, in Ireland, for the viciousness of its anti-Irish caricatures. See M. De Nie (2004) *Eternal Paddy*.
94. E. O'Malley (1978) *Singing Flame*, p. 12.
95. C. Brennan (2012) 'The Curious Career of Herbert Moore Pim.' See www.theirishstory.com, date accessed 22 July 2013.
96. M. Laffan (1999) *Resurrection of Ireland*, p. 229.
97. NLI Uncatalogued Election Ephemera, *Which Do You Choose?*, Patrick McCartan handbill, n.d. (1918?).
98. Military Archives, BMH CD 131/8/6, *The Two Policies: Sinn Fein or Parliamentarism*, by a Western Priest, Pamphlet, September 1918.
99. Military Archives, BMH CD 131/8/6, *Be Men and Vote for Freedom!*, Sinn Féin handbill, n.d. (1918?).

100. Military Archives, BMH CD 131/8/6, *Do you favour the Door-mat Policy?*, Sinn Féin handbill, n.d. (1918?).
101. Military Archives, BMH CD 131/8/6, *Do You Believe in Whining to England*, Sinn Féin handbill, 1918.
102. NLI LO P116, *The Bishop of Limerick and John Redmond*, de Valera handbill, n.d. (1917?),
103. 'Address to Edmond [sic] de Valera from the People of Bruree.' *The Clare Champion*, 7 July 1917. A contemporary pro-de Valera song described him as 'my ideal of what noble man should be … As a father, soldier, scholar, always gentle always kind.' M. Laffan (1999) *Resurrection of Ireland*, p. 112.
104. NLI LO P116, *Why You Should Support Count Plunkett*, George Plunkett handbill, n.d. (1917?).
105. NLI LO P116, *Hurrah! Hurrah! For Plunkett*, George Plunkett handbill, n.d. (1917?). The song was to be sung to the tune of 'The Boys of Wexford', thus linking Plunkett's heroism with that of the 1798 rebellion.
106. E. Manela (2007) *The Wilsonian Moment: Self-Determination and the International Origins of Anticolonial Nationalism* (Oxford: Oxford University Press) *passim*.
107. M. Skinnider (1917) *Doing My Bit for Ireland* (New York: The Century Co.) p. vii. And, as already mentioned, Arthur Griffith was uneasy about the 'tacit denial that the Irish are the peers of other white men'.
108. Military Archives, BMH CD 131/8/6, *Voter—Think*, Sinn Féin handbill, n.d. (1918?).
109. Military Archives, BMH CD 264/2/4, *Why Should You Do it, too?*, Sinn Féin handbill, n.d. (1918?).
110. Military Archives, BMH CD 264/2/4, *The Czecho-Slovaks are Demanding Independence*, Sinn Féin handbill, n.d. (1918?).
111. P.S. O'Hegarty (1924) *The Victory of Sinn Féin: How and It Won It, And How It Used It* (Dublin: Talbot Press) pp. 54–55.
112. NLI ILB 300 P24, *Free State Freaks*, n.d. (1922?).
113. NLI ILB 300 P6, Item 100, *Who is there Left?*, Anti-Treaty handbill, n.d. (1922?). This term, literally meaning Little or Effeminate John, refers to a deracinated Irish person who apes English customs. One I.R.A. veteran defined the term thusly: a 'little John Bull … anyone who aped the manners and fashions of the English as interpreted through the Anglicised Irish; who adapted his mentality, or lack of it, to theirs; who despised and, actively or passively, ignored the remnant of the older Gaelic civilization of the people.' E. O'Malley, *On Another Man's Wounds* (London: Rich & Cowan, 1936) p. 15.
114. NLI ILB 300 P13, Item 44, anti-Treaty flyer, n.d. (1922?).

115. Military Archives, BMH CD 4/9/3, *The Fenian*, No. 11 (27 July, 1922, Seventh Year of the Republic).
116. Military Archives, BMH CD, 6/36/6, *Óglaigh na h-Eireann*: *Proclamation*, 28 June 1922.
117. Military Archives, BMH CD, 6/36/9, *Address to the Dublin Brigade*, Letter from Oscar Traynor, n.d.
118. Military Archives, BMH CD 264/50/20, *Poblacht na h-Eireann*, No. 22 (24 July 1922: Seventh Year of the Republic).
119. DDA, Archbishop Byrne Papers, Box 446, Byrne Government Papers, *Daily Bulletin*, No. 163, Wednesday 11 April, Eight [*sic*] Year of the Republic [1923?].
120. NLI LO P117, *The Two Policies*, n.d. (1922–23?). The Pale was, in medieval and early modern Ireland, an enclave of English royal rule. In the early twentieth century, the term was often used to refer to an anglicised Ireland, in opposition to a more proud Irish-Ireland.
121. NLI MS 33912 (10), Piaras Béaslaí Papers, Hand-Written Notes for Pro-Treaty Speech; NLI MS 33912 (22), Piaras Béaslaí Papers, *An Bhfuil Eagla Ort?* [Are You Afraid?], pro-Treaty handbill, n.d. (1922?).
122. NLI 94109 P70, Item 12, *Simply Gamblers*, Pro-Treaty Speech by Arthur Griffith, n.d. (1922?).
123. J. Regan (1999) *Counter-Revolution*, p. 54.
124. NLI IR 94109 P70, Item 13, Kevin O'Higgins. *The New de Valera: A Contrast and some Disclosures*, March 1922.
125. K. O'Higgins (n.d.) *The Catholic Layman in Public Life* (Dublin: Catholic Truth Society).
126. NLI ILB 300 P13, Item 6, anti-Treaty flyer, n.d. (1922?); NLI LOLB 161, Item 54, *A Second Judge Toler*, Republican Political Prisoners' Committee Handbill, n.d. (1922–23?).
127. NLI ILB 300 P13, Item 38, *Holy Places in Ireland have been Violated by Vandals*, anti-Treaty flyer, n.d. (1922?).
128. NLI Uncatalogued Political Ephemera, Box 2, *To the Free State Forces*, anti-Treaty handbill, n.d.
129. See, for instance, the copies of *Poblacht na h-Eireann* [The Irish Republic] in the Military Archives, BMH CD 264/50/20 and the copies of the *Daily Bulletin* in DDA, Archbishop Byrne Papers, Box 446, Byrne Government Papers, which bore such dates as: 26 July 1922: Seventh Year of the Republic) and Friday 6 April, Eight [*sic*] Year of the Republic [1923?].
130. 'Taking Tone's Name in Vain.' *An t-Óglách: The Official Organ of the Irish Volunteers*, Vol. 4, No. 13 (2 September 1922). It is also worth noting that that publication's title called to mind both the warriors of Irish mythology and *Óglaigh na hÉireann*, the Irish Volunteers of 1913.

131. NLI Uncatalogued Historical Proclamations, 1920–29, *1916–1922—A Comparison*, Treatyite handbill, 1922.
132. O. Almog (2000) *Sabra*, pp. 21, 77.
133. This was perhaps *the* key theme in the influential writings of D.P. Moran. In *The Philosophy of Irish-Ireland* (1905), the Irish middle classes were portrayed as snobbish but shame-filled and continually aping English manners, themes continued in his now largely forgotten novel *Tom O'Kelly* (1905).

CHAPTER 3

Organised Manhood

Wellington is credited with the dictum that the battle of Waterloo was won on the playing-fields of Eton. I am certain that when it comes to a question of Ireland winning battles, her main reliance must be on her hurlers. To your *camáns*, O boys of Banba![1]

JEW REGARD FOR THE LAW

In September 1924, *Guth an Gharda* [The Policeman's Voice], a short-lived newspaper published by and for the members of the Irish Free State's nascent police force, featured a caricature entitled 'Jew Regard for the Law' (See Fig. 3.1). Punning on Irish people's similar pronunciations of 'd-u-e' and 'j-e-w', what might at first appear mere antisemitic doggerel had some deeper veins of nationalist meaning. This cartoon 'Jew' embodied a number of the somatic anxieties that were at the very core of the Irish nationalist project. This chapter is a review of the athletic and militarised strategies used to craft a more ideal image of resurgent Irish manhood that would counter those anxieties. This chapter seeks to show how such anxieties predated the 'revolution' of the 1910s and also lasted well into the 1920s.

'Jew Regard for the Law' was a means of thinking about Irish men's white, masculine identity, about the implications of political sovereignty, and about the negative gendered effects of losing that political sovereignty.

Fig. 3.1 Jew Regard for the Law, *Garda Cartoon*, 1924
Source: Guth an Gharda [The Policeman's Voice], September 1924

This cartoon was a low-culture version of what David Nirenberg analyses as 'Anti-Judaism': the use of an abstract 'Jewishness' as a category of political thought.[2] Nirenberg sees much of value in Adorno and Horkheimer's suggestion that to 'call someone a Jew amounts to an instigation to work him over until he resembles the image.'[3] Irishmen, in racist representations, had often been 'worked over' and made to resemble other supposedly inferior races. Disproving those stereotypes that compared them to other 'inferior' ethnic minorities (like Jews) was a prominent, if usually implicit, aim of Irish nationalists. *Guth an Gharda*'s cartoon presents this 'Jewish' figure as the antithesis of the stable, pure and masculine Irish nation that formal political sovereignty delivers. The policeman, unlike the 'Jew', has a correct conception of the law and of modern sovereignty; as an empowered citizen, he manages to reconcile the paradox of completely obeying the law without being meekly subservient. The hybridity and liminality of 'Jews' also serves here as a convenient counterfoil for imagining an idealised Irish body. 'Jew Regard for the Law' should thus be read as a diptych, one that contrasts the muscular and upright Irish policeman with the diminutive and weak Jewish figure. The latter's flabby and ill-matched business attire reflects his presumably underdeveloped muscles. His shuffling movements and his dirty and unkempt beard are the stark opposites of the hygienic Irish man who stands straight and proud. Irish nationalists sought to purge their own inner racial indeterminacy and so when the policeman looks back at this 'Jewish' symbol of the lack of political sovereignty, he is looking back at his own former national weakness and deformity. Recognising his lack of political sovereignty in the past serves to confirm both his political sovereignty and his healthy bodily normality in the present. By 1924 Ireland had achieved formal political sovereignty and the uniformed policeman could now easily look askance at this deformed and politically powerless 'Jew'. Just as the 'Jew's' political abnormality is mirrored by his physical deformity, so Ireland's newfound political normalisation is mirrored by a policeman whose body is almost aggressively normal. Where he once was weak and deformed like the 'Jew', now his control over a State (the Law) has redeemed him and made him whole.

There is a broader point to be made here about how a large swathe of nineteenth- and twentieth-century European nationalists focused strongly on stability, purity and strictly defined political and racial categories, while coding the obverse of all this as 'Jewish'. This was a pan-European strategic move of imagining full national sovereignty in opposition to 'Jewish' indeterminacy and weakness. As Nirenberg notes, it was in the Middle Ages that 'negative manifestations of "earthly sovereignty" took on a fleshy Jewish figure that they would never lose.'[4] In the case of European nationalist ideologies, 'Jewishness' became a figure of both powerlessness and an indeterminate and deracinated cosmopolitanism. Even Zionism constructed its images of muscular New Jews in conscious contrast with a supposedly degenerate Jewish Diaspora. Is it surprising that as both Zionism and Irish nationalism sought to prove their nation's European credentials, they should engage in so European a practice?

There is also something quite novel at work within modern nationalist anti-Judaism. Much of Nirenberg's study focuses on the antinomy of Jewish flesh and Christian spirit within European intellectual history. What the above cartoon suggests, however, is not that European nationalists assail 'Jews of the flesh'. Rather, they now seem to accuse Jews of being *of the wrong kind of flesh*. Irish nationalists were not alone in imagining 'Jews' as those who inhabit degraded bodies in pointed contrast to their own hygienic and muscular flesh. Where ancient and medieval thinkers thought of the Jew–Christian dichotomy in terms of a flesh–spirit antinomy, here the difference between sovereignty and powerlessness seems to be the difference between a healthy and muscular body (the body of a fully sovereign man) and a 'Jewish' bodily deformity (the body of an effeminate and powerless man).[5]

In one of the most famous encounters between an anxious Irish nationalist and an ill-defined figure of Judaism, the Citizen in Joyce's *Ulysses* (1922) is horrified by the 'half and half' Bloom, this racially incoherent 'pishogue' [*sic, piteog*, an effeminate man] who moves at will from one religious or national identity to another and who acquires new names only to slough them off without concern.[6] The nationalist Citizen desires stability in all things, and as such 'The challenge which Bloom poses for Irish society is radical. He is neither completely masculine nor completely feminine, but pan-sexual … As a liminal person, Leopold Bloom disrupts the complacencies of all the settled codes with which he comes into contact.'[7] But where Joyce's 'hermeneutic Jew' served to embody a more multicultural and liberated vision of Irishness, many of his nationalist contemporaries strove for a more coercively rigid and muscular sense of national sovereignty. The Citizen, as has been widely noted, was based on Michael Cusack, schoolteacher, Irish language activist and founder of the Gaelic Athletic Association (GAA). Joyce's caricature of him was not too far from the truth.[8]

The Man of the Future

As early as the 1870s, Michael Cusack was urging his students 'in the best Victorian tradition, to develop their bodies as well as their minds by participating in sport.' Cusack himself was active in rugby, cricket, handball, rowing and weightlifting, as well as taking a leading role in the recently formed Irish Champion Athletic Club. Ironically, as one historian recently observed, 'few Irish people seemed quite so committed to playing and fostering the games of the British Empire.'⁹ By the end of the decade, however, Cusack's growing interest in nationalist politics and language revival, as well as his distaste for some of the elitist trappings of contemporary Irish sport, had fomented his interest in indigenous sports.¹⁰ By 1883, Cusack was involved in the Dublin Hurling Club, which sought to promote a rationalised version of this sport.¹¹ The club held practice matches and began the process of codifying rules for hurling; at a meeting on 15 February 1883 'it was decided that at all matches played by the club that these rules should be strictly enforced and that anyone persistently breaking same should be prevented from playing.'¹² In opposition to traditional and more raucous rural games, the Dublin Hurling Club sought a 'rational' (i.e., rule-bound) sport and emphasised 'standardisation' and 'the cultivation of order.'¹³ It was Cusack's involvement with the Dublin Hurling Club and their rationalised (sanitised?) version of the game which led him to hold discussions with interested parties in Loughrea in East Galway in August 1884 about a more ordered and nationalist-inflected hurling organisation, which led to the founding of the GAA in November of that year.

Cusack's original call for supporters for this new organisation spoke of its aims as 'the preservation and cultivation of our National pastimes and for providing Rational amusements for the Irish people during their leisure hours.'¹⁴ One of the founding patrons of the GAA, T.W. Croke, spoke of how traditional pastimes were held in disregard by 'the degenerate dandies' of contemporary Ireland, who, with treasonous disregard for Irish nationality, favoured 'effeminate follies' borrowed from England. Writing on 30 October 1884, in response to an invitation to be a patron, Michael Davitt similarly linked sports to present decay and future national recuperation:

> In any effort that may be made to revive a National taste for games and pastimes such as once developed the muscular power and manly bearing of our Gaelic ancestors, I shall be most happy to lend a hand ... In this, as in so many other matters, we ought to cut ourselves adrift from English rules and patronage, and prevent the killing of those Celtic Sports which have been threatened with the same fate by the encroachment of Saxon custom, as that which menaces our Nationality under alien rule ... There are, of course, many reasons why the physique of our people is not developed as it ought to be, but there is no doubt that one reason for the degenerate gait and bearing of most of our young men at home is to be found in the absence of such games and pastimes as formerly gave to Irishman [sic] the reputation of a soldier-like and self-reliant race.¹⁵

The following year, Cusack asserted that 'no sensible person will deny that, as a Nation, we have very considerably declined physically since we gave up our National game of Hurling', and he placed this alongside other forms of national decay, in language, morals and religion.[16] Cusack also defined sports as a means of communing with a lost Irish masculinity and claimed that in his dreams 'I was living with the men of Erin of pre-Christian times. In spirit I hunted and fished with Fionn's invincible hosts from Antrim to Kerry. I hurled with the Fenians of sixteen centuries ago from Tara to Killarney. I resolved to bring back the hurling.' He claimed to have been visited in dreams by Wolfe Tone, Napper Tandy, Thomas Davis and 'Famine', all of whom urged him to revive hurling.[17] Cusack's rhetoric also drew broad links between sport and war. He believed that hurling, for instance, 'was invented by the most sublimely energetic and warlike race that the world has ever known… It teaches the use of arms at close quarters'.[18]

As well as hurling, the GAA promoted an indigenous (and largely invented) version of football.[19] In both hurling and football, the organisation came to promote a highly rationalised and even scientific sporting tradition that 'relied increasingly on precision passing, accurate shooting, quickness, guile, and teamwork, and less on brute strength.'[20] P.F. McDevitt aptly sums up the issues at stake here: 'Updated and revised, hurling and Gaelic football produced an image of Irish masculinity of which the nationalist community could be proud. The random violence of the earlier games, which had led English ruralist Arthur Young to describe hurling in 1780 as the "cricket of savages" was nominally replaced with order and virtuous manliness.' That the Irish invented their national sporting traditions, rather than accepting them en masse from England, helped to further disprove accusations that they were an inert people incapable of innovation.[21]

By the end of 1887, the GAA had 600 affiliated clubs with a membership tending to the lower-middle-class professions or those from a comfortable (20–100 acres) farming background.[22] Men in their early twenties predominated.[23] The influence of the proscribed Irish Republican Brotherhood (IRB), though, attracted early clerical hostility. Combined with the effects of the Parnellite split of the early 1890s, this almost scuppered the GAA's early successes. The Association only survived due to secretary Dick Blake's insistence that the organisation be 'non-political', by which it was meant that it remain nationalist but not under the control of any one group or party.[24] It would hence become a central pillar of Irish nationalism.[25] Whatever else changed in the GAA, muscular visions of reborn Irishness remained at the heart of the project.

By 1910 Sinn Féin's eponymous newspaper was praising the GAA as 'the maker of men—disciplined, self-controlled men—well built and square shouldered men, perfect athletes—men on whom a nation can rely in its hour of need'. Such muscular men, *Sinn Féin* declared, 'demonstrate to the world that we are not, as our enemies would have other nations believe[,] a nation of weaklings. And when we are a nation of men, we will be a free nation.'[26] As the 1912 advertisement for Whelan's selection of GAA sporting goods brazenly suggests (see Fig. 3.2), the Irish 'man of the future' would be literally rebuilt by his devotion to the native sporting tradition, with hurlies for legs and his face and mind

Fig. 3.2 *The Man of the Future*, GAA Advertisement, 1912
Source: Irish Freedom, June 1912

replaced by a *Déanta in Éirinn* [Made in Ireland] logo. Less surreally, the 1926 Gaelic Athletic Year Book urged 'all men of Irish birth' to support the GAA in their attempts to 'foster and safeguard the traditional heritage of manly vigour and racial pride against all assaults from within or without.'[27] The following year, an article in the *Gaelic Athletic Annual* recalled the weakness and national degeneration of post-Famine Ireland but presented native sports as an ideal antidote: 'The G.A.A. re-created age-long impulses which had been dead, gave a sense of power and knowledge of their latent strength to our young people, revived shattered hopes and brightened Eire's sad eyes.' *Dia Libh a Laochra Gaodhal* [God be with ye, Oh Gaelic Heroes] was this article's coda for male Irish athletes.[28] There was a popular view that Gaelic athletics were consciously militarised and an 'invaluable training grounds for a vigorous and disciplined race'.[29] Indeed, Eoin O'Duffy, whose athletic interests always ran parallel to his authoritarian nationalism, proclaimed in his unpublished memoirs that the revival of these supposedly ancient games was bringing about the revival of a strong nation. For O'Duffy, the revival of manly sporting traditions intersected with the revival of militarist nationalism: 'the Volunteers minus the G.A.A. organisation would have been negligible.'[30]

The Future, Like the Past, Is with the Fighting Man

The Irish Volunteers were founded in November 1913 as a nationalist riposte to the unionist Ulster Volunteer Force, which had been founded the previous year at the height of the Home Rule Crisis. Unlike the GAA, the Irish Volunteers' links to the Irish Republican Brotherhood did not seem to harm their early growth. Thousands attended their inaugural meeting at Dublin's Rotunda Gardens on 25 November 1913. Within a month, the Volunteers had 10,000 active members and their numbers expanded in the New Year. By May 1914, there were at least 192 Volunteer companies. Another 64 were established the following month, as the membership neared 100,000.[31]

Writing in *Irish Freedom* in July 1912, Ernest Blythe, later to be in charge of Irish health as the Free State's Minister for Local Government, discussed the contribution such a militia would make to healthy Irish masculinity. With echoes of Frantz Fanon, he began by declaring that 'The way to freedom is a sword-track through our enemies'. Reminding his readers of the Gaelic League's lesson that the nation would die without its language, he suggested that 'We need also to recollect that the nation which loses its military spirit is equally doomed.' His compatriots, he had it, 'are not virile and hardy', and he painted a picture of 'flabby' men with undue cravings for 'delicate food', made weak by their constant talking and bourgeois commercial or artistic occupations. Yet, a subterranean manliness still survived, he said, thanks both to militant nationalists 'but also those whose thoughts have gone no further than the running and leaping and hurling which they delighted in'. The future Irishmen, which physical-culture and physical-force enthusiasts such as these would birth, would be noticeable by their 'mighty lungs and muscled frames'.[32] At the close of the following year, by which time the Volunteers had become a noticeable mass movement, Blythe returned to his subject to declare: 'There is no power in politics like the armed man. He is the final arbiter'. Given that this was supposedly the case across Europe, a 'conquered' nation like Ireland thus had only one choice: 'The only thing that will loosen a conqueror's grip is the force or fear of the sword's edge … For our manhood's sake we must not merely deplore our condition, but must sweat and starve till each has a gun and can shoot to kill. It is only by thus being men that we can serve our country.' Conflating reformed masculinity with proper citizenship, Blythe concluded that 'Whatever comes[,] Ireland wants soldiers, and none is worthy of the name of Nationalist or citizen or man but the soldier.'[33] In a later *Irish Freedom* article, unsigned but utilising much the same tropes and so probably again written by Blythe, the Volunteers were described as 'the rebirth of manhood unto this Nation'. The Volunteers' 'spirit of citizenship and patriotism' had given the lie to the idea that centuries of foreign rule and colonisation had led Irish men into a cul-de-sac of 'wasting unto nothingness'. This, the author declared, had a 'spiritual effect' and pointed to a redeemed future over and against the degraded present:

> out of the materialism and sloth and decadence of so much of the Nationalism of the last decade there has come out at last the sword-sharp spirit of the fighting race. It is a great and a gallant augury for the future. The young men of Ireland are young men still, with the courage and the decision, and the fire of young men; and the sword shall not enter its scabbard again until it be either broken or victorious. In the future, as in the past, the Irish Nation shall not want for swordmen [*sic*].[34]

The 'sword' seems to be used here in an overtly symbolic and phallic register; Ireland had regained its manhood/power/phallus. While Blythe's writings here espoused a frankness that other pro-Volunteers prose lacked, they did telegraph some of the movement's essential concerns about bodies, sovereignty and resurgent masculinity.

The constitution of the Volunteers, adopted by convention in October 1914, defined the movement's objectives as securing and maintaining the rights and liberties of the Irish nation via a trained and disciplined military force united across any pre-existing party, class or sectarian divisions.[35] The *Manifesto of the Irish Volunteers* elaborated on this. Claiming that the disenfranchised Irish nation was at risk of becoming 'politically the most degraded population in Europe, and no longer worthy of the name of Nation', the *Manifesto* advocated a martial cure:

> From time immemorial, it has been held by every race of mankind to be the right and duty of a freeman to defend his freedom with all his resources and with his life itself. The exercise of that right distinguishes the freeman from the serf, the discharge of that duty distinguishes him from the coward. To drill, to learn the use of arms, to acquire the habit of concerted and disciplined action, to form a citizen army from a population now at the mercy of almost any organised aggression—this, beyond all doubt, is a program that appeals to all Ireland, but especially to young Ireland.[36]

The Irish Volunteer Fund similarly spoke of the new militia as a means for inculcating the 'duties of citizenship' through military arms. This, it was hoped, would unite Irish men 'in brotherly co-operation' and in a revived nationalist spirit.[37] *Twenty Plain Facts for Irishmen*, a handbill probably written by Thomas MacDonagh, asserted that 'It is the duty of every Irishman who desires for his country her natural right of freedom and for himself the natural right of a freeman, to be an Irish Volunteer.' As well as treading similar ground as other Volunteer statements, this handbill also tellingly collapsed national sovereignty (the nation's 'natural right of freedom') with individual male sovereignty ('the natural right of a freeman'), and so gives a good insight into a core element of Volunteer ideology. Reiterating this, the handbill harshly dismissed those who refused to align themselves with the Volunteers' programme, claiming 'there is no more to be said' of such weak and fearful men.[38]

This rhetoric continued to be used after the start of the First World War, when the Volunteers split over John Redmond's attempt to take control of the organisation as well as over the question of enlisting for the British war effort. At the time of the split, a handbill for the Irish Volunteers, the rump of the movement which opposed enlisting, presented John Redmond, and by implication those who followed his pro-imperial lead, as being split between two divided loyalties. Since Ireland was still a 'subject people', the Irish nation 'cannot with honour or safety' join with the British in this war. 'We are arming FOR IRELAND ONLY!'[39] The O'Rahilly, in his *Secret History of the Volunteers*, having established that 'the manhood of Ireland' had armed themselves to fight for Irish freedom, asserted that 'We know of only one duty, our duty to Ireland. We are Irish Volunteers, not pawns upon the chessboard of British Politics. We told Mr Redmond so, and we ceased to admit his Nominees to our Councils.'[40]

Despite the split, both sides continued to promote ideals of gendered national renewal. Addressing members of the Wexford brigade of the Irish Volunteers in 1915, Patrick Pearse lauded them as 'soldiers of Irish freedom … disciplined and armed for the service of your country'. The course of training in which the Wexford Volunteers were engaged, 'will fit you to render her precious service', 'her', of course, being the female Ireland defended by virile sons. Pearse congratulated the Wexford brigade for holding 'the most honourable name that can in our day be borne by any Irishman—the name of Irish Volunteer'.[41] This not only served to link them to the Volunteers of the 1798 rebellion but was probably also a coded reference to the other, 'dishonourable', names then being borne by Irishmen, namely National Volunteer and British recruit. Yet, against such accusations of pro-British perfidy, the pro-enlistment National Volunteers continued to present themselves as 'patriot sons', simultaneously saviours of a feminised 'dear old land' and yet also harbingers of 'a new spirit … a new awakening and love of liberty'.[42] When on parade, members of the National Volunteers were instructed to put forward an image of disciplined uniformity and 'to set a good example to their fellow-Irishmen by their good behaviour, strict maintenance of discipline, and prompt and complete obedience to orders.'[43] Such ideological practices had, in fact, been playing themselves out on a more quotidian level even before the outbreak of the Great War.

In September 1914, the Dublin branch of the pre-split Volunteers were given precise instructions about their public deportment. Volunteers were expected to march in disciplined order, not to engage in 'jeering, whistling or gesticulating at members of the public when on parade', and certainly not to enter public houses. Volunteers were to remember their status as representatives of Irish masculine honour and, most ironically, 'The system of training adopted by the Provisional Committee as set out in the British Infantry Manual 1911 must not be departed from as it is the only system authorised by Headquarters.'⁴⁴ Similarly, *The Handbook for Irish Volunteers*, whose author was listed simply as 'H' and who seems to have been a veteran of war in South Africa, had sought to help those animated by the movement's 'truly patriotic spirit' fashion themselves into 'a calm, well disciplined army'. Clean bodies and the promotion of proper personal hygiene were central to this project, as 'H' emphasised regular bathing and clean clothes, whilst railing against spitting and the sharing of other men's pipes as a major source of tuberculosis.⁴⁵

The idea that military service could have a recuperative effect on Irish men, at both the individual and the mass levels, shows how the Volunteers shared much with the GAA. And these ideas would continue to have purchase in Irish nationalist discourse for several years. Eoin O'Duffy regularly promoted such ideals within the Volunteers' successor, the Irish Republican Army. At the end of 1922, when O'Duffy was appointed Commissioner of the Garda Síochána [The Guardians of the Peace], the new police force of the Irish Free State, he continued to promote this muscular vision of Irish citizenship.⁴⁶

What Organisation, Training and Hard Work Went to the Making of that Body

In an early piece of journalistic enthusiasm for the transformative work of the Garda Síochána, it was alleged that few Irish people who saw the 'well-built, alert and spic and span Guards on parade realise what organisation, training and hard work went to the making of that body.' Continuing in a slightly voyeuristic tone, this article suggested that if one could spy on raw recruits entering the Garda headquarters in Dublin's Phoenix Park at the start of their training these men would appear to be 'fine types of manhood' but also 'like so many sheep' and just as shy. Conversely, 'If you could see the same party emerge at the close of their training, six months later, the physical and mental metamorphosis is scarcely credible. They seem to be almost different people.' The training has made each recruit 'a new man'. They now carry themselves with a military bearing and with a pride in their uniformed appearance. 'And, most important of all, they have learned the value of discipline and order. It has become part of their being.'⁴⁷ A follow-up article repeated this line about the Gardaí's valuable sense of discipline, yet also clarified a possible negative misconception: 'while obedience and discipline are sought after, a service [*sic*, servile?] and slavish docility is rightly tabooed in the force.' Like the imaginary Garda in

'Jew Regard for the Law', these 'real' Gardaí also manage to reconcile the paradox of modern citizenship. Their mass obedience to authority does not undermine their individual masculine sovereignty. Indeed, this article concluded, these men would 'go back to civil life as ideal citizens, carrying with them a sense of discipline, orderliness and law that will react favourably upon the general community.'[48]

O'Duffy was certainly partial to this kind of hyperbole. Where these articles on his training methods identified the majority of recruits as being 'either the sons of small farmers or shopkeepers' who are 'As a class … the brawn and muscle of the country, and come from its finest stock',[49] O'Duffy, with a frank acknowledgement of his own social biases, also described the 'well educated sons of the middle class peasant [*sic*] farmer' as being 'the backbone of the force.'[50] Noting that early recruits to the Garda Síochána were drawn from the ranks of the Volunteers, O'Duffy spoke of the latter as 'all that was best and manliest of the youth of Ireland' and with 'magnificent brains and brawn'. Similarly, the vigorous recruitment process for the Gardaí continued to ensure that recruits are of 'the best type mentally and physically.' In the same vein, just as sport had for several decades been a medium for a militant masculinity, so also O'Duffy put much emphasis on the Gardaí taking a strong role 'in manly combat in athletic fields.' This, he hoped, would contribute to the promotion of 'good, honest, clean and manly sport throughout the country.'[51] A GAA background was also considered helpful in applying to join the Gardaí.[52] As O'Duffy proclaimed it, the Garda Síochána were not just proponents 'of high ideals and of manly spirit' but also 'They are the guide and philosopher of the people.'[53]

Yet, this notion of the police force as a showcase for the highest ideals of national masculinity often existed alongside a far less favourable vision of Ireland. Indeed, when O'Duffy spoke of the 'manly sport' engaged in by his recruits, he went on to call it a 'necessary tonic'[54] for Irish leisure activities. His medical language highlights his fears about a sick people in need of a manly cure. Most immediately, O'Duffy had a pronounced anxiety about how his rural recruits, 'Innocent young lads from the country', could so easily develop untoward habits 'when not under supervision.' In 1923, when O'Duffy made these comments, there were 1200 Garda recruits stationed at the Phoenix Park depot on the periphery of central Dublin. They were not allowed to leave in plain clothes, for the stated reason that they would be exposed to urban 'temptations' (presumably alcohol and sex). But perhaps also there was a fear that, out of uniform, they would escape O'Duffy's supervision; 'discipline cannot be enforced so effectively as if the men were in uniform', he confessed.[55]

In his introduction to the 1928 Garda *Orders and Regulations*, which borrowed heavily from its Royal Irish Constabulary antecedents, Eoin O'Duffy hinted at some of the deeper ideological reasoning behind these coercive rules. 'Discipline', he began, 'is that quality which makes a man responsive to orders and authority' and therefore disciplined control of individual members was of utmost necessity. But in parallel to this, O'Duffy was concerned with the 'honour of the force' and just as 'individual acts of heroism, or outstanding professional achievement, reflect credit on the whole Force, so also will the moral degeneracy of even a very few of its members adversely affect the good name of the Force in general'.[56] For O'Duffy, crafting the individual members of the force into an organised and disciplined body of heroic and morally unassailable Irish men was a central plank of his muscular vision for Ireland.

Writing to the Minister for Justice, Kevin O'Higgins, in December 1926, O'Duffy made a series of revealing comments about his own views of the Irish nation and why they were in dire need of such thoroughgoing reform. Narrowing in on a history of Anglo-Irish hostility and the country's atrophy under British rule, O'Duffy identified a number of negative results. In British-administered Ireland, he believed, 'natural initiative, creative ability, even character was permitted to lie dormant, unwanted and neglected, the net result being that to-day we possess a carefully trained and well developed disctructive [*sic*] outlook and ability'. This had clear implications for the current state of Irish society: 'I am afraid that the people have been so long at war with authority that they have largely lost a proper sense of proportion and for that reason… are incapable of self-development'. The Gardaí, O'Duffy felt, would be the Irish nation's civic teachers, the ones who would take on the onerous task of imparting 'principles of citizenship' as part of a broader drive to make Ireland a 'normal state'.[57] O'Duffy's confidential memorandum fused a number of ideas and concerns that were at the heart of his work as Garda Commissioner and continued the longer discursive tradition of nationalist masculinity: the Irish nation was in need of reform, and the Gardaí would be an ideal vehicle for this reform, in the direct sense that its members could be physically moulded into new manly ideals as well as in the indirect sense that they would be exemplars to which others could aspire. O'Duffy was echoing ideas about masculinity, muscularity and citizenship that had long been espoused by the GAA and the Volunteers. Plus, the profound distrust of the Irish masses to which O'Duffy and many other early Free State elites held was clearly on display here.

Such distrust was mirrored in how the Garda elite viewed the Irish masses in general. A 1932 editorial in the *Garda Review*, presumably sanctioned by O'Duffy if not actually written by him, railed against the Irish 'man in the street' as being 'The Greatest Type of Coward' and defined by a wilful refusal to obey the law. O'Duffy, by this period, was already falling out of favour with the newly elected Fianna Fáil government and the editorial could, of course, be read in this light. O'Duffy and those who would soon coalesce around him to form the quasi-fascist Blueshirt movement viewed de Valera and Fianna Fáil as lawless republicans and closet communists (as will be discussed in Chap. 6) and these could be the law-breaking 'cowards' referred to here. Focusing on such immediate issues, however, should not blind us to the deeper history of Irish nationalists' negative perceptions of Irish citizens. The various publications aimed at the Gardaí regularly featured caricatured depictions of drunken or even subhuman Irish archetypes that were remarkably similar to earlier racist anti-Irish depictions in the British press.[58]

In one representative example, 'A Study in "Still" Life', a dishevelled rural producer of *poitín* [illicit home-distilled whiskey] stands next to his still, as the arresting Garda gazes upon him in disgust (see Fig. 3.3). The poitín-maker's clothes are patched together, much like the decrepit house in which he works. His sloping jaw, prehensile paws, oversized ears and unkempt facial hair all give him an animalistic, even simian, appearance. This is in obvious contrast to the clean uniform of the fully human Garda. A neat binary, so often used both in the vast array of cartoons analysed by de Nie as well as in 'Jew Regard for the Law', is also employed here, as the ideal of a redeemed Irishman is constructed in conscious opposition to his own degenerate past. There is still something markedly colonialist about this aspect of the Gardaí's early ideology, as if not much had changed from the time of the RIC.

Conor Brady suggests that 'There is substantial evidence that at a very early stage of planning [Michael] Collins had envisaged the new force [the Garda Síochána] almost as a direct replica of the R.I.C.'[59] Evidence such as this leads Brady to his conclusion that 'With the vital exception that it was to be unarmed, the Civic Guard [the Gardaí] was to differ little in its construction from the Royal Irish Constabulary which had preceded it.'[60] This is something of an exaggeration. There were certain significant differences between the Garda Síochána and the RIC. Aside from the fact that it was

Fig. 3.3 *A Study in "Still" Life*, Garda Cartoon, 1924
Source: Iris an Ghárda [Garda Review], 21 January 1924

an armed gendarmerie, the RIC had 10,000 members in its closing years and was often viewed with suspicion by those it policed.[61] Conversely, the Gardaí remained unarmed, had an initial membership half the size of the RIC, and generally enjoyed far better relations with local populations. Moreover, its new uniforms and symbols represented a clear break with the past and, of the 8230 recruits who passed through its training depot during the Gardaí's first decade, only 190 had served in the RIC, versus the 55% who had graduated from the IRA.[62] Nonetheless, statements such as Brady's, or Vicky Conway's subtler argument that in 'structural, and perhaps less visible ways' the Gardaí was 'little altered from the RIC' are not too wide of the mark. There was much continuity. As Conway reminds us, the more democratic model of contemporary English community policing was available as a possible alternative for the Free State.[63] The modelling of certain aspects of the Garda Síochána on the militarised and colonial RIC was a conscious choice on the part of the Free State elite. Recruits continued to undergo military-style training and in its early years the Gardaí's leadership continued to view the Irish masses in quasi-colonial terms, as a people in need of social control and, thus, ultimately in need of social engineering.[64] Indeed, the Gardaí was perhaps as close an equivalent as the Irish state ever got to what the Israeli state found in its army: a popular system of organised manhood which could be used to promote idealised images of a reborn masculinity both among its recruits and, by promoting its recruits as tutelary exemplars, among society at large.[65] In both cases, of course, the underlying presumption was that these societies were somehow degraded and so needed these palliative exemplars.

MUSKELJUDENTUM

Zionism's project of muscular self-fashioning certainly utilised some very similar mechanisms to its Irish nationalist equivalent. Jewish sports teams in early-twentieth-century Central and Eastern Europe, some of which were overtly Zionist and some not, regularly chose names that suggested a return to an ancient and forceful masculinity: *HaKoah Vienna* [The Force of Vienna], a prominent Austrian club which excelled in soccer, or *HaGibor Prague* [The Hero/Man of Prague], a Jewish water polo team which won the Czechoslovak championship in 1928.[66] Names such as Maccabi, Bar Kochba, Hasmonea, or Samson were also used. Names such as these 'demonstrate how sports was supposed to revive a past Jewish military heroism.'[67] One recent study of *HaKoah Vienna* elaborates on this, pointing out that an early goal of the organisation was 'to demonstrate to the public that Jews were the same people as non-Jews, that they could compete in will-power, physical strength, and discipline, and that the antisemitic view of the Jew as weak, deceitful, word-twisting, whining, dishonorable, and idle parasites did not conform to reality.'[68] The 'sport' of duelling, which in nineteenth-century Germany was 'a testing ground for honor and manliness', also had a fascination for many Jewish men. A large amount of German and Austrian duelling societies refused to allow Jewish members, who were felt to be effeminate men incapable of giving 'satisfaction'. Nonetheless, between 1882 and 1914, about 5% of Germans convicted for duelling were Jewish, five times their share of the national population. This was partly because Gentiles tended to find it easier to be acquitted, but was also attributable to a greater perceived need to gain 'satisfaction' for insults to Jewish honour. Theodor Herzl, for example, was a strong supporter of duelling. He fantasised about challenging leading Austrian antisemites to duels and claimed 'A half-dozen duels would very much raise the social position of the Jews.'[69] Zionism borrowed heavily from this variegated culture of European Jewish athleticism. Gideon Reuveni suggests that this can be ascribed both to 'anti-colonial' desires to disprove accusations of Jewish inferiority, as well as the general popularity of nationalist sport in Europe from the late nineteenth century onwards.[70] Indeed, the use, both of sport to create a more reputable national ideal and of names drawn from the ancient past, highlights how the invention of Zionist and Irish nationalist sporting traditions drew on conceptually similar European *and* quasi-colonial rationales.

Perhaps the most famous example of Zionism's use of sport and muscularity was Max Nordau's call for the creation of a *Muskeljudentum* [Muscle Judaism], a term he first used in a speech at the Second Zionist Congress in August 1898. Nordau was deeply affected by a 'horror of formlessness', a fear that weak and not fully masculine Jewish bodies were a reflection of Jews' ambiguous racial status.[71] Muscular Zionism was his antidote. He brashly claimed that the movement 'awakens Judaism to new life' and he spoke of creating 'a lost muscular Judaism once again'.[72] Nordau's *Muskeljudentum* would mark a return to history of the type of active, disciplined and physically impressive Jewish men represented by Simon Bar Kochba, over and against 'contemporary antisemitic representations of the Jews as scrawny, weak and inferior'.[73] Indeed, Nordau ended his famous speech at the 1898 Congress with 'the blatant and evocative image of the publicly displayed circumcised Jewish phallus as ultimate symbol of Jewish national pride as well as newfound Jewish masculinity.'[74] Whatever about such overt homoeroticism, Nordau's underlying idea of muscularity as a means of national revival quickly came to occupy a privileged position within the Zionist movement.

In 1901, Herman Jalowicz, editor of *Jüdische Turn-Zeitung* [The Jewish Gymnastics Magazine] explained the importance of sport for Zionism: 'No wonder that under such lamentable circumstances [life in the ghetto] which are the fostering soil for physical degeneration ... a lamentable human type emerged with deranged nerves and a weakened body ... Zionism is the healing serum against these miasmas of the pestilent ghetto air.'⁷⁵ Nordau himself wrote for the same magazine, elaborating on his *Muskeljudentum* vision in an article of the same name in 1900. Here he stated that 'In no other nation does gymnastics play such an important role as with us Jews. It is supposed to make our bodies and our character straight. It shall provide us with self-confidence'⁷⁶ and he again held up Bar Kochba as the muscular-historical ideal to which Zionists should return.⁷⁷

Athleticism continued to play a central role in Zionist Palestine. As a sign of the importance given to sport, tickets for popular entertainment such as the cinema or dancing were taxed at between 8% and 22%, whilst sporting events were taxed at between 0.02% and 5%, putting sport in the same class as Hebrew-language concerts and theatre performances which were also 'considered educational and valuable to the national cause'.⁷⁸ In pre-1948 Tel Aviv, the two main sporting organisations were HaPoel (The Worker) and Maccabi, ('named after the national Hebrew heroes of Hellenistic times') and the latter group defined their mission in some familiar terms. They sought to carry out 'the difficult task of curing the Jewish body, educating the young generation into national discipline and preparing it for any national calling.' By 1933, the two clubs had a shared membership of 2300 active members, comprising about 3% of the city's total population. In addition to this, sports were promoted through Tel Aviv's schools, where physical education was included as part of the curriculum. When HaKoah visited Palestine from Vienna in 1924, Tel Aviv's leading rabbis warmly welcomed 'the heroes of Israel' [i.e., the heroes of the whole Jewish nation], wishing them 'all the strength of youth, hoping that the spirit of old Israel will be fortified alongside the revived body.'⁷⁹

Outside of the narrow confines of Tel Aviv, the Maccabiah Games, which began in 1932, became a means of showcasing images of disciplined and physically strong Jewish bodies to the world.⁸⁰ Indeed, sport became a means for Israel to acquire international legitimacy as an established nation-state, what one historian calls a 'self-conscious attitude toward statehood and the insatiable need to be recognized and approved'. The Israeli desire for superiority over neighbouring Arab states was certainly expressed through sport. A 1956 article in *Chadashot Ha-Sport* [Sports News] spoke of 'Israel's superiority' in soccer, against the 'primitive' Syrians and Lebanese. And at the 1952 Helsinki Olympics, all Israeli athletes with 'foreign' names were required to change their names to more suitably Hebraic ones, as if to reiterate their recovered image of sporting Israeliness.⁸¹

In Israel, as in Ireland, sport could also easily slip into 'pseudo war-play'.[82] The Israeli Army, the 'most salient institution' in Israeli state building, continued the project of creating 'the new Israeli man and woman' and from 1948 onwards contributed to socialising new immigrants into Israeli society.[83] The obvious reality of the unresolved conflict with the Palestinians goes a long way to explaining the strong position of the army in Israeli society.[84] Israel's militaristic culture, however, should not be reduced to being a singular product of the Arab-Israeli conflict; the roots of Zionism within nineteenth-century European physical culture are also an important source of the New Jewish self-image expressed by the Israeli military.[85] The Israeli army became the 'school of the nation' but prior to the founding of the state, 'sports groups were regarded as a surrogate army', a second 'school of the nation' which was also intended to 'defend Jewish dignity.'[86] As with the rhetoric of the GAA, this again points to the blending of sport and war in the nationalist imagination.

Vladimir (Ze'ev) Jabotinsky became a strong advocate of a military ethos. He not only echoed Nordau's *Muskeljudentum* but also presaged Israeli 'cultural militarism' after 1948. Indeed, Michael Stanislawski has recently spoken of the 'breathtaking "Nordau-ization" ' that Jabotinsky's politics represented.[87] In Jabotinsky's 1930s Yiddish-language essay 'Vegn Militarizm' [Ways of Militarism], he described the military as a means to inculcate discipline, hygiene and bodily fitness, all things he felt were sorely missing in Jewish society: 'We Jews suffer from a *lack of form*' he said. Additionally, the spectacle of Jewish 'lads' marching in ordered formation was part of what would differentiate a 'nation' from 'the "masses," the "riff-raff"'.[88] His roughly contemporaneous Hebrew essay 'Ra'ayon Betar' [The Idea of Betar] continued in this vein. Promoting Betar, his newly established Baden Powell-esque youth movement, Jabotinsky again advocated the positive results of disciplined Jewish male unity. This time, however, he addressed an apparently common criticism:

> Our opponents claim that this contradicts the honor of free individuals and makes them into a 'machine'. I advise you proudly and without shame to answer: yes, a machine. For the greatest accomplishment of free men is the ability to work together in precise unison, like a machine. This is possible only for free men imbued with high culture … When we listen to a choir or an orchestra, and one hundred musicians punctiliously heed the orders of one conductor, impressing us as working totally in unison, that is proof that each individual musician has dedicated his utmost effort to the result; it is not the conductor who has forced him to do so but he himself, his own

desire for unity. This is the sort of 'orchestra' we want to make out of the entire Jewish people, and the first step toward this goal is Betar.[89]

There are a number of points worth noting about Jabotinsky's militarism, as expressed in this extended quote. First, his vision of a reborn Jewish army clearly operated within a broader discourse of Jewish national rebirth. 'Betar' was the name of the last Jewish-held fortress during the second-century Bar Kochba revolt, but is also an acronym for *Brit Trumpeldor* [Covenant of Trumpeldor]. The use of this name, therefore, echoes an ancient Hebrew masculinity as well as the heroic 'martyrdom' and revived Jewish masculinity of Joseph Trumpeldor. Both sport and the military acted as muscular expressions of a newfound autonomy and subjecthood, at the individual as well as at mass levels. Second, this points to the similarities with Irish nationalism, which also used sport and militias as vehicles for a similar reborn muscular nationalism. Zionism and Irish nationalism's shared quasi-colonial nature explains much of this; both movements sought to create proud images of muscular nationality as ripostes to anti-Irish or anti-Jewish stereotypes. Third, as the extended quote from 'Ra'ayon Betar' shows, Jabotinsky, like many Irish nationalists, was also attempting to reconcile two opposing aspects of modern subjecthood; how to create a mass obedience to authority that does not undermine individual masculine sovereignty.

Our Womanhood Is Troubling Itself Rightly Over the Woman's Place in the Community[90]

Understanding sporting organisations or various nationalist militias as machineries for inculcating a muscular and idealised masculinity, however, still leaves open the question of women's status within this nationalist project. The type of cleanly divided gender roles which the Gardaí sought to uphold, for instance, were on clear display in the *Garda Review*'s 'Woman's Realm' page, which began to appear in the early 1930s and was presumably intended for policemen's wives. The articles left little doubt as to the location of the 'woman's realm'; representative articles discussed bargain-hunting in post-Christmas sales, tips for cooking and for growing vegetables in one's garden, as well as advice on crochet, cleaning or a short piece on how to 'Cultivate a sense of responsibility in your children.'[91] More blatantly, two cartoons in early issues of the *Garda Review*'s predecessor, *Iris an Ghárda*, depicted both a feminine ideal and its stark opposite. In an October 1923 cartoon, 'A Guard acquiring a sound local knowledge by a friendly intercourse with the Village Belles', a smiling and presumably newly arrived Garda makes himself known to a local mother and daughter. Appropriately, he addresses himself to the mother, while the daughter adopts a modest pose. Conversely, in a cartoon the following March, it was two Gardaí who were averting their gaze, in an attempt to ignore a garish flapper girl in modern fur coat and high heels. The caption described her as 'The Sister that Isn't', a distressingly urban woman who was no longer under the surveillance and control of her male family members. Both cartoons, as well as highlighting the proper masculinity of the Free State's police force, also showed how this masculinity buttressed, and was buttressed by, subservient and chaste femininity.

The Garda Síochána remained a male-only institution until 1958. Even after that, female police, as in many other countries, were assigned to supposedly gender-appropriate tasks (such as cases involving children or sexual abuse). As late as the 1970s, *banghardaí* [police-women] were barred from detective work, for which they were considered unsuitable, and were paid less than their male equivalents.[92] Already in 1937, however, the *Garda Review* was commenting on the possibility of female recruitment to Ireland's police force. The *Review* claimed to be neither in favour of nor opposed to such proposals, and merely interested in ascertaining the facts. While theoretically recognising that there may be a diverse set of crimes in which women officers could play a role, particularly cases involving 'women complainants in certain types of offences', (a euphemism for prostitution) the *Garda Review* denied the efficacy of female police in reality. Dealing with this kind of urban crime, it was claimed, 'is for a man hard at any time and often pretty revolting, and in this latter regard we cannot conceive the nature of the work so often associated with women criminals as being suitable for a woman, as we believe that the finer instincts and susceptibilities with which nature has endowed women would be in constant revolt.' In other words, only men could have the emotional strength to face such stark realities. At the close however, this article did allow that women police *might* be suitable for cases involving children, but even then remained sceptical that they would be more efficacious than a 'woman probation officer or welfare worker unassociated [*sic*] with the police.'[93]

In the GAA, Michael Cusack certainly did not envisage women taking an active role. He felt women should remain passive spectators of Irish sports, attending games in their 'gala attire to flash looks and smiles of approval on their rustic knights.' Cusack's idealisation of gender divisions was not all that different, then, from that of Baron Pierre de Coubertin, founder of the modern Olympic Games, who felt women's sport was 'against the laws of nature' since 'the eternal role of woman in this world was to be a companion of the male and mother of the family, and she should be educated towards those functions.'[94] Nonetheless, An Cumann Camógaíochta [The Camogie Association], an organisation promoting hurling's female equivalent, was founded in February 1905 with Máire ní Chinnéide as president and espousing a similar nationalist line to that of the GAA.[95]

Contradicting his caricatured image as a dour republican fundamentalist,[96] Brian O'Higgins unambiguously praised camogie-playing women in a poem printed in *Irish Freedom* in 1912. O'Higgins recorded his pride at how women playing this sport sharply offended the snobbish and anglicised elites of Dublin: 'The hockey-loving ladies, with an accent all their own / At sight of young *Camóguidheacht* [camogie] are heard to wail and moan.' '*Camóguidheacht go Bráth*' [Camogie for Ever] was O'Higgins concluding message.[97] Úna Ní Fhaircheallaigh (Agnes Farrelly), a leading proponent of camogie and president of An Cumann Camógaíochta from 1935 onwards, certainly saw the sport as part of a larger project of male *and* female revival.[98] Placing people like Ní Fhaircheallaigh in a broader history of both 'Gaelic feminism' and women's sports, Ríona Nic Congáil has suggested that the predominantly middle-class and university-educated women who invented camogie were motivated by similar desires of national rebirth to those of their male counterparts, albeit minus the overt emphasis on powerful muscularity: 'Within the future-oriented discourses symptomatic of the early century, camogie was envisioned as a means of enhancing the health of the next generation and discouraging Ireland's most talented young women from emigration to England and North America.'[99] Nonetheless, the rules drawn up for camogie by Máire Ní Chinnéide and Cáit Ní Dhonnchadha, along with the latter's brother Tadhg Ó Donnchadha, continued to reflect a supposedly innate female gentleness. Camogie was to be played on a smaller field than hurling and with a lighter ball.[100] Even with this conservatism, some of the earliest players of camogie hid their hurlies under their coats when traveling to games, for fear of public ridicule. Their organisation stagnated until, tellingly, a man, Sean O'Duffy, oversaw its relaunch in 1911.[101] O'Duffy recognised that women playing sports publicly 'was, in many quarters, considered little short of sinful' and recommended that 'we need to be very careful that no girl [*sic*] will appear in national athletic or cycling sports in any way which would appear repulsive to the national or Catholic ideas of the people of the country.'[102]

In this, Ireland did not buck any international trends. Tony Collins has pointed out that while women were active in the traditional rural *games* of pre-capitalist Europe, they were often systematically barred from the rationalised *sports* that emerged in the Victorian period.[103] Modern sport, Collins observes, was founded on

> a rigid differentiation between men and women, the masculine and the feminine, the sexually normative and the transgressive ... Sport was therefore not merely a pastime for men, it was by its very definition masculine. Games were used to define who was and who was not a true, heterosexual man. It was part of the socialisation of boys into men, a central feature of the process of 'making men'. It separated them from girls and femininity.[104]

In other words, sport, like nationalism, remained the primary preserve of men.

A similar tension existed in Cumann na mBan, a military organisation which shared many members with An Cumann Camógaíochta. At the most basic level, this tension can be seen in how the group's name was translated. Though it literally means 'The Women's Association', Tom Barry pointedly remembered them as 'The Woman's Auxiliary'. While he praised their dedication, his choice of words reinforced the idea that they were subservient to the active men of the Volunteers. Similarly, Ernie O'Malley, reflecting a common view among male nationalists, described how Cumann na mBan was an organisation dedicated to providing first aid and organising fund-raising and social events. He also recalled how 'Cumann na mBan girls' would cook and clean for Volunteer meetings.[105] Cumann na mBan's own scheme of organisation took a similar position, listing the group's activities as being primarily related to first aid and medical care as well as supplying food, with intelligence work and military drilling relegated to the end of their list.[106] Elsewhere, though, Cumann na mBan proved less willing to demur. In a 1915 pamphlet, Cumann na mBan described themselves as 'the most vigorous and enterprising of all the movements that have grown out of the idea of arming and drilling the nation.' While the pamphlet spoke with hope for the future leaders of Ireland emerging out of the 'young, daring and self-sacrificing men' of the Volunteers, it also declared that 'The destiny of small nations always finally depends on their women.'[107] Cumann na mBan's 1921 constitution pledged to support the broader nationalist struggle whilst not forgoing the group's autonomy.[108] A pamphlet from the same period criticised the glacial pace of female emancipation in Ireland and strongly reminded male Irish nationalists that the 1916 Proclamation gave full rights of citizenship to Irish women: 'That right in Ireland means the right to work and to fight, to suffer and to give.'[109] Even more audaciously, Constance Markievicz, wrote that 'Ancient Ireland bred warrior women ... Today we are in danger of being civilized by men out of existence ... Women are left to rely on sex charm, or intrigue and backstairs influence.... It is advisable', argued Markievicz, to bring out the 'masculine side of women souls.' And in a 1915 speech, she urged the Irish Women's Franchise League to 'leave your jewels and gold wads in the bank, and buy a revolver.'[110] Markievicz's leading role in the Easter Rising represented the practical application of these ideas.

Perhaps more representative of broader nationalist sentiment, though, was Terence MacSwiney. As early as 1914 he had praised Cumann na mBan's push for gender equality whilst also admonishing women for not embracing that sense of self-reliance that was usually recommended for men. His suggestion that nationalist women emulate the wife of Wolfe Tone, however, gives a strong indication of the tension at work here.[111] Women had a right to political freedom and a rightful part to play in the nationalist movement. They could even situate themselves within a similar schema of nationalist time as men.[112] Yet, they should remain within set gender roles, like the wife of a canonical figure like Tone. The Cumann na mBan uniform was another obvious site for this tension. Above the waist it was a military tunic similar to that worn by their counterparts in the Volunteers, but below the waist was a modest ankle-length skirt.[113] In Cumann na mBan, active public womanhood co-existed alongside conservative archetypes and in this sense, Cumann na mBan's attempts to forge a female space within a broader male-centric militarised milieu often meant that that milieu went unquestioned. Cumann na mBan were ultimately complicit in facilitating the Volunteers' masculine self-image, confirming Ríona Nic Congáil's suspicion that 'Gaelic Feminism' was an 'inconsistent and often contradictory' phenomenon.[114]

There were some similar tensions within the *Muskeljudentum* project. Women were 'conspicuously absent in the vast majority of discursive practices and representations of the muscle Jew ... Simply put, it was Jewish men who were supposedly not strong enough, healthy enough, and fit enough— as measured by the European benchmark—to build a modern nation.'[115] When Rafael Halperin founded the first professional bodybuilding gym in

Israel in 1949, he named it Shimshon [Samson], continuing a set pattern of Zionist sports as a means of reviving ancient and biblical masculinity. Seven years later, he opened a special gym for women, but called it 'Venus', after the Greek goddess of love. Thus, women were here symbolically denied a part in the muscular national rebirth.[116] They were not placed within a trajectory of Israelite history. As with Ireland, and indeed much of the world, sport in Israel remained a predominantly male preserve.

The same trend could be seen with the Israeli Army. 'Although the Israeli Army is still perceived as the main mechanism for building a *national* identity, in particular it has become the basis of a *male* self-image and a source for *male* social mobility in society.'[117] The Defence Service Law of 1949 set up some clear demarcations between male and female service. Conscripted women would only serve for two years, as opposed to men's three, and exemptions were to be granted to married women, pregnant women, mothers and women who declared that their religion prevented them from serving. Exemptions for men were, and are, far less forthcoming.[118] Women were also excluded from combat units and the more distinguished military positions, which in turn served to exclude women from one of the most prestigious social institutions in Israel. As one of Israel's leading sociologists concludes, 'The military itself is basically a macho and male-oriented subculture.'[119] During times of 'active wars' moreover, which have occurred at least once a decade since 1948, Israeli society 'is divided basically into two major cultures: the warrior society of men and the home front society of women.'[120] Notwithstanding some obvious differences (the army occupies a status in Israeli society for which Ireland has no real equivalent) Zionism and Irish nationalism did both conform to a larger pattern in the modern world, that of the 'reciprocal relationship between militarism and masculinity'.[121]

This chapter has sought to understand the anxieties that nationalists expressed over their own predominantly male bodies and how this was linked to contemporary debates over political sovereignty. Addressing the recent fashion for academic studies of the body, David Harvey outlines some of the pressing reasons why such concerns have come to the fore in scholarly research, whilst also arguing against slipping into the trap of viewing 'the body as the measure of all things'. As Harvey notes, 'the body is not a closed and sealed entity, but a relational "thing" that is created, bounded, sustained, and ultimately dissolved in a spatiotemporal flux of multiple processes.'[122] This issue of 'space', the spaces through which nationalist bodies pass, is the subject of the next chapter.

Notes

1. Quote attributed to Patrick Pearse. D. Ryan, ed. (1917) *The Story of a Success, Being a Record of St. Enda's College, September 1908 to Easter, 1916* (Dublin: Maunsel) pp. 40–41. A *camán* is the stick used in hurling. *Banba* is a mythical name for the Irish nation
2. D. Nirenberg (2013) *Anti-Judaism: The Western Tradition* pp.1–12. See also Jeremy Cohen's conceptually similar argument about 'Hermeneutic Jews'. J. Cohen (1999) *Living Letters of the Law: Ideas of the Jew in Medieval Christianity* (Berkeley CA: University of California Press,
3. '[T]he fact that someone is called a Jew acts as a provocation to set about him until he resembles that image.' M. Horkheimer, T. Adorno (2002) *Dialectic of Enlightenment: Philosophical Fragments* (Stanford CA: Stanford University Press) p. 153; D. Nirenberg (2013) *Anti-Judaism*, p. 240.
4. Ibid., p. 211.
5. I am hesitant in my language here, because I am not willing to go so far as to say that the flesh–spirit antinomy is completely absent in this strand of nationalist thought. It is perhaps more accurate to say that the normative bodies of white Christians have a physiognomic role, alerting us to their deeply felt normative national spirit (a spirit, of course, from which Jews are allegedly alienated).
6. J. Joyce (1986) *Ulysses* (New York: Random House) pp. 240–283.
7. D. Kiberd (2009) *Ulysses and Us: The Art of Everyday life in Joyce's Masterpiece* (New York: W.W. Norton) p. 189. See also Frank Felsenstein's argument that the imaginary 'Jew' 'threatens to overturn and confound the fabric of the social order by the uneasiness that his being brings, although perhaps he unwittingly mirrors the cracks and tensions already inherent there. He is the perpetual outsider whose unsettling presence serves to define the bounds that separate the native English*man* from the alien Other.' F. Felsenstein (1995) *Antisemitic Stereotypes: A Paradigm of Otherness in English Popular Culture, 1660–1830* (Baltimore MD: Johns Hopkins University Press) p. 3. Emphases added.
8. 'The evidence from the real Cusack's letters and speeches, and from what we know of his career, suggests that Joyce's parody was only slightly exaggerated.' W.F. Mandle (1987) *The Gaelic Athletic Association and Irish Nationalist Politics, 1884–1924* (Dublin: Gill and Macmillan) p. 2.
9. Ibid., p. 1; P. Rouse (2009) 'Michael Cusack: Sportsman and Journalist' in M. Cronin, W. Murphy, P. Rouse, eds. *The Gaelic Athletic Association, 1884–2009* (Dublin: Irish Academic Press) p. 47.
10. W.F. Mandle (1987) *Gaelic Athletic Association*, pp.1–2.

11. McDevitt provides a concise summary of hurling for neophytes: 'a combination of lacrosse and field hockey in which a hard, leather ball (called a "sliotar") is struck with a wooden, ax-like club (called a "caman" [*sic*, camán]) toward a "H"-shaped goal'. P.F. McDevitt (2004) *May The Best Man Win: Sport, Masculinity, and Nationalism in Great Britain and the Empire, 1880–1935* (New York: Palgrave MacMillan) p. 15.
12. NUIG, Michael Cusack Papers, P95/12, Minutes of Dublin Hurling Club.
13. W.F. Mandle (1987) *Gaelic Athletic Association*, p. 33.
14. NUIG, Michael Cusack Papers, P95/39, P. Lee (1986) 'Cusack: The Founder of the G.A.A' in *Oscailt Oifigiúil: Teach Mhichíl Chísóg Carn Co. An Chláir* (Co. Clare: GAA).
15. GAA (1987) *The Gaelic Athletic Association for the Preservation and Cultivation of our National Pastimes*, 2nd edn (Dublin: A&E Cahill).
16. GAA (n.d) *Constitution and Rules of Games of Gaelic Athletic Association* (Dublin: Alley & Co).
17. W.F. Mandle (1987) *Gaelic Athletic Association*, p. 2. Wolfe Tone and James Napper Tandy were both late-eighteenth-century nationalists. Davis was a nationalist active in the early nineteenth century.
18. *Celtic Times*, 26 February 1887. Quoted in P.F. McDevitt (2004) *May The Best Man Win*, p. 19.
19. Ibid., p.16; Tony Collins points out the invented nature of most modern games called "football": 'The use of the word "football" before the twentieth century should not be assumed to be a synonym for Association football or soccer ... all pre-modern forms of football allowed some combination of handling, throwing and kicking the ball.' T. Collins (2013) *Sport in Capitalist Society: A Short History* (New York: Routledge) pp. 12–13.
20. P.F. McDevitt (2004) *May The Best Man Win*, p. 31.
21. Ibid., p. 16.
22. M. Cronin, M. Duncan, P. Rouse (2009) *The GAA: A People's History* (Cork: The Collins Press) p. 142.
23. T. Hunt (2009) 'The GAA: Social Structure and Associated Clubs',in M. Cronin,; William Murphy, Paul Rouse, eds. *The Gaelic Athletic Association, 1884–2009* (Dublin: Irish Academic Press, 2009) *Gaelic Athletic Association*, p. 188.
24. M. Cronin et al. (2009) *A People's History*, p. 147.
25. G. Ó Tuathaigh (2009) 'The GAA as a Force in Irish Society: An Overview',in Cronin et al., eds, *Gaelic Athletic Association*, p. 242.
26. 'Oisin's Address to his Clann'. *Sinn Féin*, 14 May 1910. Quoted in S. Banerjee (2012) *Muscular Nationalism: Gender, Violence and Empire in India and Ireland* (New York: NYU Press), p. 47. See also the 1908 *Sinn Féin* article on 'Muscular Sinn Fein'. Ibid., p. 45.

27. GAA (1926) *Gaelic Athletic Year Book, 1926: A Complete Compendium of Irish Athletic Records* (Dublin: The Gaelic Press).
28. GAA (1927) *The Gaelic Athletic Annual, 1927–28* (Kilkenny: Kilkenny Journal).
29. GAA Archives, GAA/Prog/1887 to GAA/Prog/1944, *All Ireland Football Final Programme*, 17 September 1937.
30. NLI, Eoin O'Duffy Papers, MS 48300/2, 'Reminiscences', unpublished autobiography by Eoin O'Duffy, Chapters IV and V.
31. For a background of the founding of the Volunteers, and for the source of these membership statistics, see M. Hay (2009) *Bulmer Hobson and the Nationalist Movement in Twentieth-Century Ireland* (Manchester: Manchester University Press), pp. 110–128.
32. Earnán de Blaghd [Ernest Blythe] (July 1912) 'Men and Arms' in *Irish Freedom*.
33. Earnán de Blaghd [Ernest Blythe] (December, 1913) 'Arms and Drill' in *Irish Freedom*.
34. Unsigned (January 1914) 'The Rebirth' in *Irish Freedom*.
35. NLI ILB 300 P2, Item 92, *Constitution of the Irish Volunteers, Adopted at the First Irish Volunteer Convention*, 25 October 1914. For the original draft version, see NLI, Bulmer Hobson Papers, MS 13174 (1), Proposed Constitution of the Irish Volunteers, Passed at special meeting of the Provisional Committee, 10 October 1914.
36. NLI, Bulmer Hobson Papers, MS 13174 (2), *Manifesto of Irish Volunteers*, n.d. (1913?).
37. UCDA, de Valera Papers, P150/449 *The Irish Volunteer Fund*, 16 December 1913. Published in *The Irish Volunteer*, 7 February 1914.
38. NLI LO P115, Item 4, *Twenty Plain Facts for Irishmen*, undated handbill (1914?).
39. NLI ILB 300 P7, Item 19, *The Duty of Irish Volunteers*, undated handbill (1914?). Capitalisation in original.
40. The O'Rahilly (1915) *Secret History of the Volunteers: Tracts for the Times, No.3*. 3rd edn (Dublin: Irish Publicity League).
41. NLI, Pearse Papers, MS15556, Speech by Commandant P.H. Pearse, 26 September 1915.
42. T.A. Higgins (1914) *The Rise of the Irish National Volunteer Movement* (Belfast: United Irish League, 1914).
43. Military Archives, Bureau of Military History, Contemporary Documents, 52/2/11, The Volunteers: Sunday's Great Demonstration: The Inspector-General's Orders, 29 March 1915.
44. NLI, MacDonagh Family Papers, MS 20643/3, Irish Volunteers: Dublin City and County Board, Order signed by M.J. Judge, Hon. Secretary, 16 September 1914.

45. Irish Volunteers (1914) *The Handbook for Irish Volunteers: Simple Lectures on Military Subjects* (Dublin: M.H. Gill).
46. For background on O'Duffy's appointment, see F. McGarry (2005) *Eoin O'Duffy: A Self-Made Hero* (Oxford: Oxford University Press) pp. 113–114.
47. NLI, Eoin O'Duffy Papers, MS 48284, *The State's Young Police Force in the Making: Training of a Civic Guard Described*, undated press cutting [circa 1923–24]. In the first two years of its existence, Ireland's independent police service was titled 'The Civic Guard', before formally taking on the Irish-language name which still remains in place today.
48. Ibid.
49. Ibid.
50. NLI, Eoin O'Duffy Papers, 'The Garda Siochana: The Story of Ireland's Marvellous New Police Force—Chapter Two.' *Northwest Police Journal*, Vol. VIII, No. III, February 1931.
51. 'Foreword' in *Aonach an Gharda* [Garda Festival] *Souvenir Programme*, 14–16 July 1926.
52. F. McGarry (2005) *O'Duffy*, pp. 118–119.
53. NLI, Eoin O'Duffy Papers, Eoin O'Duffy (incorrectly named as Even O'Duffy) 'The Story of the Garda Siochana: Irish History in the Making—Chapter One.' *Northwest Police Journal*, Vol. VIII, No. II, January 1931. The *Northwest Police Journal* was published in Washington State.
54. 'Foreword' in *Aonach an Gharda* [Garda Festival] *Souvenir Programme*, 14–16 July 1926.
55. NAI TAOIS/ 3108, *Gárda Siochána: Supply of Uniforms*, Letter from Garda Commissioner to Secretary, Ministry of Home Affairs, 15 June 1923.
56. *Orders and Regulations for the Instruction and Control of the Garda Síochána. As Approved by the Minister for Justice* (Dublin: The Stationery Office, 1928). For some of the antecedents of this, see also: *Official Standing Orders and Regulations for the Government and Guidance of the Dublin Metropolitan Police, as Approved by His Excellency the Lord Lieutenant* (Dublin: Her Majesty's Stationery Office, 1889); *Standing Rules and Regulations for the Government and Guidance of the Royal Irish Constabulary, Sixth Edition, as Approved by his Excellency the Lord Lieutenant* (Dublin: His Majesty's Stationery Office, 1911).
57. UCDA, Kevin O'Higgins Papers, P197/170, *State of National Emergency: The Garda—Armed or Unarmed*, Confidential Memo to Minister for Justice from Eoin O'Duffy, 6 December 1926.
58. See, for example, the cartoons in *Guth an Ghárda*, 28 August 1924, 11 September 1924 and 9 October 1924; *Garda Review*, September 1926.

    For the British antecedents of this, see M. de Nie (2004) *The Eternal Paddy: Irish Identity and the British Press, 1798–1882* (Madison, WI: University of Wisconsin Press).
59. C. Brady (2000) *Guardians of the Peace* (London: Prendeville Publishing) p. 45.
60. Ibid., p. 43.
61. Ibid., p. 1. Conway points out that the RIC's size fluctuated depending on the level of contemporary political unrest, with the ratio of police to population always being greater than in the rest of the United Kingdom. V. Conway (2014) *Policing Twentieth Century Ireland: A History of The Garda Síochána* (London: Routledge) p. 13.
62. V. Conway (2014) *Policing*, p. 27; D.J. O'Sullivan (2007) *The Depot: A History of the Garda Síochána Depot at the Phoenix Park, Dublin* (No Place of Publication: Navillus Publishing) p. 142. O'Sullivan was a Garda Chief Superintendent and this book is described as 'Published with the approval of Mr. Noel Conroy, Commissioner of The Garda Síochána.'
63. V. Conway (2014) *Policing*, pp. 27–29.
64. The pre-existing RIC Policeman's Manual was used in training until 1942, when the Garda Síochána Manual was first published. Ibid., p. 32.
65. Conway talks of this as the 'view that the police had an important role to play in personifying the image of independent Ireland.' Ibid., p. 40.
66. For an analysis of how such muscular ideals straddled Zionist/non-Zionist lines, see J. Jacobs (2007) 'Jewish Workers' Sports Movements in Interwar Poland: Shtern and Morgnshtern in Comparative Perspective' in J. Kugelmass, ed. *Jews, Sports and the Rites of Citizenship* (Urbana IL: University of Illinois Press) pp. 114–128; J. Bunzl (2006) 'Hakoah Vienna: Reflections on a Legend' in M. Brenner, G. Reuveni, eds. *Emancipation Through Muscles: Jews and Sports in Europe* (Lincoln, NE: University of Nebraska Press) pp.106–115; M. Brenner (2006) 'Why Jews and Sports' in M. Brenner, G. Reuveni, eds. *Emancipation*, p. 1.
67. G. Reuveni (2006) 'Sports and the Militarization of Jewish Society' in M. Brenner, G.Reuveni, eds.*Emancipation*, p. 47.
68. J. Bunzl (2006) 'Hakoah Vienna', p. 113.
69. S.A. Riess (2012) 'Antisemitism and Sport in Central Europe and the United States, c. 1870–1932' in L.J. Greenspoon, ed. *Jews in the Gym: Judaism, Sports and Athletics* (West Lafayette, IN: Purdue University Press) pp. 99–100.
70. G. Reuveni (2006) 'Sports and the Militarization' p. 44.
71. T.S. Presner (2007) *Muscular Judaism: The Jewish Body and the Politics of Regeneration* (London: Routledge) p. 47.
72. Ibid., p. 1.
73. Ibid., pp. 2–3.

74. M. Stanislawski (2001) *Zionism and the Fin de Siècle: Cosmopolitanism and Nationalism from Nordau to Jabotinsky* (Berkeley CA: University of California Press) pp.93–94.
75. M. Zimmerman (2006) 'Muscle Jews versus Nervous Jews' in M. Brenner, G. Reuveni, eds., *Emancipation*, p. 17.
76. Ibid., pp. 4–5
77. T.S. Presner (2007) *Muscular Judaism*, p. 3.
78. A. Helman (2007) 'Zionism, Politics, Hedonism: Sports in Interwar Tel Aviv' in J. Kugelmass, ed. *Jews, Sports, and the Rites of Citizenship*, p. 96.
79. Ibid., p.100.
80. N. Spiegel (2012) 'Sporting a Nation: The Origins of Athleticism in Modern Israel' in L.J. Greenspoon, ed. *Jews in the Gym: Judaism, Sports, and Athletics* (West Lafayette IN: Purdue University Press) pp. 189–196.
81. A. Helman (2008) 'Sports in the Young State of Israel' in E. Mendelsohn, ed. *Jews and the Sporting Life: Studies in Contemporary Jewry XXIII* (Oxford: Oxford University Press) pp. 108–111
82. M. Brenner (2006) 'Why Jews and Sports', p. 3.
83. B. Kimmerling (2001) *The Invention and Decline of Israeliness: State, Society, and the Military* (Berkeley, CA: University of California Press) p.6. For an overview of militarism and its links to Jewish identity across the modern period, see: D. Penslar (2013) *Jews and the Military: A History* (Princeton, NJ: Princeton University Press).
84. For an overview, see: B. Kimmerling (2008) *Clash of Identities: Explorations in Israeli and Palestinian Societies* (New York: Columbia University Press) pp. 132–153.
85. G. Reuveni (2006) Sports and the Militarization, p. 44.
86. Ibid., pp. 48–56.
87. M. Stanislawski (2001) *Zionism*, p. 194.
88. Ibid., pp. 216–217. Emphases in original.
89. Ibid., p. 219.
90. T. Mac S. [Toirdealbach Mac Suibhne, i.e. Terence MacSwiney] (31 October 1914) 'Irish Womanhood: Wolfe Tone's Wife: A Model for Cumann na mBan.' *Fianna Fáil: A Journal for Militant Ireland*, Vol. 1, No.6.
91. These articles were in the September 1932 and February 1937 issues.
92. V. Conway (2014) *Policing*, pp. 82–83.
93. 'Women Police.' *Garda Review*, May 1937.
94. M. Cronin, et al. (2009) *People's History*, p. 320.
95. Ibid., pp. 323–328.
96. R. Dudley Edwards (2006) *Patrick Pearse: The Triumph of Failure*, 2nd edn (Dublin: Irish Academic Press), p. 158; B. Feeney (2002) *Sinn Féin: One Hundred Turbulent Years* (Dublin: O'Brien Press) p. 171.

97. Brian na Banban [Brian O'Higgins] (September 1912) 'Camóguidheacht go Bráth', *Irish Freedom*.
98. R. Nic Congáil, (2010) *Úna Ní Fhaircheallaigh agus an Fhís Útóipeach Ghaelach* [Úna Ní Fhaircheallaigh and the Gaelic Utopian Vision] (Dublin: Arlen House) pp. 320–350.
99. R. Nic Congáil, 2013) '"Looking On For Centuries From the Sideline": Gaelic Feminism and the Rise of Camogie', *Éire-Ireland*, Volume 48, Nos. 1 & 2, 170.
100. Ibid., p. 173.
101. M. Cronin et al.(2009) *'People's History* pp. 323–328.
102. R. Nic Congáil (2010) *Úna Ní Fhaircheallaigh* pp. 336–337.
103. T. Collins (2013) *Sport in Capitalist Society* pp. 38–39.
104. Ibid., pp. 42–43.
105. E. O'Malley (1936) *On Another Man's Wounds* (London: Rich & Cowan) p. 70; E. O'Malley (1978) *The Singing Flame* (Dublin: Anvil Books) p. 21.
106. Military Archives, Bureau of Military History, Contemporary Documents, 202/5, Cumann na mBan: Scheme of Organisation, n.d. (circa, 1921–22).
107. NLI LOLB 161, Item 26, *The Volunteers, the Women, and the Nation*, Cumann na mBan Pamphlet, 1915.
108. NLI EPH B13, Cumann na mBan Constitution, n.d. (circa 1921).
109. NLI LOLB 161, Item 5, Cumann na mBan Pamphlet, n.d. (circa 1919–21).
110. S. Banerjee (2012) *Muscular Nationalism*, p. 89.
111. T. Mac S. [Toirdealbach Mac Suibhne, i.e. Terence MacSwiney] (31 October 1914) 'Irish Womanhood: Wolfe Tone's Wife: A Model for Cumann na mBan.'
112. See, for instance, Military Archives, Bureau of Military History, Contemporary Documents, 200/2/2, E. de B. [Elizabeth Bloxham?]. *A Call to Irishwomen*, undated pamphlet, which linked the honour and distinction enjoyed by women in ancient Ireland with the Proclamation's promise of a more gender-equalitarian future.
113. As depicted in *The Irish Volunteer*, 1 April 1916. The conservative clothing favoured by Cumann na mBan members can be seen in the photograph of Elizabeth Bloxham and others attending a secret meeting sometime before 1922. Military Archives, BMH Contemporary Documents, 216/3.
114. R. Nic Congáil (2013) 'The Rise of Camogie', p. 169.
115. T.S. Presner (2007) *Muscular Judaism*, p. 12.
116. A. Helman (2008) 'Sports in the Young State', p. 107.
117. U. Klein (2003) 'The Military and Masculinities in Israeli Society' in P.R. Higate, ed. *Military Masculinities: Identity and the State* (Westport, CT: Praeger) p.198.

118. Ibid., p. 192. In practice, however, men attending a *Yeshiva* [a rabbinical seminary] can gain exemptions from their national service.
119. B. Kimmerling (2008) *Clash of Identities*, p. 150.
120. Ibid., p. 149.
121. J. Hopton (2003) 'The State and Military Masculinity' in P.R. Higate, ed. *Military Masculinities*, p. 113.
122. D. Harvey (2000) *Spaces of Hope* (Berkeley, CA: University of California Press) p. 98.

CHAPTER 4

The Genders of Nationalist Space

It is nothing but love of country that rouses us to make our land full-blooded and beautiful where now she is pallid and wasted. This, too, has its deeper significance.[1]

LYING IN STATE/A STATE IN THE MAKING

This chapter begins with an end: the 1915 funeral of Jeremiah O'Donovan Rossa. Born in 1831, O'Donovan Rossa was a veteran of the Irish Republican Brotherhood and a famously satirical journalist who had mostly lived in exile in New York since his release from prison in 1871.[2] On 29 June 1915 he died at St Vincent's Hospital on Staten Island and another IRB 'exile', John Devoy, took charge of his funeral arrangements. Notwithstanding O'Donovan Rossa's wishes to be buried alongside his father in his native Rosscarbery in West Cork, Devoy orchestrated to have his Fenian comrade interred in the more suitably nationalist surroundings of Dublin's Glasnevin Cemetery. The funeral, on 1 August 1915, took on all the trappings of an official state event. It provided Pearse with the occasion for his famous speech on 'our Fenian dead'. It brought together the various radical factions of Irish politics who, a year later, would execute the Rising. It was, in many ways, a dress rehearsal for the Rising itself. It was also, though, an event pregnant with a gendered conception of nationalist space. Devoy's immediate call for a publicly supported funeral, for instance, neatly welded the erotic to the nationalist in its description of O'Donovan Rossa's return to an Irish space: 'It was always his fond hope, his heartfelt wish that his remains should be borne across the seas to his beloved Ireland, and that he should be laid to rest upon the bosom of that land which he loved so well; that his ashes should mingle with the ashes of his forefathers, while his spirit wandered freely among the hills and glens of his beloved Erin.'[3] The return of O'Donovan Rossa's body for burial in his homeland reiterated the almost sacral centrality of Irish soil. His burial in Dublin's Glasnevin Cemetery served to place him, quite literally, alongside other dead (mostly male) patriots. It also reaffirmed Dublin's centrality, over and above rural backwaters like West Cork.[4]

While Devoy may have been the initiator of this event, though, it was the Volunteers who ultimately took control of it. And within the Volunteers, Thomas MacDonagh, under the auspices of the impromptu O'Donovan Rossa Funeral Committee, ensured that this would be a closely stage-managed event.[5] Upon initial arrival in Dublin on 27 July, O'Donovan Rossa's body was brought to the Pro-Cathedral at Marlborough Street, where Volunteers guarded him 'like silent soldier sentinels at the bier of a dead king.'[6] The next day, his body was brought to City Hall, where it lay in state until Sunday, 1 August.[7] Then, directly following a mass at the Capuchin Church in Dublin's north inner city, a several-mile-long funeral procession wound its way through Dublin's urban spaces.[8] It moved along the north side of the Liffey River, across to the entrance of City Hall, and moved down Dame Street to College Green (home of Ireland's lost independent parliament), before crossing back over the river and advancing up a street which, in MacDonagh's handwritten orders, was pointedly not called Sackville Street.[9] MacDonagh's tersely worded command for each battalion of the Volunteers was to 'supply to the General Staff 3 section or Squad commanders (armed) and 30 men to *clear and hold Grattan Bridge, Parliament Street and Cork Hill.*'[10] That Irish men, in Irish uniforms, would take control of the urban spaces of Dublin city, as they served as military escort to the funeral of a dead patriot, clearly had important political overtones. 'The procession through Dublin was a veritable march of triumph'[11] and on 1 August 1915 the Irish Volunteers 'virtually policed Dublin for the day.'[12]

There were also precise instructions for the sequence in which various groups would join the cortège. The Volunteers took the vanguard as well the rear. The Irish Citizen Army, the GAA and the Gaelic League were afforded representation, as were the National Volunteers (though suspicion due to their support for the British war effort perhaps explains why they were relegated to marching with the women and children of Cumann na mBan and Na Fianna Éireann).[13] This sequencing, and the hierarchies that went along with it, were to be maintained by marshals along the route of the procession.[14]

Having reached Glasnevin Cemetery, Volunteers formed a cordon, both at the entrance and, in numbers four-deep, along the path to the grave, ensuring that Volunteer authority would be visible to all in attendance.[15] MacDonagh also provided a map to his fellow organisers, with precise instructions for where each group would be positioned. The various nationalist groups occupied strategic points across the entire cemetery with a clear hierarchy reflected in which of them were allowed to be positioned closest to the grave.[16] The numbers in attendance for this 'gigantic propagandistic exercise'[17] reached the hundreds of thousands and those deemed worthy of a place close to the grave would have been able to hear Pearse's famous speech. Pearse's declared aim in his eulogy to O'Donovan Rossa was 'to formulate the thought and hope that are in us as we stand around his grave.' Pearse spoke of the 'communion' those present felt with this 'brave and splendid Gael' and his 'proud manhood'. His aggressive conclusion was that:

> Life springs from death; and from the graves of patriot men and women spring living nations. The Defenders of the Realm have worked well in secret and in the open. They think that they have pacified Ireland. They think that they have purchased half of us and intimidated the other half. They think that they have foreseen everything, think that they have provided against everything; but the fools, the fools, the fools!—they have left us our Fenian dead, and while Ireland holds these graves, Ireland unfree shall never be at peace.[18]

Brian Murphy's analysis unselfconsciously reflects the nationalist and highly gendered mood of this moment: 'These well known words, and the huge crowds that attended the funeral, have often been taken as inaugurating a *mass rallying of men* to the Republican banner'[19] (notwithstanding Pearse's mention of 'patriot men *and women*').

Writing a few days before 1 August, Terence MacSwiney asked what lessons could be drawn from O'Donovan Rossa's life. MacSwiney's answer strongly reflected both MacDonagh's funeral arrangements and the nationalist bombast of Pearse's speech: 'He [O'Donovan Rossa] must be happy, too, to look on us. For we recall the time in early days when he told us how he exhibited a rifle and other weapons on his premises to prove to his timid friends that they were entitled to possess arms; and now he can see us marshalled in thousands as soldiers and carrying our weapons bravely in the sun.'[20] Where once Irish men were weak and fearful, now they are strong, militant and willing and able to take control of Irish spaces. They draw inspiration in a sort of nationalist communion, as they (or at least a select few) mass around the fresh grave of 'our Fenian dead'. As Devoy recalled, 'it was the most imposing demonstration ever held in Ireland' and 'It was splendidly managed, perfect order and discipline prevailed from start to finish and it had a great effect on the country.'[21] Space, more particularly the disciplined control of space, was clearly a central element in the O'Donovan Rossa funeral.

SPACE, POWER AND GENDER

To imagine an independent Ireland is, in a very real sense, to imagine something spatially novel and 'space' as a distinct category should feature in any thorough analysis of Irish nationalism. Borrowing from the terminology of Neil Smith, Irish nationalism was an attempt to move from 'relative space' (Ireland's status as an internal part of the United Kingdom) to 'absolute space' (a separate and spatially coherent nation-state).[22] And for many Irish nationalists, the vaguely defined 'relative space' of pre-independence Ireland mirrored the nation's ill-defined racial and gendered identity. John Tosh persuasively argues that modern male power 'has resided' in men's 'privileged freedom to pass at will between the public and the private.'[23] Frank Mort similarly notes how moving 'easily across the whole city and experience[ing] its diversity' are the 'traditional rights of privileged men.' Tellingly, one recent commentator observes that many an early-twentieth-century Irishman 'felt no great investment in a setting which his people did not own.'[24] If control over space and the ability to move freely through public and private spaces are perceived as defining characteristics of modern men, it is unsurprising that Irish men's lack of control over Irish spaces came to be seen as emblematic of a deeper lack of masculine power. In the words of one Israeli scholar, debates over borders and space are often connected 'to the contours of the national body' [*le-kavai ha-mit'ar shel ha-guf ha-le'umi*].[25] The space of Ireland was often coded as a female body and thus British colonialism was imagined as something akin to rape or (at the least) adultery.²⁶ In this vein, creating an absolute space over which Irish men would be in clear control was of a piece with crafting a more powerful sense of decolonised Irish masculinity. This entailed performing a gendered Irishness in public so as to demonstrate Irish men's ownership of the public space; such performances not only 'proved' the space was Irish, but the primary preserve of men as well.

Zionism, targeting Diasporic Jews, had to deal with an even more extreme version of this kind of spatiality. Jews were perhaps the spatially undefined people par excellence and Zionism sought to create a spatially coherent nation-state to end the anomalous condition of what Gabriel Piterberg terms the Diaspora's 'infinite temporal and spatial permutations'.²⁷ Taking control of the national space of Palestine was conceived as a palliative for Jewish men. *We came to the land to build it and to be built by it*, as a popular Zionist song of the early twentieth century proclaimed.²⁸ Promoting a similar vision, the Zionist poet Shaul Tchernichovsky's 'Shadows Are Spreading' [*Nitshu Tzlalim*] identified martial masculinity with sovereignty over the space of Palestine and, consequently, a national rebirth:

On the Jordan and in Sharon	*al ha-Yarden u-va-Sharon*
Where the Arabs camp,	*sham Aravim chonim*
This will be our land!	*lanu zot ha-aretz tihiye!*
You, too, are among the builders!	*gam atah ba-bonim*
And some day the standard-bearers will arise,	*ve-yom yakumu nos'ei-degel*
Do not betray them!	*al tim'alah ma'l*
To your weapons among the heroes,	*el Kelei zaynecha ba-giborim*
Our sun shall rise.	*ki shimeshenu ya'al.*²⁹

Anti-colonial nationalism, as Partha Chatterjee notes, often 'creates its own domain of sovereignty within colonial society well before it begins its political battle with the imperial power.' By acting thusly, Chatterjee suggests, 'the nation is already sovereign, even when the state is in the hands of the colonial power.'³⁰ Zionists sought to do something conceptually similar; they sought to control specific spaces of Palestine even before achieving formal state power. The *tiyul*, the tour through Palestine, became something of a ritual among younger Zionists. Often organised through the Society for the Protection of Nature in Israel, these tours became a way of reinforcing Israelis' stability and the Zionist ownership of the national space.³¹ Attias and Benbessa aptly call this 'the voyage as a sign of being anchored'.³²

Nomenclature was another familiar means of establishing Zionist ownership. Meron Benvenisiti, the former deputy-mayor of the city alternatively known as Jerusalem, Yerushalayim (in Hebrew), Al-Quds (in Arabic) and Urshalim (in the Hebraicised Arabic favoured by the Israeli state), has called the 'Hebrew map' which his father drew up, 'a renewed title deed'³³ for the ownership of Israel-Palestine. After 1948, the Negev Naming Committee established by the Israeli government was tasked with Hebraicising the names used on the original modern map of Palestine, drawn up in 1913–14 by Herbert Horatio Kitchener and T.E. Lawrence via the Palestine Exploration Fund. Kitchener, Benvenisiti comments, might have been saddened if he had seen all his work undone. 'But the legendary empire builder—son of an English colonist in Ireland—would have understood the logic of the Israeli bureaucratic campaign. After all, that is precisely how the British had behaved in every region they chose to colonize—from Ireland in the seventeenth century to the plateaus of Kenya in the early years of the twentieth; in Canada, Australia, and Rhodesia.'³⁴ Intriguingly, Benvenisiti boldly asserts that 'Only those who have experienced the dichotomous environments of Sarajevo, Beirut, *or Belfast* can truly comprehend the phenomenon of the "white patches" on the mental maps carried around in the heads of the Jews and Arabs of Eretz Israel/Palestine.'³⁵ And just as in Ireland, this focus on Jewish ownership of Palestine was a vehicle for gendered and regenerative projects.

As the two previous chapters demonstrated, a 'return to history' was a major element in early-twentieth-century Irish nationalist thought. This highly gendered practice, seen as a means of reconnecting to a masculinity destroyed by British rule, also had some distinctly spatial elements. This can be seen in the notes produced for a May 1903 Gaelic League tour from Dublin to Galway. The Gaelic League had been founded in 1893 with the aim of reviving the Irish language, as well as promoting homegrown industries and social reform. By the turn of the century, it had become one of the most important cultural organisations in Ireland.³⁶ In the brochure produced for those taking part in their 1903 tour, precise instructions were given for how Gaelic Leaguers should experience the recovered Irish space through which they passed:

> As you come to the different stations mentioned in this series of notes, fix their Irish names—and their meanings—in your memory, and use the

Irish names in future, always, when referring to these places. CLUAIN-SIOLLACH (Clonsilla—the Meadow of the Sallies), not far from which is *Cnuca* (Castleknock) where *Fionn Mac Cumhaill*'s father was killed. From him (*Cumhaill*) is named *Rath-Cumhaill* (Rathcool), a few miles away.

There was a clear didactic quality to this. Gaelic League day trippers were being taught about Ireland and instructed in how to feel rooted in its past, present and future. Tellingly, though, it is only the description of Irish-speaking Galway that includes actual living people, albeit ones presented in an exotic light: 'Crossing the River Corrib by the West Bridge (tram line) you come to Salthill. Leaving the tram line at left corner of Lower Dominick Street, you arrive at Cladach—the village of fishermen, who are rather conservative in habits and manner, but who use Gaelic as their ordinary speech.' As Benjamin Harshav has said of the representation of the *shtetl* in modernist Yiddish literature, Irish-speaking villages are here 'unmistakably reconstructed from a distance ... Both the writer and his readers are already modern city-dwellers who believe in "Culture, Progress, Civilization" and look back at the small town as at a museum exhibit.'[37] The brochure ended with the hope 'May God strengthen us and we will make Ireland free' [*Go Neartuigidh Dia Sinn and Go Saoirimis Èire*].[38]

As will be discussed more fully in the next chapter, language revival regularly intertwined with notions of a resurgent Irish masculinity. As the notes for the 1903 Tour make clear, Gaelic League tourists from Dublin were urged to feel connected both to the ancient masculinity of Fionn Mac Cumhaill, one of the most archetypal figures from Irish mythology, as well as to the 'museum exhibits' of the Irish-speaking periphery. The residents of the Gaeltacht, predominantly poor farmers who spoke a language previously maligned as backwards, were now praised as the living repositories of a recovered Gaelic manliness. Experiencing both the Gaeltacht and its residents was a means to strengthen (i.e., re-masculinise) the Irish nation.

There was 'a spatialized notion of memory'[39] at work here and, for the Gaelic League, what was at stake was the belief that the memory of Ireland's ancient manly heroism was embedded in certain spaces of Ireland. Reconnecting to these spaces was a means of reconnecting to these embedded memories and would thus ultimately allow for a reconnection with this ancient heroic masculinity. Moreover, by moving through these spaces, by demanding that Irish rather than English names be used, the predominantly male, urban leadership of the Gaelic League could demonstrate their ownership of Ireland. The League was 'building up', its president Douglas Hyde proclaimed in 1914, 'a little Irish nation, which would become big some day—he hoped, please God, so big as to absorb the entire island.'[40]

The Gaelic League's examination papers also urged students to think in terms of a recovered time and space and to explore their bonds with heroic men from the national past.[41] In the 1907 exam, under the heading 'Irish History' [Stair na hÉireann], students were asked 'What caused the Festival of Tara to be founded? What was its nickname? When was it in existence?' [*Cé chuis Feis na Teamhrach ar bun? Cad é (cé, goidé) an leas-ainm a bhí uirri? Cathain (cé 'n uair) a bhí sé 'na beathaidh?*] and then told 'Write a short account of the life and acts of Cormac Mac Airt', [*Sgrí'ig (sgríobh) cúnntas gearr ar beathaidh & ar ghníomharthaibh Cormaic Mhic Airt*], a mythical high-king of Ireland.[42] Intriguingly the exams were labelled as coming from the Gaelic League's *An Gléas Sgoláireachta* [Educational or Scholarship System], as if the Gaelic League was part of an embryonic state, with its own educational system (even if this 'state' could still not agree on a standardised form of the language). In the British state intermediate system, which had begun (under pressure from language activists) to offer Irish exams, there was a similar phenomenon. In the 1905 senior grade honours Irish exam, compiled by Úna Ní Fhaircheallaigh, the first question was to translate the following into Irish:

(a) The Brehon laws were in force in the country from very early times.
(b) In 1586, the English poet Spenser received a grant of 3028 acres in County Cork...
(d) The Norsemen began to ravage Ireland about the end of the eighth century.
(e) 'This is the land of brave men and generous women,' said the stranger.[43]

Again, the historical image is one of brave men, here accented with 'generous women', presumably meaning that these women restricted themselves to providing for the culinary needs of their militarily active menfolk.

The degree to which history and geography featured so heavily in what was ostensibly a language exam reinforces the idea that reconnecting with the ancient language was perceived as a means of reconnecting with the redeemed space and heroic time of Ireland. The Anglocentric sense of time and imperial understanding of space appearing in a typical contemporary British Ministry of Education Intermediate history and geography exam further highlights this:

3. Give a brief narration of Fairfax's campaign in Kent and Essex during the Second Civil war....
8. Where are the following places, and what are their respective capitals: Malta, Cyprus, Baluchistan; Sierra Leone; Mauritius; Jamaica; Newfoundland

or

8. Give the names and situations of the six leading seats of shipbuilding in the United Kingdom.
9. Give the boundaries of India; and state its area and population approximately.[44]

Save Your Land[45]

Given the deep roots that gendered notions of spatial control had within Irish nationalism, it is unsurprising that such concerns were again to the fore from 1916 onwards. Scholars have long noted that performance, symbolism and control of Dublin's urban space were key elements in the Easter Rising. Historians have spoken of it as 'the last 1848-style rebellion in European history', in which nationalists took to the barricades and waited to be shot down, or even as a completely symbolic event lacking in any realistic military goals.[46] While the Rising may have been a series of tactical mistakes, Declan Kiberd discusses how it became a kind of spatio-symbolic victory:

> from a symbolic perspective, taking possession of the most important building on Dublin's main street was an effective action—something that put a halt to ordinary communication in the city and that thus would affect the life and imagination of the masses. It is not difficult to show the link between 1916 and the theatre; it was as a drama that the leaders themselves imagined the revolution, and it was as a drama, not as a military campaign, that it entered the public domain.

> [*ó thaobh na siombalaíochta de, b'éifeachtach an gníomh seilbh a ghlacadh ar an bhfoirghneamh ba thábhachtaí ar phríomhshráid Bhaile Átha Cliath—rud a chuirfeadh deireadh le gnáthchumarsaid na cathrach agus a rachadh i bhfeidhim ar shaol agus an shamhlaíocht an ghnáthphobail da réir. Ní deacair an bhaint idir 1916 agus an drámaíocht a léiriú; mar dhráma ann féin a shamhlaigh na ceannairí an réabhlóid, agus ba mar dhráma, ní mar fheactas míleata, a chuaigh sé i mbéal an phobail ó shin*].[47]

Pushing this analysis to its outer reaches, James Moran calls the Rising 'Guerrilla Theatre', in that 'an idealistic group of men and women, who also realised the power of the theatre, decided to practise what they had been preaching in the playhouse, and take control of the centre of Dublin.'[48] As with Sean Treacy and Dan Breen's history lessons, though, it is doubtful that the rebels were thinking of the theatre as the violence of the rebellion got under way. As outlined in Chap. 2, it is important to differentiate between the experiential reality of the Rising as opposed to the *post facto* construction of a more idealised vision of that reality. The 'Rising' in 1917 had some marked differences to the Rising in 1916. What came to be a defining feature in later popular perceptions was the symbolism of Irish men (and some women) taking control of a number of Dublin's key public spaces and the manner in which this symbolism prefigured Irish political sovereignty. As with the construction of images of heroic martyrdom, Pearse et al. were again complicit in the narratives that would later emerge.

Control of the GPO on O'Connell/Sackville Street on the north side of the city and Boland's Mills on the south side gave the rebels control of the two main entrance points into the city centre. Positions at the Jacob's factory and the Irish Citizen Army's control of St Stephen's Green should have cemented this control. In *War News*, the newspaper produced by the rebels,[49] the various militias were described as 'dominating' the city. 'The Republican forces everywhere are fighting with splendid gallantry' *War News* wishfully claimed, and 'The populace of Dublin are plainly with the Republic'. This had a clear political symbolism, if only at the municipal level: 'The Irish troops hold the City Hall and dominate the Castle' and British troops were described as being 'everywhere repulsed'. *War News*, of course, was produced before the violence reached its zenith and thus represents not an accurate snapshot of reality but a glimpse at the political desires of the rebels. Most telling of all, *War News* was designed to look like a British informational bulletin, as if it were being circulated by an already extant state. Even its banner headline served to suggest that the Irish Republic was already a reality: 'STOP PRESS! "War News" is published to-day because a momentous thing has happened. The Irish Republic has been declared in Dublin, and a Provisional Government has been appointed to administer its affairs.'[50] And the Provisional Government were, of course, all men. In another case, despite the obvious tactical downsides to doing so, the rebels who seized St Stephen's Green at the very centre of the city, dug trenches as if they were the soldiers of just another sovereign European nation-state fighting in the Great War.[51] As with broader nationalist attitudes towards violence, the idea that Irish sovereignty could be 'proven' through violently taking control of space points to a clear war-time influence.

A similar state-centric imaginary appears to have been at work in Pearse's various addresses to the people of Dublin during the rebellion. He gave himself the unwieldy title of 'Commandant-General Commanding-in-Chief of the Army of the Irish Republic, and President of the Provisional Government' and spoke of 'the gallantry of the soldiers of Irish Freedom, who have, during the past four days, been writing with fire and steel the most glorious chapter in the later history of Ireland.' In his surrender notice to the British forces Pearse still defiantly spoke of 'the glorious stand which has been made by the soldiers of Irish freedom during the past five days in Dublin' which he felt would be 'sufficient to gain recognition of Ireland's national claim at an international peace conference'.[52] Pearse claimed that the rebels 'have redeemed Dublin from many shames, and made her name splendid among the names of cities.' Though facing military defeat, he added, 'I am satisfied that we have saved Ireland's honour.'[53]

As was argued in the previous chapters, such projections of militarised strength and the claim that the nation's degraded honour needed to be saved or redeemed had specific meanings within Irish nationalism. Not only were such tropes related to the country's quasi-colonial status, they were also a means of projecting an idealised and highly gendered image of Irish men coming together in heroic defence of a nation that was coded as female. What is worth further emphasising here, however, is the manner through which the control of space came to be seen as a suitable means for achieving all this. These were concerns familiar to Zionists, for whom masculinity merged with militarist posturing and it was widely felt that control over a clearly defined space would redeem Jewish men. Writing in his diaries in June 1895, the Zionist leader Theodor Herzl, for instance, equated control of an absolute national space with a redeemed national masculinity:

> The Promised Land, where it is all right for us to have hooked noses, black or red beards, and bandy legs without being despised for these things alone. Where at last we can live as free people on our own and die in peace in our own homeland. Where we, too, can expect honour as a reward for great deeds; where we shall live at peace with all the world, which we shall have freed through our own freedom, enriched by our wealth and made greater by our greatness.[54]

Interestingly, not only does Herzl appear to accept the antisemitic idea that Jewish men have congenitally weak bodies, he also appears relatively comfortable with that bodily weakness. However, as the notion of a *Muskeljudentum* [muscular Judaism], most commonly associated with Max Nordau, came to predominance within the movement, Zionists began to feel that settlement in Palestine would lend itself to a more thoroughly physical reform of Jewish men.[55]

As early as October 1882, one of the first Zionist settlers, Vladimir (Ze'ev) Dubnow, wrote to his brother, the famous historian Simon Dubnow, warning him: 'Don't laugh, this is not a delusion ... The Jews will yet arise, weapons in hand (if need be); and, in a loud voice, they shall proclaim themselves the lords and masters of their ancient homeland.' Anita Shapira summarises such views thusly: 'Russia belonged to the Russians; and, by the same token, Palestine belonged to the Jews. For that reason, from the moment Jews landed in Jaffa harbor, they did not behave like a small minority dependent on the good grace of the majority. Rather, their comportment was befitting of persons who were the *rightful lords and masters of the land*'.[56] Such images, of strong men taking control of their supposedly rightful inheritance, were often contrasted with their mirror opposite, the ghetto Jew, whose spatially undetermined status was mirrored by an allegedly weak body. In an introduction which he wrote for Chaim Nachman Bialik's poem 'In The City of Slaughter' (itself a harsh polemic on ghetto life) Vladimir Jabotinsky asserted that 'The Ghetto despised physical Manhood, the principle of male power as understood and worshipped by all free peoples in history.' In contrast to this image of degraded and unfree ghetto life, Jabotinsky spoke 'of triumphant, invincible, rebellious Manhood, of the arm that wields the sword, of muscles of granite and sinews of steel.'[57] For people like Jabotinsky, of course, such a powerful and reborn masculinity could only come through abandoning the ghetto in favour of a normative national sovereignty in the Land of Israel. Being masters of the land whose control over the national public space would be undisputed, was clearly of importance to both Irish nationalists and Zionists. Irish nationalism, the Marxist-Zionists of Ha-Shomer Ha-Tzair [The Young Guard] jealously reported in the later 1940s, was 'the struggle of a people *on its land.*'[58]

By the summer of 1916, as the Rising began to receive a post facto legitimisation, and as idealised images of the 'martyrs' were constructed, the perception that it was a heroic moment of Irish men taking control of Irish spaces, and that this prefigured Irish political sovereignty, came to dominate popular perceptions. One early pamphlet spoke of the Easter Rising as 'the solemn moment when Ireland, a strong man armed, entered the clangorous halls of war, and, with drawn sword, demanded that nationhood, which seven centuries of tyranny have been unable to destroy'. The same pamphleteer looked askance at suggestions that it was a mere riot when, instead, 'It was a carefully-planned seizure of the capital of Ireland by soldiers well equipped, well led, and well disciplined'. Soldiers who 'equal in discipline and courage any army engaged in the [Great] war.'[59] Another contemporary observer described the rebels' actions as motivated by 'manly patriot pride' and linked this to a categorically Irish sense of space: The rebels fought 'Not by the far-off Dardanelles / Nor slimy Tigris banks / Nor mid the din of Pagan yells' rather, 'For Ireland's rights they died' and 'On Ireland's soil they died.'[60] This mixing of the spatial and the masculine with militant nationalism would come to be a defining feature of Irish nationalist rhetoric during the War of Independence. Already in 1917, as the first Easter Rising prisoners were being released on amnesty, a poem by the nationalist writer Alice Milligan intimated that the gendered sense of control over public space would soon extend over the whole country.[61]

FROM THE RISING TO THE WAR OF INDEPENDENCE

As Sinn Féin regrouped in 1917, their new constitution began by declaring 'the people of Ireland never relinquished the claim to separate Nationhood' and the party promised to 'Make use of any and every means available to render impotent the power of England to hold Ireland in sujection [*sic*] by military force or otherwise.'[62] English rule threatened to 'crush and stifle the country' and Ireland had become 'England's milch-cow', feminised, subservient and exploited (milked?) for resources.[63] The same year, an electoral handbill for de Valera asserted that 'The bugle note is sounding' which would 'save our land from slavery's thrall'. This new pride was 'Inspiring Hope where hope had fled' across the national space. It was 'Throughout our Isle resounding ... O'er valley, hill and mireland.'[64] It seems that 'mireland' was not merely a sloppy misspelling but an intentional neologism conveying the sense of decay in an Ireland over which Irish men were not sovereign. Indeed, Sinn Féin's 'Manifesto to the Irish People', issued for the 1918 General Election, spoke with hope that 'Ireland is faced with the question whether this generation wills that she is to march out into the full sunlight of freedom, or is to remain in the shadow of a base imperialism that has brought and ever will bring in its train naught but evil for our race.'[65] Michael Flanagan said that the Irish 'stand erect now' and no more 'the chains bind and fetter our own beautiful dark Rosaleen.'[66] Once these chains were dismantled, the feminised space of Ireland would herself be redeemed. And with it Irish men would also be redeemed.

Talk of sickness, barrenness and fertility abounded in contemporary propaganda. Arthur Griffith, pushing for a programme 'to re-build the nation', claimed Ireland had become 'the most deforested country in Europe', the nation's soil had become less productive, and the people's health had been impaired. Conversely, with national freedom would come re-forestation, which would allow Ireland to 'gain in health, in beauty, and in wealth', the Irish would become 'rooted in the soil', and the population would rise to 16 million.[67] Similarly, J.J. Walsh and Liam de Roiste claimed 'A Free Ireland would not, and could not, have hunger in her fertile vales and squalor in her cities'. They also spoke of how 'A Free Ireland would drain the bogs, would harness the rivers, would plant the wastes'. 'Freedom is the condition of sane life' de Roiste and Walsh claimed, and so not only would the people become sane, but Irish sovereignty would also restore sanity and order to the geography of Ireland.[68] Various Sinn Féin publications from this period spoke of the spaces of Ireland as being in some way deficient due to a lack of Irish political sovereignty. Irish cities were 'ugly', the countryside was 'barren of flowers' and cottages were 'dirty'. All of this had detrimental effects on the Irish population.[69] Ireland's advantageous geographical position was underutilised. Instead, it was a 'barren bulwark'[70] under British rule whilst, 'from the sanitarian view-point', this was 'perhaps the most backward country in Europe.'[71] The procreative connotations of this language points again to the supposed unnaturalness of a female Ireland now made barren because *she* is not ruled by *her* true lover.

After the first Dáil was established in 1919, it sought financial aid through the sale of bonds. Investments in these bonds, the new TDs promised, would 'Recover Ireland for the Irish. Re-people the land … Drain the bogs. Save the boys and girls of Ireland.' Individual investors were told 'You can restore Ireland's health, her strength, her beauty, and her wealth.'[72] Contemporaneously, Michael Collins, the Minister for Finance who oversaw the Dáil bonds spoke of Ireland as 'a barren waste' in an open letter co-signed by Arthur Griffith. The money from bonds would ameliorate this and would 'make Ireland morally and materially strong and self-supporting.' Collins and Griffith presented this as being part of a broader change in control over Irish space: 'After centuries of repression the Irish Nation has burst from the dungeon in which it had been hidden away from the knowledge and conscience of mankind. Its freedom and its future have become a prime concern to Europe and America. Ireland is now a question of world-politics'.[73] Thus, Ireland would no longer be an enslaved nation and the national space, under that normative Irish political control, would be also restored to its rightful dignity.

Sandra Sufian, in her highly innovative study of Zionist medical politics, talks of how Palestine was also viewed as a 'pathological landscape' and that 'Healing the pathological features of the land of Palestine was essential for healing the Jewish nation. Both were constitutive, interactive elements in the transformative project of Zionism.'[74] As a leading figure in Kupat Holim, the health insurance provider of the Zionist project, summed it up: '*leyashev* [to settle] means *lehavri* [to heal]'.[75] Just as Jews outside of Palestine were seen as somehow deficient, so also the Land of Israel was deficient if it itself was missing Jewish sovereignty. The space and the people would be redeemed together.[76]

BETWEEN PRAGMATISM AND PARTITION

In a 1918 interview with the *Christian Science Monitor*, later republished as a Sinn Féin pamphlet, Eamon de Valera summed up many of these inter-related themes of gender, power, and space. The Irish, he declared, sought 'to be free ... not to have a master.' He also threatened that 'we would fight to the last man to maintain that independence.' Once the 'enforced partnership' with England was ended, however, a new friendship of equals, of 'independent neighbours' could emerge, 'each respecting the rights and interests of the other'. In the same interview, though, de Valera also touched on another problem related to the national space. Asked about 'the general Sinn Fein attitude towards Ulster', he asserted that 'Sinn Fein regards as brothers Irishmen of every creed and every class provided they accept the one test of citizenship, that they place Ireland and her interests before those of any other nation.' His qualified ecumenism notwithstanding, de Valera disparaged Ulster Protestants as 'the garrison party... proud to have upheld an enemy's flag for 300 years.' His pointed question (pointed both for the interviewer and for the people who would soon be the Northern Irish) was 'Are these Irishmen or Englishmen—which?'[77] These issues would very much come to the fore in 1922 and 1923.

The Treaty reinforced the partitioning of Ireland, first legislated in the 1920 Government of Ireland Act. Thus, those who opposed the Treaty presented it as a continued fettering of the national space or as a mutilation of an anthropomorphised Ireland. Interestingly, Ireland here was symbolised as a male body and partition was compared to the horrors of castration. Partition was feared as irreversible and a 'Conspiracy to dismember Ireland'.[78] Ireland would be 'permanently torn in twain' and 'permanently dismembered'.[79] There was an underlying suggestion that this personified Ireland would lose male virility along with its north-east corner. Much was made of the suggestion that the loss of Ulster would prevent the possibility of communing with heroic nationalist men who came from that province: 'Ulster gave us Hugh Roe O'Donnell, Owen Roe O'Neill, Henry Joy McCracken, Henry Monroe, Jimmy Hope, W[illiam] Orr, and John Mitchel … Is this the Province that at the bidding of a foreign Government shall be severed from the Irish Nation?'[80] Mary MacSwiney described it as a form of national castration: 'cutting away from Ireland and making a British shire the land of Red Branch Knights of old—the home of the O'Neills and the O'Donnells, of Red Hugh and Shane the Proud'.[81] Partition would be 'national suicide' and 'the name of Ireland would pass from the roll of Nations'.[82] The Irish Free State would be nothing more than 'a vassal state'.[83]

In similar terms, the Treaty was depicted as offering a wholly inferior version of freedom and, nationalist castration-anxieties aside, some familiar themes of dutiful sons protecting a national mother were utilised. An open letter signed by leading anti-Treaty figures, including Liam Mellows, Ernie O'Malley and Tom Barry, called on former comrades to return to their allegiance to the Irish Republic and 'thus guard the Nation's honour from the infamous stigma that her sons aided her foes in retaining a hateful domination over her.'[84] Republican journalist Frank Gallagher [Proinnsias Ó Gallchobhair] spoke of the Treaty as a violation of 'The sanctity of our national independence declared by the Sovereign National Assembly in January, 1919' and a violation of 'The territorial integrity of Ireland, which has outlasted history itself.' The Treaty, Gallagher claimed, would impose upon Ireland 'alien authority in a more deadly and degrading form' than that which previously existed. Instead of a sovereign republic, the Irish would have 'a British King for their President and a British Colony for their nationhood.'[85] The 'ancient, beloved, unchanged name' of Ireland would be replaced by 'the Irish Free State', comparable to the 'hideous enslavement' of not only the Congo Free State but also of the

Orange Free State, conquered by Britain and reduced to the status of 'a minor province inside the Dominion of South Africa.'[86] The deeper concerns about Ireland's continued presence in the British Empire were acutely evident in one anti-Treaty handbill's declaration that 'The Irish people are as white as the English people. They are at least equal to the English in physique, intelligence, morals and culture.'[87] Without full control over the national territory, the Irish would be denied the full political sovereignty that was the preserve of white men. They would remain racially inferior in the eyes of the world. Ireland, 'a parent Nation with a distinct racial identity and more ancient than Britain herself', obviously did not deserve this treatment.

The pro-Treaty side, unsurprisingly, took a different view of things. In a series of speeches in late 1921 and early 1922, as the Civil War loomed, Arthur Griffith defended the Treaty in which he had been so closely involved. On 19 December 1921, he spoke of it as a 'Treaty of equality', the first official document to recognise Ireland's equality with England. Perhaps more importantly, though, the Treaty was a return to a lost Irish sovereignty: 'We have brought back the flag. We have brought back the evacuation of Ireland after 700 years by British troops, and the formation of an Irish Army. We have brought back to Ireland her full rights and powers of fiscal control.' The following month, Griffith described Ireland as being 'a quaking bog for 300 years where there was no foothold for the people of Ireland'. Now though, with the Treaty, the Irish have 'solid ground upon which to stand' and 'a foothold in their own country.' Pointing to some of the gendered issues at stake, Griffith's 12 March speech to Treaty supporters in Dundalk was titled 'Masters in Our Own House', referencing the idea of patriarchal control of the national-familial household.[88]

That the Treaty, whatever its shortcomings, gave Irish men spatial control over the national territory and thus ended the nation's anomalous status, was a recurring theme in pro-Treaty arguments. If the Irish 'want to be free nationally, to govern your self in your own way, for your own good' then they should vote for the Treaty.[89] The Treaty would guarantee 'Full control of all our resources' as well as an Irish army and police force.[90] The Irish educational system would be Irish-controlled.[91] There would be 'An IRISH STATE organisation to express the will and the mind of the Nation. A recognised place as a separate State among the Nations'[92] and 'An Irish legal system, controlled and administered by Irish*men*'.[93] The Treaty 'gives us full control' and a 'resurgent Ireland'[94] and 'every means to render impotent the power of England to hold Ireland.'[95] Above all, it gave the nation 'Freedom.'[96] The Treaty would end Ireland's status as a relative space and would copper-fasten its international legitimacy as an absolute space.

Given that, by the close of 1922, a physical state with functioning institutions did exist, these were to prove hard arguments to counter. The Irish Free State did have a recognised international status and did institutionalise Irish control over (most) of the national territory. As even one anti-Treaty pamphlet conceded, this was an 'important advance … upon any previous Home Rule Bills or Acts.'[97] Indeed, what stands out in hindsight is how narrow the differences could be between the pro-Treaty side and the more moderate anti-Treaty forces orbiting de Valera. De Valera's much-debated *Document No.2*, which sought to reconcile political sovereignty with Ireland's continued place in the Empire, and which became a major point of discussion during the Treaty debates, offered something remarkably similar to the Treaty itself. De Valera did seek to remove any oath to the British Crown and asserted that 'the legislative, executive, and judicial authority shall be derived solely from the people of Ireland', suggesting that these partially symbolic issues were of greater importance to him. Both the Treaty and *Document No. 2* promised that Ireland would contribute to Britain's national debt (something de Valera later railed against in the Economic War) and, most importantly, both recognised partition.

Irish nationalist and Zionist obsessions with space thus ultimately pose something of a paradox: unfettered control over an absolute national space was clearly of concern to these national movements, yet both ultimately acquiesced in a partition of the national space. In the Irish case, this is partly explainable by the long history of a sense (albeit, at times, a vague and fragile one) that the north-east of Ireland was in some ways different from the rest of the island, a difference primarily attributable to the twin forces of religion and industrialisation.[98] Compounding this, by the time of the truce in the War of Independence in July 1921, a de facto unionist state was already in place in six of the nine counties of Ulster.[99] Irish nationalists were thus faced with the choice between a relatively full sovereignty over most of the island, or to gamble for a disputed sovereignty over the whole island. Unsurprisingly, the former proved more appealing. J.J. Walsh, for instance, described his support for the Treaty in terms of this unfettered nationalist control over an Irish space: 'I came to the conclusion that if we included the 3/4 million West British cuthroats [*sic*] that had dominated the Country and claimed they owned 2/3 of it, they would again influence over [*sic*] our national policy. The Irish language and all that pertained to it would go by the board ... and everything we have fought for through 800 years would be smashed to atoms and swallowed up in the British Empire.'[100] Sovereignty, the need for national-cultural homogeneity as a precursor to national unity and the desire for some kind of spatial separation from Britain, are all adverted to here. De Valera would continue to engage in anti-partition rhetoric after 1922, even going so far as to warn the binationalist Zionist Judah Leb Magnes about partition's evils in 1937: 'I do not know the Palestine problem as you know it, but from a knowledge of what partition means in Ireland now ... I regard partition as perhaps the worst of the many solutions that have been proposed.'[101] Despite this, de Valera was willing to admit, in an unguarded moment in the 1960s, that 'France was France without Alsace and Lorraine ... Ireland is Ireland without the north'.[102]

Notwithstanding the irredentist tendencies which (re-)emerged after 1967,[103] Zionists prior to 1948 were also noticeably amenable to partition. The UN decision to partition Palestine in November 1947 was greeted with 'an unparalleled outburst of jubilation among Jews in Palestine'.[104] This willingness to acquiesce in a Solomonic solution and to accept something less than all of Palestine had some deep roots. In *Auto-Emancipation*, Leo Pinsker had called for the creation of a 'single refuge' that would be 'politically assured'. This would replace the 'many refuges' as part of his project of 'national regeneration'. Pinsker longed for a singular and politically sovereign absolute space in contrast to the perennial relative spaces of the Diaspora. Yet, it was not at all pre-determined that this regenerative space would be in Palestine:

> If we would have a secure home, so that we may give up our endless life of wandering and rehabilitate our nation in our own eyes and in the eyes of the world, we must above all, not dream of restoring ancient Judaea ... The goal of our present endeavour must not be the "Holy Land", but a land of our own. We need nothing but a large piece of land for our poor brothers; a piece of land which shall remain our property, from which no foreign master can expel us ... Perhaps the Holy Land will again become ours. If so, all the better, but *first of all*, we must determine—and this is the crucial point—what country is accessible to us, and at the same time adapted to offer the Jews of all lands who must leave their home a secure and unquestioned refuge which is capable of being made productive.[105]

Similarly, Herzl's seminal 1896 text on *Der Judenstaat* [The Jews' State] was indifferent as to whether this state should be founded in the biblical homeland.[106] For Herzl, as for Pinsker, it was more important that Jews would be 'settled in their own state' and 'We shall at last live as free men on our own soil, and die peacefully in our own homes.'[107] The national regeneration that would arise out of the newfound dignity accorded to Jewish men owning their own national space was of more importance than biblical ideals. Herzl was famously willing to imagine this Jewish sovereign space in Uganda rather than Palestine, or even in spaces *near* Palestine such as Cyprus or the Sinai Peninsula.[108] This, however, prompted a serious controversy within the Zionist movement, one that was eventually won by the Tzyonei Tzyon [Zionists of Zion], for whom a modern Jewish state could be built only in the emotive, autochthonous space of Eretz Yisrael [The Land of Israel].[109] Yet for all these claims of rebuilding sovereignty in the biblical homeland, the Jewish state that eventually emerged in "Israel" was not in the same space, from Dan to Beersheba,[110] usually described in the Bible. Even in the case of the right-wing Revisionists orbiting Ze'ev Jabotinsky, with their popular refrain 'There are two banks of the river Jordan / this one is ours and so is this' [shtei gadot le-yordan/ zu shelanu zu gam ken], their objective to move across the river was more rhetoric than reality.[111] The supreme irony of the conflict over national space in Israel-Palestine is that the State of Israel exists in the space of the Philistines, the Palestinians' putative ancestors, whilst the West Bank largely corresponds to the space of ancient Judea and Samaria.[112]

Such ironies and paradoxes were perhaps irrelevant. Achieving an undisputed sovereignty over the national space was a central plank of both nationalist projects. This sovereignty was often coded as being somehow masculine in nature and Zionists and Irish nationalists sought legitimacy, both in the standard political sense and in the sense of a national masculinity redeemed and legitimised by the acquisition of sovereignty over an internationally recognised absolute national space. Achieving that undisputed male sovereignty, that 'place in the sun',[113] was central to both movements. Thus, a willingness to accept partition lurked in the background of both ideologies, as both of them accepted borders laid down by imperial concerns as part of their respective projects to acquire international legitimacy. In reference to the fact that the maps of Palestine, which have so animated Zionists and Palestinian nationalists, were actually drawn up by late-nineteenth-century British imperial officials, Rachel Havrelock notes 'the degree to which imperial geographies influenced the map of the

Jewish and the Palestinian national homes' and that one of the functions of 'national lore' is that it 'domesticates the lines drawn across the world by empires.'[114] What John Regan calls the Irish state's 'management of partition' had a comparable function: it 'not only served the interests of southern [Irish] nationalism, but also those of interdependent relationships with Britain and with Ulster unionism.'[115]

In the Israeli case, 'the lack of congruence between the political space of the state and the cultural space of the nation' [*et choser hahalima bein ha-merchav ha-politi shel ha-medina le-bein ha-merchav ha-tarbuti shel ha-umma*] remained an unresolved 'story of dichotomy and ambiguity' [*sipur shel shniut ve-dumashma'ut*]. This was a story that would come back to haunt Zionist politics after 1967.[116] In the Irish case, however, this remained a more-or-less finished project: 'the southerners chose to protect power positions inside the *staatsnation*, rather than press for the irredentist *kulturnation* ... In the southern nationalist imagination, Ulster did not exert in 1922 (nor, for that matter, again in 1968–97) the mobilizing power of a "Kosovo" or a "Kashmir" '.[117] Nor, I would add, a Judea and Samaria.

John Maher has argued that Zionism and Irish nationalism are two ideologies that share a concern with 'land as language' and 'language as land'.[118] Having focused here on how masculinity manifested itself in conceptions of land and spatial sovereignty, the next chapter will focus on language.

Notes

1. T. MacSwiney (1921) *Principles of Freedom*, p. 7.
2. O'Donovan Rossa had been arrested in 1865 for his involvement with the Fenians. He was released in early 1871 on condition that he leave the UK. His exile was only interrupted by a brief decade around the turn of the century, when Cork City Council granted him a sinecure.
3. Quoted in W. O'Brien, D. Ryan, eds. (1953) *Devoy's Post Bag: Volume II, 1880–1928* (Dublin: C.J. Fallon) p. 436. Margaret O'Donovan Rossa had a similar view of her father's return to Ireland: 'The return of O'Donovan Rossa to Ireland was as the return of a king to his people—a victorious king returning to a loyal people'. M. O'Donovan Rossa (1939) *My Father and My Mother Were Irish* (New York: Devid-Adair) p. 179.
4. 'The last of the great Fenians is being brought back to green Erin, the land of his love to be laid to rest in the historic Cemetery of Glasnevin, where so many of his comrades in the Republican movement are also

sleeping ... it is certainly most fitting that he should take his last long sleep side by side with those heroic comrades of his whose life and deeds will for ever remain a source of the noblest and loftiest inspiration for Irish Nationalists.' O'Leary Curtis (August 1915) 'Among His Comrades.' *Fianna* [Warriors], No. 2 [New Series].
5. The Committee was dominated by the Volunteers. Their slogan, emblazoned on their letterhead, was 'Oh do not fear for Ireland, For she has soldiers still.'
6. M. O'Donovan Rossa (1939) *My Father*, p. 177.
7. Ibid., p. 178.
8. J. Devoy (1969) *Recollections of an Irish Rebel* (Shannon: Irish University Press) p. 332. One contemporary account spoke of the funeral procession as 'exceeding ten thousand' people with multiple numbers watching, and taking an hour to pass any point. It allegedly came through College Green at 3 p.m. but not arrive at Glasnevin Cemetery until 6 p.m. 'O'Donovan Rossa's Funeral' (7 August 1915) *Irish Volunteer*.
9. NLI, MacDonagh Family Papers, MS 44337/4, Handwritten note by Thomas MacDonagh on routes for O'Donovan Rossa Funeral. In the late nineteenth century the main thoroughfare in Dublin's north inner city was named Sackville Street. Attempts from the 1880s onwards to change its name to the more suitably nationalist O'Connell Street, after Daniel O'Connell, prompted controversy. Though the street's name was not officially changed until 1924, it was still unofficially called O'Connell Street from this time onwards. Y. Whelan (2001) 'Monuments, Power and Contested Space: the Iconography of Sackville Street (O'Connell Street) before Independence (1922). *Irish Geography*, Vol. 34, No.1, pp. 11–33. MacDonagh, of course, used the nationalist name. To do otherwise would be to admit English ownership of an Irish space.
10. NLI, MacDonagh Family Papers, MS 20643/20, *Order of Commandant General Thomas MacDonagh*, undated letter printed on O'Donovan Rossa Funeral Committee Notepaper (July 1915). Emphases added.
11. M. O'Donovan Rossa (1939) *My Father*, p. 179.
12. 'O'Donovan Rossa, Jeremiah' (2009) *Dictionary of Irish Biography* (Cambridge: Cambridge University Press, 2009).
13. NLI, MacDonagh Family Papers, MS 20643/20, Handwritten description of funeral procession.
14. NLI, MacDonagh Family Papers, MS 44337/4, Handwritten note by Thomas MacDonagh on routes for O'Donovan Rossa Funeral.
15. NLI, MacDonagh Family Papers, MS 44337/4, Handwritten note by Thomas MacDonagh on routes for O'Donovan Rossa Funeral.
16. NLI, MacDonagh Family Papers, MS 20643/20, Rough hand-drawn map of Glasnevin Cemetery. It also appears that graveside passes were

issued to potential attendees, ensuring that only a select few would be allowed come close to O'Donovan Rossa's grave. See the copy of one of these passes, issued by the Wolfe Tone Memorial Committee. NLI, John L. Burke Papers, MS 36124, *Pass for O'Donovan Rossa Funeral*.

17. R. Dudley Edwards (2006) *Patrick Pearse: The Triumph of Failure*, 2nd edn (Dublin: Irish Academic Press) pp. 235–236.
18. P.H. Pearse (1996) 'While Ireland Holds These Graves' in M. McLoughlin, ed. *Great Irish Speeches of the Twentieth Century* (Dublin: Poolbeg Press) pp. 38–40.
19. B. Murphy (1991) *Patrick Pearse and the Lost Republican Ideal* (Dublin: James Duffy) p. 47. Emphases added. Margaret O'Donovan Rossa described her father's funeral in similarly masculine, nationalist terms: 'To one more hero of this glorious land had Ireland's sons paid tribute.' M. O'Donovan Rossa (1939) *My Father*, p. 181.
20. NLI IR 94109 P1, Item 3, Terence MacSwiney. *Rossa: Born 1831, Died 1915, Buried Glasnevin Cemetery Dublin, Sunday, August 1st, 1915* (Dublin: O'Donovan Rossa Funeral Committee, 1915) 2nd edn. The date on MacSwiney's article is listed as 25 July 1915 and this appears to have been a pamphlet issued in advance by the Committee to publicise the funeral.
21. J. Devoy (1969) *Recollections*, p. 332.
22. N. Smith (2008) *Uneven Development: Nature, Capital, and the Production of Space*, 3rd edn (Athens GA: University of Georgia Press) pp.115–116 and *passim*.
23. J. Tosh (1999) *A Man's Place: Masculinity and the Middle-Class Home in Victorian England* (New Haven CT: Yale University Press) p. 2.
24. D. Kiberd (2009) *Ulysses and Us: The Art of Everyday Life in Joyce's Masterpiece* (New York: W.W. Norton), p. 81.
25. A. Kemp (2000) 'Ha-Gvul Ke-Pnei Yanos: Merchav ve-Toda'ah Le'umit Be-Yisrael' [The Border as a Janus Face: Space and National Consciousness in Israel]. *Teoria u-Vikoret* [Theory and Criticism]. Vol. 16, p.13.
26. E. Madden, M.D. Lee (2008) 'Geography and Gender in Irish Studies' in M.D. Lee, E. Madden, eds. *Irish Studies: Geographies and Genders* (Cambridge: Cambridge Scholars Publishing) p. 6. Madden and Lee, observing the 'insistent feminization of the land in Irish literature', trace this conceptualisation to 'the analogy of colonialism and rape'.
27. G. Piterberg (2008) *The Returns of Zionism: Myths, Politics and Scholarship in Israel* (London: Verso) pp.128–129. This focus on absolute space is one of the elements that gave Zionism a distinct advantage over binationalism and Diaspora Jewish nationalisms, which remained rooted in notions of relative space and thus tacitly accepted notions of Jewish difference, rather than the normalisation and rehabilitation which mainstream Zionism promised.

28. D. Biale (1997) *Eros and the Jews: From Biblical Israel to Contemporary America* (Berkeley CA: University of California Press) pp. 182–183.
29. The original Hebrew version of this poem can be found in the Hebrew version of *Land and Power*, A. Shapira (1992) *Cherev ha-Yonah: ha-Tzyonut ve-ha-Ko'ach, 1881–1948* [The Dove's Sword: Zionism and Force, 1881–1948] (Tel Aviv: Am Oved) pp. 54–55. As with Trumpeldor in the previous chapter, note the use of 'givorim', meaning heroes or men, a pun that suggests that by re-embracing an ancient heroism, Jewish men would also re-embrace a lost manliness. Note also that Hebrew is a gendered language, and so Tchernichovsky addresses his poem to a male *Atah* (you), rather than a female *At*.
30. P. Chatterjee (1993) *The Nation and Its Fragments: Colonial and Postcolonial Histories* (Princeton NJ: Princeton University Press, 1993) p. 6.
31. O. Ben-David (1997) 'Tiyul (Hike) as an Act of Consecration of Space' in E.Ben-Ari, Y. Bilu, eds. *Grasping Land: Space and Place in Contemporary Israeli Discourse and Experience* (Albany, NY: State University of New York) pp. 129–145.
32. J. Attias, E. Benbessa (2003) *Israel, the Impossible Land* (Stanford: Stanford University Press) p. 174.
33. M. Benvenisiti (1999) *Sacred Landscape: The Buried History of the Holy Land since 1948* (Berkeley CA: University of California Press) p. 2.
34. Ibid., pp. 22–23.
35. Ibid., p. 1. Emphases added.
36. The League's aims are outlined here: NUIG Stephen Barrett Papers G3/1476, *Reasons Why You Should Join the Gaelic League*, n.d.; NLI MS 18254, Folder 6, Letter from the General Secretary of the Gaelic League, on behalf of the Executive Committee, to the General Synod of the Church of Ireland, 1910. Their activities are discussed more fully in Chap. 5.
37. B. Harshav (1993) *Language in Time of Revolution* (Berkeley CA: University of California) p. 4.
38. NLI IR 49162 P45, *Connradh na Gaedilge: Turas go Gaillimh, Bealtaine 31, 1903* [The Gaelic League: Tour to Galway, May 31, 1903]; See also NUIG, Stephen Barrett Papers, G3/1152, *Turas an Oireachtais, 1909: Teamhair na Ríogh* [Tour of the Gathering (of the Gaelic League), 1909: Royal Tara].
39. J. Boyarin (1994) 'Space, Time, and the Politics of Memory' in J. Boyarin, ed. *Remapping Memory: The Politics of TimeSpace* (Minneapolis, MN: University of Minnesota) p. 12.
40. NUIG, Stephen Barrett Papers, G3/1190, *The Gaelic League and Politics: Pronouncement by Dr. Douglas Hyde*, 15 December 1914.
41. Compare this with the similar manner in which Zionist history textbooks, overseen by Ben-Zion Dinur [Dinaburg], later a prominent historian at the Hebrew University, put great emphasis on the Land of Israel as the

central fulcrum of Jewish space and time. D.A. Porat (2008) 'Between Nation and Land in Zionist Teaching of Jewish History, 1920-1954'. *Journal of Israeli History*, Vol. 27, No. 2, 253-268.
42. NLI, Pearse Papers, P 7643, *Irish First Year Exam*, April 1907. The Gaelic League's 'Education System' even offered English exams!
43. NLI, Pearse Papers, P 7643, *Intermediate Education Board for Ireland: Examinations, 1905, Senior Grade, Irish, Honours*, 17 June 1905.
44. NLI, Pearse Papers, P 7643, *Intermediate Education Board for Ireland: Examinations, 1906, Junior Grade, Honours, History and Geography*. The exams contained in NLI, Pearse Papers, P 7643 were presumably those used at St. Enda's College.
45. Military Archives, BMH CD 264/2/4, *Save Your Land*, undated Sinn Féin handbill (1918).
46. F. McGarry (2010) *The Rising, Ireland: Easter 1916* (Oxford: Oxford University Press) pp. 120-121.
47. D. Kiberd (1993) *Idir Dhá Chultúr* [Between Two Cultures] (Dublin: Coiscéim) p. 59.
48. J. Moran (2005) *Staging the Easter Rising: 1916 as Theatre* (Cork: Cork University Press) pp. 28-29.
49. Copies of *War News* quickly became souvenirs of the Rising. See the advertisement for E.H. Stoker, Grafton Street, which was offering 'Rebellion Souvenirs' including the last remaining copies of *Irish War News* for five guineas, in Military Archives, BMH CD 227/3/11, *The Sinn Fein Leaders of 1916*, undated pamphlet (1916?).
50. Military Archives, BMH CD250/1/2, *Irish War News*, Vol.1, No.1 (25 April 1916).
51. F. McGarry (2010) *The Rising*, p. 130.
52. NLI, Pearse Papers, MS15453, Notice of Surrender of P.H. Pearse, 29 April 1916.
53. Military Archives, BMH CD 264/1/2, *Last Bulletin Issued by Commandant Pearse from Headquarters, G.P.O., Easter Week 1916*, undated poster (circa 1919).
54. Quoted in A. Shapira, trans. W. Templer (1999) *Land and Power: The Zionist Resort to Force, 1881-1948* (Stanford CA: Stanford University Press). p. 10.
55. T.S. Presner (2007) *Muscular Judaism*.
56. A. Shapira (1999) *Land and Power*, pp. 55-56. Emphases added.
57. M. Stanislawski (2001) *Zionism and the Fin de Siècle: Cosmopolitanism and Nationalism from Nordau to Jabotinsky* (Berkeley CA: Univeristy of California Press, p. 194.
58. CZA, Printed Matter Collection, DDI/5447, *Resistance? Yes! Suicidal Terror—No!*, HaShomer HaTzair handbill, n.d. (circa 1945). Emphases in original.

59. Military Archives, BMH CD 127/4, *To Your Places, Slaves! A Striking Pronouncement on the Easter Insurrection by Rev. Father Yorke, San Francisco*, undated pamphlet, circa 1916–17.
60. Military Archives, BMH CD 227/37/10, *Songs & Poems: The Rebels who fought and died for Ireland in Easter Week, 1916*, undated pamphlet (1917?).
61. Military Archives BMH CD 264/45/1, Alice Milligan. *The Home Coming (Lewes to Dublin, June 18th, 1917)*, undated handbill/poem.
62. Military Archives BMH CD 105/8/1, Sinn Féin Constitution, n.d. (1917?).
63. Military Archives BMH CD 176/1/3, *Farmers! Your turn now*, undated Sinn Féin pamphlet (1917?).
64. Military Archives BMH CD 176/1/3, *The Dead Who Died for Ireland*, de Valera Handbill/Poem, n.d. (1917?).
65. Military Archives BMH CD 95/4/1, *General Election: Manifesto to the Irish People*, n.d. (1918?)
66. Military Archives, BMH CD 131/8/6, Rev. Michael Flanagan. *The Two Policies: Sinn Fein or Parliamentarism*, September 1918. *Róisín Dubh*, alternatively translated as Black-Haired Little Rose or Dark Rosaleen, was another female name for an abstract vision of the Irish nation.
67. A. Griffith (n.d.) *To Re-Build the Nation*. For a copy of this pamphlet, see: Military Archives, BMH CD 227/25/37.
68. NLI Uncatalogued Political Ephemera, Box 2, *Do You Realise What A Free Ireland Will Be Like*?, undated handbill for J.J. Walsh and Liam de Roiste (1918?).
69. W.P. Hackett (1921) *Character and Citizenship*. For a copy of this pamphlet, see: Military Archives, BMH CD 250/4/15.
70. NLI ILB 300 P2, Item 2, *The Message of Dail Eireann to the Free Nations*, January 1919.
71. R. O hAodha (1921) *Hygiene*. For a copy of this pamphlet, see: Military Archives, BMH CD 250/4/7.
72. NLI ILB 300 P2, Item 47, *You Can Buy Dail Eireann Bonds To-day*, undated handbill (1919?).
73. NLI ILB 300 P2, Item 33, undated open letter from Michael Collins and Arthur Griffith. Griffith is listed as 'acting president', suggesting the letter was published some time during de Valera's visit to the US in 1919 and 1920, when presidential duties were taken on by Griffith.
74. S.M. Sufian (2007) *Healing the Land and the Nation: Malaria and the Zionist Project in Palestine, 1920–1947* (Chicago: University of Chicago Press) p. 63.
75. Ibid., p. 39.
76. G. Piterberg (2008) *Returns of Zionism*, p. 94.

77. Military Archives, BMH CD 131/8/6, *Eamonn* [sic] *De Valera states his case* undated Sinn Féin pamphlet. Reprinted from the *Christian Science Monitor*, 15 May 1918.
78. NLI Uncatalogued Political Ephemera, Box 1, *Sensational Discovery*, undated anti-Treaty handbill (1922?).
79. NLI ILB 300P, Item 36, *Do you want an Ireland permanently torn in twain?*, undated anti-Treaty handbill.
80. NLI ILB 300 P12, Item 16, *Ireland One and Indivisible*, undated anti-Treaty handbill.
81. Military Archives, BMH CD 250/6/17, Address by Máire Nic Suibhne T.D. to Àrd Fheis Sinn Féin, 16 October 1923.
82. NLI ILB 300P, Item 29, *Sinn Fein*, undated anti-Treaty handbill.
83. Military Archives BMH CD 6/36/9, *Address to the Dublin Brigade*, Undated Open Letter from Oscar Traynor (1922?); NLI 3076 TX, Item 23, Civil War-era anti-Treaty cartoon, n.d.
84. Military Archives BMH CD 6/36/6, *Oglaigh na hEireann: Proclamation*, 28 June, 1922.
85. Military Archives, BMH CD 250/6/13, Proinnsias Ó Gallchobhair. *By What Authority?*, Undated Pamphlet, (1922?).
86. NLI IR 94109 p 5, Item 25, *What the Treaty Means* (Dublin: Republic of Ireland, n.d.).
87. NLI ILB 300 P13, Item 85, *Arguments for British Domination?*, undated anti-Treaty handbill.
88. A. Griffith (n.d.) *Arguments for the Treaty*. For a copy of this pamphlet, see: Military Archives, BMH CD 131/8/21
89. NLI ILB 300 P13, Item 87, *Do You Want to be Free*, undated pro-Treaty handbill.
90. NLI ILB 300 P13, Item 86, *The Two Paths*, undated pro-Treaty handbill.
91. NLI, Piaras Béaslaí Papers, MS 33912 (12), *Shadow or Substance*, undated pro-Treaty handbill (1922?).
92. NLI ILB 300 P13, Item 88, *What the Peace Treaty Gives Ireland*, undated pro-Treaty handbill.
93. Ibid., Emphases added.
94. NLI, Piaras Béaslaí Papers, MS 33912 (12), *Resurgent Ireland*, undated pro-Treaty handbill (1922?).
95. NLI, Piaras Béaslaí Papers, MS 33912 (12), *The Power of England*, undated pro-Treaty handbill (1922?).
96. NLI, Piaras Béaslaí Papers, MS 33912 (12), *Our Purpose*, undated pro-Treaty handbill (1922?).
97. NLI IR 94109 p 5, Item 25, *What the Treaty Means* (Dublin: Republic of Ireland, n.d.).

98. G. Martin (1999) 'The Origins of Partition' in M. Anderson, E. Bort, eds. *The Irish Border: History, Politics, Culture* (Liverpool: Liverpool University Press) pp. 83–84. See also: M. Laffan (1983) *The Partition of Ireland: 1911–1925* (Dundalk: Dundalgan Press/Dublin Historical Association) p. 3; J. Regan (2013) *Myth and the Irish State* (Dublin: Irish Academic Press, 2013), p. 51 and *passim*.
99. M. Laffan (1983) *Partition of Ireland*, p. 77.
100. G. Martin (1999) *Origins of Partition*, p. 71.
101. CAHJP, Judah Leb Magnes Papers P3/2424, *Letter from Eamon de Valera to Judah Leb Magnes*, 10 September 1937.
102. J. Regan (2013) *Myth*, p. 73. Tellingly, the 1938 Fianna Fáil electoral newspaper declared 'Fianna Fáil has undone the conquest in three quarters of the national territory[.] Your support is needed now to complete the work'. The rest of the paper, though, whilst twice mentioning how partition would end some time in the future, offered no concrete policies for achieving this. Military Archives BMH CD 6/51/12, *Victory Election Bulletin*, Fianna Fáil Electoral Newspaper, 1938. De Valera, Regan accurately notes, 'raised partition as an electoral issue but did not at any time form constructive policies intent upon remedying it. Rather, de Valera's irredentism is best understood as an attempt to monopolise the issue, forestalling extra-constitutional ambitions in that quarter… Like many of his generation, for practical purposes de Valera was "*a twenty-six counties man*" dedicated to the existing state before all else.' J. Regan (2013) *Myth*, p. 148. Emphases added.
103. See, for example: M. Feige (2009) *Settling in the Hearts: Jewish Fundamentalism in the Occupied Territories* (Detroit: Wayne State University Press); I. Zertal, A. Eldar (2007) *Lords of the Land: The War over Israel's Settlements in the Occupied Territories, 1967–2007* (New York: Nation Books).
104. A. Shapira (1999) *Land and Power* p. 353
105. L. Pinsker (1882/1973) 'Auto-Emancipation: An Appeal to his People by a Russian Jew' in A. Hertzberg, ed. *The Zionist Idea: A Historical Analysis and Reader* (New York: Atheneum) pp. 197–198. Emphases in original.
106. J. C. Attias, E. Benbassa (2003) *Israel, the Impossible Land*, trans. S. Emanuel (Stanford: Stanford University Press), p. 146.
107. T. Herzl (1946) *The Jewish State: An Attempt at a Modern Solution of the Jewish Question* (New York: American Zionist Emergency Council) pp. 153, 157. This is a reprint of the 1896 edition.
108. Y. Conforti (2014) 'Searching for a Homeland: The Territorial Dimension in the Zionist Movement and the Boundaries of Jewish Nationalism.' *Studies in Ethnicitiy and Nationalism*, Vol. 14, No. 1, 36–54.

109. A. Saposnik (2008) *Becoming Hebrew: The Creation of a Jewish National Culture in Ottoman Palestine* (Oxford: Oxford University Press) pp. 41–63; B. Kimmerling (1983) *Zionism and Territory: The Socio-Territorial Dimensions of Zionist Politics* (Berkeley, CA: University of California Press/Institute of International Studies) p. 9.
110. 1 Kings 4:25 states: "And Judah and Israel [i.e., the Southern and Northern tribes of Israel] dwelt safely, every man under his vine and under his fig tree, from Dan even to Beersheba, all the days of Solomon." The coastal plain, which makes up the bulk of the modern Israeli state, corresponds far more to the space inhabited by the Philistines according to the Bible (cf. 1 Samuel 7:14).
111. R. Havrelock (2011) *River Jordan: The Mythology of a Dividing Line* (Chicago: University of Chicago Press) p. 234.
112. For a discussion of the selective use of the Bible in Zionism, see: N. Masalha (2007) *The Bible and Zionism: Invented Traditions, Archaeology and Post-Colonialism in Israel-Palestine* (London: Zed Books).
113. A. Shapira (1999) *Land and Power*, p. 54.
114. R. Havrelock (2011) *River Jordan*, p. 218.
115. J. Regan (2013) *Myth*, p. 62.
116. A. Kemp (2000) 'Ha-Gvul Ke-Pnei Yanos: Merchav ve-Toda'ah Le'umit Be-Yisrael' [The Border as a Janus Face: Space and National Consciousness in Israel]. *Teoria u-Vikoret* [Theory and Criticism]. Vol. 16 (2000) 13.
117. J. Regan (2013) *Myth*, p. 61.
118. J. Maher (2012) *Slouching Towards Jerusalem: Reactive Nationalism in the Irish, Israeli and Palestinian Novel, 1985–2005* (Dublin: Irish Academic Press) pp. 35–66 & 163–210.

CHAPTER 5

National Sovereignty, Male Power and the Irish Language

Oh! that this hero-spirit were stronger than it is! Oh! that men could be brought to realize that they are Men, not animals,—that they could be brought to realize that, though "of the earth, earthy," yet there is a spark of divinity within them! And men *can* be brought to realize this by the propagation of a literature like that of the Gael,—a literature to which nature-love and hero-love shall form the keywords, a literature which shall glorify all that is worthy of glory,—beauty, strength, manhood, intellect, and religion.[1]

PATRICK PEARSE AND THE GENDER OF LANGUAGE

In the spring of 1914, fearing for the future of St Enda's College (his perennially cash-strapped nationalist hothouse) Patrick Pearse agreed to go on an extended trip to the US, hoping there to gain funds from wealthy nationalist-minded Irish-Americans. The trip was partly organised through the Irish Republican Brotherhood, an organisation Pearse had just joined and his involvement with which would lead, two years later, to his execution.[2]

In an open letter to the boys of St Enda's sent from the United States, Pearse said he hoped his pupils had all been working hard since returning from their Easter holidays. He reassured his charges that he had been telling American audiences 'what fine fellows you are.' And he let them know that upon his return he would regale them all with exciting tales of the 'sea-sharks and land-sharks' encountered on his voyages. In other words, he made the kinds of statements and observations one would expect from a radical liberal Edwardian educator, which is what he was in so many ways. At the end of his letter, however, Pearse made a seemingly more unusual announcement to his students: 'Remember that that rifle is still unwon. I want to give it away this summer but it can only be given on condition that some boy wins it by a genuine effort to speak Irish.'[3]

It is partly because of this support for youthful violence, evident in both his politics and his writings, that Pearse has not always received the warmest of appraisals from Irish historians. Ruth Dudley Edwards famously presented him as a generally extreme figure and called this letter to his students one of his 'manifestoes', and 'militaristic'.[4] Marianne Elliot has spoken of Pearse as a kind of political necrophiliac[5] and Sean Farrell Moran, in his attempt at Freudian biography, depicted Pearse as an irrational character whose 'overwhelming interest in things Irish' was an Oedipal response to his emotionally distant English father.[6] More recently, historians like Joost Augusteijn have reappraised Pearse. Without denying the violence inherent in his politics, Augusteijn presents a more sophisticated and multifaceted view of Pearse, emphasising the positive (such as his progressive economics and liberal approach to education) alongside the negative.[7] Augusteijn's work, though, is still an empirical project and a conventional political historiography.

This chapter seeks to construct a quite different appraisal of Pearse, and of Irish nationalism and the Irish-language movement in general. This is an appraisal that takes the symbolism inherent in Pearse's letter as its starting point. The gift of a rifle to the best student of Irish at St Enda's points to a deeper and more complex issue in contemporary Irish nationalism: the notion that Irish men had been emasculated by the slow process of anglicisation. No longer speaking Irish, they were alienated from their true national spirit; they were deficient and deformed and as such were no longer real men. The movement to revive the Irish language was thus imagined as a process of reasserting a purified male power and was often associated with a recovery of sovereignty and strength. Pearse's gift of a rifle had a clear layer of symbolic male power; only when a boy had proved his mastery of his true native tongue would he be ready to wield this weapon. Both the rifle and the language were symbols of a resurgent Irish national masculinity.

Similar concerns had already appeared in Pearse's famous essay 'The Murder Machine', published in 1913 but culled from earlier articles. An extended discussion of the British educational system in Ireland (the eponymous 'Machine'), the essay declares this system to be worse than 'an edict for the general castration of Irish males.'⁸ Where education should inspire and 'harden', Pearse alleged that British state schools instead work to 'tame' and 'enervate'. The result is that Irishmen are 'not slaves merely, but very eunuchs.'⁹ He also argued, in a possible hint at the physical act of castration, that the current educational system was akin to chopping off parts of children's bodies.¹⁰ A year later, in a speech delivered in Philadelphia during his tour of the US, Pearse again talked of how an anglicising education was 'emasculating our boys and corrupting our girls.' He saw this as clear evidence of an English government conspiracy to enslave Ireland and cut off future generations from a proud history. Thus, Irish schoolboys 'were not taught to be brave, to be strong, to be truthful, to be self-reliant and to be proud.'¹¹

Pearse, however, had a clear plan for halting this national castration of Irish boyhood: 'A new education system has to do more than restore a national culture. It has to restore manhood to a race that has been deprived of it. Along with its inspiration it must bring a certain hardening. It must lead Ireland back to her sagas.'¹² Within a system based on fosterage, the supposed educational system of ancient Ireland, boys should be encouraged to 'recreate and perpetuate'¹³ the traditions of legendary Irish heroes.¹⁴ This programme, of course, was to be carried out through Irish, as an integral part of bringing emasculated Irish boys back into contact with the language and their true, manly heritage. This, as Elaine Sisson has shown, was the prevailing ethos at St Enda's College.¹⁵

Masculinity and the Gaelic League's Return to History

Pearse was by no means the first Irish-language activist to draw out these connections between language, power and gender. Sarah McKibben has shown how, even as early as the sixteenth century, Irish was being linked to ideals of correct manliness whilst anglophone culture was feared as an emasculating influence.¹⁶ Pearse's arguments about national castration echo the views of Thomas Davis (1814–1845): 'To impose another language on such a people is to send their history adrift amongst the accidents of translation ... 'tis to cut off the entail of feeling and separate the people from their forefathers by a deep gulf—tis to corrupt their very *organs*... The language of a nation's youth is the only easy and full speech for its manhood and for its age.'¹⁷ A desire for revival and a recurring fear that the language would soon disappear, which have long been features of Irish-language discourse, are probably recurring tropes in the history of any language that remains in a perpetual minority status.[18]

Certainly, the ideas of national decay and (via the Irish language) national revival were already implicit in the ideology of the Gaelic Union, a precursor of the Gaelic League. The Union's membership card, for instance, depicted Ireland as a dark and decrepit land, whilst also suggesting the possibility of linguistic rejuvenation with the familiar symbol of a distant rising sun.[19] Presumably these were the ideas a Gaelic Union member was to carry close to his or her body, along with their membership card. The inaugural issue of the Gaelic Union's *Irisleabhar na Gaedhilge* [The Gaelic Journal][20] featured a poem with the pleading title '*Go Mairidh na Gaedhil*' ['May the Gaels Live']. Though insisting that 'Now the Gaels are alive in Ireland!' [*Anois tá na Gaedhil in Eirinn beo!*] and 'Gaels and the Irish language are in Ireland yet' [*Tá Gaedhil agus Gaedhilig in Eirinn fós*] there is an anxiety about racial and linguistic decline perceptible throughout the poem. Its declaration that 'It is not true that the land or the language are in decline/It is not true that our spirit is quietly spent' [*Ní fíor go bh-fuil an tír no an teanga dul a bh-feogh'/Ní fíor go bh-fuil ár meanmain caithte go fóill*] signposts a reluctant recognition that things are not as they should be.[21] Highlighting how easily these fears could take on gendered overtones, an 1889 letter to the moderately nationalist *Freeman's Journal* claimed that if the Gaelic Union and the more antiquarian-oriented Society for the Preservation of the Irish Language were not successful, 'we will be absorbed by "our stronger sister", and Ireland soon will be West Britain.'.[22]

The gendered components of these anxieties only became fully apparent, though, with the founding of the Gaelic League in 1893. As a contributor to the League's *Fáinne an Lae* [The Dawning of the Day] asserted in 1898, for instance: 'It is a language which, on account of its almost unchanging character, enables us who use it now to think the thoughts, and feel the feelings, and live, as it were, in the same time with our forefathers who trod the earth and breathed the air of this country twenty—thirty centuries back.'[23] An 1899 speech reprinted in *An Claidheamh Soluis* [The Sword of Light] similarly presented the language not only as a means of communing with the nation's male ancestry and romanticised spaces, but also as a link to a mythical past. Without this link the Irish would be a deficient people, lacking an important element of their heritage:

for every Irishman the ancient tongue had untold interest. It was the language written in their hills, their glens and in the romances of their country. It summoned back the soul of olden times; the echo of silent hearts; the golden chain that bound with the past. (Applause.) The customs, beliefs and dreams of their forefathers were embalmed in it; it preserved undying the image of Ireland clothed in the ancient Druid romances. Hence, the extinction of such a language would be to them an irretrievable loss—a gap in the continuity of their national being; the cutting off of their intellectual life; the cutting off of their religious life, their sacred traditions and romances, and their martyrs' struggles.[24]

All this talk of 'cutting off' strongly echoes Pearse's view that anglicisation was a form of national castration. A year later, Rev. Michael O'Hickey, a prominent clerical supporter of the Gaelic League and professor of Irish at St Patrick's College, Maynooth, decried the low level of resistance to the absence of the Irish language in primary education. 'Are the Irish people going to endure this?' he rhetorically asked. 'If so they deserve the worst that has ever been said of them. They are a people without spirit, without national self-respect, without racial pride, a poor, fibreless, degenerate, emasculated, effete race—eminently deserving of the contempt of mankind.'[25] Patrick Forde, a student of O'Hickey's at Maynooth,[26] showed his teacher's influence when he claimed that, speaking only English, 'we can never be perfect men, full and strong men, able to do a true man's part for God and Fatherland.' Forde, in his most purple of prose, went on to describe the Irish language as, again, a means of communing with a historic Irish masculinity:

> I don't ask you to go a-hunting after tit-bits of curious information, to become dry antiquarians, to peep and botanise upon the grave of mother Erin! Look to your forefathers, read of them, speak of them; not in unworthy mendicant eloquence, nor yet in vulgar boasting about our ancient glories while we squat down in disgraceful content with our present degeneracy, nor least of all in miserable petty controversy with the hireling liars who calumniate our dear Ireland. No! but to learn from them what you ought to be, what God destined Irishmen to be![27]

If an Irish man could be perfected only by speaking the language of his forefathers, without this language he would be, as another Gaelic League pamphlet phrased it, 'a self-degraded and denationalized being who is proud of being mean and who glories in being abject.' Once such an abject young Irish man learnt Irish, a language of which he was previously ashamed, he would gain pride and self-respect from the knowledge that his 'Celtic ancestors were worthy of the vigorous and refined language they spoke'. He would learn that Ireland has produced 'sages who in wisdom and learning were not surpassed by men of any nation in the world' and 'warriors who in valour might vie with the proudest of other lands.'[28] The return to Irish was thus posited as a return to a more glorious and heroic sense of Irish identity, before the humiliation of being deprived of state power and linguistic purity by British colonial rule.

The claims to be returning to a mythical Gaelic Ireland could also be reworked to accommodate a vision of women's liberation. Where British imperialism was often justified on the grounds that it was a benevolent means to protect native women from their 'savage' menfolk, the 1917 work *Women in Ancient and Modern Ireland* by C. Maire Ní Dhubhghall (Crissie M. Doyle) instead argued that oppression of women was an English invention, one that would be promptly dismantled with the full return to an Irish Ireland. As Áine Ceannt declaimed in her introduction to this book: 'In reading of Ireland's glorious past we find the women taking their *rightful place* in Arts, Literature, Legislation, and even in the making of War. The Irish woman of to-day is debarred from entering on many a sphere which she would desire. Are we competent to take our proper place in the New Ireland which is dawning for us? Let us see to it that we be worthy successors of *Brighid, Maebh* and *Gráinne Mhaol.*'[29] Both Ceannt and Ní Dhubhghall mapped a number of different schemas of time onto each other. The future return to Irish rule would not just be a return to a glorious recovered Irish past, but also a return to an old/new Gaelic gender equality. Nor were Ceannt and Ní Dhubhghall the only ones to think along these lines. In an essay entitled 'The Social Position of Women', Eoin MacNeill claimed no ancient and few modern countries had matched the 'enviable position' of women in ancient Ireland.[30] It was only in contemporary America, MacNeill claimed, that women had achieved such ancient Irish equality. Thus, for MacNeill the 'return' to ancient Gaelic Ireland was also an embracing of American-style modernity.[31] This essay, however, does not appear to have been published. Nor were such ideas at the forefront of MacNeill's thinking in the 1920s, when he was a prominent government minister of the Free State.

A perhaps more accurate sense of Irish revivalists' views of women can be seen in the Gaelic League's 1905 *Simple Advice* pamphlet, which warned: 'A woman or girl who goes about at any time in a slatternly way, with rough and uncombed hair hanging in disorder, *does not look like a civilised human being, but like a wild Indian.* No respectable female should neglect herself thus' and 'slovenly ways, whether in man or woman, do harm to Ireland by exposing our people to contempt.'[32] As a general palliative, Gaelic Leaguers were urged to 'study the history of *civilised nations*' and there they would find that 'the possession of a national language makes for the mental, moral and material efficiency of a people.'[33] It is quite telling that the League's views of women here intersected with a certain uneasiness about the Irish nation's racial status.

Colonialism, Postcolonialism and Language

Ireland in the 1890s and 1900s, like the rest of late-nineteenth-century Europe, displayed *fin-de-siècle* anxieties of decay, degeneration and racial decline. Late-nineteenth-century social Darwinism prompted some serious questions for Irish nationalists and language activists, playing into fears of degeneracy, weakness and an uncertain future for a racially and linguistically impure nation:

> Where did that [Darwinism] leave Ireland and the Irish? As a healthy living race ploughing a singular path? Or as a failing race whose soul was weakened due to population decline after the Great Famine? Where did it leave the Irish language? As an energetic living language or as a polluted, besmirched dialect that would not be successful? Where did it leave the Hiberno-English of the people, the new emerging dialect, a mix of English and Irish?
>
> *[Cár fhág sé [Darwineachas] sin Èire agus na Gaeil? Mar chine beo sláintiúil ag treabhadh leo ar chonair aonair? Nó mar chine teipithe a raibh an t-anam ag dul as de réir mar a laghdaigh líon an chine tar éis an Ghorta Mhóir? Cár fhág sé sin an Ghaeilge? Mar theanga bheo bhríomhar nó mar chanúint smálaithe thruaillithe nach mbeadh aon rath uirthi? Cár fhág sé Gall-Ghaeilge na ndaoine, an chanúint nua sin a bhí ag teacht chun cinn ar mheascán den Bhéarla agus den Ghaeilge í].*

At the very heart of this, Brian Ó Conchubhair persuasively argues, were a set of anxieties about *Béarlachais* [a pejorative term for a heavily anglicised Irish language], and the idea that a degenerated patois reflected a deeper racial degeneration.[34]

As previous chapters have argued, anxieties about Irish people's vaguely defined racial status had a determining impact in late nineteenth- and early twentieth-century Irish nationalist thought. The Gaelic League, with its imagined return to an idealised and linguistically pure past, was a 'defensive shield' [*sciath chosanta*] against such anxieties.³⁵ The desire to project a stronger and more respectable image of Irish manhood was also part of an anti-colonialist project to refute the idea, popular in the late nineteenth century, that the Irish were a racially inferior people and incapable of self-rule. A common contemporary perception, as Ó Conchubhair observes, was the belief that 'He who spoke only English, was under an English mental control' [*An té a labhair Béarla amhain, ba faoi smacht Shasana a bhí a mheabhair*].³⁶ Learning Irish was thus a way to slough off the indignity of colonial control and to disprove the negative stereotypes of British rule.

Anxieties about the Irish people's racial status certainly underpinned much of the Gaelic League's ideology. Speaking in Belfast in late 1899, the League's president (and the future president of the Irish state) Douglas Hyde was cheered when he defensively asserted that 'The Irish were not negroes or uitlanders; *they were people with a past*, and had a great past behind them.'³⁷ He would later say that the return to Irish was a return to the country's 'pure Aryan language.'³⁸ Hyde was certainly also worried by the racial implications of the impure *Béarlachais* popularly spoken by most Irish people:

> If by ceasing to speak Irish our peasantry could learn to appreciate Shakespeare and Milton, to study Wordsworth or Tennyson, then I would certainly say adieu to it [the Irish language]. But this is not the case. They lay aside a language which for all ordinary purposes of every day life is much more forcible than any with which I am acquainted, and they replace it by another which they learn badly and speak with an atrocious accent, interlarding it with barbarisms and vulgarity.³⁹

For Hyde, as for most of the Gaelic League, the grammatically impure, the racially impure and national degeneration were three anxiety-inducing subsets of a broader whole.

Irish revivalists implicitly accepted the various accusations that lay behind anti-Irish biases, that the Irish were a racially weak people, lazy and incapable of self-rule and self-control.⁴⁰ They inverted these stereotypes, however, into accusations against the British rule they now claimed had caused this situation. This process can be clearly seen in Cesca Chenevix Trench's [Sadhbh Trinseach] classic 1913 diptych (see Fig. 5.1). A promotional poster for that year's Seachtain na Gaeilge [Irish-Language Week], it contrasted a healthy and sovereign Irish-speaking Ireland alongside an

Fig. 5.1 *On Which Side Are You?*, Gaelic League poster, 1913
Source: NLI EPH G11

anglicised and thus denationalised land. On the right, craven and pathetic, wrapped in a Union Jack, sits an utterly feminised Ireland. She is reduced to begging as, all around her, boatloads of emigrants leave what has now become no longer a true Ireland but a mere 'West Britain'. Indeed, the country itself has been castrated, with the western seaboard, home of the last true Irish speakers, chopped off. Conversely, in the opposing image, Ireland is clad in heroic clothing and proudly displays a weapon as a symbol of martial strength. Indeed, the 'woman' on the right has perhaps become a man, or at least an upright and more powerful woman, by virtue of his/her return to the Irish language. And just as a purified language makes the Irish nation whole, so the land is here made whole; the national castration has been reversed. Language revival has also undone the waves of emigration; the now linguistically stable figure of 'Éire' holds back the ships with ropes, which pictorially suggest a sense of physical stability and rootedness. A purified Irish language has redeemed the space of Ireland and made it whole.

As with the 1917 poster of Eamon de Valera (see Fig. 2.1), which depicted him as a proud ancient Irish woman and which was discussed in Chap. 2, *On Which Side Are You?* is open to contrasting interpretations. For more conservative nationalists it reinforced the soothing ideal of the nation as a poor and defenceless mother in need of 'her' virile sons' protection. According to such a reading, the poster expresses a conservative gender order. It reinforces a message of male public action and feminine passivity. The image on the left, though, is more ambiguous. It offers up a vision of active femininity, of women playing a key role in the maintenance of national sovereignty. Yet, it also continues to rehearse the idea of the nation as an abstract and timeless woman. Cesca Chenevix Trench had moved away from her Anglo-Irish Protestant background as she embraced republicanism and a bohemian lifestyle, and clearly her poster could mean different things to conservative male Gaelic Leaguers than to their feminist colleagues. It is also a work that points to the limits of achieving a female-centric politics within a set of tropes originally determined by the exigencies of what remained a male-centric nationalist project.

P.J. Mathews has observed of the 'classic post-colonial situation' of the Gaelic League that 'emerging nationalists felt obliged to refute the imperial conception of Irish culture by idealizing it and exaggerating its inherent morality, but in the process often replicated in nationalist guise the very colonial thinking which they sought to dislodge.'[41] There is perhaps not much to separate the first reading of *On Which Side Are You?*, of a linguistically sovereign Ireland, from contemporary imperialist notions of politics and power. We can see a similar problem at work in claims emphatically arguing that if the Irish were not a savage or uncivilised people, they must then be a noble and purely European people. One Gaelic League publication spoke of how 'Except Basque, Irish is the most ANCIENT LANGUAGE in Europe' and far more grammatically pure than English. Yet, despite this picture of the Irish language's superiority over English, this handbill also put a strong emphasis on the positive views, regarding the Irish language, of leading English scholars, as well as European academics, such as Prof. Stanley Lane-Poole, 'a great English linguist', and Kuno Meyer, a German professor at the University of Liverpool.[42] A similar desire for British and European respect can be seen in Rev. O'Hickey's pamphlet of February 1900, already quoted. O'Hickey demanded that the Irish Parliamentary Party should 'insist that what has been granted in Wales to the Cymric [i.e., *Cymraeg*, Welsh] speech shall be granted to … the far nobler speech' of Irish. This should go hand in hand with a popular movement of cultural and linguistic revival: 'Let it not be said that the Irish are behind the Finns, the Flemish, the Greeks, the Hungarians, the Poles, the Bohemians, the Provençals, the Bretons, the Welsh &c., &c., in national spirit, in pride of race, in love of their past, in devotion to their ancestral speech.'[43] In other words, let it not be said that the Irish were not white Europeans.

The idea that the Irish people, lacking in state sovereignty, had ceased to be European, or were at least at risk of doing so, underpinned this rhetoric. Not only did the Irish have to disprove that they were a deficient people, they also had to *prove* that they were European. The return to Irish was thus not only a return to history, but also a return to Europeanness and to the political sovereignty and self-control that marked one as a true white European.[44] A handbill dating from about the first decade of the century, adding masculinity to this mix, spoke of how the Gaelic League 'aims at fitting Ireland for a place in the brotherhood of nations. Ireland a nation will enrich the world, like a strong, healthy-hearted man. Ireland an imitation will impoverish the world and be a drain upon it, like a feeble, dull-witted person [like a woman?].'[45] The Gaelic League claimed that Ireland in the seventeenth and eighteenth centuries was 'in much more vital and intimate contact' with Europe than it had been after anglicisation: 'In fact, just in proportion as the Irish language began to fall into disuse and to be replaced by English, did we gradually lose contact with Europe. One of the most obvious lessons to be learned from our history is that to be European we must first of all be Irish.'[46] Learning Irish was a way of proving one's Irishness as well as proving that the Irish were as good as the English, or indeed as good as any other European nation. The revival of a purified Irish, one Gaelic Leaguer claimed, 'would do for the Irish[-speaking] Irishman what it had done for the poor unlettered Finn walking dumb behind his plough for six centuries; for the Czech, a serf in his own land in mind and body to his German master; for the Fleming and for the Croat.'[47] Moreover, within this newly redeemed and unambiguously European Irish-speaking space, there were specific rules of how to act, many of them markedly gendered.

The Rules of the New Gaelic Space

The 1901 Gaelic League pamphlet *Irishwomen and the Home Language* contained some severe strictures on women's role in the language movement, an involvement that at first glance seemed like a paradox. On the one hand, the pamphlet claimed that 'the women of our race are dignified and decorous; they shrink from mingling in a melee, and retiring into the inner courtyard, they leave the scene of strife in the outer world to the sterner sex.' Yet, contradicting this, women still had an important role to play: 'The heavy responsibility rests with them of deciding the fate of the language'. The solution to this apparent paradox was that women's 'mission is to make the homes of Ireland Irish[-speaking]. If the homes are Irish the whole country will be Irish. The spark struck on the hearthstone will fire the soul of the nation.' Anne McClintock argues that nations rest on a masculine sense of identity, as well as masculine hopes, humiliations and memories. Where women are given a role in the nationalist movement' it is as symbolic bearers of the nation and its traditions, thus affording them a *political* role even as it evacuates that role of possibilities for public agency or tangible political action. It is for this reason that McClintock says 'all nationalisms ... are dangerous' since all of them represent 'relations to political power and to the technologies of violence.'[48] The objectives sought by the nationalist movement are, in reality, biased towards the interests of an elite male leadership. In the Irish case, one of those ideals was that in the future Gaelic state, men would hold sway in public and women would be restricted to the private sphere of the marital home. In these private spaces, women would devote themselves to the task of raising the next generation of nationalist men, a task that would leave them little time for involvement in public politics. The nation might be publicly symbolised as a woman, but the state, in practice, remained male.

Irishwomen and the Home Language, however, was written by a woman, Mary E.L. Butler. There is an obvious contradiction here. In a prominent platform afforded to her by a very public organisation, a woman issues this call for women to not 'mount a platform and hold forth in public.' In fact, Butler was carving out a specific role for women in Irish life, and she made barbed and less-than-subtle comments about male Gaelic Leaguers along the way: '... if there is one thing for which our countrymen are remarkable, it is inconsistency. We, their countrywomen, know them pretty well, and understand them if anyone does, and we are therefore not surprised to find most of them making no attempt to carry their theories into practice, and to bring their home life into harmony with their platform utterances.' And while her admonition that language activism be 'waged not by shrieking viragoes or aggressive amazons, but by gentle, low-voiced women' working in the home tended to reinforce gender stereotypes, as well as a gendered split between feminine private spaces and a masculinised public sphere, it also helped to gain women an input they may have otherwise been denied.[49] The Gaelic League, however, made demands not only of women, but also of men. One set of these demands related to the proper attire for Gaelic public spaces.

Shane Leslie, an aristocratic convert to both Catholicism and the Gaelic League, was one of the strongest advocates for men to wear 'traditional' clothing. The Irish nation, he felt, faced a clear danger from 'The monstrous fashions of Queen Ann and the Georgean [*sic*] period' and from 'servile imitators' of the same. Alongside the movement to revive Irish, Leslie hoped that 'the manly vesture in which their fathers lived and died'[50] would also be revived and 'The sooner the high ancestry of the Irish kilt is accepted the better.'[51] Similarly, in 1900, one Gaelic Leaguer went so far as to seek out Pearse's counsel as to what should be the proper attire for an Irish man. Pearse had recently viewed a collection of sixteenth-century clothing at the National Museum that had left him sadly unimpressed: 'one would at first sight take them for a rather clumsily made and ill-treated pair of modern gentlemen's drawers.' Wearing them, one would 'run the risk of leading the spectators to imagine that you had forgotten to don your trousers.' Such a spectacle, Pearse feared, would undermine the 'dignity' of a Gaelic League celebration. Thus, 'I should much prefer to see you arrayed in a kilt, although it may be less authentic, than in a pair of these trews.'[52] All of this has obvious echoes of the kilts that became fashionable in Britain in the early nineteenth century as part of what Hugh Trevor-Roper termed 'The Invention of Scotland.'[53] That Irish nationalists would engage in a similar 'invented tradition' is hardly surprising. What is surprising is their awareness of how historically false this was. Even Leslie, who held that 'we can confidently regard the kilt as a genuine development of the original dress of the Gaels', also accepted that 'our evidence is piecemeal.'[54]

For Pearse, though, it was not a question of historically accurate clothing, but of the image that such clothing projected: 'If you adopt a costume, let it, at all events, have some elements of picturesqueness'. Leslie had similar ideas. He urged that the *Oireachtas* [the annual *Assembly* of the Gaelic League] would be an ideal place for 'twenty or thirty young men ... to appear together in the kilt (and it appears that there are a great many men over Ireland who are waiting for a lead).' J.J. Lee observes that 'The preoccupation of "Irish-Irelanders" with legitimising their aspirations by invoking alleged precedents from the celtic mists have misled some observers into portraying them as simple reactionaries. In fact, far from prisoners of the past, the modernisers created the past in their image of the future.'[55] With varying degrees of openness, Leslie and Pearse were both constructing a vision of a modern, manly, and independent Ireland. It is also worth considering how this was a means of promoting Irish industrial development. Hyde believed that 'the language revival is having the healthiest result upon the industries of the country' because each 'convert' to the Gaelic League 'determines to be as Irish as he can, from head to toe, and insists on being clad in Irish tweed, and upon wearing an Irish-made hat and Irish-made boots.'[56]

Indeed, it was more common for men than women to wear 'traditional' clothing, and to use this as a way to project an image of recovered Gaelic heroism, again reflecting the clear male biases of the language revival. At the 1910 *Oireachtas*, the feminist republican magazine *Bean na hÉireann* [The Irish Woman] reported that there were 50 men, who 'looked to great advantage in the old Irish dress', whilst only 20 women were similarly attired.[57] And this despite the fact that it was a rule of the *Oireachtas* that 'No prize will be awarded to any competitor who is not dressed in clothes of Irish material and manufacture.'[58] This marks an important difference between Irish nationalism and other postcolonial nationalisms. In the latter, controlling women's clothing was often considered of far greater importance. Thus, women would 'display the signs of national tradition' with their clothing (even if that tradition was only recently invented) 'and therefore would be essentially different from the "Western" woman.'[59] Conversely, men, the active public leaders, would embrace Western, 'rational' dress. These practices trod a fine line between regarding women as receptacles of conservative tradition and yet also as targets for men's sexual gazes. That Gaelic Leaguers never engaged in this practice (though did seek to control women in other ways) highlights one additional manner in which Irish nationalism differs from its postcolonial cousins.

Additionally, by taking to the streets in curious outfits, male Gaelic Leaguers were on the verge of engaging in a dangerously performative spectacle. Such performances can make men the subject of the spectator's gaze (a role usually reserved for women) and thus undercuts male hegemony.[60] This perhaps explains the short life of the Gaelic League's kilt. As Leslie himself noted, 'We are sometimes told that there are a great many lunatics in Ireland besides those in confinement. They are generally classified as the slightly deranged who advocate teaching Irish, the rather madder who actually speak it, and lastly the entirely mad who combine the language with the Irish kilt.'[61] The dream of a nation united in their wearing of 'manly' Irish costumes was perhaps, as Pearse feared, open to too much mockery and never attracted a large following.

More popular than this nationalist fancy dress, though, and representing an even more fundamental personal transformation, was the popular practice of changing one's name. This was also linked to a desire for a redeemed and purified Irish identity. It was the process whereby John Leslie, a landed nobleman, Oxford-graduate and first cousin of Winston Churchill, became Shane Leslie, sometimes spelling it 'Seaghan Leslaigh'. Percy Fredrick Beazley, the son of Irish immigrants in Liverpool, became Piaras Béaslaí, Gaelic Leaguer, Volunteer, pro-Treaty Sinn Féiner and Michael Collins' hagiographer. Patrick Pearse, son of a Birmingham stonecutter,[62] became Pádraic MacPiaras, as well as adopting pen names redolent of a recovered Gaelic ideal; Colm O Conaire and Cuimin O Cualain.[63] Pearse was again picking up on ideas popular throughout the Irish-language movement.[64]

Changing one's name was a common means of reinforcing ownership over one's own identity and of expressing a purely Gaelic subjecthood as opposed to the inchoate nature of being inwardly Irish but with an externally English label. This was in fact a quite common practice in various national contexts across Europe: 'The generations before 1914 are full of great-nation chauvinists whose fathers, let alone mothers, did not speak the language of their sons' chosen people, and whose names, Slav or Magyarized German or Slav testified to their choice.'[65] It was certainly also a common practice in Zionism.

David Grün, for instance, a native of rural Poland, became David Ben-Gurion, as part of his sloughing-off of his East European origins. He would later claim 'I have forgotten that I am Polish.'[66] His successor as Israeli Prime Minister, Moshe Sharret, born Moshe Shertok, had also abandoned a Yiddish name along with a Diasporic past. And one Goldie Myerson, a native of Belarus, adopted the more suitably Hebraic Golda Meir.[67] Adopting new Hebrew names, and expecting others to do the same, was a central part of negating the Diaspora and forging a new Israeli identity.[68] As the right-wing Israeli poet Uri Tzvi Greenburg once sardonically asked 'How is it possible that this Jerusalemite body was born in Poland' [*ech efshar she-guf yerushalmi ze noled be-polin*].[69]

In Zionism this also had a distinctly masculine aspect. The Israeli poet Avot Yeshurun, for instance, abandoned his birth name, Yechiel Perlmutter (which, as well as advertising his Diasporic and Yiddish origins, was also a name with clearly feminine overtones).[70] His new name, which can mean either 'Fathers are Watching Us' or 'Fathers of The People of Israel',[71] was thus part of his new masculine Zionist identity.[72] Another instructive case is that of 'The First Hebrew Child', Ben-Tsiyon Ben-Yehuda, son of Eliezer Ben-Yehuda. The elder Ben-Yehuda was a central figure in the 'revival'[73] of modern Hebrew, albeit one whose importance has perhaps been exaggerated. He was born Eliezer Yitzhak Perlman, but, upon moving to Ottoman Palestine, adopted a name with less obviously Yiddish and mercantile origins; his new name translates as Son of Judea. His son, who grew up barred from speaking any language but Hebrew, was given a name meaning Son of Zion, reflecting his new identity rooted in the soil of the biblical homeland. In adulthood, though, he changed his name to Itamar Ben-Avi, meaning Date Tree (a Zionist symbol) Son of My Father. Ben-Avi can also mean Son of A.B.Y. (his father's initials).[74] Both father and son were clearly involved in a process of self-invention, creating new names and new ideals for men rooted in the soil of a Hebrew-speaking homeland.

In fact, the early Zionists had '…. a proclivity to redefine themselves with names that denote firmness, toughness, strength, courage, and vigor', names such as Yariv [antagonist]; Oz [strength]; Tamir [towering]; Bar Adon [son of the master, or masterful]; and even Bar Shilton [fit to govern].[75] Much like in the revival of Irish, Zionists, by 'reviving' Hebrew, sought to prove their masculine strength and, more importantly, to prove to themselves and others that they were indeed *Bar Shilton*. While Gaelic name-changing never took on so overtly masculine a tone, it did serve to present an image of recovered national identity. Given how obviously gendered this feeling of Irish national resurgence could be in other situations, it is reasonable to presume a masculinist element at work within Gaelic name-changing too.

In 1899, presenting evidence to a government inquiry into education, Douglas Hyde argued that the nation had become ashamed of their Irish names. Hyde let it be known that he, and indeed the Gaelic League in general, believe 'that no good can result to national character from such a state of things as that [shame of Irish names].' Moreover, 'No wise Government, unless it was deliberately playing the game to weaken the people, would have allowed such a tone of mind as that to have arisen.'[76] Four years later, in an attempt to have mail addressed in Irish accepted, Hyde sent a volume to the Post Office 'giving the correct forms of Irish names which are now being widely adopted, and the *vulgarised and corrupt forms* which are also in vogue.'[77] The same year, Neilí ní Bhriain [Nelly O'Brien], a leading figure in the Gaelic League's Dublin-based *Craobh na gCúig Cúigí* [Branch of the Five Provinces], spoke with pride of the 'good old Irish names' of her three sons, Donough, Phadrig and Fionn.[78] Like Hyde, Ní Bhriain/O'Brien was a Protestant, as were a disproportionate number of *Craobh na gCúig Cúigí*,⁷⁹ and it would not be a stretch to imagine that such an 'Irish' practice served to reaffirm their contested sense of national identity. Indeed, Hyde liked to regularly say that the Reverend R.R. Kane, a staunchly unionist Protestant cleric from Belfast, had confessed to him that 'he could never forget his "real name" was Ó Catháin.'⁸⁰ Name-changing was also a complex practice, capable of expressing a number of quite different ideals. Hyde adopted the pen name *An Craoibhín Aoibhinn* [The Pleasant Little Tree-Branch], which points to a far less militarised, less forceful vision of a de-anglicised scholarly identity.⁸¹

It was not only Protestants, though, or those with an English ancestry⁸² (both of whom were at risk of being placed outside the boundaries of the nation) who engaged in this practice. Patrick Ingoldsby, one of the main organisers of the Gaelic League's annual language parades, became Pádraic Mac Giolla Iosa (lit. Patrick son of the servant of Jesus). Nor was it only men who changed their names. Agnes Farrelly, a feminist, educator and one of the few female figures in the early leadership of the Gaelic League, decided, after her first visit to the Irish-speaking Aran Islands, that she would now rather be known as Úna Ní Fhaircheallaigh, instead of her birth name, Agnes Mary Winifred Farrelly.⁸³ Ríona Nic Congáil has observed that 'Gender equality in public and social life was central to Ní Fhaircheallaigh's utopian vision of Ireland's future' [*Bhí an comhionannas inscne sa saol poiblí agus sóisialta lárnach i bhfís útóipeach Ní Fhaircheallaigh do thodhchaí na hÉireann*].⁸⁴ Much like the return to a glorious, manly past, re-worked in feminist directions by some women language activists, this change in names perhaps also symbolised a return to a better, more equal Ireland. Nonetheless, like the Gaelic League in general, which had an 'overwhelmingly male' leadership (about 90%) in 1903 and 1913,⁸⁵ this practice points to an ideology that was far more masculine in nature than feminine.

*Ha-Ivrit: Gesher Le-Chaim Be-Yisrael*⁸⁶

That Hebrew revivalists engaged in a similar practice to that of their Irish contemporaries is unsurprising. Both drew on a similar set of ideas about history and national revival and both sought to counter similar stereotypes about deformed language as a sign of a deeper national deformity. Even the titles of two of the most important Hebrew and Irish revivalist publications are remarkably similar; *HaShachar* [The Dawn], edited by Peretz Smolenskin in the 1870s and 1880s, and the Gaelic League's *Fáinne an Lae* [The Dawning of the Day]. Both titles suggest a return to some lost national ideal after a long night (or nightmare?) of exile or foreign control. Smolenskin saw Hebrew as a palliative for the Jewish people. It was 'a suitable language for a people who found themselves in a moribund situation' [*hi halashon hamat'ima le'am hamatzui be-matzav gesisa*'].[87] Michael Gluzman's Foucault-influenced study of the canonical works of modern Hebrew, from Smolenskin in the late nineteenth century to David Grossman at the end of the twentieth, argues that, even as early as the 1880s, Hebrew literature regularly 'described the Jewish man as one who was in exile not just from his Land but also from his body and his masculinity' [*t'iarah et ha-gever ha-yehudi ce-mi she-goleh lo rak me-aretzo elah gam ma-gufo ve-mi-gavriuto*]. Much of this Hebrew literature focused on a supposed 'defective masculinity' [*gavryut peguma*] of the Jew's body in opposition to the masculinity of the New Jew that would be 'anti-Diasporic, Zionist, manly' [*anti-galuti, tzioni, gavri*].[88] Arieh Saposnik's discussion of the lived experiences of those involved in the emergent modern Hebrew-language culture in late-Ottoman Palestine shows that many of them had highly negative views of 'an unhealthy Diaspora and its decaying culture.' These early Hebrew-speaking Zionist settlers saw their work in part as a break from a weak and effeminate Yiddish-speaking Diaspora.[89]

In general, anxieties about the lack of a single shared Jewish language expressed a set of deeper fears about Jews' racial ambiguities. At the forefront of these anxieties, was Yiddish. This language, with its diverse roots in German, Hebrew and various Slavic languages, 'seemed to bear out nineteenth-century racist European notions that people speaking a hybrid language were somehow inferior and incapable of clear, intelligible, and sophisticated thought.'[90] As with so much else in Zionism, this linguistic anxiety bore more than a passing resemblance to contemporary antisemitism. Sander Gilman identifies this as a linguistic racism: 'The Other cannot every truly possess "true" language and is so treated.'[91] The allegedly corrupt nature of Jewish discourse (whether in an indigenous tongue or in the use of Gentile languages by Jews) was an antisemitic accusation with a long pedigree, and elsewhere Gilman observes, with a note of resignation: 'Is it of little wonder that modern Hebrew developed a set of sociolinguistic practices which were the antithesis of this ancient stereotype?'[92] Many Zionists certainly felt that Jews were linguistically flawed and saw Hebrew as the means to correct this.

Ben-Gurion, for instance, while pragmatically accepting that other languages might have to be used within the Zionist movement, felt that only Hebrew could guarantee 'our future as a healthy nation, united in its land.'[93] A poster produced after 1948 by the Israeli Ministry of Education and Culture promoted the use of the national language by talking of 'not seventy languages, one language, Hebrew'[94] [*lo shiv'im lashon, lashon achat, ivrit*], a biblical reference to the 70 nations of the postdiluvian world. Thus, in opposition to a confusing and inchoate Babel of tongues, Zionism would mark a return to a nation 'of one language and of common purpose.'[95] With unalloyed harshness, a poster from the Israeli Army's cultural unit depicted European languages such as Hungarian, Romanian, and Polish as a multitude of signposts that lead to the darkness of the concentration camps. In contrast, Hebrew was a single signpost pointing to a bright, bucolic vision of Palestine.[96] 'The language serves to create a single heart for all parts of the nation' [*ha-lashon ba'ah livro lev echad le-col. chelekei ha-umma*], the culture ministry declared, in a quote ascribed to the national poet, Chaim Nachman Bialik.[97] Eric Hobsbawm has spotted the congruence between early-twentieth-century debates over racial purity (with their attendant 'horrors of miscegenation') and the contemporary nationalist focus on linguistic purity.[98] Zionists saw Yiddish, and the diversity of Diasporic tongues in general, as signs of racial indeterminacy. Much like the Irish nationalist concern that *Béarlachais* was a living symbol of a worryingly diluted national identity, Yiddish became a signifier that Jews were everywhere a minority and nowhere a cultural, linguistic or politically sovereign majority. Echoing such ideas, Yosef Chaim Brenner, novelist and prominent Zionist, conflated the speaking of Yiddish with an 'inability to function "normally" ' and 'the worst aspects of diasporic life.' Even more blatantly, the poet Avraham Sholonsky spoke of the 'catastrophe of bilingualism' as being a form of national tuberculosis.[99] Hebrew would thus be the obvious national cure.

That a revival of the Hebrew language would cure Jews of sickness and decay was also a central idea in Yonatan Ratosh's 1943 essay, *Ketav Al Ha-Noar Ha-Ivri* [Epistle to the Hebrew Youth], a foundational document of the so-called Canaanite Movement. The 'Caananites' sought to create a modernised Israelite identity, rooted in the biblical homeland, to replace completely the Jewish Diaspora, thus taking the Zionist notion of *Shlilat Ha-Golah* [Negation of the Diaspora] to a logical if eccentric conclusion.[100] Ratosh talked of how 'a chasm of different opinions and alienation' [*amok hatehom ve-hazarut*] separated the proud

Hebrew-speaking pioneers from a degenerated Diaspora. Those who spoke Hebrew, Ratosh believed, had freed themselves from the 'mental neuroses' [*tavsichim nefashot*] of the Jewish Diaspora, a Diaspora that, implicitly, was Yiddish-speaking. This recovered sense of Hebrew-speaking pride, Ratosh believed, stemmed from a new life rooted in 'The Hebrew Homeland' [*ha-moledet ha-ivrit*].[101] As with the Gaelic League, Hebrew revivalists saw their project as one of reconnecting to a heroic past and to a lost national and linguistic purity, and thus as a means of ameliorating their nation's contemporary weaknesses and racial indeterminacy. Rather than being unique, as some historians have claimed, this was something Zionism clearly shared with Irish nationalism.[102]

Gender and the Irish Language After 1922

The idea that a link exists between a lost language and a gendered national deficiency has had a long half-life in Ireland. At the 1932 Sinn Féin Ard Fheis, the head of the party, Brian O'Higgins (Brian Ó hUiginn), delivered a tirade about the English government, which displayed the 'reasoning of the Devil himself' [*ciall an diabhail féin*] in its diabolical schemes to destroy Irish national identity. Such schemes, he claimed, had led to the situation whereby 'It is not only in the body that Ireland is connected to the Foreigner [i.e., the English] but also in consciousness and in mind' [*Ní i gcorp amháin atá Éire ceangailte le Gallaibh acht i n-aigne agus i meóin chomh maith*]. He continued his theme, albeit in apologetic English:

> And now I must speak to you in this other tongue that is a living and constant reproach to us, a constant reminder that we are an enslaved nation, that we are bound body and mind to our one and only enemy in the whole world, and that to be free we must come back to the truth, build up from the foundations again and make ourselves fit for freedom when it comes.[103]

While Sinn Féin were, by this point, little more than a fringe element in Irish politics, their leader was here expressing a common notion about the intersecting of masculinity, sovereignty and a purified Irish language.[104] Similar symbols and rhetoric appear in the publications of *Glún na Buaidhe* [The Victorious Generation] and the more fascist-oriented *Ailtirí na hAiséirghe* [Architects of the Resurrection], two important if short-lived post-1922 Irish-language groups.[105] As late as 1967, the journalist Peter Lennon was still able to observe that 'for more than thirty years we've been led to believe that the magic potion which was to restore dignity, identity, and confidence, to a mutilated republic was the revival of our ancient tongue.'[106]

Perhaps this focus on language as a symbol of recovered Gaelic masculine ideals, however, could help to explain one of the most obvious paradoxes in the history of Irish nationalism. Irish nationalists clearly displayed a strong anxiety about the decline of Irish, and yet, since 1922, the Irish state has proved singularly incapable of reviving this language. Given how interventionist this state could be in other areas (citizens' sex lives, choice of reading material and leisure habits), this failure is perplexing and requires explanation. This is more pressing when we recall that the 'revival' of Hebrew went hand-in-hand with a quite coercive suppression of Yiddish in British Palestine and later in the State of Israel.[107] Why did Hebrew succeed where Irish did not?

In a consciously didactic work that seeks to garner lessons for twenty-first-century Irish from twentieth-century Hebrew, Muiris Ó Laoire notes how the grammatically pedantic approach to Irish has often been in contrast to that facing Hebrew in Israel: 'immigrants and Israelis were not overly concerned about mistakes and about "bad Hebrew" and did not need to help the language in its own path of development' [*nach raibh inimircigh agus muintir Iosrael róbhuartha faoi bhotúin agus faoi "drochEabhrais" agus níorbh fholáir nó gur chabhraigh sé sin ina shlí féin le dul chun cinn na teanga*].[108] Notwithstanding their coercive approach, Zionists could also show a pragmatism toward language, recognising the need to not control all aspects of the language. Addressing the Fifth National Conference of the Brigade of the Defenders of the Language, in Tel Aviv in 1929, for instance, Prof. Joseph Klausner warned his audience to stop obsessing over grammatical mistakes in modern vernacular Hebrew. Such errors, he declared, 'are not mistakes at all when you write modern Hebrew … stop scaring us constantly that we are writing with mistakes because in phrase X in *Mishna Y* and in *Midrash Z*, the phrase is different.' While he took issue with the use of Yiddish sentence structures, common among the 'Simple people in Eretz-Israel', he also felt that 'A limited number of barbarisms [i.e., words borrowed from other languages] is natural: no language was ever developed without a conscious or subconscious influence of another language.' Evoking some of his deeper concerns, Klausner concluded that he sought, not the language of 'a fishwife in the marketplace', but rather that 'We must speak and write as free men in their own language and not as slaves to Isaiah and Rabbi Yehuda ha-Nasi.'[109] Though we should not ignore the obvious material factors acting against the Irish revivalists (the need to retain English as a commercial language in a country so heavily dependent on trade with Britain) or in favour of Hebrew (the need to find a common language for the ingathering of polyglot 'exiles'), neither should we downplay the role of ideology.[110]

A focus on the Irish language as a living thing, as something capable of change and of borrowing from other languages, would perhaps have defied the purpose of its revival and purification in the first place. Perhaps the purpose was always to engage in the act of symbolic defiance which *relearning* Irish necessitated, rather than recreating the language as a run-of-the-mill vernacular. The ongoing act of learning Irish acted as a clear symbol of the harm done by colonial rule and of the need for elite action to rectify this. And it is questionable how committed all Irish nationalists were to reviving Irish as opposed to merely using it as a means of reconnecting to a pure, nostalgic and harmonious pre-anglicisation Irish past. Unlike Hebrew in Palestine and later in the State of Israel, Irish remained a language to be appreciated for its symbolic content.

In any case, reviving the language was hardly the only unfulfilled goal of Irish nationalists. Nor was it the only 'goal' that could also be interpreted as actually acting as a vehicle for deeper concerns. Breaking economically from the British was another, and that is the subject of the next chapter.

Notes

1. P.H. Pearse (1898) 'The Intellectual Future of the Gael' in *Three Lectures on Gaelic Topics* (Dublin: M.H. Gill) p. 55. Emphases in original.
2. K. Clarke, H. Litton, ed. (1991) *Revolutionary Woman: Kathleen Clarke, 1878–1972: An Autobiography* (Dublin: The O'Brien Press) p. 43.
3. NLI, Pearse Papers, MS 21084, Undated Open Letter to the Boys of Scoil Éanna. Given that Pearse only visited the US once, and that the letter mentions the boys' recent Easter break, this letter must date from the spring of 1914.
4. R. Dudley Edwards (2006) *Patrick Pearse: The Triumph of Failure*, 2nd edn (Dublin: Irish Academic Press) p. 196.
5. M. Elliot (2003) *Robert Emmet: The Making of a Legend* (London: Profile Books). It is never entirely clear if Elliot intended this as an accusation of real, repressed sexual desires or just as an accusatory metaphor for Pearse's views of history.

6. S. Farrell Moran (1994) *Patrick Pearse and the Politics of Redemption: The Mind of the Easter Rising, 1916* (Washington DC: Catholic University of America Press) p. 46 and *passim*.
7. J. Augusteijn (2010) *Patrick Pearse: The Making of a Revolutionary* (London: Palgrave Macmillan). Tellingly, Augusteijn says that it was 'the virtual end of political violence in Northern Ireland' that allowed for a better understanding of Pearse.
8. P.H. Pearse (1966) *Political Writings and Speeches* (Dublin: Talbot Press) p. 7.
9. *Ibid.*, pp. 8–9.
10. Ibid., p. 32.
11. NLI, Pearse Papers, MS33702, *Stenographic Copy of Speech Delivered by Padraic Henry Pearse, Philadelphia*, 1914.
12. P.H. Pearse (1966) *Political Writings*, p. 41.
13. *Ibid*, pp. 20–25.
14. *Ibid*, p. 38.
15. E. Sisson (2004) *Pearse's Patriots: St. Enda's and the Cult of Boyhood* (Cork: Cork University Press).
16. S. McKibben (2010) *Endangered Masculinities in Irish Poetry, 1540–1780* (Dublin: UCD Press).
17. Quoted in NLI IR 49162 P57, *The Case for Irish* (Dublin: Conradh na Gaedhilge, n.d. [1929?]. Emphases added.
18. D. Kiberd (2001) *Irish Classics* (Cambridge MA: Harvard University Press) p. 25.
19. NUIG, Stephen Barrett Papers, G3/291, Gaelic Union Membership Card.
20. *Irisleabhar na Gaedhilge* literally translates as 'The Irish Language Journal'. The translation that this bilingual publication used, however, was *The Gaelic Journal*.
21. 'Go Mairidh na Gaedhil'. *Irisleabhar na Gaedhilge/The Gaelic Journal*, Vol. 1, No. 1, November 1882. As if to reinforce the idea that the Irish language would help to root the Irish nation in their homeland, the poem's author is named simply as *Leath Chuinn* [The Northern Half of Ireland].
22. NUIG, Stephen Barrett Papers, G3/106, Press Cutting: F.J. Healy, 'The Departing National Characteristics of the Irish Nation', *Freeman's Journal*, 5 January 1889. This letter prompted at least two positive responses: Ed. Finneran, 'Ireland's Departing Characteristics', *Freeman's Journal*, 8 January 1889; Taenga Gaedilge [*sic, Teanga Gaedilge?* i.e., The Irish Language]; 'The Irish Language Movement', *Freeman's Journal*, 7 January 1889.

23. *Fáinne an Lae*, Vol. 1, No. 5, 5 February 1898, quoted in B. Ó Conchubhair (2009) *Fin de Siècle na Gaeilge: Darwin, An Athbheochan agus Smaointearacht na hEorpa* [Irish Language *Fin de Siècle*: Darwin, the Gaelic Revival and European Intellectual Thought] (Indreabhán: Cló Iar-Chonnachta) p. 25. Ó Conchubhair calls this idea: 'language as a treasury of history' [*teanga mar thaisceadán na staire*].
24. 'The Value of the Irish Language and Literature,' *An Claidheamh Soluis*, Vol. 1, No. 38, 2 December 1899. Quoted in Ó Conchubhair (2009) 'Fin de Siècle', p. 22. This article was an account of a public meeting in Carraig an Ime [Carriganimmy] in Cork.
25. M. O'Hickey (1900) *Irish in the Schools* (Gaelic League Pamphlets, No. 3).
26. T. McMahon (2008) *Grand Opportunity: The Gaelic Revival and Irish Society, 1893–1910* (Syracuse NY: Syracuse University Press) p. 77.
27. P. Forde (1900) *The Irish Language Movement: Its Philosophy* (Gaelic League, Pamphlets, No. 21).
28. P.F. Kavanagh (1901) *Ireland's Defence: Her Language* (Gaelic League Pamphlets, No. 23).
29. C.M. Ní Dhubhghaill (1917) *Women in Ancient and Modern Ireland* (Dublin: The Kenny Press) Emphases added. Brighid, Maebh and Grainne Mhaol are, respectively, St Brigid, a fifth/sixth-century saint and one of Ireland's three patron saints, Queen Maeve, a heroic figure from Irish mythology, and Grace O'Malley, as mentioned in Chap. 2, was a sixteenth-century 'pirate-queen' about whom a large body of mythology has grown up.
30. Gail Bederman has strongly argued that, in the context of the US in the late nineteenth and early twentieth centuries, such an imagined return to a pure and primitive masculinity was a means of actually reinforcing quite contemporary, and in the American case, racist ideals of manliness. G. Bederman (1995) *Manliness and Civilization: A Cultural History of Race and Gender in the United States, 1880–1917* (Chicago: University of Chicago Press). A similar process is observable here. As Forde said, 'Do the so-called blessings of Protestant English liberty suffice for us? Or are we on the other hand, a totally distinct and superior race, ever zealous for the better gifts that God made the soul of man to desire and enjoy … Are we mere planters and marchmen of the Pale, or are we Celts, Gaels, Irish? 'P. Forde (1900) 'Irish Language Movement'. The examples of Ceannt, Doyle and MacNeill, though, show that this return to a primitive past could go in a number of directions.
31. NLI MS 13167, Bulmer Hobson Papers, *The Social Position of Women*, handwritten essay by Eoin MacNeill, n.d.
32. C. O'Conor-Eccles (1905) *Simple Advice: To be followed by all who desire the good of Ireland, and especially by Gaelic Leaguers* 2nd edn. Emphases added.

33. NUIG, Stephen Barrett Papers, G3/1476, *Reasons Why You Should Join The Gaelic League*, n.d.
34. B. Ó Conchubhair (2009) 'Fin de Siècle', pp. 97–100.
35. *Ibid*, pp. 6, 8.
36. *Ibid*, p. 15.
37. 'Dr. Douglas Hyde in Belfast—The Educative Influences of the Irish Language, Eloquent Lecture in the Ulster Hall', *An Claidheamh* Soluis, Vol. 1, No. 41 (23 December 1899). Quoted in *Ibid*, 21. Emphases Added.
38. NLI MS 18436, Xerox copies of material formerly in the papers of John Quinn, *Autograph draft of paper by Douglas Hyde on the Gaelic League*, 1905.
39. 'A Plea for the Irish Language,' *Dublin University Review*, April 1885, quoted in B. Ó Conchubhair (2009) *Fin de Siècle*, p. 88.
40. S. Garrigan Mattar (2004) *Primitivism, Science, and the Irish Revival* (Oxford: Clarendon Press) pp. 13–14.
41. P.J. Mathews (2003) *Revival: The Abbey Theatre, Sinn Féin, The Gaelic League and the Co-Operative Movement* (Cork: Cork University Press) p. 45.
42. NUIG Stephen Barrett Papers, G3/1060(1), *What the Irish Language Is: Some Facts*, undated handbill. Capitalisation in original. See also NUIG Stephen Barrett Papers, G3/1061, *Views of some men of light and leading upon the Irish Language*, undated pamphlet (probably 1899).
43. M. O'Hickey (1900) 'Irish in the Schools'.
44. This draws on David Myers' similar arguments about a Zionist return to history. D.N. Myers (1995) *Re-Inventing the Jewish Past: European Jewish Intellectuals and the Zionist Return to History* (Oxford: Oxford University Press).
45. NUIG Stephen Barrett Papers, G3/1476, *Reasons Why You Should Join the Gaelic League*, n.d.
46. NUIG Stephen Barrett Papers, G3/1197, *Connradh na Gaedhilge: The Case for Irish*, n.d.
47. 'Notes', *An Claidheamh Soluis*, Vol.1, No. 17, 8 July 1899, quoted in B. Ó Conchubhair (2009) *Fin de Siècle*, p. 41.
48. A. McClintock (1993) 'Family Feuds: Gender, Nationalism and the Family.' *Feminist Review*, No. 44, pp. 61–80.
49. M. Butler (n.d.) *Irishwomen and the Home Language* (Gaelic League Pamphlets, No. 6),
50. NLI MS 23378, Shane Leslie Papers, Press Cutting: Seaghan Leslie, 'A Word on the Kilt', n.d.
51. NLI MS 23378, Shane Leslie Papers, Press Cutting: Seaghan Leslaigh, 'The Irish Kilt', n.d.

52. P.H. Pearse, S. Ó Buachalla, ed. (1980) *The Letters of P.H. Pearse* (London: Colin Smythe) pp. 22–23. The original, including Pearse's drawing of the 'trews', can be viewed at NLI P6431, Pearse Papers, Letter from Pearse to J. O'Kelly, 26 October 1900.
53. H. Trevor-Roper (2012) 'The Invention of Tradition: The Highland Tradition of Scotland' in E. Hobsbawm, T. Ranger, eds. *The Invention of Tradition* 2nd edn (Cambridge: Cambridge University Press) pp. 15–42. See also: H. Trevor-Roper (2009) *The Invention of Scotland: Myth and History* (New Haven, CT: Yale University Press).
54. NLI MS 23378, Shane Leslie Papers, Press Cutting: Seaghan Leslie, 'A Word on the Kilt' n.d.
55. J.J. Lee (1973) *The Modernisation of Irish Society* (Dublin: Gill and MacMillan) p. 141.
56. NLI MS 18436, Xerox copies of material formerly in the papers of John Quinn, *Autograph draft of paper by Douglas Hyde on the Gaelic League*, 1905.
57. 'At the Oireachtas,' *Bean na hÉireann*, Vol. 1, No. 19 (May 1910).
58. NUIG, Stephen Barrett Papers. G3/1141, *Clár Oireachtas 1905* [Programme of the *Oireachtas*, 1905].
59. P. Chatterjee (1993) *The Nation and Its Fragments: Colonial and Postcolonial Histories* (Princeton NJ: Princeton University Press) p. 9. See also: the discussion of 'Fashion, Clothes, Jewellery, Purdah [gender segregation]' in C. Gupta (2001) *Sexuality, Obscenity, and Community: Women, Muslims, and the Hindu Public in Colonial India* (New York: Palgrave) pp. 140–150; and the discussion of Palestinian women's traditional clothing and men's wearing of Western suits with the *keffiyeh* scarf that 'expressed the Palestinians' identity with their land, and their solidarity with their leaders, calling for independence' from the 1930s onwards. W. Kamel Kawar, T. Nasir (1980) 'The Traditional Palestinian Costume.' *Journal of Palestine Studies*, Vol.10, No. 1, 118–129.
60. M. Leeds Craig (2014) *Sorry I Don't Dance: Why Men Refuse to Move* (Oxford: Oxford University Press) p. 8. Pointing to how selective an anxiety this is, Craig has astutely noted that 'Watching men play sports, however, is an entirely different matter. It is a comfortable sight for men and a thrilling one. When men watch athletics, they gaze upon the creation of male heroes, whose existence bolsters the general idea of male supremacy.'
61. NLI MS 23378, Shane Leslie Papers, Press Cutting: Seaghan Leslaigh, 'The Irish Kilt,' n.d.
62. Interestingly, Pearse's English father was born James Pierce, which he changed in 1892 to the more Irish 'Pearse.' S. Farrell-Moran (1994) *Patrick Pearse*, p. 22.

63. R. Dudley Edwards (2006) *Triumph of Failure*, pp. 92, 97.
64. See, for example, *A Gaelic League Catechism* (Gaelic League of London, n.d.) where it was claimed that 'Irish surnames have been largely altered to suit English pronunciation, and most of them have dropped the O and Mac. Irish Christian names, such as Patrick, Bridget, Conor, Brian, etc., are being replaced by English ones—John, William, Elizabeth, Henry, etc.' (All are names of English monarchs!)
65. E. Hobsbawm (1991) *Nations and Nationalism Since 1780: Programme, Myth, Reality* (Cambridge: Canto/Cambridge University Press) p. 39.
66. Quoted in G. Eyal (2006) *The Disenchantment of the Orient: Expertise in Arab Affairs and The Israeli State* (Stanford, CA: Stanford University Press) p. 140.
67. It is also worth remembering that in Judaism, the practice of adopting a Hebrew name has deep historical roots. As Rabbi Joshua Trachtenberg observed in 1939: 'Outstanding among those beliefs that are universally characteristic of the religion of superstition is the conviction that "a man's name is the essence of his being" (one Hebrew text says "a man's name is his person" and another, "his name is his soul"). This doctrine elevated the process of naming a child into one of major importance. The name carried with it all the associations it had accumulated in history, and stamped the character of its earlier owners on its new bearer, so that the choice of a name was fraught with grave responsibility.' J. Trachtenberg (1939) *Jewish Magic and Superstition: A Study in Folk Religion* (New York: Behrman's Jewish Book House) p. 78.
68. B. Harshav (1993) *Language in Time of Revolution* (Berkeley CA: University of California Press) p. 167; O. Almog (2000) *The Sabra: The Creation of the New Jew* (Berkeley, CA: University of California Press) pp. 91–95.
69. Quoted in M. Gluzman (2007) *HaGuf HaTzioni: Le'umiyut, Migdar u-Miniyut ba-Sifrut ha-Ivrit ha-Chadashah* [The Zionist Body: Nationalism, Gender and Sexuality in Modern Hebrew Literature] (Tel Aviv: Ha-Kibbutz Ha-Meuchad).
70. *Perlmutter* means 'Mother of Pearl' in Yiddish.
71. Often believed to be linked to the adjective *Yesharim*, meaning straight or upright, *Yeshurun* is a biblical Hebrew word that can mean a romanticised name for the Land of Israel, the People of Israel, or the Patriarch Jacob.
72. N. Seidman (1997) *A Marriage Made in Heaven: The Sexual Politics of Hebrew and Yiddish* (Berkeley CA: University of California Press) p. 118. Seidman also cautions, though, that there was an ambiguity to this. *Avot*, she suggests, is redolent of the Yiddish term *Tatelekh* (Little Fathers), a term for young boys which Yeshurun/Perlmutter's mother used with him as a child. Yeshurun thus consciously recognised that he had a

Hebrew adulthood whilst not forgetting his Yiddish childhood. See also A.X. Jacobs (2013) 'Hebrew Remembers Yiddish: Avot Yeshurun's Poetics of Translation' in L. Rabinovitch, S. Goren, eds. *Choosing Yiddish: New Frontiers of Language and Culture* (Detroit: Wayne State University Press) pp. 295–313.

73. Much as in the case of Irish, 'revival' is a problematic term to use for the establishment of modern Hebrew. Ríona Nic Congáil has observed that much of the practices of the Irish-language movement are clear cases of invented traditions, and has seen something quite telling in one Gaelic Leaguer's claims about the *'re*creation of a *new* Irish-Ireland' (Nic Congáil's emphases) R. Nic Congáil (2010) *Úna Ní Fhaircheallaigh agus an Fhís Útóipeach Ghaelach* [Úna Ní Fhaircheallaigh and the Gaelic Utopian Vision] (Dublin: Arlen House) pp. 88, 72. The linguist Ghil'ad Zuckermann has gone even further and claimed that it is untenable to speak of the majority language of the State of Israel as 'Hebrew'. Rather he calls it Israeli [*Yisra'elit*], a 'Semitic-European hybrid language' [*sefat-col'a'im Shemit-Eropit*] that contains significant Yiddish-influences within it and is only 120 years old. 'Af Achad Lo Medaber Ivrit' [Nobody at all speaks Hebrew]. *NRG-Ma'ariv*, 25 December 2008.

74. B. Harshav (1993) *Language*, p. 107. See also, the discussion of David Shimoni's (Shimonvits) 1920 short story 'Ben-Artsi', in G. Toury (1990) 'The Hebraization of Surnames as a Motive in Hebrew Literature.' *Actes du XVIe Congrès international des sciences onomastiques Québec, Université Laval, 16–22 août 1987* (Québec: Presses de l'Université Laval) pp. 545–555. In this story, the eponymous character has adopted a name that means Son of My Land, thus simultaneously suggesting masculinity, individualism, agrarian labour and rootedness in the national homeland.

75. A. Elon (1971) *The Israelis: Founders and Sons* (Middlesex: Penguin) p. 120. Quoted in N. Seidman (1997) *Marriage*, p. 117.

76. *The Irish Language and Irish Intermediate Education, III: Dr. Hyde's Evidence* (Gaelic League Pamphlets No. 13). For a copy of this pamphlet, see: NUIG, Stephen Barrett Papers, G3/1186. This pamphlet is undated, but the Vice-Regal Inquiry into Irish and Intermediate Education sat from 11 February to 23 January 1899. P.J. Mathews, (2003) *Revival*, p. 36.

77. NLI MS 18254, Papers of Douglas Hyde relating to the Gaelic League, Folder 5, Letter from Douglas Hyde to Unspecified Recipient, 3 April 1905. Emphases added. Hyde addresses his recipient as "Lord", perhaps suggesting that he was writing to the Postmaster General or Lord Lieutenant.

78. NLI MS 28909, Douglas Hyde Additional Papers, Folder 2, Letter from Neilí ní Bhriain to Douglas Hyde, 5 December 1905.
79. T. McMahon (2008) *Grand Opportunity*, pp. 114–115.
80. Ibid., p. 18.
81. The practice of name-changing was harshly derided in one of the more memorable scenes of Myles na gCopaleen's classic satire of romantic visions of rural, Irish-speaking life, *An Béal Bocht* [The Poor Mouth]. In a chapter devoted to the pretensions of urban Irish-language activists on a trip to the Gaeltacht, the narrator recalls that these visitors 'had another virtue that we had not had since losing our true Gaelicness.' [*Bhí bua eile acu nach raibh againne riamh anall ó chailleamar an fíor-Ghaelachas*]; they abandoned their original names, and instead adopted idealised names that projected a more perfected vision of themselves. One visitor, 'who was quiet, docile, innocent, gave himself the title "The Merry Billy-Goat", notwithstanding that he had never hit anyone and was not merry' [*a bhí ciúin ceansa neamhurchóideach, thug sé air féin "An Pocán Meidhreach," d'ainneoin nár phoc sé aoinne agus nach raibh sé meidhreach.*]. M. na gCopaleen (1999) *An Béal Bocht, nó An Milleánach: Drochscéal ar an Drochshaol Curtha in Eagar le Myles na gCopaleen* [The Poor Mouth, or The Millenarian: A Terrible Tale of the Terrible Life edited by Myles na gCopaleen] (Cork: Mercier Press) p. 44. There is a bilingual play on words here between *pócan* [A male goat] and *phoc* [past tense of *poc*, to hit a ball], calling to mind the English 'Fuck'. Thus, the visitor perhaps also gave himself the title "The Merry Billy- Goat", notwithstanding that he had never fucked anyone' This vulgarity, as well as problems of easy translation, are perhaps why it is omitted from the standard English version. F. O'Brien (1996) *The Poor Mouth: A Bad Story about the Hard Life* (Normal IL: Dalkey Archive Press/Illinois State University) p. 52.
82. In 1904, one Joseph Grimes wrote anxiously to Eoin MacNeill, seeking help 'to get the correct Irish form of my surname'. Grimes had previously thought that his name 'was English in in [*sic*] origin, but I place reliance on your opinion to the contrary, and am encouraged to investigate the matter.' UCDA, Eoin MacNeill Papers, LA1/J/309(4), Letter from Joseph Grimes to Eoin MacNeill, 18 March 1904. This file contains a number of letters from correspondents seeking MacNeill's advice about the 'correct' Irish version of their name. MacNeill's responses, however, which presumably include recommendations for how to do this, do not appear to have survived.
83. R. Nic Congáil (2010) *Ní Fhaircheallaigh*, pp. 35, 70. Nic Congáil, though, presents this transformation without comment, stating simply 'O'Farrelly (or Ní Fhaircheallaigh as she started to call herself at this

time) spent five summers altogether on Inis Meáin' [*Chaith O'Farrelly (nó Ní Fhaircheallaigh mar a thosaigh sí ag tabhairt uirthi féin timpeall an ama seo) cúig shamhradh i ndiadh a chéile ar Inis Meáin*].
84. Ibid., p. 29.
85. T. McMahon (2008) *Grand Opportunity*, p. 95.
86. In a poster encouraging recently arrived immigrants to register for evening classes in Hebrew, Hebrew was called 'A Bridge to Live in Israel' ['Ha-Ivrit: Gesher Le-Chaim Be-Yisrael'] CZA, Posters Collection, KRA/254, undated poster.
87. M. Gluzman (2007) *HaGuf HaTzioni*, p. 16.
88. *Ibid*, pp. 13, 18. The words used here by Gluzman for 'man' and 'masculinity' (*gever* and *gavriut*) can also mean hero and heroism; the return to masculinity is thus also a return to heroism. As noted earlier, this is a play on words regularly used in Zionist literature.
89. A. Saposnik (2008) *Becoming Hebrew: The Creation of a Jewish National Culture in Ottoman Palestine* (Oxford: Oxford University Press) pp. 189–190.
90. Y. Chaver (2004) *What Must Be Forgotten: The Survival of Yiddish in Zionist Palestine* (Syracuse, NY: Syracuse University Press) p. 10.
91. S. Gilman (1986) *Jewish Self-Hatred: Antisemitism and the Secret Language of the Jews* (Baltimore, MD: Johns Hopkins University Press) p. 15.
92. S. Gilman (1991) *The Jew's Body* (New York: Routledge) p. 3.
93. Y. Chaver (2004) *What Must be Forgotten*, p. 20.
94. CZA, Posters Collection, KRA/303, undated poster.
95. Genesis 11:1.
96. CZA, Posters Collection, KRA/462, undated poster.
97. CZA, Posters Collection, KRA/361, undated poster.
98. E. Hobsbawm (1991) *Nations*, p. 108.
99. Quoted in Y. Chaver (2004) 'What Must be Forgotten', pp. 20, 25, 104–105.
100. T. Segev (1986) *1949: The First Israelis* (New York: The Free Press) pp. 244–245.
101. Y. Ratosh (n.d.) *Ketav Al Ha-Noar Ha-Ivri* [Epistle to the Hebrew Youth]. See: National Library of Israel, S 441647.
102. D.N. Myers (1995) 'Re-Inventing the Jewish Past'. Yael Chaver goes much further than Myers, suggesting that 'Unique among national movements, Zionism might be said to have been conceived in language.' Y. Chaver (2004) *What Must be Forgotten*, p. 2. Aside from the fact that all nationalisms are, in some way, conceived in language (indeed, how can one have an ideology that is not carried out through language?), this is also problematic for the simple fact that many national movements are

conceived figuratively in language, as well as literally. Aside from Irish nationalism, there is also Greek nationalism, as Chaver herself discusses.

103. NLI MS 36124, Item 8. John L. Burke Papers, Brian O'Higgins (1932) *Gáir-Chatha Gaedheal* [Battle Cry of the Gael]: *Sinn Féin and Freedom* (Dublin: Sinn Féin Bureau). Consciously or not, O'Higgins was echoing Cathal Brugha's belief, expressed in Dàil Éireann in 1922, that English is 'The language of their masters.' Moreover, de Valera, in a speech in 1917, began by declaiming 'that he would be ashamed to address his audience in the language of the foreigner, but after a brief introduction in Irish he triumphed over his shame.' This seemed to be a common tactic, one that simultaneously accepted that nationalist audiences could not understand Irish, whilst also reiterating the language's symbolic value. Both quoted in M. Laffan (1999) *The Resurrection of Ireland: The Sinn Féin Party, 1916–1923* (Cambridge: Cambridge University Press) p. 237.

104. See, for instance, de Valera's 1936 speech in Enniscorthy in which he warned that 'we would be deficient as Irish people if we did not speak our ancestors' language' [*do bheadh easnamh orainn mar Eireannaigh mara mbeadh teanga ár sinnsear á labhairt againn*]. NLI LO P101, *National Discipline and Majority Rule: Three Speeches by Eamon de Valera*, Fianna Fail Pamphlet No. 1, 1936.

105. See, for example, NLI IR 32341 P16, Cathal Ó Sándair (n.d.) *Tusa agus an Ghaedhilg* [*You and the Irish Language*]: *A Word to the Worker*, Paimpléid Reatha Uimhir 12 [Pamphlet Series Number 12] (Dublin: Glún na Buaidhe); NLI IR 32341 P16, Máire Ní Dubhsláine. *A Chailíní, Èistigidh! nó* [*Oh Girls, Listen! or*] *For Girls Only* [Dublin: Craobh na hAiséirghe, 1942?]; R.M. Douglas (2009) *Architects of the Resurrection: Ailtirí na hAiséirghe and the fascist 'new order' in Ireland* (Manchester: Manchester University Press). To my knowledge, no academic study of *Glún na Buaidhe* has yet been produced.

106. Quoted in Lennon's 1967 documentary *The Rocky Road to Dublin*. And as one recent sophisticated analysis has discussed, in Northern Ireland after 1972 republican internees and prisoners regularly drew links between power and language. D. Mac Giolla Chríost (2012) *Jailtacht: The Irish Language, Symbolic Power and Political Violence in Northern Ireland, 1972–2008* (Cardiff: University of Wales Press/Gwasg Prifysgol Cymru) pp. 98–101. Mac Giolla Chríost notes that adopting Irish names was a central element of the 'performativity' of the *Jailtacht* [a melding of Jail and Gaeltacht] Irish-language prison argot.

107. : A. Saposnik (2008) *Becoming Hebrew, passim;* Y. Chaver (2004) *What Must be Forgotten*, pp. 93–129.

108. M. Ó Laoire (1999) *Athbheochan na hEabhraise: Ceacht don Ghaeilge?* [The Hebrew Revival: A Lesson for the Irish Language?] (Dublin: An Clóchomhar) p. 40.

109. Yosef Klausner, 'Ancient Hebrew and Modern Hebrew' (1929). Barbara Harshav, trans., in Harshav (1993) *Language*, pp. 208–215. In an interesting postscript to this, Klausner's grandson, Amos, would later recall attending a Menachem Begin rally with his grandfather. To the amusement of Klausner junior, Begin, who spoke a more literary Hebrew than the younger generations, gave a speech about the emerging arms race in the Middle East and announced that 'If I was prime minister now, everyone, everyone would be *arming* us, every-one' [*lu ani ha'iti rosh hamemshala ka'et, culam, culam hayu mezaynim otanu, cul-am*]. Unbeknownst to Begin and Joseph Klausner, though, the verb *le-zayen* [to arm] had, for a younger generation, taken on a new sexualised meaning. Thus, the leader of the Israeli opposition appeared to be saying 'If I was prime minister now, everyone, everyone would be fucking us.' Amos Klausner remembered this as a key moment in abandoning his family's right-wing politics. In adulthood he moved to a kibbutz, abandoned his surname in favour of a new name meaning 'strength' and as Amos Oz he would become one of the dominant figures in contemporary Hebrew fiction. A. Oz (2002) *Sipur al Ahava ve-Choshekh* [A Tale of Love and Darkness] (Jerusalem: Keter Publishing) pp. 479–481.
110. Ó Laoire (1999) *Athbheochan*, p. xiii.

CHAPTER 6

Fianna Fáil, Masculinity and the Economics of National Salvation

Economic forces make for the obliteration of the Irish nation.[1]

THE ECONOMIC HISTORY OF THE LAND OF ERIN

This chapter begins with a fairy tale. 'Once upon a time, there lived in Ireland a man who grew wheat.' At first, this man lived a harmonious and autarchic life, selling his crops to the other men of Ireland, who, in turn, 'made boots and clothes for him.' Unfortunately, though, this peaceful all-male economy was soon destroyed by the market forces of international capitalism. The land had become a dumping ground for cheaply made foreign goods and the men of Ireland 'ceased to get a livelihood out of the trade, and they grew thin', whilst international capitalists grew fat. Emigration increased, but this only exasperated the situation. Those who left found work overseas producing mountains of commodities, which were added to the cheap goods already flooding into Ireland, all to the benefit of the same foreign capitalists. Those men that had stayed in Ireland, because they lacked the money to leave, sank further into despair. Then, one day, there appeared a prophet in a top hat, a very thinly veiled W.T. Cosgrave, who promised to save the men of Ireland. Cosgrave, however, was not only a devious Free State politician, he was also a weak man. He was secretly in league with 'the Knights of the Compass and Square and Ring' (i.e., the Freemasons) and he grovelled before them. And they rejoiced at the terrible work he had done, opening up Ireland ever more to their rapacious capitalism. Meanwhile, the remaining men of Ireland, now languishing in a workhouse, were moving from despair to anger. They had begun to see the solution to their problems. If the men of Ireland could all be provided with their own means of production, they could make enough to provide for themselves and their families. As the wheat farmer observed, while looking at the rich farm land outside the workhouse, 'I could have grown good food for ye all, and it's not here I'd be to-night, with a shoemaker and his toes sticking out, and a tailor with no seat in his breeches, swilling watery German porridge and eating watery Russian bread.' Indeed, like all fairy tales, this one also had a happy ending: 'IRISHMEN! Let us end that story! Henceforth we will utilise the resources God gave us to provide a livelihood for our own people in our own land. VOTE FIANNA FÁIL.'[2]

Fig. 6.1 *The Economic History of the Land of Erin*, Fianna Fáil pamphlet, 1932
Source: NLI LO P111: Item 11

The Economic History of the Land of Erin, one of the most idiosyncratic pieces of electoral literature ever published by a mainstream Irish political party, was a four-page pamphlet produced by Fianna Fáil as part of their successful campaign for the 1932 general election. It was in the aftermath of that electoral victory that de Valera's party entered into the 'post-colonial wrangle'[3] known as the Economic War or, more formally, the Anglo-Irish Trade War. Between 1932 and 1938, the Irish government intentionally defaulted on annuities owed by Irish farmers to the British government under the terms of the 1891 and 1909 Land Acts. As per the 1922 Anglo-Irish Treaty, the new Free State had promised to continue handing over the annuities to the British government. By the 1930s, however, these repayments absorbed 3 % of Irish national income. In the summer of 1932, after the newly elected Fianna Fáil government refused to hand over the payments, the British government imposed tariffs of 20 % on Irish livestock imports. When this proved insufficient to raise the necessary £5 million, the tariffs were raised to 40 % on livestock imports and 30 % on other agricultural imports. The Irish government had already responded in kind, introducing tariffs on British imports into Ireland.[4]

The Economic History of the Land of Erin signposts some core concerns of that 'war', ideas that were at the heart of Fianna Fáil's policies during this period: the Irish nation had been emasculated by the economics of British rule. Irish men, rather than being able to provide for their wives and children and pursue a stable economic life rooted in the soil of their homeland, instead suffered a precarious existence subject to the whims of British market forces. Thus, it was only by securing their access to the land that Irish men could be made productive and whole again. Tellingly, women are absent from the narrative, hinted at only through the misery that men suffer when they cannot provide for their families.

These key elements of Fianna Fáil's idealised image of Irish agrarian masculinity had long had currency within Irish nationalism. Anne Kane, for instance, argues that many of the central agrarian tropes of Irish nationalism—anti-landlordism, an affinity for owning land over renting it, and the ideal of the 'Strong Farmer' (private property owners with large farms of 50 acres or more)—were invented during the intense rural agitation of the Land War (1878–1882). With more than a hint of de Valera, Kane places the Strong Farmer ideal within a broader nationalist vision: a 'rural society of small independent family-sized farms, which provided a modest livelihood of "frugal comfort" free from want and privation and preserved the family as the essential unit of production.'[5]

What Kane only hints at, though, is that Irish agrarianism was a highly gendered phenomenon. The Irish Strong Farmer was a man who was rooted in his soil; he was independent, self-reliant, productive and able to provide for his wife and family. As an owner-occupier, the Strong Farmer could avoid the emasculating indignity of paying rent for another man's land. As was discussed in Chap. 4, control over the space of Ireland regularly intersected with gender in the Irish nationalist imagination. In the 1920s and 1930s, Fianna Fáil's agrarian project drew on the same gendered discourse, but with an emphasis on the individual private-property owner rather than the macro-level of national sovereignty.

Cultivation in Both Meanings of the Word

Zionism also looked to agrarianism as a means of masculine and national salvation and the Zionist *Sabra* had some interesting similarities to the Strong Farmer ideal in Irish nationalism. Sabra or, in Hebrew, *Tzabar*, is a species of cactus and just like this cactus the Sabra would flourish in the Land of Israel. He would have a tough exterior but would be tender on the inside.[6] Zionists also used terms such as *Etrogim* [Citrons] and Gideons, or *ha-matmid he-hadash* [The New Matmid], 'the Jewish farmer who channels all the passion of a zealous yeshiva student, a *matmid*, into the study of agronomy.'[7] All these names, of course, carry connotations of strength, physical and national renewal, rootedness in the soil, and a return to a biblical past. The Sabra would be physically strong, with deep roots in the soil of the homeland, and was usually a resident of a socialist kibbutz. Zionist agrarianism sought to effect changes in Jews' bodies and psyche through agricultural work[8] and those who worked in agriculture were granted a position 'in the top ranks in the prestige hierarchy' even if this symbolism rarely translated into control of political power, which continued to be held by 'city-dwelling party bureaucrats and leaders.'[9]

The Sabra was a muscular man whose strength would be an asset to the re-born modern Jewish nation and was intended to allow both individual and nation to survive in the harsh modern world. The same was supposedly true of the Irish Strong Farmer. Kimmerling notes that the extreme hardship of Zionist agricultural work was transmogrified into 'an epic of heroism and sacrifice.' This hard work was consciously seen as contributing to both collective and individual identity. The heroic individual created by this was *adam ha-yishuv* [the man of the Jewish settlement], said to embody a sense of self-effacing responsibility to the collective.[10] Additionally, much as the image of the Irish Strong Farmer was constructed in opposition to narratives of economic humiliation under British rule, so also the Sabra was constructed in conscious opposition to images of Diasporic Jews. Agrarianism would birth a 'gentile Jew', liberated from the supposed weakness and economic parasitism of Diasporic Jews. Zionism stressed both the humiliation experienced by Jews in exile from their land, as well as a sense that Diasporic non-Zionist Jews were a national embarrassment, unlike the Sabras, proud Hebrews and new Jews of the Zionist kibbutzim.[11]

The kibbutzim, in marked contrast to Ireland's overtly male-centric agrarianism, often espoused a rhetoric of gender equality. This did not always carry over into quotidian practices, though, and the hardworking and agrarian 'new Jew' was conventionally depicted as a muscular man. Indeed, in 1921, Ada Fishman, a leading feminist Zionist, pointed out how women were often restricted to the private sphere of the home and thus barred from the national palliative of public work.[12] Reinforcing this, the Zionist agricultural hero was usually imagined as a virile and young male pioneer, setting off to a frontier settlement to make the land bloom (see Fig. 6.2[13]). Women, conversely, were often imagined within the Zionist project as 'the nation's womb', the ones who would create a Jewish demographic boom and thus a future Jewish majority over the Arab population.[14] It is this reality that leads David Biale to comment that 'As long as Zionism was seen as the creation of a virile New Man against the allegedly feminine impotence of exile, women would have difficulty finding a truly equal place.'[15] This was true in the world of agricultural work no less than elsewhere.

If the Strong Farmer ideal can be placed in a discursive context stretching back to the 1880s and the Land War, then the Sabra and the associated themes of exile and return, abnormality and a return to normality through physical labour and 'productivisation' can be traced back even further. The *Haskalah*, the European Jewish Enlightenment, which began in German lands in the late eighteenth century before radiating out into Eastern Europe in subsequent decades, had an enormous influence on Zionism. The Haskalah proposed the 'productivisation' of the Jews, by which it meant moving Jews from the 'useless' occupations of commerce and moneylending to trades and agriculture. Productivisation put a large emphasis on the social and moral benefits of labour, on state intervention into the economy, and it ultimately became 'the stock-in-trade of Zionists'.[16] Derek Penslar, in his analyses of Zionist productivisation, highlights the obvious influence of the *Haskalah*. Penslar, though, also places it in a broader

Fig. 6.2 *To The Galilee!*, Poster for the Jewish National Fund (JNF), 1938
Source: CZA KRA/13

context of European social reform, fear of the lower classes and a supposedly disinterested sympathy for non-white peoples: 'Jews and savages were to undergo a process of "cultivation" in both meanings of the word: cultivation of the soil, producing, in time, a cultivated, civilized being.'[17]

Penslar notes the strong influence here of modernist theories of social engineering and political economy.[18] Despite the fact that the social relations favoured (socialist kibbutzim and capitalist private property) were drastically different, it is still the case that Zionists and Irish nationalists shared a view that agriculture was a way to create a more stable image of national masculinity. And this points to the strong influence of physiocratic and Enlightenment thinking about agriculture as the most stable form of economic activity.[19]

Yet, the comparison of the Sabra and the Strong Farmer can only go so far. One recent call for an 'economic turn' in Jewish history has noted that 'the general image of the Jew is overloaded with tropes and motifs taken from the sphere of economics.'[20] Indeed, anti-Jewish stereotypes were often built on accusations of involvement in non-productive labour or, more infamously, Shylock-esque Jewish usury.[21] Whether due to internalised self-hatred or a conscious anti-Diasporic strategy, the Zionist creation of an agrarian ideal appeared to accept these stereotypes. The Sabra would be a physical refutation of economic antisemitism.[22] This points to some of the most important differences between Zionist agrarianism and its Irish nationalist equivalent. Indeed, contrasting the divergent approaches to agrarianism highlights the very limits of the comparative model explored throughout this book. Where Zionist agrarianism was a response to a set of antisemitic representations, Irish nationalism instead reified the material realities of a peripheral agrarian economy. The Sabra ideal was an attempt to create a new and more honourable economics whereas the Strong Farmer was an attempt to make an already existing reality more humane; as Fig. 6.2 shows, the Sabra looked to the future; the Strong Farmer was a redeemed link in a chain stretching back into the past. This helps to explain two major differences between the Sabra and the Strong Farmer.

First, private property did not feature as much in Zionist thinking. Zionists were more concerned with issues of 'national ownership' and mass rootedness. As Gershon Shafir has pointed out, the ostensible 'socialism' of the kibbutz movement should be seen as a product of Palestinian realities rather than more abstract utopian ideologies. Since the goal of Zionism was Jewish control over as much of Palestine as possible, the kibbutz served as a model for a collective Jewish control over the land in the face of Palestinian Arab resistance.[23] The Strong Farmer was more concerned with individual concerns, regaining 'his' land, stolen from 'him' by British interlopers.

Second, the muscular Sabra was always more overtly homoerotic than the Strong Farmer.²⁴ The Strong Farmer was a family man, modest and presumably Catholic, but the Zionist settler, by definition, had to be young and unmarried since 'he' could not safely bring a young family to a frontier farm. He needed to be imagined as young, virile and strong enough to work the land. The Sabra was also imagined as being literally reborn, again connoting youth, unlike the Strong Farmer who was imagined as taking back a land that was rightfully his so as to settle his family there. The Sabra was a new and erotically charged ideal that Jews should aspire to (feel attracted to?) whereas the Strong Farmer was more a means of legitimising an already existing or slowly emerging reality on the periphery of British capitalism.

THE HUMILIATING RULE OF CUMANN NA NGAEDHEAL

When Fianna Fáil was founded in 1926, a prevalent desire for a more stable and proud image of Irish agrarian manhood still existed. A postwar slump, as well as poor weather conditions, had led to decreased agricultural prices.²⁵ Cumann na nGaedheal, in power since the Civil War, had remained staunchly committed to the interests of the large grazier ranch-farmers, who had strong reasons for desiring that Ireland remain an agricultural appendage of the British economy. Agriculture employed over half the Free State's workforce, and accounted for 86 % of exports.²⁶ Of these exports, 98 % went to Great Britain and Northern Ireland (a total of £51.8 million) and live cattle exports made up over a third of this figure. The 25,000 grazier farmers were thus one of the dominant forces in 1920s Ireland and Cumann na nGaedheal's economic policies were tailored to fit their concerns.²⁷ This, though, was politically dangerous. Downward trends in global economics were such that the '1920s were not the most opportune decade for a newly independent nation'²⁸ and the 'overdependency on one economic sector and indeed one class of farmer to pull the Irish economy along in its train also left Cumann na nGaedheal extremely vulnerable to an economic downturn.'²⁹

Even prior to the global crash of 1929, Cumann na nGaedheal's economic policies were undermining the party's popularity: 'it must be remembered that the abandonment of the economic goals of the national revolution struck hard at an important source of Cumann na nGaedheal's legitimacy.'³⁰ Wages fell precipitously in the 1920s for farm labourers and urban workers, whilst the Cumann na nGaedheal government reduced expenditure on unemployment benefits, pensions, national health insurance, and public works programmes. Emigration reached a 40-year high in 1929. Trade unions were also systematically undermined, and Labour's Thomas Johnson accused the government of working to weaken the labour movement and ban strikes. This was no idle accusation; in 1923 the Free State government issued a circular to the Garda Síochána ordering them to 'get tough with unions'.[31] All this would only increase after 1929.[32] Poverty was widespread before the Wall Street Crash and a number of infamous cases of death through starvation were only the most visible manifestations of something far larger. 'It was increasingly clear that Cumann na nGaedheal was protecting the financial self-interests of the class it represented, while the rest of the nation could, quite literally, starve.'[33]

The rank and file of Cumann na nGaedheal, more in tune with Irish social realities, did seek to change party policy accordingly. The October 1924 'Statement of Views' of the party's Standing Committee highlighted the continued popularity of autarchic, Sinn Féin-style economics. The party leadership was reminded that the 'brief of Cumann na nGaedheal is for the common people of Ireland, and what the common people want under the Free State is to abolish ascendancy, to undo the Conquest and resume the course of their national life *as masters in their own land.*' The document admitted, however, that the party members' 'influence on Government policy and its power to effect patronage has been negligible if not nil.'[34] When the Minister for Post and Telegraphs, J.J. Walsh, resigned from Cumann na nGaedheal in protest against the party's refusal to implement protectionist tariffs he alleged that the party 'has gone bodily over to the most reactionary elements of the state who will henceforth control its policies. Followers of Arthur Griffith's economic teaching will now be forced to subordinate their life-long conviction to the dictates of people whose only concern appears to be the welfare of England'.[35] These were exactly the kinds of economic sentiments to which Fianna Fáil would soon appeal. The Minister for Local Government, Ernest Blythe, however, felt grassroots criticism reflected 'the state of mind which is responsible for a good deal of harm in this country' and was due to members joining in the 'ignorant and irresponsible chorus' of the rest of the country.[36] Infamously, Patrick McGilligan confessed that 'people may have to die in this country and may have to die through starvation' if it meant his government could balance its budget.[37]

Fianna Fáil's economic policy adeptly tapped into this growing sense of disillusionment with a party increasingly seen as arrogant, insensitive and out of touch with the 'plain people'. Shortly after being elected, de Valera declared in the Dáil that Irish workers 'should not merely be wage slaves or simply spending their lives to make money for somebody or other.' In contrast to this 'wage slavery' there was 'a vague suggestion that one day they might be working for themselves, possibly in rural Ireland, where the sturdy self-sufficient farmer was held up as the ideal.'[38] In 1930, Seán Lemass, one of Fianna Fáil's leading economic voices, said his politics were concerned with 'the plain, good, honest-to-God working men whose interests were neglected' by Cumann na nGaedheal.[39] Acquiring land had been, since the 1880s, the only guaranteed access to social status in rural Ireland and had overtly masculinist overtones.[40] While Cumann na nGaedheal acted as the party of the already established grazier farmers, Fianna Fáil positioned itself as 'the vehicle for the economic and social advancement of the "small man" ', much as Sinn Féin's economic policy during the War of Independence had 'offered the small man the possibility of becoming a slightly bigger man if only he would bide his time, and fall in behind the national independence struggle.'[41] The stage had been set for the return of a comforting Strong Farmer ideology.

Fianna Fáil's Agrarian Masculinity

The suggestion that Fianna Fáil would restore economic dignity to the 'men of no property'[42] was, in fact, a perennial feature of the party's propaganda in the 1920s and 1930s. Fianna Fáil's first constitution defined the party's aims, *inter alia*, as 'To make the resources and wealth of Ireland subservient to the needs and welfare of all the people of Ireland'; 'To make Ireland, as far as possible, economically self-contained and self-sufficing'; 'To establish as many families as practicable on the land'; 'By suitable distribution of power to promote the ruralisation of essential industries as opposed to their concentration in cities.'[43] At Fianna Fáil's first public meeting, at the La Scala Theatre,[44] Dublin, on 16 May 1926, de Valera himself declared 'I have said it before, and I repeat here, and I believe that most *right-thinking men* will agree with me, that it is a primary duty for any government in any civilised country to see that men and women will not starve, and that little children will not starve, through opportunity for useful work being denied *the bread-winner*.'[45] Already at their founding, productive family men, along with their wives and children, held a prominent place in the party's rhetoric. The same year, at the party's first Árd Fheis, Frank Aiken, recently decamped from the IRA, issued a circular to delegates defining the party's goals. Aiken talked of 'using of every honourable political and cultural weapon which will bring us forward one inch on the right road to the achievement of a strong and self-reliant Gaelic Independent Republic.' He also claimed that '80 per cent. of the people of Ireland are at heart Republican and hate, as much as any member of Sinn Fein, to see us losing our national identity, our language, our self-respect, our riches, and our young men and women.' He claimed people had been fooled by the Treaty's 'false promises' that 'Ireland would become prosperous'. Instead, since Cumann na nGaedheal came to power 'there has been a steady rapid growth of everything that is abhorrent to *every decent Irishman*'.[46]

In 1927, as Fianna Fáil prepared for their first general election, these ideas took centre stage. The party claimed 'The Farmer's Welfare is the Nation's Welfare. The Nation's Welfare is the Farmer's Welfare.'[47] One electoral pamphlet described Cumann na nGaedheal's rule as 'Five Years of Poverty and Panic' and asked 'Workers, Fathers of Unemployed Sons and Daughters, which will you choose ... The Party of Unemployment ... or, The Party of Work.'[48] A handbill claimed that de Valera had saved Ireland from the 'terrible menace' of conscription in 1918 but 'the Irish People are again faced by a terrible Menace: Bankruptcy and Starvation. They are looking to Eamon de Valera to save them. And he will.' Voters were reminded that the Fianna Fáil candidates had 'One Allegiance Only!'[49] Agricultural labour was given a privileged status; it was understood to be the preserve of men, and these masculine tropes were mixed with ideals of national loyalty and redemption.

These ideas, of course, had been central tropes in Sinn Féin's economic propaganda in the years between the Easter Rising and the Civil War.[50] When de Valera was first elected to public office, in the East Clare by-election of 1917, one of his pieces of electoral literature depicted him as a virile young farmer, just waiting for a chance to replace the worn-out old men of the Irish Parliamentary Party: 'The Irish Party is old and worn out, and the Electors must put in new men to do Ireland's work, as the farmer must hire new men to do his ... As times change new methods are required to meet them; the farmers avail of new kinds of machinery to harvest their crops; let them also avail of new men to save Ireland's national harvest. The Irish Party is out of date—Sinn Fein is the new implement to your hands.' The leaflet ended with the claim that 'The Tithes were Beaten IN IRELAND and Landlordism was Beaten IN IRELAND when you

"KEPT A FIRM GRIP ON YOUR HOMESTEADS."'[51] In other words, the very act of being a strong self-reliant (male) farmer, property-owning and rooted in the soil, was a nationalist act benefiting the whole community. Sinn Féin claimed, in 1917, that their economic ideas were 'the only virile, healthy policy before the country at the present time; the only policy that your enemies are powerless to subvert for their own ends.'[52] As Frank Aiken presented it in 1926, 'The policy I have in mind is simply a development of the old 1917–1921 policy of Sinn Féin self-reliance brought up to date in order to meet the changed conditions.'[53] That Fianna Fáil could present themselves as heirs to this tradition of gendered economic salvation only added to their legitimacy.

More worryingly, from the point of view of Fianna Fáil, these ideas were also being appropriated by socialist republicans like Peadar O'Donnell and pushed in far more radical directions. A 'catechism' produced by O'Donnell's supporters in East Galway laid out some of their claims:

> How did England establish a claim to the land of Ireland? By robbery.
> What is rent? Rent is a tribute of slavery enforced by the arms of the robber-landlord.
> What is a landlord? A landlord is a descendant of a land robber.
> Who pays rents to landlords? Only slaves.[54]

Writing in the IRA's *An Phoblacht* [The Republic] in the summer of 1926, O'Donnell spoke of the need for 'defence of peasant farmers' in opposition to annuities, which were termed 'this robbery of children to meet the call of British interests',[55] thus suggesting that the annuities were an invasion not just of the land but also of the family home. These were ideas with obvious similarities to those of the emergent Fianna Fáil. The following year, though, O'Donnell nailed his ideological colours more firmly to the mast. National economic salvation should be achieved 'not by appeasing hunger by crusts of bread, nor relieving cold by doled out cast-off clothing, but by the organizing of the people to seize power to make bread and clothing available, according as the labour of the nation and our resources can afford them. That, then is our task—to seize power, so that the people may be worthy of themselves.'[56]

For O'Donnell, opposition to the annuities was to be part of a much broader, much more radical restructuring of Irish property relations, albeit one still couched in the same language of agrarianism and the reversal of national economic humiliation.[57] What O'Donnell sought to achieve was clearly expressed in his pamphlet, *For or Against the Ranchers?*, published in the early years of the Economic War: 'The youth of the small farmer areas must get into the fray quickly. All that they have a right to demand of life this country can give them ... Take over the ranches; they are yours. Workers and Working Farmers—Unite! Long live the Workers' and Working Farmers' Republic!'[58] O'Donnell's vigorous campaign against annuities was certainly attracting enough attention by the late 1920s for his public appearances to be monitored by the Garda Síochána.[59] The superficial similarities between Fianna Fáil and Peadar O'Donnell would feed into a convenient set of accusations used by Cumann na nGaedheal.

Masculinity and the Cumann na nGaedheal Red Scare

Fianna Fáil first came to power in 1932, having won 72 seats against Cumann na nGaedheal's 57 in that year's general election, enough to allow them to install a minority government with the external support of Labour's seven seats. Irish politics in this period, as has been widely discussed, was characterised by a large-scale red scare.[60] Cumann na nGaedheal propaganda, out of a mix of genuine fears and cynical party politics, portrayed de Valera and his new party as secret communists who would bring chaos in their wake. What has been less discussed is how this fear of communism was linked to Irish male identity; Fianna Fáil's erstwhile Bolshevism was supposedly a threat to men's right to own property and, thus, a threat to social order and a man's ability to provide for his family.[61]

'Farmers Keep a Firm Grip of Your Homesteads', warned one Cumann na nGaedheal advertisement, which appeared, appropriately, in the local paper of de Valera's constituency. The (presumably male) farmers were warned not to 'endanger your claim to the ownership of your land' by being 'fooled' by Fianna Fáil's policies regarding the land annuities. Even if the annuities were a burdensome yoke, Cumann na nGaedheal argued that 'every payment you make brings nearer the day when the land will be absolutely your own.' Conversely, 'Fianna Fail believes that everybody else in the country has as good a right to YOUR land—the land for which your fathers and grandfathers have paid by the toil of years—as you have' and if 'you put Fianna Fail in power, you are putting in men who hold that YOUR land belongs fundamentally to other people.' Fianna Fáil were accused of being 'land-grabbers' and the advertisement ends by asserting 'You beat the grabbers before. Beat them again by voting for Cumann na nGaedheal.'[62] Privately held land was presented as part of Irish men's patrimony, the ownership of which linked men back to their forefathers. And the accusation of 'land-grabbers' drew on strongly felt nationalist traditions that linked male identity to independent land-ownership, and linked landlords, rent and the loss of land to both personal and national emasculation.

Another piece of Cumann na nGaedheal propaganda from 1932 accused de Valera of being 'Un-Irish and Un-Catholic' and stated that 'his theory of state ownership of the Land is opposed to Catholic teaching.' Voters were thus warned to 'Beware! least [*sic*, lest?] by putting Fianna Fáil into power you enslave yourselves.' The pamphlet then gave details of what a Fianna Fáil-run Ireland might look like: the farmers would find themselves in 'an economic position worse than existed when the power of landlordism was at its height' and those not forced into bankruptcy would subsist on a diet of 'Indian meal porridge all year and every year'.[63] Therefore, Fianna Fáil would undo the manly independence of Irish farmers and return Irish society to both the indignity of tenant-farming and the unappetising misery of the food handed out as relief during the Famine. *Slavery*, as discussed in earlier chapters, was a charged accusation in Irish nationalist thought, often constructed in opposition to an ideal of proudly masculine national *freedom*. As used in the 1930s, it served to suggest that Fianna Fáil's economics would return Ireland to a state of enervating national humiliation. G.C. Bennett, Cumann na nGaedheal TD for Limerick, was aghast that Fianna Fáil would 'undo all that our forefathers fought for and won' and warned that 'Surely an Irish government is not going to undo the great work that was accomplished ... to make the position of the Irish farmers secure in *his* [*sic*] homestead.'[64]

Fianna Fáil were regularly accused of pursuing an anarchic and alien ideological programme. As early as the Civil War, Kevin O'Higgins, emerging as a dominant Treatyite voice, attacked de Valera as a practitioner of 'Mexican Politics', calling to mind not only the social strife then underway in that country but also de Valera's family background. The anti-Treatyites were 'a motley coalition which contains within itself elements so conflicting that it can only be held together on a destructive programme'.[65] By labelling them as 'Mexicans' O'Higgins could dismiss republicans' ideology as alien to the Irish social, economic and gender order. An obvious way to score political points from de Valera's Hispanic origins, this would occur with regularity in condemnations of Fianna Fáil. At a Fine Gael meeting in August 1934, Cosgrave claimed an end to law and order was being 'brought about by a son of Mexico.'[66] During the 1932 general election, voters were warned to 'Remember Spain and Mexico. Take no risks.' Instead, 'Vote Cumann na nGaedheal which has maintained Catholic Principles, given the country peace and order, outlawed armed revolt and communism'.[67] A Cumann na nGaedheal poster from the same election suggested that Fianna Fáil was a cover for the IRA and showed an ominous and masked gunman, with his weapons 'from Russia', 'made in Spain' and of 'Mexican Brand'.[68] And the famous 1932 *We Want No 'Reds' Here*! poster garishly depicted the Irish tricolour being smothered under the solid red of a communist flag.[69]

The small number of foreign investors Fianna Fáil did attract to Ireland in the 1930s were attacked by Richard Mulcahy, who asked 'How many factories have been opened with the names of Matz, Gaw, Lucks, Galette, Wigglesworth, Woodington.' Similarly, Patrick McGilligan harshly criticised a new razor blade factory because, of the two investors, 'one is a gentleman who came to this country from Palestine via Great Britain and the other is a man who came from Belfast via Tanderagee' (a village between Belfast and the border with the Free State). This situation, he claimed, was partly attributable to Lemass' supposed Huguenot background, in contrast to that of McGilligan who presented himself as 'a native Irishman without any tinge of foreign blood in me at all.'[70] Thus, McGilligan and Mulcahy blended a racialised ideal of Irish masculinity with antisemitism, anti-Protestant sectarianism, and anti-English resentment.

Cumann na nGaedheal's successors would have recourse to much the same rhetoric. A 1933 Fine Gael handbill, for instance, claimed the new party had been founded to remedy the fact that '[t]housands of Irish boys and girls are to-day leaving their schools to begin their working lives without any prospect of employment.' Echoing the idea that Fianna Fáil were an alien influence, the handbill claimed 'It is not an Irish Policy nor one conceived by Irish Minds which to-day … Creates more unemployment day by day at the port of Dublin, by killing our foreign markets; Ruins the farming industry; Stifles the growth of Irish industrial development, by destroying the people's purchasing power; Reduces the people to living on relief.' Fine Gael's proposed solution was to 'awaken a spirit of self-reliance, dignity and discipline in the rising generation and inculcate through Young Ireland [Fine Gael's youth wing] the ideal of voluntary public service as an essential part of citizenship'.[71] Thus, in opposition to the dangerous cosmopolitanism of Fianna Fáil, Fine Gael offered a return to order and national self-reliance.

Cosgrave claimed in the same year that if Fine Gael won the 1933 general election, 'I will immediately end the economic war. I will thus re-open their markets to farmers, and re-establish their capacity to pay their way' and, in a less than oblique accusation about Fianna Fáil's attitudes to a man's property rights, the 'remission of Land Annuity payments [under a Fine Gael government] will be accompanied by an absolute guarantee of the farmer's title to *his* land.'[72] Late in the Economic War, a Fine Gael handbill claimed that Irish men 'are poorer because, under this Government prices have risen' and compared the spending of the 'wives of two working men' on either side of the border, supposedly demonstrating that the 'Northern Ireland workingman's wages buy more than yours.'[73] Voting Fine Gael would thus make working men more capable of providing for their wives and would solidify their power in the home.

In opposition to the image of Fianna Fáil as duplicitous, deracinated and dangerous, Cumann na nGaedheal and Fine Gael portrayed themselves as paragons of order. Anti-communism was a central part of this. When this failed to stop Fianna Fáil in 1932, they changed tack. Putting a new emphasis on W.T. Cosgrave's positive masculine virtues, Cumann na nGaedheal foregrounded their leader's honesty, straightforwardness, and candour. Refusing to pay the annuities was presented as a dishonest and dishonourable act that sullied the name of Ireland internationally.[74] Cosgrave, an honest man and an honest Irish leader, was the trope that replaced anti-communism in their propaganda: 'COSGRAVE WILL END THE [Economic] WAR. COSGRAVE will give you peace with honour and without more sacrifice. COSGRAVE is the only man in Ireland who can save Ireland and save you … A win for Cosgrave is a win for you.' By claiming that he would be the one to end the Economic War and end the dastardly and dishonest politics of Fianna Fáil, 'Cosgrave's reelection was thus presented as a necessary step in the restoration of the nation's honour.'[75]

These ideas and accusations would also be regularly used by the more fascist elements orbiting Fine Gael. The Army Comrades Association, the first incarnation of the Blueshirts, saw communism 'as a creeping danger, which, if permitted to percolate through the social fabric, cannot but prove itself an enemy of religion and ordered society. Particularly it may become an unsuspected danger to the farming population and other property owners, small as well as large.'[76] Speaking at the graveside of a recently deceased Blueshirt in Cork in the summer of 1934, Eoin O'Duffy claimed farmers in Ireland, 'known throughout the ages for their honesty', were now in as bad a position as they had been during the Famine, despite Ireland's agricultural land being 'as fertile as ever'. Evoking the gendered cultural memory of the Land War, he told of how, under Fianna Fáil, 'the bailiffs were turned loose on our people. Cattle and furniture were seized, our people were put into gaol illegally, and bludgeons and batons were used against them. The farmers had to bear all that, and they had to face black ruin at the same time. Their security of tenure of their homes was gone.'[77] Fianna Fáil had damaged men's status at the head of their households and de Valera 'does not understand the people of this country because he is a half-breed.'[78] Like his fellow colleagues in Fine Gael, O'Duffy tapped long-standing anxieties about racial indeterminacy, masculinity, and Irish national humiliation.

The Economic War and the Restoration of National Dignity

Cutting across the supposed Civil War divides of Irish politics, Fianna Fáil would also draw heavily, and perhaps more adeptly, from the same masculinist language. As with Cumann na nGaedheal, Fine Gael and the Blueshirts, de Valera's party would also draw on the diffuse discursive field of Irish nationalism and its tropes of 'slavery', 'humiliation', 'freedom' and 'redemption', as well as the idealisation of male private-property-ownership. As the previous chapters have shown, these tropes expressed deeply gendered ideals of national and masculine revival. Fianna Fáil's political strategies, as Richard Dunphy argues, 'combined an element of politically inspired economic populism with a successful moral and ideological offensive'.[79] Gender, the ideal of the Strong Farmer, and the degree to which Fianna Fáil skilfully convinced Irish men that they could reverse their humiliation were all central planks in those strategies. Not least is the fact that in their first five years in power Fianna Fáil distributed 353,000 acres of agricultural land amongst 25,802 (predominantly male) allottees.[80]

Even prior to coming to power, Fianna Fáil had claimed that not paying the annuities would save £3 million and 'This saving alone would put the FARMERS OF IRELAND on their feet again instead of into the Workhouse.'[81] Oscar Traynor, a prominent member of Fianna Fáil in Dublin, felt that it was in fact Cumann na nGaedheal who were espousing foreign ideology: they 'have not hesitated to sacrifice the economic interests of our people to a blind adherence to the theory of so-called Free Trade', their economic philosophy had destroyed Ireland and they 'have fairly earned the title of Imperialists'. Indeed, 'Poverty and decay have been the fruits of British rule whether it operated direct from London or through a Cumann na nGaedheal Government here.' Only 'a native Government with the national outlook of Fianna Fáil' could redeem Ireland.[82] Cumann na nGaedheal's rule had been 'The Greatest Failure in Irish History' and voters were urged to ask:

> Is the country better or worse because they have ruled? Is our wealth greater? Has production increased? Has the standard of living of our people been raised? Or is it that industries which were flourishing in 1922 have since disappeared; that farmers who could then pay their way are now facing bankruptcy; that thousands are unemployed; that poverty and destitution are widespread with a consequent heavy drain on public funds for the relief of distress. Each individual voter must ask *himself* these questions *and satisfy himself* as to the correctness of *his* conclusions before making up *his* mind how *he* will vote at the General Election.'[83]

As the choice of language makes clear, Fianna Fáil imagined the Irish electorate as a male-only field.

A poster from the 1932 election contrasted the harsh misery of unemployed men with the colossal number of presumably cheap imports flooding the country. A vote for Fianna Fáil it was brashly claimed, would 'End Unemployment' and so relieve men's despair.[84] Cumann na nGaedheal supporters had voted for prosperity but instead got an 'Agreement to pay an Annual Tribute of Over £5,000,000'.[85] Instead of supporting those who 'creep over to England and in all humility, kneel down and beg for the rich man's crumbs' voters should vote for a party that will support local industry and thus 'The earnings of every person on the land can be increased by £16 a year'.[86] Fianna Fáil thus positioned themselves as real men, heroic and dignified, in opposition to spineless and servile men like W.T. Cosgrave. During the same election campaign, at an outdoor meeting in Ennis, Thomas O'Donnell, a local supporter of de Valera, said Cumann na nGaedheal had made 'beggars' of the Irish people, a statement with which the audience strongly agreed. O'Donnell also claimed that ten years of Cumann na nGaedheal rule had been the worst time economically since the Famine.[87] In 1933, after Fianna Fáil had begun to refuse to pay the annuities, the newly formed Fine Gael came out strongly against this policy.

Thus, a Fianna Fáil poster from that year's general election made much political capital out of the accusation that Fine Gael were 'defeatists', weak-willed and foolish puppets of the British government.[88]

In April of 1932, as the Fianna Fáil government began to publicly contemplate retaining the annuities, the British government reminded their Dublin counterparts that, in their view, Ireland was legally bound to repay them. De Valera, clearly annoyed by this, felt the need to inform J.H. Thomas, the British Secretary of State for Dominion Affairs, that the 'suggestion in your despatch that the Government of the Irish Free State contemplates acting dishonourably cannot in justice be let pass.' De Valera informed him that the 'pages of the history of the relations between Great Britain and Ireland are indeed stained by many breaches of faith, but I must remind you the guilty party has not been Ireland'.[89] When Britain imposed retaliatory tariffs on Irish imports, Thomas Johnson, leader of a Labour Party then in loose alliance with Fianna Fáil, wrote an open letter to J.H. Thomas. Ireland was potentially a 'weak nation', Johnson said, and he went on to accuse Thomas of 'showing the masses of Irish nationalists that political self-government means nothing real if Ireland's economic life remains at the mercy of British fiscal policy'. He felt that Thomas needed to remember that 'The terrible story of the famine years of 1846–7–8 is ingrained in the minds of the Irish people. Amongst the bitter memories left by the famine, the present generation feels most keenly the knowledge that, whilst thousands of their grand and great grand parents [*sic*] lay on the roadsides or in their hovels to die literally of starvation, ship load after load of corn was being shipped to England in order to pay rent to landlords.' Both Fianna Fáil and the Irish Labour Party, Johnson pronounced, were united by their opposition to 'the pagan social order which now exists'. Both parties sought 'to ensure that the wealth producing powers and resources within the country shall, in the first instance, be used to provide the people with a little more than the starvation diet and indecent living standards which one-third of our people are forced to endure'.[90] Such ideas of national economic humiliation were central to the Economic War:

> Apart from being a financial burden, the payment of the annuities was heavy with political implications. There was a widespread feeling that the payment of money to the UK Government for land which was Irish in the first place was both profoundly unjust and an insult to national pride. Indeed, the real significance of the annuities issue is probably political rather than economic; the mythology surrounding the question touched upon the farmer's

> ideological perception of *himself* as the descendant of the cruelly expropriated, restored to *his* rightful inheritance.[91]

And it was this perception that the annuities were an insult to national (male) pride which attracted support far beyond the small farmer community.

In an article explaining Ireland's stance in the Economic War to an American readership, Seán T. O'Kelly, Minister for Local Government, claimed that in 1801 Ireland had entered the Union with Britain 'comparatively rich' but 'emerged poor'. This end result, he argued, was due to the landlord system, where the agents of absentee landlords 'let the land to the farmers usually at such exorbitant rents that the latter rarely succeeded in wresting from the soil anything more than a most miserable subsistence for themselves and their families.' Since 1922, Ireland had enjoyed only 'a strictly limited freedom' and so he presented the Economic War as an expression of national freedom as well as an amelioration of past economic humiliations.[92] Fianna Fáil were thus implementing an economics of masculine revival. That same year, speaking at a Commonwealth Conference partly dedicated to ending the Economic War, O'Kelly told the other delegates that 'Our aim is the aim of all organised States, namely, to provide such economic conditions in our country as will allow the greatest number of our people to live there in peace and comfort.' Interfering with these aims was 'the anomaly of one-sided development which has caused a country relatively rich in natural resources to be the one country in Europe whose population has steadily decreased for almost a century.' A different version of the speech, presumably an earlier draft, stated: 'our economic position is in many respects unlike that of the other States here represented. Our economic development has hardly begun. We are still, and shall be for some considerable time to come, engaged in the task of building up the elements of an economic life suitable to the conditions of our people.'[93]

Fianna Fáil's Minister for Finance, Seán MacEntee, had similar views. Prior to his party's first electoral victory, he had dismissed the annuities as being nothing but 'a free gift [to Britain] of £3,000,000 a year'; to continue to bestow such a gift 'means continued emigration for our young people. It means unemployment and impoverishment for those who remain at home.' Were it not paid, the money could instead be devoted to native agricultural development. MacEntee also believed that there was 'no embezzlement in retaining what is legally and morally one's own.' Because

Britain had destroyed Irish industry and stolen land to give as reward to soldiers, he felt that it was 'fantastic to maintain that Ireland is under a moral obligation to recoup England for the wages of her Cromwellian and Williamite soldiers.'[94] After the 1932 election MacEntee would state that the annuities 'are nothing more or less than the old rents imposed by landlords and their predecessors'. He claimed that under British rule 'Good lands were turned into cattle ranches and the ancient owners were driven into the bogs and mountains' and 'the original occupiers of the soil were reduced to a position of servitude the most degraded ever imposed on a helpless people.' MacEntee also warned against any suggestions that politicians like the British Dominions Secretary had any feelings of goodwill or affection toward Ireland: 'The love they feel is the love that a weasel has for a rabbit when he holds it by the throat and sucks its blood.' English leaders' true feelings could actually be found, he suggested, in 'the furious indignation expressed when Irish leaders stopped the tribute.'[95]

Interestingly, despite the view that they were the same as landlords' rents,[96] the Fianna Fáil government continued to collect the annuities from farmers, even if they were not subsequently handed over to the British state. An internal government memorandum from late 1932 identified various proposals for what to do with the Land Annuities and also discussed why the annuities could not be completely remitted:

> The introduction of such legislation will immediately raise in an acute form the problem of the landless men. It will give point in purpose to the agitation which is being carried on by Peadar O'Donnell's Organisation for the non-payment of Annuities. It is possible that behind the ostensible objective of this Organisation there may be a further purpose, that of creating that insecurity of title which would justify a demand for the ultimate appropriation of all land by the State. In the position which would be created by the introduction of the legislation referred to, every labourer would be demanding his five or ten acres, and the question of land distribution would certainly arise in a revolutionary form.[97]

Drawing on the work of the Greek Marxist Nicos Poulantzas, Richard Dunphy has defined Fianna Fáil's economics as the 'status quo anti-capitalism' common to the *petite bourgeoisie*.[98] The danger with O'Donnell was that he might reveal the contradictions of this ideology as he de-emphasised the status quo of male property ownership in favour of a radical anti-capitalism. Fianna Fáil's policies required a delicate balancing act, as they sought to tap into the same economic grievances as O'Donnell, but with fundamentally different goals in mind. Indeed, Seán Lemass, Minister for Industry, had supposedly told Peadar O'Donnell that Fianna Fáil would only take up the annuities issue provided doing so would not undermine the right to private property.[99] O'Donnell's hoped-for revolution would harm Fianna Fáil's vision of a nation of male owner-occupiers, 'bread-winners', rooted in their own land and able to provide for their wives and children in frugal self-sufficiency.

ECONOMIC REVOLUTIONS ON THE GLOBAL PERIPHERY

A series of coal-cattle pacts from 1935 onwards marked the beginning of the end of the Economic War.[100] The Anglo-Irish Trade Agreement in 1938, which allowed Irish farmers to again have free access to British markets, was the final act of the 'war'.[101] Even by 1937, when the 'war' was supposedly still extant, 50% of Irish imports were coming from Britain, with 97% of Irish exports going in the opposite direction.[102] In 1938 Irish cattle exports to Britain were worth £8,400,000. By 1939 they were over £10 million, less than what they had been in 1931 but double their value for 1934. Under the terms of the agreement, though, the British could intervene at any time with import quotas if they felt that British farmers' interests were threatened. As Mary Daly observes, the 'wording of this clause indicates that the balance of advantage rested with Britain; the key consideration was the stability of the British market, not market stability for Irish farmers.'[103] Elsewhere, though, Daly has said the trade agreement should be deemed an 'Irish victory' because, as well as dealing with the issues of ports and annuities, 'the overall package brought consensus among the dominant forces in Irish politics and society. This consensus marked the end of Fianna Fail economic radicalism, demonstrated by the 1938 founding of Clann na Talmhan [Family of the Land], a party representing small farmers of the west.'[104]

Which poses the question: if this was an 'Irish victory', which Ireland was victorious? Certainly large cattle farmers, again granted privileged access to British markets, gained much from this. But those smaller farmers who felt the need to form Clann na Talmhan clearly did not think their interests had won out.[105] Nor, in general, did those who supported Fianna Fáil out of a wish to see Ireland slough off its peripheral economic status as part of the broader movement towards independence, find that their goals were achieved. As Daly herself says it was 'the dominant forces in Irish politics and society'[106] who were happy with the 1938 settlement, because it was this elite who primarily gained from it.

This, though, was an unsurprising conclusion to the Economic War. Fianna Fáil's enthusiasm for self-sufficiency and smallholders had been gradually waning since the mid-1930s. Seán Lemass, Minister for Industry and Commerce and never a strong supporter of de Valera's vision for rural Ireland,[107] 'secretly wished for a way of removing incompetent farmers from the land'. Minister for Lands Seán Moylan openly declared that it was 'a mistake to give land to landless men.'[108] Fianna Fáil had sought to implement a popular set of policies, but ended up trapped in an ideological cul-de-sac. Their ideology was partially anti-capitalist and yet also conservative. The party attacked how large farmers used their land, whilst also seeking to grant more Irish men the dignity of private land-ownership. And it sought to do all this in a relatively small island with a finite supply of agricultural resources. Fianna Fáil sought to be radical and conservative at the same time, and was ultimately more of the latter than the former, settling for the status quo and a loose consensus with Fine Gael.[109]

The conclusion of the Economic War was also unsurprising for another reason, one related to the nature of Irish modernisation and thus also related to the nature of Irish nationalism; Ireland's continuing peripheral status within the global economy. Ireland had long been 'locked' into a system of economic path-dependency, a provider of agricultural raw materials for British markets in a global division of labour.[110] This was not, as Irish nationalists would later claim, a devious plot by British policy-makers to prevent Irish economic success.[111] Rather, it was a much more impersonal function of Ireland's continuing status in a broader economic and political system. The Irish economy in the nineteenth century and the first half of the twentieth century remained primarily dedicated to providing agricultural products for British markets. And this phenomenon did not disappear during the supposed revolution of 1916–1923.

In parallel to this, a nationalist culture emerged that also saw the Irish as preternaturally suited to agricultural work; indeed agriculture was seen as a means of redeeming Irish men. This is perhaps one of the most salient examples of the manner in which, as Declan Kiberd suggests, Irish nationalists remained trapped within the very codes they sought to oppose.[112] Irish nationalists lauded rural life and a clean-living frugality even as that romanticism reinforced their country's peripheral and subservient status as a producer of raw agricultural goods for John

Bull's industrialised cities. The Strong Farmer ideal and the gendered valorisation of private property that went along with it were partly the product of broader transnational economic forces. W.T. Cosgrave promoted agriculture over all else, arguing it was the 'spring and fertiliser of many other forms of industry *natural to an agricultural country such as this is.*'[113] Even de Valera, who sought to end Ireland's peripheral economic status, sought to do so primarily via agriculture, the very sector that reinforced the country's economic 'servitude', rather than through rapid and heavy industrialisation, as other 'developmentalist' states would seek to do in the twentieth century. A recent work that seeks to understand Irish historical development in the context of the country's broader global status has spoken of the 'limits of independence' in Ireland.[114] Neither of the two dominant parties in post-1922 Ireland were quick to abandon the ideas of Irish agrarian manhood and so perhaps de Valera and Cosgrave also reveal not just the limits of independence, but the limits of an Irish nationalism whose form and content was so strongly determined by the country's gradual modernisation on the agrarian periphery of the global economy.

Zionism also began on the periphery of Europe, both in the economic sense of 'peripheries' as well in a more cultural register, and Zionism also developed an idealised image of agrarian life. However, there were only between 5000 and 8000 people who fitted the description of Sabras in the 1930s; at their height, in the years immediately after 1948, they never amounted to more than 20,000.[115] Nor did the kibbutzim ever attract more than a small percentage of what remained a predominantly urban, capitalist society. This is in stark contrast to Ireland, where, in 1926, 53 % of the population worked in agriculture, of whom about one-fifth fitted the bill of Strong Farmers.[116] Where Irish nationalism's agrarian ideal, as argued above, reified and legitimised an already existing status-quo of individual property-ownership,[117] the Sabras and the members of the kibbutz movement, many of whom were radical socialists, sought to break with a mostly imaginary vision of parasitical Jewish economic life devoid of physical work in the Diaspora.[118] Mainline Irish nationalism did not carry out an economic revolution for the simple reason that it never really sought to do such a thing. Zionism, even socialist Zionism, did seek a much greater break with the Jewish economic past, though its vision of that past was built on a foundation of easy stereotypes. Yet Zionists failed to attract more than a small minority to live in kibbutzim and so did not effect an economic revolution either. Zionism and Irish nationalism emerged on the periphery and, in differing ways, ended up emulating the core. David Biale's analysis highlights how Israel's international status became something roughly analogous to that of Ireland:

> Political Zionism was based on late nineteenth-century notions of sovereignty that are less and less relevant to today's world. The 'spring of small nations' in Eastern Europe after World War I infected the Zionist quest for power. Yet, just as these hopes were dashed in Eastern Europe by the Nazis and the Soviets, so the dream of full Jewish sovereignty today has had to accept severe limitations. Despite the proliferation of small independent countries since World War II, the world is increasingly dominated by the large powers and a widening network of international corporations. Even nations blessed with strategic resources cannot escape the entanglements of the world political economy; sovereignty for small nations too often means dependence on the major powers.[119]

This chapter has discussed the Irish state's attempts to realise a long cherished vision of Irish agrarian masculinity, one whose roots go back to the 1880s. This discussion had at its heart not only the nature of that vision, but also the state's own limits in imposing it. In the same vein, the final chapter will discuss how the Irish state sought to control Irish people's leisure activities as part of a broader vision of nationalist self-fashioning. Again, this will be a discussion of both the nature of that vision and of the scope and limits of the newly independent state's power to force Irish people to live up to that ideal.

Notes

1. D.P. Moran (1905) *The Philosophy of Irish-Ireland* (Dublin: James Duffy) p. 23.
2. NLI LO P111: Item 11, *The Economic History of the Land of Erin*, Fianna Fáil pamphlet, 1932. Also available in UCDA, de Valera Papers, P150/2096.
3. C. Ó Gráda (1997) *A Rocky Road: The Irish Economy since the 1920s* (Manchester: Manchester University Press) p. 5.
4. C. Ó Gráda (1994) *Ireland: A New Economic History, 1780–1939* (Oxford: Oxford University Press) p. 412.
5. A. Kane (2011) *Constructing Irish National Identity: Discourse and Ritual During the Land War* (New York: Palgrave Macmillan) p. 230. Kane is here quoting David Jones (1995) *Graziers, Land Reform, and Political Conflict in Ireland* (Washington DC: Catholic University of America Press) p. 132.

6. Ironically this species of cactus is not native to Palestine, but was introduced from Latin America in the eighteenth century!
7. O. Almog (2000) *The Sabra: The Creation of the New Jew*, trans. H. Watzman (Berkeley, CA: University of California Press) p. 4; D. Penslar (1991) *Zionism and Technocracy: The Engineering of Jewish Settlement in Palestine, 1870–1918* (Bloomington, IN: Indiana University Press) p. 8.
8. D. Biale (1997) *Eros and the Jews: From Biblical Israel to Contemporary America* (Berkeley CA: University of California Press) pp. 182–183.
9. B. Kimmerling (2001) *The Invention and Decline of Israeliness: State, Society and the Military* (Berkeley, CA: University of California Press) pp. 90–91.
10. *Ibid*, p. 91.
11. O. Almog (2000) *The Sabra*, pp. 76–82.
12. D. Biale (1997) *Eros*, p. 187.
13. The Hebrew text of this poster declares the JNF's support 'For Hebrew settlement in the Land of Israel' [*la-yishuv ha-ivri ba-aretz*]. It goes on to speak of the JNF's support for the project for 'redemption of the territory' [*gaulet ha-karka*], something that contributes 'to the revival of the Jewish nation on their land' [*le-tekumat yisrael al admato*].
14. B. Kimmerling (2008) *Clash of Identities*, p. 149.
15. D. Biale (1997) *Eros*, p. 187.
16. D. Biale (1987) *Power and Powerlessness in Jewish History* (New York: Schocken Books), pp. 103, 107, 131.
17. D. Penslar (2001) '*Shylock's Children: Economics and Jewish Identity in Modern Europe* (Berkeley CA: University of California Press) p. 40.
18. Ibid, p.81; D.Penslar (1991) *Zionism and Technocracy, passim.*
19. 'The leitmotif of redemption drew upon Western physiocratic ideas, which stressed that a nation's wealth derived from the land and that a healthy economy was dependent upon scientifically proved agricultural methods'. S.M. Sufian (2007) *Healing the Land and the Nation: Malaria and the Zionist Project in Palestine, 1920–1947* (Chicago: University of Chicago Press) p. 32.
20. G. Reuveni (2010) 'Prolegomena to an "Economic Turn" in Jewish History' in G. Reuveni and S. Wobick-Segev, eds. *The Economy in Jewish History. New Perspectives On The Interrelationship Between Ethnicity and Economic Life.* (New York: Berghahn Books) p. 1.
21. D. Penslar (2001) *Shylock's Children*, pp. 11–49; for a review of the Shylock image and its history, see: D. Nirenberg (2013) *Anti-Judaism: The Western Tradition* (New York: W.W. Norton) pp. 269–299; F. Felsenstein (1995) *Antisemitic Stereotypes: A Paradigm of Otherness in English Popular Culture, 1660-1830* (Baltimore MD: Johns Hopkins University Press) pp. 158–186.
22. O. Almog (2000) *The Sabra*, p. 77.

23. G. Shafir (1996) *Land, Labor and the Origins of the Israeli-Palestinian Conflict, 1881–1914* (Berkeley CA: University of California Press) pp. 146–186.
24. As Almog evocatively describes the Sabra: 'The image was first modelled after Soviet propaganda posters, which portrayed a stereotypical muscular Soviet laborer; later inspiration was drawn from Hollywood's leading men, such as Gary Cooper, John Wayne, and Johnny Weismuller.' O. Almog (2000) *The Sabra*, p. 79.
25. R. Dunphy (1995) *The Making of Fianna Fáil Power in Ireland, 1923–1948* (Oxford: Oxford University Press) p. 50.
26. T. Dooley (2004) *'The Land for the People': The Land Question in Independent Ireland* (Dublin: UCD Press) p. 4.
27. R. Dunphy (1995) *Fianna Fáil Power*, pp. 20–21.
28. M. Daly (1992) *Industrial Development and Irish National Identity, 1922-1939* (Syracuse NY: Syracuse University Press) p. 13.
29. J.M. Regan (1999) *The Irish Counter-Revolution, 1921–1936: Treatyite Politics and Settlement in Independent Ireland* (Dublin: Gill & Macmillan), p. 308.
30. C. McCabe (2011) *Sins of the Father: Tracing the Decisions that Shaped the Irish Economy* (Dublin: The History Press Ireland) pp. 58–59.
31. M.E. Daly (1992) *Industrial Development and Irish National Identity, 1922–1939* (Syracuse NY: Syracuse University Press, 1992) p. 37.
32. R. Dunphy (1995) *Fianna Fáil Power*, pp. 55–63.
33. C. McCabe (2011) *Sins of the Father*, p. 71.
34. J.M. Regan (1999) *Counter-Revolution*, p. 213. Emphases added.
35. M.E. Daly (1992) *Industrial Development*, pp. 35–36.
36. J.M. Regan (1999) *Counter-Revolution*' pp. 210–211.
37. R.M. Douglas (2009) *Architects of the Resurrection: Ailtirí na hAiséirghe and the Fascist 'New Order' in Ireland* (Manchester: Manchester University Press) pp. 7–8. As Douglas has said, this was 'perhaps the most asinine statement ever made by an Irish public representative.'
38. K. Allen (1997) *Fianna Fáil and Irish Labour, 1926 to the Present* (London: Pluto Press) p. 21. It is unfair, though, to label this vision of 'sturdy, self-sufficient farmer[s]' as something vague. It was, as is argued throughout this chapter, a vision of Irish life that, for rural Irish men, drew on familiar and strongly felt economic experiences.
39. R. Dunphy (1995) *Fianna Fáil Power*' p. 125.
40. T. Dooley (2004) *'The Land for the People': The Land Question in Independent Ireland* (Dublin: UCD Press) pp. 3–4.
41. R. Dunphy (1995) *Fianna Fáil Power*, pp. 41, 31.
42. 'Without going into the debate over the true content of [Wolfe] Tone's remarks, the phrase had, by the 1920s, become part of the ideological arse-

nal of the *petite bourgeoisie*. The "men of no property" were in fact the "men of little property", hoping for more land, a bigger home market for their products, or, in the case of the landless labourers or lower-middle-class professionals, an opportunity to set themselves up as farmers or to reap the advantages of social advancement which they hoped the newly independent state would offer.' Ibid, p. 47.
43. NLI LO P103, *Cóiriú Fhianna Fáil* [Constitution of Fianna Fáil].
44. The La Scala Theatre, on Prince's Street, was close to the GPO on O'Connell Street, thus Fianna Fáil was launched in a location almost certainly chosen for its clear symbolic value. T.P. Coogan (1993) *Eamon de Valera: The Man Who Was Ireland* (New York: Harper Collins) p. 386.
45. Quoted in UCDA, de Valera Papers, P150/2048, *A Brief Outline of the Aims and Programme of Fianna Fáil*. Emphases added. After five years of Fianna Fáil rule, an open letter from de Valera spoke of his satisfaction 'that in our society all citizens, men and women, are entitled to an adequate means of livelihood, and [that he considered] that it is just that fathers of families should receive such a wage as would be sufficient for their reasonable domestic needs.' *Address to the Electors*, Fianna Fáil handbill, 1937.
46. UCDA, Archives of the Fianna Fáil Party, P176/23, *Fianna Fáil: A Call to Unity*, 19 June 1926. Emphases added.
47. UCDA, de Valera Papers, P150/2048, *All-Ireland Agricultural Conference, Held at Jury's Hotel, Dublin, on 3rd February 1927, Speech Delivered by Eamon de Valera*.
48. NLI, Uncatalogued Commerce Ephemera, Box 1, *Five Years of Poverty and Panic*, Fianna Fáil election pamphlet, 1927.
49. UCDA, Archives of the Fianna Fáil Party, P176/827, Fianna Fáil election handbill, 1927.
50. See, for example, Military Archives, Bureau of Military History, Contemporary Documents, 131/8/3, Labhras Mag Fhionnghail. *The Land Question* (Dublin: Sinn Fein—Leaflet No. 8, n.d.); Military Archives, BMH CD, 264/2/4, *Save Your Land*, n.d.
51. Military Archives, BMH CD 227.7.B1 (M), *Electors of East Clare!*, 1917. Capitalisation in original.
52. NLI Uncatalogued Historical Proclamations 1910–19, *Leaflet No.7: War on the Cattle Trade*, Sinn Féin pamphlet, August 1917.
53. UCDA, Archives of the Fianna Fáil Party, P176/23, *Fianna Fáil: A Call to Unity*, 19 June 1926; similarly de Valera spoke of Fianna Fáil as 'an organization of destiny—an organization which is a fitting successor to the great Sinn Féin Organization which existed from 1917 to 1921.' UCDA, de Valera Papers, P150/2048, *Statement by Eamon de Valera, T.D., at 2nd Annual Árd Fheis of Fianna Fáil, as President of that Organization*.

54. Quoted in P. O'Donnell (1963) *There Will Be Another Day* (Dublin: Dolmen Press) p. p. 95.
55. *An Phoblacht*, 4 June 1926. Quoted in R. English (1994) *Radicals and the Republic: Socialist Republicanism in the Irish Free State, 1925–1937* (Oxford: Clarendon Press) p. 90.
56. *An Phoblacht*, 25 March 1927. Quoted in R. English (1994) *Radicals*, p. 82.
57. Terence Brown, for example, has said that implicit in O'Donnell's work was 'a sense that Gaelic Ireland in the west is the authentic heroic Ireland in a way that confirms rather than contradicts the conventional image of the west as "certain set apart." The power of this conventional image was perhaps so great that it affected as intelligent a social commentator as Peadar O'Donnell'. T. Brown (1985) *Ireland: A Social and Cultural History, 1922-85* 2nd edn (London: Fontana) p. 94. Quoted in R. English (1994) *Radicals*, p. 83.
58. NLI IR 308 P7, Peadar O'Donnell. *For or Against the Ranchers? Irish Working Farmers in the Economic War*, n.d. (1932?).
59. NAI TAOIS/S 8336, Land Annuities: Non-Payment Campaign, 1928–31, *Confidential Memorandum from Garda Superintendent, Kinsale*, 17 May 1928; NAI TAOIS/S 8336, Land Annuities: Non-Payment Campaign, 1928–31, *Secret Memorandum from Garda Chief Superintendent, Letterkenny*, 12 February 1929.
60. J.M. Regan (1999) *Counter-Revolution*, pp. 279–304; F. McGarry (2005) *Eoin O'Duffy: A Self-Made Hero* (Oxford: Oxford University Press) pp. 170–199.
61. John Regan has hinted at this in his assessment that anti-communism was built on the same foundations as Catholic moral paranoia. 'The case against communism was primed on the same ground. It was a powerful corrupting influence, invisible, and for that all the more potent ... Communism and sexual immorality were also interchangeable concepts.' and 'The communist, like the devil, was at his most dangerous when he could not be seen: after all the greatest trick the devil ever pulled was convincing the world he did not exist.' J.M. Regan (1999) *Counter-Revolution*, pp. 283, 358.
62. *Clare Champion*, 6 February 1932. Capitalisation in original. The 'grabbing' that the advertisement was denouncing was a proposed land tax on richer farmers.
63. *Voters! You have a solemn responsibility*, Cumann na nGaedheal Pamphlet, 1932. http://irishelectionliterature.wordpress.com. Accessed 4 June 2013.
64. *Dáil Debates*, Vol. 60, 13 February, 1936, p. 724. Quoted in T. Dooley (2004) *Land for the People*, p. 104. Emphases added.
65. UCDA, Kevin O'Higgins Papers, P197/137, *Mexican Politics*, article by Kevin O'Higgins, n.d. 1922?]

66. Quoted in J.M. Regan, *Counter-Revolution*, p. 364.
67. *Voters! You have a solemn responsibility*, Cumann na nGaedheal pamphlet, 1932.
68. NLI EPH F57, *No Goods Taken From Window!*, Cumann na nGaedheal poster, 1932. Another 1932 poster depicted de Valera opening up the door of a vault, out of which appeared the grotesque and savage men of the IRA and the leftist *Saor Eire* [Free Ireland]. The caption read 'Don't Let This Happen, Vote for Cumann na nGaedheal.'
69. NLI EPH F54, *We Want No 'Reds' Here!*, Cumann na nGaedheal poster, 1932.
70. Quoted in M.E. Daly (1992) *Industrial Development*, p. 105.
71. NLI LO P117 Item 119, *Músgail do Mhisneach a Bhanba*, Fine Gael election handbill 1933. The title of this item is also quite telling. It was a commonly used nationalist slogan that translates as 'Rouse your Courage, oh Banba' [a romantic name for the ancient Irish nation].
72. *No Land Annuities Till November 1934*, Cumann na nGaedheal handbill, 1933. Emphases added; http://irishelectionliterature.wordpress.com. Accessed 4 June 2013.
73. UCDA, Patrick McGilligan Papers, P35/193, Fine Gael election handbill, 1937. Another version of this item claimed 'YOU pay more and more, BUT the farmer and his labourer get less and less.'
74. C. Meehan (2010) *The Cosgrave Party: A History of Cumann na nGaedheal, 1923–33* (Dublin: Royal Irish Academy) p. 146.
75. J. Knirck (2012) 'A Cult of No Personality: W.T. Cosgrave and the Election of 1933.' *Éire-Ireland*, Volume 47, Nos. 3&4,. 65, 75, 82.
76. J.M. Regan (1999) *Counter-Revolution*, p. 326. Regan notes that 'This was classic treatyite rhetoric in the style of its best exponent, Kevin O'Higgins'.
77. NAI, JUS/93/4/5, *Blueshirt Press Cuttings*: 'Graveside Oration: General O'Duffy & Government's Responsibility', *Cork Examiner*, 16 August 1934.
78. J.M. Regan (1999) *Counter-Revolution*, p. 347.
79. R. Dunphy (1995) *Fianna Fáil Power*, p. 26.
80. T. Dooley (2004) *Land for the People*, p. 207.
81. NLI Uncatalogued Election Ephemera, *Fianna Fáil (Republican Party) Provides the Remedy*, n.d. (1927?). Capitalisation in original.
82. NLI LO P111, Item 19, *To Each Elector of North Dublin*, Open Letter from Oscar Traynor, n.d. (1929?). A election pamphlet for Oscar Traynor and other Fianna Fáil candidates from the 1933 election was entitled 'The Men for North City' [Traynor's constituency] and stated 'Let us tell the world that the men of Dublin who gave the lead in every national effort, stand now solidly for Ireland's rights.' It is not clear, of course, if 'the men of Dublin' refers to the Fianna Fáil candidates, or to an all-male vision of the

electorate. NLI LO P111, Item 20, *The Men for North City*, Fianna Fáil pamphlet, n.d. (1933)
83. NLI Uncatalogued Political Ephemera, Box 1, *The Greatest Failure in Irish History*, Fianna Fáil electoral pamphlet, n.d. (1931?) Emphases added.
84. This poster is reprinted in J.J. Lee, G. Ó Tuathaigh (1982) *The Age of de Valera* (Dublin: Ward River Press/Radio Teleſís Éireann) p. 65.
85. NLI LO P111, Item 9, *Free State Supporters!*, Fianna Fáil leaflet, 1932.
86. NLI Uncatalogued Political Ephemera, Box 1, *Listen!*, Fianna Fáil electoral pamphlet, n.d. (1932?)
87. 'Mr. De Valera in Clare', *Clare Champion*, 13 February 1932.
88. NLI EPH E37, *Give Fianna Fáil a Clear Majority*, 1933.
89. UCDA, de Valera Papers, P150/2176, Letter from Eamon de Valera, Minister for External Affairs, to British Secretary of State for Dominion Affairs, 5 April 1932.
90. NLI MS 27685/1, Seán T. Ó Ceallaigh Papers, An Open Letter to the Right Honourable J.H. Thomas M.P., from Senator Thomas Johnson, n.d. Johnson mentions a conference, with which Thomas is involved as Dominions Secretary. This is almost certainly the Commonwealth conference in Canada, in July 1932.
91. R. Dunphy (1995) *'Fianna Fáil Power'*, pp. 96–97. Emphases added.
92. 'The Irish Land Annuities'. *New Outlook*, December 1932. The original can be viewed in NAI TAOIS/S 10841.
93. NLI MS 27685/1, Seán T. Ó Ceallaigh Papers, *Speech by Mr. Seán T. O'Kelly, Head of the Irish Free State Delegation.*
94. UCDA, Seán MacEntee Papers, P67/134, *Ireland's Right to the Land Annuities*, n.d. [circa 1929–32].
95. UCDA, Seán MacEntee Papers, P67/141, *Short Notes on the Irish Land Purchase Annuities: How they Originated and the present Position*, October, 1932.
96. Col. Maurice Moore. *Short Notes on the Irish Land Purchase Annuities: How They Originated and the Present Position* (n.d.). Quoted in R. English (1994) *Radicals*, p. 117.
97. NAI TAOIS S/2888, *Land Annuities: Relief for Annuitants, 1932–4*, Memorandum from the Minister for Finance, 11 November 1932.
98. R. Dunphy (1995) *Fianna Fáil Power*, pp. 39–40. Dunphy's focus on Fianna Fáil as a petty bourgeois party holds a lot of water, but in his drive to create an analysis of the party grounded in comparative analyses, he ignores those things which are specifically Irish about Fianna Fáil; the obsession with land ownership and suspicion of the rich and of capitalism in general can also be ascribed to the cultural memory of the Famine, the landlord system and the difficulties inherent in Ireland's status as a agricultural periphery of the British economy. It also fails to adequately explain the par-

ty's support from the working classes and richer industrialists. I would tend to agree more with Kieran Allen's focus on Fianna Fáil as a populist party aiming for cross-class support for a project of native capitalist development. K. Allen (1997) *Fianna Fáil*, p. 10. Allen's argument, however, tends towards the teleological. He presumes de Valera had a concrete idea of the type of capitalist state an independent Ireland would be, rather than seeing de Valera, and Fianna Fáil, as exhibiting a dynamic ideology split between capitalism and a fear of capitalist excess. The form of capitalism that emerged reflected the complexities, contradictions and tensions of de Valerian nationalism, as well as broader social struggles, rather than capitalism being something monolithic and already fully formed. The latter is what Nicos Poulantzas would probably call a 'historicist' argument. N. Poulantzas (1978) *State, Power, Socialism* (London: New Left Books).
99. R. Dunphy (1995) *Fianna Fáil Power*, p. 97.
100. K. Allen (1997) *Fianna Fáil*, p. 42.
101. The looming threat of Hitler was perhaps *the* motivating factor for Britain in ending this 'war'. As one commentator observed in the *New Statesman*, whilst simultaneously hinting at Irish nationalist concerns, 'The bully remains a bully until he is frightened by a bigger bully.' *New Statesman and Nation*, 20 August 1938. Quoted in C. Ó Gráda (1994) *New Economic History*, p. 416.
102. M. Cronin (2000) 'Golden Dreams, Harsh Realities: Economics and Informal Empire in the Irish Free State' in M. Cronin, J. Regan, eds. *Ireland: The Politics of Independence* (London: Palgrave-MacMillan) p. 162.
103. M.E. Daly (2002) *The First Department: A History of the Department of Agriculture* (Dublin: Institute of Public Administration) pp. 196–197.
104. M.E. Daly (1992) '*Industrial Development*', p. 170.
105. As Dooley observes 'Clann na Talmhan did best in areas where Fianna Fáil had failed to deliver upon its earlier election promises of more land acquisition and division'. T. Dooley (2004) *Land for the People*, p. 208.
106. M.E. Daly (1992) *Industrial Development*, p. 170.
107. Bryce Evans provides some intimate details of the divisions within Fianna Fáil between Lemass, whose economics leaned towards industrialisation, and Seán MacEntee, who was cut from agrarian cloth. B. Evans (2011) *Seán Lemass: Democratic Dictator* (Cork: The Collins Press) pp. 71–110.
108. C. Ó Gráda (1997) *Rocky Road*, p. 146.
109. This is part of what Regan has aptly called 'The Consensus of Irish Nationalist Politics'. J. Regan (1999) '*Counter-Revolution*', pp. 373–383.
110. D. O'Hearn (2001) *The Atlantic Economy: Britain, the US and Ireland* (Manchester: Manchester University Press). For the idea of a global capitalist division of labour, see: H. Chang (2002) *Kicking Away the Ladder: Development Strategy in Historical Perspective* (London: Anthem Press);

K. Pomeranz (2000) *The Great Divergence: China, Europe, and the Making of the Modern World Economy* (Princeton NJ: Princeton University Press); I. Wallerstein (2011) *The Modern World-System I: Capitalist Agriculture and the Rise of the European World-Economy in the Sixteenth Century*, 2nd edn (Berkeley CA: University of California Press)
111. This was a regular theme in Arthur Griffith's writings. See, for example, A. Griffith (n.d.) *Sinn Féin Pamphlets No. 3: England's Colossal Robbery of Ireland, The Final Relations of the Two Countries since the Union. Extract from Mr. Arthur Griffith's Speech, made at No. 11, Lower O'Connell St., Dublin, on 22nd Oct., 1906* (Dublin: National Council); A. Griffith (n.d.) 'How Ireland has "Prospered"'.
112. D. Kiberd (2009) *Ulysses and Us*, p. 204. Kiberd says of Gerty McDowell and The Citizen, minor characters in Ulysses: 'Gerty's problem ... is rather like that of the nationalists in 'Cyclops': her rebellion is doomed because it is trapped in the very codes it opposes.'
113. J.M. Regan (1999) *Counter-Revolution*, p. 146. Emphases added.
114. M. Coakley (2012) *Ireland in the World Order: A History of Uneven Development* (London: Pluto Press) pp. 155–158. See also, Mike Cronin's discussion that Ireland's continuing ties to the British economy in the 1920s and 1930s could be labelled 'informal empire'. Breaking economically with Britain would have required a level of economic 'pain', Cronin says, that few were willing to countenance. M. Cronin (2000) Golden Dreams, pp. 144–163.
115. O. Almog (2000) *The Sabra*, p. 3.
116. R. Dunphy (1995) *Fianna Fáil Power*, pp. 39–40.
117. 'The Fianna Fáil agricultural policy, which has often been hailed as a radical assault upon the big estates, actually reinforced the private ownership of land more than ever—before the party, inevitably, and without too much fuss, bowed to the laws of capitalist economic development and gave up the struggle to multiply the ranks of the small farmers, accepting land clearance.' Ibid., pp. 23–24.
118. As Ezra Mendelsohn shows, by the closing years of the nineteenth century we can easily speak of a Jewish proletariat in Tsarist Russia, mainly working in workshops and small-scale factories. E. Mendelsohn (1970) *Class Struggle in the Pale: The Formative Years of the Jewish Worker' Movement in Tsarist Russia* (Cambridge: Cambridge University Press) pp. 1–26. This, of course, does not sit comfortably with easy stereotypes about Jewish economics in the Diaspora.
119. D. Biale (1987) *Power and Powerlessness*, p. 169.

CHAPTER 7

Regulating Sex, Gender and Leisure in the Irish Free State

> This is the society we, who were born in the Thirties, inherited. We were told that we were the sons of revolutionary heroes, and that our role now was to be one of gratitude, well-behaved gratitude. What was expected of us now was a new kind of heroism—heroic obedience.[1]

THE HEIR TO GENERATIONS OF CONSERVATISM

The Israeli sociologist Baruch Kimmerling, borrowing from the signal work of Max Weber, argues for the idea of a 'unique "fingerprint" that distinguishes each state-society complex and is created through interaction between the state and civil society.'[2] In the case of Israel, Kimmerling talks of the pre-1948 Jewish community in Palestine as a 'state in the making'. A direct result of the existence of this proto-state, he feels, was that after 1948, 'the boundaries between "state" (i.e., the central political institutions) and "society" (non-political but exclusive ethnic institutions) were completely blurred, as institutionalization of political organizations and leadership intensified social control and surveillance.' Kimmerling thus identifies the essence of the Israeli 'fingerprint' as being determined by state–society relations that predated the formal birth of the state. This led, he feels, to a situation wherein the Israeli state sought to impose its dominance in society by forging alliances with those groups that would help it maintain its initially fragile hegemony.[3]

Kimmerling builds on this by talking of how individual states display a 'state's logic', by which he means 'the basic codes, conditions, rules of the game, and practices that are unaffected by changes of government, administration, or even entire regimes.' Zionism, as previous chapters have shown, was a concerted effort to construct a more idealised image of Jewish masculinity (the 'New Jew') as well as a coercive programme to make Jewish men fit that image. These were some of the foundational 'codes' of Israeli society and the project to create a new Jewish man continued to have a strong influence after 1948. Moreover, the new state's elite were presented to the public as exemplars of redeemed Jewishness and they, in turn, could use that image to copper-fasten their power. This has led several scholars to present the early Israeli state as, at best, a shallow democracy, or even as a Bolshevik-type regime in which a small old-timer elite group ruled the state under the premise of democracy.[4]

The Irish Free State, a similarly shallow democracy, also had a nationalist 'fingerprint' that, to a large degree, determined its early politics. This was a markedly masculinist, nationalist and Catholic 'fingerprint.' Michael Laffan has pointed out that 'The catholic [sic] nature of independent Ireland was never sought by nationalists but once it had been imposed and had become a fact of life many people were attracted by the opportunity of building in the twenty-six counties a more thoroughly catholic [sic] state than a united Ireland could ever have become'.[5] The Church was a convenient ally for the weak hegemony of a post-Civil War state and certainly the intensely Catholic climate of the Free State cannot be understood outside of the immediate context of partition, which had ensured a population close to being homogenously Catholic. Nonetheless, as was argued in earlier chapters, the stridently Catholic rhetoric employed by Irish nationalism, in areas such as martyrology (Chap. 2) or debates over private property (Chap. 6), often served to legitimise what were also markedly secular state-building projects. Indeed, Perry Anderson has recently pointed out that Ireland and Israel, along with India, could be seen as representing 'a distinct sub-group' in the history of twentieth-century nationalism, due to the manner in which they merged nationhood and religion.[6] Additionally, as with Zionism and Israel, the Irish state's masculinist fingerprint was in utero well before 1922 and this fingerprint would leave a lingering mark on Irish society well after 1922.

Even before the founding of the state, the key roles played by women were being suppressed in favour of a smooth narrative of men united in the singular cause of the nation. The postcards in Fig. 7.1, produced just

Fig. 7.1 *Gendering the Memory of the Rising*, Postcards c. 1917
Source: NLI, MacDonagh family papers MS 44337/7

a few months after the Rising, show how even at this early date, images of active public men were coming to predominate. Sean Heuston is here depicted as an active agent of nationalist military power. Conversely, Constance Markievicz, who had commanded a rebel position during the Rising, is pictorially domesticated and placed at a familial hearth with an ornately feminine bridal gown substituted for her military uniform. Where Heuston stares boldly out from the camera, Markievicz modestly averts her gaze. These postcards reflected some broader patterns in contemporary nationalist politics.

As was mentioned in Chap. 2, P.S. O'Hegarty's *The Victory of Sinn Féin*, an early history of the War of Independence and Civil War, took a harsh line on women's involvement in contemporary Irish politics.[7] Women, O'Hegarty felt, had been irreparably damaged by their wartime experiences, which had the effect of 'cutting [them] loose from everything which their sex contributes to civilisation and social order.'[8] He primarily blamed

Cumann na mBan for this development since, unlike *Inginidhe na hEireann* [The Daughters of Ireland], they had violated the gendered division of labour of Irish nationalist politics.[9] These women were 'Furies',[10] he claimed, and he blamed them for the excesses of the Civil War, when their 'hysterical' dedication to Republicanism violated the bond of brotherhood that had previously prevailed between nationalist men. 'Left to himself, man is comparatively harmless' but 'It is woman ... with her implacability, her bitterness, her hysteria, that makes a devil of him. The Suffragettes used to tell us that with women in political power there would be no more war. We know better now. We know that with women in political power there would be no more peace.'[11]

O'Hegarty's ideas were representative of a broad swathe of Treatyites[12] and pointed to a longer debate in Irish nationalism about women's equality and the role women should play in a future Irish state. While women were afforded a certain amount of freedom, there was much tension between those male and female nationalists who supported this against those who wished to restrict women's freedom. Ultimately, this was to be a debate that feminists lost. W.T. Cosgrave, newly installed as President of the Executive Council of the Irish Free State, pined for a gendered public–private split. He felt that rather than being involved in anti-Treaty politics, women 'should have rosaries in their hands or be at home with knitting needles.'[13] Eamon de Valera, who a decade later would take power, backed away from fully supporting the radical anti-Treatyites: 'I must be the heir to generations of conservatism', he informed Mary MacSwiney. 'Every instinct of mine would indicate that I was meant to be a dyed-in-the-wool Tory or even a Bishop, rather than the leader of a Revolution'.[14] Though gender politics did not go back to the way they were before women's suffrage, there was a general backlash against women's involvement in politics and public life.[15] Just as there was to be no revolution in labour relations, or in economics in general, a revolution in gender relations was not to take place in post-1922 Ireland. This chapter is a study of what happened next and a study of how Irish politics after 1922 cannot be divorced from events before that year. States are often imagined as male projects and the masculinist 'fingerprint' of the Irish state has deep historical roots.

The Irish Civil War ground to a slow halt in 1923. With the end of this physical war, the Irish state (re-)embarked on a more abstract moral war to redeem a degraded nation. It has become common among Irish historians to describe the period after 1922 as a 'counter-revolution', the period of enforced calm after the revolutionary upheaval.[16] What such views ignore, however, is the degree to which 'counter-revolutionary' elements (coercion, soft authoritarianism) had long existed within the 'revolutionary' project with its utopian visions of a better society and a meritocratic national revival. As discussed in the introduction, the degree to which this was so calls into question the analytical utility of such terms as 'revolution' or 'counter-revolution' as tools for understanding the complex interactions of change and continuity across late-nineteenth- and early-twentieth-century Ireland. In fact, the Irish Free State's moral war was underpinned by a number of key concerns that had already proven popular within the nationalist movement and would come to dominate the soft-authoritarian[17] political landscape of the Irish Free State: there was something profoundly wrong with Irish people and their public behaviour. Now, however, an independent Ireland could tackle this (self-hating) malaise via a programme of thorough social reform. One of the first 'battles' in this renewed 'war' was Frank Duff's assault on Montgomery Street.

The War on Monto

Prior to 1922, the red-light district centred on Montgomery Street in Dublin's north inner city, commonly known as 'Monto' and immortalised as Joyce's Nighttown, was already a source of moral panic in Ireland. Frank Duff, a civil servant in the Free State's Department of Finance and the founder of the lay Catholic organisation The Legion of Mary, led a campaign in the years immediately after independence to have Monto shut down.[18] Through the Ministry for Local Government, Duff was able to arrange a meeting with W.T. Cosgrave, the minister at that department, in the summer of 1922.[19] Cosgrave arranged for Duff and his fellow campaigners to have access to 76 Harcourt Street in Dublin's south city centre. Renamed Sancta Maria, the building had formerly been the head offices of Sinn Féin and now was to be used as a hostel for 'fallen' women. No taxes or rent were payable on the building for the first three months of their tenancy and Duff also received a donation of £25 from E.P. McCarron, Secretary of the Department of Local Government.[20] 'Business' in Monto had already gone into decline by 1922, partly due to the departure of the British garrison.[21] Initially, Duff's plan was for prostitutes to be won over through a mixture of visitations, religious retreats and the promise of assistance in finding regular employment.[22] When this proved less than successful, Duff began to work with the Garda Chief Commissioner. 'A large-scale police raid was organized for midnight on 12 March 1925 under the supervision of Colonel David Neligan and Captain Ennis of the Detective Branch.'[23] The leadership of the Dublin police were 'quite willing to take a hand in extirpating'[24] Monto, and indeed this raid and the arrest of 100 people during it did bring an end to open prostitution (at least in that part of Dublin).[25]

Prostitution had, in the nineteenth century, been a social and moral issue, but, as Maria Luddy observes, 'Prostitution in early twentieth-century Ireland became bound up with the cause of Irish independence. The prostitute became a symbol of British oppression and the means by which the British soldier infested the Irish nation with physical disease and immorality.'[26] There existed a popular view in pre-1922 Ireland that prostitution was widespread due to the presence of British soldiers. This not only served to confirm comforting notions of Irish moral superiority, but also became an emotive symbol of British social and political control. Just as Ireland was controlled politically by London, so also British soldiers exploited foolish Irish girls: 'the politicisation of prostitution and venereal disease embraced and gave voice to nationalist concerns of the dominance of English culture in Irish society.'[27] Luddy, though, also sees the concerns with prostitution after 1910 as being a reaction against another type of 'public' woman, the suffragist, and an argument over whether it should be men or women that had the right to deal with prostitution: 'In some ways the debate was more an argument about authority than about the practical means of ridding the city of its prostitutes.'[28] These two explanations (opposition to prostitution as an opposition to English rule and opposition to prostitution as a reaction against suffrage) are certainly not mutually exclusive. Both are arguments about Irish men's power and their control over a newly sanitised Irish public sphere. This complexity can be seen in the work of Frank Duff.

Duff was clearly motivated by familiar nationalist concerns. Looking back from the 1960s, he recalled his shame at the international reputation Dublin was acquiring. In 1905 the *Encyclopaedia Britannica* had named Dublin as one of the worst cities in Europe for prostitution, which led Duff to exclaim, 'Such was the sad fame to which our genuinely good city had attained'. Moreover, he feared licentiousness for the way it seemed to confirm the Irish nation's ambiguous 'white' racial identity. Prostitution in Dublin, Duff confessed, was 'carried on more publicly than even in the south of Europe or in Algeria.'[29] One of Duff's sympathetic biographers and confidantes also put much emphasis on Montgomery Street's 'unenviable reputation that extended far beyond the boundaries of the country.'³⁰ The continuing existence of so well known a red-light district cut across any idealised notions of Ireland's ordered society. Reinforcing this, the clearance of Monto went 'almost unremarked in the press',³¹ as if even to admit its existence was too large a step. Gary Boyd, in his provocative study of Dublin's urban geography, points to some of Frank Duff's gender- and class-based concerns. Duff, Boyd suggests, saw Monto as an arena of 'weirdness and unnaturalness' and he traces this to the way in which different social classes regularly mixed in this area (and often mixed only in this area). Perhaps more importantly, though:

> The area also contained a further gender inversion. Unlike the city which was controlled by city fathers, according to Duff, Monto was governed by a powerful matriarchy of madams who controlled both prostitutes and clients … These social distortions, furthermore, seemed to be embodied and signified in the transformations exercised upon the built fabric of the area as it descended into poverty. In Monto, in common with much of the north-inner city, the alleyways and service lanes, designed as subservient spaces to the main streets of the Georgian townscape, assumed an equal functional importance, despite obvious differences in width and architectural treatment. Ground floor hallways, for example, often became shortcuts between parallel streets, opening up a myriad of alternative routeways so that the edges of the private zone did not begin at the front door of the house but, rather, whole blocks of tenements became almost infinitely penetrable.³²

Which is to say, that Monto contradicted the kinds of long-standing notions about public order and masculine spatial sovereignty discussed in Chap. 4.

Monto was also perceived as a living symbol of the failure of Irish men; their failure to protect Irish women, their failure to control Irish women, and their failure to control themselves in the face of sexual temptation. The undoing of these failures was a motivating factor for Duff. Presenting evidence to the Inter-Departmental Committee of Inquiry Regarding Venereal Disease in 1926, Duff took umbrage with any suggestion that prostitutes were not the primary cause of venereal disease in Ireland. He spoke of 'the prostitute lying in wait in cities to tempt men. Behind all Venereal Disease the prostitute lies hidden somewhere.'³³ There was a profound distrust of female 'reprobates'³⁴ present in Duff's actions. In the case of the hospitals treating venereal diseases, Duff felt patients should be divided 'along lines of respectability', lest the 'abominable' women infect the 'respectable girls' and 'first-fall cases'. To treat them together, he felt, increased the 'great danger of corruption.' Conversely, Duff supported a system wherein 'the moral appeal is stronger, undesirable visitors are kept away, and patients are not permitted to leave the Hospital during treatment.'[35]

There was a noticeable violence to all of this. Duff recalled that during one of his earliest visits to Monto, on 13 July 1922, he had to convince six women that, should they join his retreat, they would 'not be forced to remain against their will'.[36] Coercion, though, was precisely what Duff did engage in, in what were euphemistically called 'Enclosed Retreats.' In one account, Duff provided a detailed overview of the standard method employed:

> The girls are taken straight from their evil life. All of them have been drinking. Half-a-dozen came in to the Hostel actually drunk. The nerves of all are on a tension, yet they are subjected to a three-day Retreat in the closest confinement. The garden even is not used. The Retreatants spend their day between the Oratory, the dormitory, and one large room which has to serve alike as dining-room, common-room, and grounds; and nevertheless no difficulty is experienced in keeping in hand, and the spiritual results are of the first order.[37]

Given that many of these women likely had alcohol addictions, the isolated three-day 'enclosed retreats' probably bordered on psychological torture. Moreover, potential 'retreatants' were harassed by Duff, 'followed into their haunts week after week and in innumerable cases year after year, before being prevailed upon to enter the Hostel'.[38] Surveillance was a recurring feature. Even after leaving the hostel, a woman would be 'visited regularly and made to feel that she is an object of solicitude. This is all-important for the perseverance of many.'[39]

On a number of occasions Duff let slip the raw violence inherent in the clearances of Monto. In one anecdote, having been contacted by an anxious mother who feared her missing daughter had become a prostitute, Duff recalled that he forced his way into a brothel in Monto and went room to room seeking this missing girl. 'I was warned I could not roam around the house like that. I disregarded this injunction, told the woman [the brothel's madam] with whom I was conversing that I would not be long in going through and pushed past her down the hall and up the stairway.' When the madam's son confronted him, 'I said I did not mean to make myself a nuisance, but that I thought the woman down below was only being disobliging and that I knew the owners would never object if they were told the nature of my errand.'[40] That an adult man forcing his way into a brothel might have violent intentions, and that the madam might have legitimate fears of him, does not seem to have occurred to Duff.

Frank Duff also had a propensity for militaristic language. Large retreats organised for prostitutes were called 'Councils of War' and were held in 'our little GHQ'. A red-light district was 'the Danger Zone' and Duff talked of going there 'in force—a sort of invasion' during which there was a 'mighty roundup' of women and 'Legionary warfare against the place'. The police raid on Monto in 1925 was 'The Last Assault.'[41] Duff acknowledged that, even prior to this police raid, 'The *material* for the Retreats has been obtained almost entirely by raids or personal canvass in the houses where the girls live.'[42] Male control over this space was thus forcefully imposed. Thomas O'Flynn, a priest and supporter, recalled that Duff 'was no meek and mild plaster saint. I have heard it said that in his day he could "floor" [knock out with a punch] the toughest troublemaker in the hostel. Though not above average height he was deep chested, sturdily built and generally strong physically, a strong swimmer in his day, and a potentially promising athlete.'[43] Clearly, he was a suitably muscular man who could properly control recalcitrant women. Moreover, as if to symbolise a newfound masculine control over the spaces of Monto, 'By the 1930s, the entire area had been razed, many of the street names changed, two of its streets completely obliterated and its maze-like warren of alleys and routes replaced with orthogonal and highly visible blocks of flats placed within open space and each with a single entrance'.[44]

Frank Duff's 'assault' on Monto certainly had extreme overtones. Rather than being an aberration, though, this represented the outer limits of some broader patterns of 1920s and 1930s Ireland, patterns that could be traced back to the later nineteenth century. First, Duff's actions and beliefs highlight the distrust that the emerging Irish elite had of the popular classes, particularly of women. Second, they show how the state actively sought to construct what James Smith calls 'the Nation's Architecture of Containment',[45] a statist power coded as male power that would allow for greater social control whilst also bolstering an idealised image of Ireland. Underpinning this was the idea that 'the real threat to chastity and sexual morality resided in the bodies of women. Thus moral regulation, by Church and state, attempted to impose standards of idealised conduct, particularly on women, that would return the nation to purity.'[46] Third, the case of Frank Duff highlights the conceptual problems of speaking of 'the state' in post-1922 Ireland. As Duff's actions show, it is often difficult to tell where 'the state' ended and 'the Church' began. What can appear to be a religious project (moral renewal led by the Legion of Mary) was often secular at its core (the construction of an idealised national image, the control of women, and the maintenance of male power within a strict gender order, assisted by the police and government ministers). Indeed, the willing support Duff received from the state contrasts sharply with the Church's on-going suspicions of him.[47]

This newfound state power, though, was not only directed at supposedly wayward women. There were also attempts made to rectify the ostensibly immoral behaviour of men, as happened with the Intoxicating Liquors Commission in 1925 and the subsequent Intoxicating Liquors Act in 1927.

Ireland Sober Is Ireland Free

Anxieties about alcohol and alcoholism and a desire to restrict, if not fully prohibit, the availability of alcohol had long been recurring themes in Irish nationalist discourse. These were common features, for example, in the ideology and practices of the Gaelic League, and various Irish militias, militaries and police forces. In one of the more outré examples of this, de Valera blamed the Civil War on alcohol. He claimed that 'As long as the Volunteers avoided drink they stood together and were invincible. It was only when drink crept in that our morale was lost and we fell asunder.'[48] More than that:

> It has been a greater curse to our people than perhaps anything else. Personally, I believe that it was at the bottom of the Treaty. (Applause). Our people during the interval of the Truce, when they were taken back, and when they had come from arduous work with the columns, were treated [i.e., had alcoholic drinks bought for them] here, there and everywhere, and the abstinence they had practiced during the hard times was given up, and you know that if you want men with spirit and determination—men like Cathal Brugha—you will get them from the men who do not drink.[49]

Like many stereotypes, there was a limited amount of truth to the prevalent accusations about Irish drunkenness. Alcohol consumption in early-twentieth-century Ireland, however, was slightly below the English average[50] and by the broader standards of the British Isles, the level of

Irish alcohol consumption was far from abnormal. An analysis of the motivations and ideologies behind the Free State government's legislation in this area should be grounded in the realisation that there was a noticeable gap between accusations of mass Irish drunkenness, and reality.[51] The Free State's legislation in this area was part of a broader project of social engineering, of fashioning idealised images of Irish men and women. It was a project to refute one of the most commonly held stereotypes about the Irish. It should also be seen, though, as an example of the limits of that project.

The Intoxicating Liquor Commission began its work in March 1925 under the chairmanship of John J. Horgan, a well-known figure in legal, business and politically right-of-centre circles in Cork.[52] As well as Horgan, the Commission was made up of three senators (Evelyn Costello, J.T. O'Farrell and John O'Neill), three Dáil deputies (James Craig, James Murphy and Richard Wilson), Rev. John Flanagan, a Catholic cleric and J.J. McElligot, a senior civil servant. Its secretary was John Duff, a civil servant and the brother of Frank Duff. In an early meeting of the Commission, John Duff reported that there were 13,000 businesses licensed to sell alcohol in the Irish Free State, one for every 230 citizens. The comparable statistics for England/Wales and Scotland were one for every 400 and one for every 695, respectively. John Duff felt these statistics warranted 'a thorough and close investigation into the social and economic effects' of this 'plethora of licensed premises.' Carrying out this investigation was the stated purpose of the Commission, and a secondary purpose was to come up with standardised, nationwide rules for the sale of alcohol.[53]

Many of those who submitted evidence to the Commission desired stringent legislation to limit the availability of alcohol. Thomas Somerville Lindsay, a member of the Council of the Church of Ireland Temperance Society, felt 'there is a very strong body of public opinion behind us in the desire for further restrictions in Ireland in the drink traffic. We feel that the liquor traffic has to be very stringently controlled and that the existing restrictions are not sufficient.'[54] Various Protestant and Catholic temperance societies presenting evidence to the commission called for all public houses to be closed on Sundays, the rescinding of licences for the sale of alcohol in ordinary grocery shops (known as 'mixed-trading'), and a reduction by one half of the number of public houses in the state.[55] The Commission, though, issued a vaguer and less draconian set of recommendations: An overhaul of the confusing legislation on alcohol sales; a reduction in the number of licensed premises, with demographics, level of business and cleanliness of each pub to be deciding factors in who would be allowed to remain open; generous compensation for those who lost their licence; a reduction in opening hours; and a strengthening of laws restricting the sale of alcohol to drunk persons.

Interestingly, the final report of the Commission displayed a remarkable pragmatism about what the state could and could not achieve. 'The essential functions of the law' it said 'are to preserve order, maintain justice, and protect the community. It is not the function of the law to make people good.' To attempt to use the state's legal machinery for the purposes of moral reform—'to abolish extravagance by sumptuary laws, to suppress idleness, prostitution and gambling'—was something that would supposedly 'bring the law into contempt'. The commissioners, though, did reserve '[t]he right to interfere with the drunkard', since this was 'the right to interfere with a public nuisance'. Their fear, though, was that such a programme, if handled badly, 'would unduly restrict the satisfaction of a natural and legitimate appetite by *reasonable and moderate men* who do not abuse their rights.' The Commissioners were also unimpressed by the zealousness of some witnesses, diplomatically described as having 'little practical knowledge of the problems with which they were dealing.' As the Commissioners pointed out: 'Those who most strongly condemn the publichouses would do well to remember that in most of our Irish villages it is, for better or worse, the poor man's club, and nearly always the only one available.'[56]

In contrast to Monto and issues of control over women's sexual bodies, where the full machinery of the state could be utilised, it is revealing that more sober heads prevailed on this issue of men's right to drink alcohol. The pragmatic reforms suggested by the Commission also reflected the limits of social reform, when such reform cut across private economic interests. Already in 1921, one supporter of temperance legislation had remarked that 'The magnitude of the drink evil in Ireland is increased by the fact that temperance reformers have to fight against one of the strongest organisations in the country, banded together together [*sic*] by hoops of gold to defend a traffic that when ill-regulated is a menace to all true citizenship.'[57]

The push for a more rigorous control of alcohol, if not even outright prohibition, was stymied (but never fully blocked) by the economic clout of such organisations as the Irish Brewers Association, the Licenced Grocers and Vintners Association, the Hotel, Restaurant and Catering

Association of Ireland and the Irish Tourist Association.[58] Thomas Callan MacArdle, a prominent brewery owner, admitted that Ireland suffered from a population that included 'weaklings who have no self-control'. But he also argued strongly against government interference, believing that the Church, rather than the state, should take on the task 'to strengthen their moral fibre.'[59] When the government enacted legislation based on the Commission's recommendations, various business groups again lobbied the government. In one collective submission, the 'Licensed Trade of the Saorstat [Free State]' asserted that 'The licenced trader's house is his castle' and criticised 'puritanical' restrictions made by 'a very small minority population ... who, if they had their way, would stop at nothing short of Prohibition from which GOD SAVE IRELAND'.[60] The Hotel, Restaurant and Catering Association of Ireland went so far as to suggest amendments to the proposed legislation, whilst merchants from Kilkenny, Kerry and Cork threatened that pressure would be brought to bear against political parties that supported 'the obnoxious licensing legislation of the past few years.' They also sought 'to restore the trade to its former position of respect in the National life' and the government was reminded how strong a force publicans and licensed shopkeepers were within Cumann na nGaedheal.[61] Reflecting publicans' political power, the local government in Killarney passed a resolution echoing their strong opposition to 'iniquitous Government interference with the Licenced Trade Industry.'[62]

Conversely, organisations such as the Irish Association for the Prevention of Intemperance, whose motto was 'Ireland Sober is Ireland Free', as well as the Pioneer Total Abstinence Association, the Cork Women's Christian Temperance Association, and the World Women's Christian Temperance Union, lobbied the government either to strengthen the proposed legislation, or to push it further in the direction of even greater restriction.[63] This was all to no avail. Temperance was often seen internationally as something of a female movement.[64] This seems to have also been an issue here since, as the names of the groups just mentioned suggest, women were to the fore in contemporary Irish temperance activism. Thus, state control of alcohol could be dismissed as an unpopular infringement of men's right to drink alcohol or an infringement of male publicans' property rights. The collective economic weight (and hence also political weight) of the brewers, publicans and shopkeepers also ensured that it was these interests that would have more influence. It is also worth noting that it was lay-led groups that were at the forefront of these calls for temperance, not the 'Church' per se. The Catholic hierarchy tended to be more moderate in their publicly expressed views on this issue, and had a more intimate relationship with the political elite. And this limited ability of Catholic lay groups to influence government legislation again counters any easy stereotypes about direct religious control over the Irish state. Indeed, the Jesuit-led Pioneer Total Abstinence Association was relatively ineffectual in the years after 1922 and was rarely taken seriously by those in political power.[65]

Attempts to enforce rigid control of alcohol, to create a totally sober nation, broke under the combined weight of economic self-interest, the prominent role of alcohol in Irish popular culture, and the latter's link to men's drinking culture. In fact, Tom Inglis has observed the key role that male drinking played in the maintenance of Irish social order: 'As much as the Church and school served to develop a rigid system of sexual morality, the pub, in later life, served to maintain this morality, albeit in a more convivial but nevertheless highly ritualistic and disciplined manner.'[66] Public houses, 'masculine purgatories'[67] until the later twentieth century, were the places wherein Irish men policed each other, where they performed an ideal of cross-class solidarity and where they reinforced their sense of manly power through a ritualised drinking culture. The push for something bordering on prohibition in Ireland was thus an attempt to change deep-rooted aspects of Irish social organisation, social control and the Irish gender order. It ultimately proved too large a step for the state to take. There was quite a different result, though, in the area of literary censorship, where the state was able to go further in controlling another popular leisure activity.

The Clean Tradition of the Irish Press

As with their anxieties about alcohol, the Free State government started to address the issues of censorship by first appointing a commission to study the matter and to make recommendations for suitable legislation. Aggressively titled 'The Committee on Evil Literature' and established in February 1926, this commission's make-up again reflected a broadly defined Church/state consensus. Chaired by Robert Donovan, a professor of English literature at University College Dublin, the commission also included two Opposition TDs (William Thrift and Thomas O'Connell), a Catholic priest (James Dempsey) and a Protestant cleric (Rev. J. Sinclair Stevenson). Appointed by the Minister for Justice, Kevin O'Higgins, their drily worded task was 'to consider and report whether it is necessary or advisable in the interest of public morality to extend the existing powers of the state to prohibit or restrict the sale and circulation of printed matter.' To this end, a general announcement soliciting contributions was issued in the press. The Committee dispatched special invitations to organisations such as the Catholic Truth Society of Ireland, the Christian Brothers, and the Church of Ireland Young Men's Christian Association, as well as educational organisations like the School Masters' Association and the Irish National Teachers' Organisation (INTO). There was almost unanimous agreement on the part of those submitting evidence that the current legislation was inadequate and that this had profound moral consequences for Ireland.[68]

Richard Devane, a Jesuit priest and veteran of the campaign against Monto (who had also established a reputation as a pro-active, if highly conservative, Catholic social reformer) was the only individual witness to be personally invited by the commission.[69] A year earlier, writing in the *Irish Ecclesiastical Record*, Devane observed that 'our new-won powers to legislate according to Irish ideals and Catholic standards' made it possible to deal with what he termed 'indecent literature and unsavoury publications'. Indeed, the moral horror underpinning Devane's views surfaced in the very language used. He spoke of 'the cross-Channel unclean press' and 'the reptile press'. He believed that, with the law reformed, 'we could deal satisfactorily with the cross-Channel looseness, grossness, and vulgarity that are nowadays being propagated with impunity throughout the country, by prosecuting bookstalls, booksellers, and newsvendors engaged in the sale of this unclean and vulgar literature, throwing on them the whole onus of what they sell.' The worst element of this 'unclean' literature, for Devane, was the promotion of contraception, something he believed was rife in the Free State: 'Advertisements of manuals of immorality, of immoral appliances, and of diabolical books, mostly written by women, are becoming quite common in what is appropriately styled the "gutter press", which is dumped by the ton each week on the Dublin quays.' He urged Catholic dock workers to refuse to handle these 'tainted goods'. Though he generally agreed that 'the clean tradition of the Irish Press ... has upheld morality in the face of many inducements from cross-Channel purveyors of filth', Devane also suggested that a 'black-list' of banned publications be compiled by the Irish government, as other governments had done ('I have the Australian and Canadian lists beside me as I write'). Probably referencing Joyce's *Ulysses*, Devane wanted the list to begin with 'the notorious volume of a well-known degenerate Irishman ... Indecency is indecency even though the cunning hand of some degenerate artists pretends to hide its nakedness under the transparencies of a seductive style.'[70] His testimony to the Committee covered similar ground; he railed against 'the growing circulation of these cross-channel filthy weeklies', and also dismissed any objections to censorship that he felt came from 'loose-thinking and loose-living gentlemen' who intentionally 'confuse the liberty with the license of the Press.' Quoting Pope Leo XIII, Devane sought to draw a stark distinction between the right to speak the truth (which should never be hampered) and the erroneous assumption that one has a right to speak falsehoods. Hinting at some of his social biases, Devane felt a clear distinction should be drawn here because 'by far the greater part of the community is either absolutely unable, or able only with great difficulty, to escape from illusions and deceitful subtleties, especially such as flatter the passions.'[71]

Devane represented the outer reaches of a mainstream viewpoint. Pointing to the intertwined relationship between state and Church, his pro-censorship missives were 'suggested' by the Justice Minister, Kevin O'Higgins, 'who is conscious to excite an atmosphere in advance so as to facilitate legislation'.[72] There was almost unanimous agreement on the part of those submitting evidence to the Committee on Evil Literature that the current legislation was inadequate, that Ireland was being flooded by 'imported newspapers' that reported on 'incidents of an immoral and degrading nature', and that there was 'indiscriminate advertisement and circulation' of literature promoting birth control. The Catholic Truth Society, a lay group specially invited to submit evidence, took direct issue with publications advocating 'neo-Malthusian birth control' in that the latter allows sexual intercourse to be divorced from procreation and therefore is 'a very deliberate and shameless form of mutual masturbation.' This was an obviously Catholic position to take. Unlike the more statist Devane, the Catholic Truth Society felt the Church, rather than the Free State, should take the lead in tackling these issues of 'moral welfare'.[73] In subsequent years the Society would regularly correspond with state officials, demanding that the latter act to fulfil the Catholic wishes of the former.[74] Charles Eason, proprietor of the one of the country's largest booksellers and newspaper distribution companies, similarly agreed that the Church should play the dominant role in suppressing the 'reading of immoral papers' in Ireland. Though Eason, like Thomas Callan MacArdle before him, had presumably more mundane economic reasons for urging 'voluntary action' rather than state legislation or censorship.[75]

The final recommendations of the Committee, however, were far closer to the suggestions of Devane than those of Eason. The Committee proposed that existing laws be amended so as to give a wider interpretation of the terms 'indecent and obscene'; that recent British legislation which regulated the reporting of court cases be adopted in Ireland; that a 'Board or Committee' be set up to censor books (the committee would be drawn from religious, educational and literary and artistic fields); that those who published 'prohibited' books be fined and/or imprisoned; and that only 'authorised persons' be allowed to buy publications promoting birth control.[76] Within a year, Kevin O'Higgins sought the 'authority of the Executive Council ... to proceed with the preparation of a bill to be introduced in the Autumn [of 1927], giving effect generally to the recommendations of the Committee.'[77]

By the end of the decade, Devane's 'black-list' would be legally enforced by the state and censorship would reach such extremes that some of the highest regarded works of twentieth-century literature would find their way onto the Irish Free State's *Register of Prohibited Publications*.[78] The primary issues, though, seem to have been sex, representations of sexuality, and publications that promoted women's use of birth control. Works by the eugenicist and sexologist Havelock Ellis and by birth control advocate Marie Stopes recurred regularly on the *Register*, as did works with such telling titles as *Birth Control Methods*, *Marital Hygiene* and *What Every Mother Should Know*. Women's bodies and the desires of a male-dominated state to control those bodies were never far from the legal surface.

Yet, while literature explaining the use of contraception was now banned, contraception itself remained legally available. This paradox was discussed in December 1932, when James Geoghegan, Minister for Justice of the newly installed Fianna Fáil government, met with a delegation representing the Catholic hierarchy. The bishops pointed out the 'illogical' fact that 'any publication advocating the sale of contraceptives' could be banned whilst 'the sale of apparatus of this kind in the State' was still permitted. The bishops themselves made reference to 'the Report of the Committee on the Criminal Law Amendment Acts (1880–85)'. Geoghegan also referenced this report and its recommendations:

> The Minister stated that he would like to see a Bill go through which would bring the law into accord with the best Catholic practice and teaching on those subjects, it being understood, of course, that the legislation would

need to be practicable and readily workable and that possibly many provisions otherwise desirable might have to be omitted because of the difficulty of giving effect to them through the machinery of the police and the judicial system. Their Lordships [i.e., the Catholic bishops] agreed.[79]

The report in question was the so-called Carrigan Committee report, a highly instructive moment in the history of Irish sexuality, male political power, and the on-going project of gendered nationalist self-fashioning in the Irish Free State.

The Carrigan Committee

The Carrigan Committee was chaired by the eponymous William Carrigan, a senior member of the judiciary, and included a Jesuit priest (Rev. John Hannon S.J.) and the Dean of Christ Church Cathedral (Rev. H.B. Kennedy) as well as a surgeon, Francis J. Morrin. Unlike previous such commissions, two women were also included in the committee: Mrs Jane Power, a Commissioner of the Dublin Union, and Miss V. O'Carroll, Matron of the Coombe Hospital. Formed in June 1930, the Committee's designated task was:

> to consider whether the following statutes require amendment and, if so, in what respect, namely: The Criminal Law Amendment Act, 1880, and The Criminal Law Amendment Act, 1885, as modified by later statutes; and to consider whether any new legislation is feasible to deal in a suitable manner with the problem of juvenile prostitution (i.e. prostitutes under the age of 21).

However, the Committee decided to push beyond these narrow jurisprudential boundaries. Defining their focus as 'the secular aspect of social morality which it is the concern of the State to conserve and safeguard for the protection and well-being of its citizens', Carrigan and his colleagues sought 'to collect sufficient information from such authentic sources as would enable us to determine whether the standard of social morality is at present exposed to evils, which the existing laws of the Saorstát, for the suppression and prevention of public vice, are inadequate to check'.[80]

In all, the Committee held 20 meetings between 20 June 1930 and 10 August 1931. Submissions were sought from the Garda Commissioner, Eoin O'Duffy, the Irish Vigilance Association, the St. Vincent de Paul Society, the National Society for the Prevention of Cruelty to Children, and, of course, the ubiquitous Jesuit, Richard Devane.[81] As with previous such commissions, there was again a consensus among those giving evidence that something had gone wrong in Irish society; 'The testimony of all the witnesses, clerical, lay and official, is striking in its unanimity that degeneration in the standard of social conduct had taken place in recent years.'[82] Devane was present at the Committee's fourth meeting, on 1 July 1930, and like Frank Duff (who had presented his evidence a week earlier, on 27 June 1930), Devane agreed that prostitution was rife in Ireland. For Devane, it was temporary migration to England, as well as the new fashion of dance halls, which had 'ruined' these 'girls'.[83]

Dance halls were a common scapegoat for the supposed decline in standards of public morality in contemporary Ireland. Eoin O'Duffy's submission, which became 'the framework around which the report was built',[84] suggested that 'dance halls are responsible for a good deal of immorality amongst the youth.' O'Duffy was disturbed by the absence of supervision over such places and felt they could be made 'respectable' by stricter regulation. In any case, O'Duffy, long an advocate for a more active and muscular masculinity,[85] was perplexed why 'athletic young men should spend beautiful Summer evenings indoor [*sic*] in such fashion.'[86] On the issue of prostitution, O'Duffy blamed the dangers inherent in female adolescence: 'Between those ages (13–18) sexual passions are so predominant that they are most difficult to subdue, and females [*sic*] are affected with natural weaknesses. They have not the physical strength or strength of will to resist suggestions which so strongly appeal to their senses.' Once 'fallen', O'Duffy saw such women as 'a source of temptation to men, and their conduct will influence those of their own sex with whom they come in contact'. Conversely, 'for the class of men known as bullies [i.e., pimps], and for all offences against girls under 13 years of age, I take the responsibility of very strongly recommending the "cat" [a cat-o'-nine-tails whip]—not a few strokes, but the most severe application the medical advisor will permit, having regard only to the physical condition and health of the offender.'[87]

O'Duffy also outlined 24 separate recommendations for legal reform, again mainly focusing on dance halls. He called for annually renewable licences for dance-hall owners. He urged that licences to be renewed should require endorsement by 'six respectable householders in the immediate locality'. He suggested that the 'local Clergy, any householder and the Garda [*sic*, Gardaí]' should have the right to legally object in court to the granting of licences or renewals; in other words, the Church, the state and male property-owners would together enforce morality. Gardaí should also have the right to enter dance halls at any time, without prior warrants.[88] Moreover, 'It should be a condition that licences may be revoked at any time during the year by District Justices on a well-founded complaint from the Garda or two responsible householders', 'the character of the applicant should be a determining factor in the granting of a licence' and a residence qualification should be used to prevent outside 'undesirables' from setting up dance halls.[89]

The recommendations of the Carrigan Report itself were remarkably similar. They urged stricter regulation of dance halls via licences that would be renewed and reviewed annually. No licence should be issued unless the applicant was of a 'good character'. They recommended that contraception be banned, along the lines of the 1920 Dangerous Drugs Act 'except under exceptional circumstances.'[90] Echoing Duff and Devane's recommendations that prostitutes be sent to special 'homes' for treatment, the report urged that 'Girl offenders' [i.e., those aged 16–21] should be dealt with via a borstal system. The Committee also agreed with O'Duffy's recommendations about the flogging of offenders, but left it unclear if this punishment should be reserved for men only. Additionally, they suggested that 'persons found guilty should be black-listed officially by publishing their names and addresses, the description of the offence, the Court of trial, and the sentence imposed.' Concluding that there could be 'no doubt that gross offences are rife throughout the country' the Committee urged a 'Frank recognition of this fact' which, they felt, would 'create a state of healthy public opinion helpful to the Government in purging the State from these evils.'[91]

This, though, would prove too much for the state. In a December 1931 memorandum sent to all members of the Executive Council, the secretary of the Department of Justice outlined his minister's anxieties: 'The Report contains very sweeping statements as to the standard of morality in this country and unless the Council are satisfied that these statements are justified, and this is a point on which the Minister has some serious doubts, it may not be considered wise to give currency to the damaging allegations made by the Committee.' The legislative reforms were described as legally unworkable, something ascribed to the fact that 'no Judge either of the High Court or Circuit Court' was invited to appear before the Committee.[92] Similar views prevailed within the new Fianna Fáil government, which came to power the following year: 'On the whole the Report should be taken with reserve. It leaves the impression that the authors did not face their task in a judicial and impartial frame of mind ... It contains numerous sweeping charges against the state of morality of the Saorstat and even if these statements were true, there would be little point in giving them currency.'[93] Nationalist elites had long sought to construct an idealised image of order and harmony. The Carrigan Report's 'frank' discussions of Irish sexuality cut across these putative notions of Irish national purity and thus proved too contentious.[94] The report was suppressed and never published, a decision supported by the Catholic hierarchy and by the Church generally.[95] Indeed, as late as 1974, the then Minister for Posts and Telegraphs, Conor Cruise O'Brien, was only allowed access to the report on condition that he not refer to it in public.[96] The same year, Cruise O'Brien's Labour colleague, Senator John Horgan, was refused any access to the report.[97]

Dancing at the Crossroads[98]

Notwithstanding the suppression of the Carrigan Report, some of its less extreme recommendations were subsequently implemented. Following the completion of the work of the Carrigan Committee, another committee was established, this time under the direct supervision of the Minister for Justice. The purpose of this informal cross-party committee was to make specific recommendations for legislation, and it was active both before and after Fianna Fáil's ascension to power in February 1932.[99] A memorandum circulated to the Executive Council in June 1934 asserted that the 'Minister for Justice is anxious'[100] to implement Geoghegan's recommendations, out of which two important pieces of legislation emerged: The Public Dance Halls Act and The Criminal Law Amendment Act, both implemented in February 1935.

The Criminal Law Amendment Act provided for new penalties for rape and for the 'Defilement of girl[s] under fifteen years of age' and for those between 15 and 17 years of age. The Act also stipulated that those convicted of the 'Offence of keeping a brothel' be fined or imprisoned, as also would 'Every common prostitute who is found loitering in any street, thoroughfare, or other place and importuning or soliciting passers-by for purposes of prostitution or being otherwise offensive to passers-by'. In line with Frank Duff and Eoin O'Duffy's views of prostitutes as female seductresses of male victims, no criminal charges were thought necessary for those men soliciting prostitutes. Most famously though, this Act banned the importation and sale of contraceptives in Ireland, with fines of up to £50 or prison sentences of up to six months being stipulated.[101] Contraception was defined as 'any appliance, instrument, drug, preparation or thing, *designed, prepared, or intended* to prevent pregnancy resulting from sexual intercourse between human beings.' Geoghegan and his Committee had 'decided that there should be no prohibition of drugs or substances *capable of use* for contraception, and limited their recommendations to contraceptive appliances.'[102] Whether done intentionally or not, this left open a legal loophole that would allow for the sale of contraception, provided the ostensible *intent* was not the prevention of conception. In the 1960s, this loophole allowed women to buy the contraceptive pill, provided their stated intent was to use it for non-contraceptive purposes such as menstrual regulation.[103] Similarly, family planning clinics could distribute condoms from the late 1960s onwards, provided they were not 'for sale', but rather were given as gifts to 'clients making donations to the clinic.'[104] These were obvious legal veneers, but the central point of banning contraception in 1935 was, itself, to create a politically useful veneer that the Irish, unlike their neighbours across the St George's Channel, were a nation who observed sexual respectability and a strict gender order.

A comparable dissimulation was underway in the Public Dance Halls Act. A report compiled by the Garda Deputy Commissioner at the end of the 1930s admitted that the various sexual crimes known to the Gardaí ('infanticide, indecent assaults, concealment of births and defilement of young girls') almost certainly do not 'arise from causes connected with public dancing'. The report also disputed the claims that 'there is excessive drinking at Public Dances' and noted that 'It is generally admitted that the younger generation are far more sober than their predecessors'. Moreover, the report confessed, 'It must be admitted that in so far as the commercial hall is concerned the reports indicate that their proprietors are men of good character who do their best to see that dances are properly conducted.' Conversely, in the case of dances in Parish Halls rather than commercial venues, 'the supervision on dancing is rather strict and does not call for comment.'[105]

These calmer views of Irish rural dances are starkly at odds with those of Richard Devane. He saw dance halls as a 'moral and national menace' and claimed they were bastions of drunkenness and even worse: 'Not only is drink taken by the men but girls [*sic*] are induced to do so. Hence the orgies one sees so often reported in the Press and which centre round the dance-halls.' The parish priest in Newbridge in Kildare, one Fr. Brophy, called two local dance-halls 'Synagogues of Satan'. Devane spoke of them as 'man-traps' and physically dirty places; notions of sanitised space were central, if subtle, elements in his thinking.[106] Uncharacteristically, Devane approvingly quoted the stricter regulations enforced in Britain, whereby dance halls were more closely monitored by the authorities: 'There is a spirit of discipline in all this that it would be well we should copy, if for no other reason than to teach many of our young folk a sense of restraint and discipline, of which they seem scarcely to have a rudimentary idea.' Whereas Devane saw Irish public spaces as increasingly polluted by dance halls, British authorities, he believed, had properly disciplined their public spaces. His conclusion was that the 'moral health of the [Irish] Nation is not quite sound and shows signs of being gradually undermined ... There is a general languor and *malaise* in the body corporate which seem to imply a general poisoning of the national system.' Pushing this medical metaphor, Devane urged: 'Remove the source of infection and a surprising recovery will soon take place ... We need the hand of a national surgeon, of a strong Minister, to rid us of its poisoning influence and so to lead to the restoration of our normal moral health. God send it soon.'[107]

The Public Dance Halls Act trod a fine line between the anxieties of the likes of Devane and the far more staid realities. After this Act's passing, all dance halls were licensed and the issuing of licences depended on 'the character and the financial and other circumstances of the applicant', as well as the age of potential customers and the facilitating of full Garda supervision and inspection. All licence applications could also be disputed by the Gardaí or by members of the public.[108] This legislation was perhaps not the 'national surgeon' for which Devane was praying. Nonetheless, it does echo his concerns about control of sanitised public spaces, control of women, and the promotion of idealised archetypes of male and female behaviour. Again, Devane represented the outer limits of a broadly held consensus.

Where Does the State End and the Church Begin?

The intensely Catholic nature of public life in post-1922 Ireland and the strong role played by Catholicism in Irish national identity would seem to be two of the most obvious differences between Irish nationalism and Zionism. Indeed, a number of recent histories have explained the austere politics of morality in post-1922 Ireland by focusing overwhelmingly on Catholic elements.[109] That these works have emerged in the context of a supposedly post-Catholic Ireland[110] is not a coincidence. The Church, of course, was not an innocent bystander to the legislation of the 1920s and 1930s. Nonetheless, whether done consciously or not, Catholic-centric explanations serve not only to place a disproportionate amount of blame on the Church, they also serve to exculpate the state. Thus, in the context of a society that has ostensibly moved away from Catholicism, oppressive social control can be historiographically represented as something *Catholics* were responsible for *in the past*, whilst the state, then as now, remains blameless. This has obvious political ramifications.

As this chapter has sought to demonstrate, however, the Irish state was strongly invested in projects of male power and social control. Moreover, this was not something that began in 1922, when a Catholic state emerged. The campaign to shut down Monto, the campaigns against alcohol and public dancing, the restrictions on contraception and book publishing, all echoed and drew from earlier nationalist concerns about public space, public order and masculine control. This legislation, most especially in the area of alcohol, also sought to counter anti-Irish stereotypes and craft a more soothing image of the nation.[111]

There is a long history of Church–state co-operation in Ireland as the Church, the state, and the Catholic elite together sought to 'police' a supposedly unruly society:[112] 'the Church was a major source of political stability in modern Irish society' and 'it regularly preach[ed] submission to the power of the state'.[113] Maurice Curtis points out that the major changes wrought by the French Revolution and the Industrial Revolution had made the Catholic Church across Europe identify with 'the parties of order and authority.'[114] The Church was certainly a willing ally of the Irish state; in the aftermath of not only the Civil War but the entire period of crisis from 1912 onwards, both sought to return to some sense of societal normality. Additionally, 'Vigilantism [i.e., Catholic control of the Moral Order] and nationalism were not strange bed-fellows; both sought a certain kind of purification.'[115]

These desires for purification and large-scale social reform, as well as revived masculine power, were key components in both Zionism and Irish nationalism in the late nineteenth and twentieth centuries. As already mentioned, this gendered 'fingerprint' had a long-term impact on the Israeli state and society. Margalit Shilo has shown how the demand for female suffrage within Zionism posed larger, and perhaps more dangerous, questions for a male-dominated movement: 'suffragettes in each and every place did not just criticise the civil status of the women but sought to give birth to a new social order' [*sufrajistim be-kol etar ve-etar lo rak bikru et ha-maamad ha-izrachi shel ha-isha eleh bikshu le-brua seder chavrati chadash*]. Drawing on Louise Ryan's work on gender and Irish nationalism, Shilo goes on to argue that in Zionism, as in its Irish equivalent, 'the nationalist movements strengthened masculinity and kept women in the domestic sphere, with neither of them [Irish nationalism and Zionism] ever having the opposite effect of contributing to a strengthening of women' [*ha-tenu'ot ha-le'umiot he'etzimu et hagaveriut ve-hish'iru nashim be-techum ha-bayit, ach lo achat haita la-hen gam ha-shepa'ah hafucha ve-hen tarmu le-ha'atzamat nashim*].[116] Both Zionism and Irish nationalism did indeed have leading female activists, and these activists, as Shilo points out, may have seen national liberation and gender liberation as interrelated goals.[117] Theirs, however, remained minority voices in a male-dominated project.

It is unsurprising, then, that obsessions with gender order and social control were noticeably present in both the Yishuv and, after 1948, the State of Israel. Bat-Sheva Margalit Stern's analysis of Zionist beauty pageants in Mandate Palestine, for instance, identifies these events as means of controlling women's bodies, as well as part of the broader project of creating the 'new Jew'.[118] In opposition to a much cherished image of Israel as an egalitarian society, the sociologists Baruch Kimmerling and Nitza Berkovitch both note that 'women have been constructed not as equal citizens' in Israel, 'but first and foremost as mothers and wives.'[119] And as discussed in Chap. 6, it is similarly doubtful if socialist kibbutzim were ever the bastions of gender equality that romantic accounts portrayed. As one recent account has shown, the notion that motherhood was women's natural role was pervasive in Israel.[120] In this, the kibbutzim reflected broader trends. Even before the founding of the state, pro-natalist ideas were prominent in Zionist politics and the burden was placed predominantly on women. Jacqueline Portugese ascribes this to an ongoing demographic battle with Palestinians as well as a patriarchal 'ideology of familism' that 'permeates all sectors of Israeli society.'[121]

Honing in on the Israeli Women's Equal Rights Law of 1951, Baruch Kimmerling notes that the preamble states 'from the beginning of the movement to return to Zion, the Jewish woman was *a loyal companion* to the early immigrants and settlers'. Presenting the Equal Rights Law to the Knesset, the Ministry of Justice declared that 'in fulfilling her duty and privilege as a Hebrew mother cherishing the young generation and educating them … the Hebrew woman and mother continues the great tradition of the Israeli heroine'. Israeli women, Kimmerling concludes, 'are thus considered to have been merely companions to the founding fathers, not "pioneers" themselves.'[122] Citizenship in Israel, as in many other polities, was subtly coded as male and Zionism was a project predominantly for and by (Ashkenazi Jewish) men.[123] Orit Rozin similarly suggests that the Israeli state was coded as male. In the early years of the state, Israeli women (many of whom were veteran residents of Israel-Palestine) were removed from employment and replaced by newly arrived male immigrants. As Rozin argues: 'Despite their egalitarian principles, it simply did not occur to Mapai's [*Mifleget HaPoalim Eretz Yisrael*, lit. Party of the Workers of Israel, the Israeli Labour Party] male leaders that women could or should be involved in making policy that affected them.'[124] Many of the female immigrants who arrived after the founding of the state were accused, by Israeli elites, of engaging in prostitution[125] or were perceived, in terms familiar to Irish politics, as 'aggressive, alcoholic, cunning, immoral, lazy, noisy, and unhygienic.' Kimmerling talks of 'the anxiety over loss of control and surveillance over all these new populations' and argues that 'In order to meet these threats, the state was organized as a highly centralized and all-encompassing institution.'[126] The parallels (and contrasts) with Ireland are obvious: in both cases, certain (predominantly female) groups were classed as a danger to the national order and the control of these groups served to exemplify the new state's power and authority. A deeper anxiety about national degeneracy was at work in both cases.

Zionism's egalitarian socialist roots did serve, *somewhat*, to temper its attitudes towards women.[127] This is in obvious contrast to the undeniably strong influence of a conservative Catholicism on Irish nationalism's gendered project of social control. Catholicism undeniably played a major role in post-1922 Irish nationalism, but this should not distract from the fact that its primary role was often to legitimise a secular project of masculinist social engineering which, legitimising veneers aside, was quite comparable to the similar Zionist project of fashioning the 'new Jew'. As Tom Inglis notes, in twentieth-century Ireland, there may have been debate about 'the State, political parties, trade unions and other national organisations,' but the Church was not to be publicly criticised. State policy could always be openly criticised, as opposed to Church dogma. Thus, by outsourcing sexual morality to the Church,[128] by having the Church lead the push for changes in censorship, alcohol consumption, sexual legislation and the control of leisure activities, the Irish state was able to better pursue its project of social control, surveillance and national reform. The Church's divine legitimacy served to ordain a state-project of constructing a rigidly defined, nationalist, and male-centric gender order.[129]

Notes

1. Peter Lennon, quoted in *Rocky Road to Dublin* (dir. P. Lennon, 1967).
2. B. Kimmerling (2001) *The Invention and Decline of Israeliness: State, Society and the Military* (Berkeley, CA: University of California Press) p. 58.
3. Ibid., p. 65–68.
4. Ibid., p. 9; O. Rozin (2011) *The Rise of the Individual in 1950s Israel: A Challenge to Collectivism* (Waltham, MA: Brandeis University Press).
5. M. Laffan (1983) *The Partition of Ireland: 1911–1925* (Dundalk: Dundalgan Press/Dublin Historical Association) p. 117.
6. P. Anderson (2013) *The Indian Ideology* (London: Verso) p. 146.
7. Joan Landes talks of 'the masquerade through which the (male) particular was able to posture behind the veil of the universal.' Thus, 'when women during the French Revolution and the nineteenth century attempted to organize in public on the basis of their interests, they risked violating the constitutive principles of the bourgeois public sphere ... Worse yet, women risked disrupting the gendered organization of nature, truth, and opinion that assigned them to a place in the private, domestic but not the public realm ... women's (legal and constitutional) exclusion from the public sphere was a constitutive, not a marginal or accidental feature of the bourgeois public from the start.' J. Landes (1998) 'The Public and the Private Sphere: A Feminist Reconsideration' in J. Landes, ed.. *Feminism, the Public and the Private* (Oxford: Oxford University Press) p. 143.
8. P.S. O'Hegarty (1924) *The Victory of Sinn Féin: How and It Won It, And How It Used It* (Dublin: Talbot Press) p. 57.
9. Ibid., p. 56.
10. Ibid., p. 102.
11. Ibid., pp. 104–105. Interestingly, though, in 1912 O'Hegarty had come out strongly and unapologetically in favour of women's emancipation. P.S. Ó h-Éigeartaigh (September 1912) 'The Emancipation of Women.' *Irish Freedom*.
12. J.M. Regan (1999) *The Irish Counter-Revolution, 1921–1936: Treatyite Politics and Settlement in Independent Ireland* (Dublin: Gill and Macmillan) pp. 180–181.
13. L. Ryan (2002) *Gender, Identity and the Irish Press, 1922–1937: Embodying the Nation* (New York: Edwin Mellen) p. 213.

14. UCDA, de Valera Papers, P150/657, Letter to Mary MacSwiney from Eamon de Valera, 11 September 1922.
15. L. Ryan (2002) *Embodying the Nation*, pp. 212–221; M. Ward (1983) *Unmanageable Revolutionaries: Women and Irish Nationalism* (London: Pluto Press) pp. 156–198.
16. John Regan's *The Irish Counter-Revolution* is perhaps the best-known proponent of this view.
17. J.H. Whyte suggests that Church–state relations should also be understood in the context of what he terms 'the authoritarian strain in Irish culture', something that manifests itself in deference to clergy, the arrogance of elite politicians, coercive father–son relationships and the education system. J.H. Whyte (1971) *Church and State in Modern Ireland, 1923–1970* (Dublin: Gill and MacMillan) pp. 21–23. John Regan has similarly noted the wariness of democracy shared by both Cumann na nGaedheal/Fine Gael and Fianna Fáil in this period. J.M. Regan (1999) *Counter-Revolution*.
18. John McGahern would later sum up the Legion of Mary as 'a kind of legalized gossiping school to the women and a convenient pool of labour that the priests could draw on for catering committees ... it was founded by one of our countrymen, Frank Duff ... it was organized on exactly the same pattern as Communism: a presidium at the top and widening circles of leadership all the way down to the bottom'. J. McGahern (1963/1983) *The Barracks* (London: Faber & Faber) p. 163.
19. H. Firtel (1985) *A Man For Our Time: Frank Duff and The Legion of Mary* (Cork: Mercier Press) pp. 40–41.
20. F. Duff, D. McAuliffe, ed. (1961) *Miracles on Tap* (New York: Montfort Publications) p. 32; T. O'Flynn (1981) *Frank Duff: As I Knew Him* (Dublin: Praedicanda Publications) p. 33.
21. M. Luddy (2007) *Prostitution and Irish Society, 1800–1940* (Cambridge: Cambridge University Press) p. 216.
22. DDA, Lay Organisations Section, Box 1, *The Work at 76 Harcourt Street*, Undated Memorandum probably written by Frank Duff; DDA, Lay Organisations Section, Box 1, Undated Memorandum (probably written by Frank Duff).
23. F. Kennedy (2011) *Frank Duff: A Life Story* (London: Continuum) p. 82.
24. L. Ó Broin (1982) *Frank Duff: A Biography* (Dublin: Gill and Macmillan) pp. 25–26.
25. D. Ferriter (2009) *Occasions of Sin* (London: Profile Books) p. 150. As Ferriter points out, though, slightly less open prostitution continued in the St Stephen's Green area, just across the Liffey. *Ibid*, p. 152.
26. M. Luddy (2007) *Prostitution*, p. 156.

27. Ibid., p. 157.
28. Ibid., p. 161.
29. F. Duff (1961) *Miracles*, p. 117.
30. T. O'Flynn (1981) *As I Knew Him*, p. 32.
31. M. Luddy (2007) *Prostitution*, p. 227.
32. G.A. Boyd (2006) *Dublin, 1745–1922: Hospitals, Spectacle and Vice* (Dublin: Four Courts Press) pp. 188–189.
33. *Report with Appendices of the Inter-Departmental Committee of Inquiry Regarding Venereal Disease* (Dublin: The Stationery Office, 1926).
34. Ibid.
35. Ibid. As Foucault said, 'the hospital is increasingly conceived of as a base for the medical observation of the population outside.' M. Foucault (1995) *Discipline and Punish: The Birth of the Prison* (New York: Vintage Books) p. 212.
36. F. Duff (1961) *Miracles*, p. 10.
37. DDA, Lay Organisations Section, Box 1, *The Work at 76 Harcourt Street*, Undated memorandum by Frank Duff.
38. DDA, Lay Organisations Section, Box 1, Undated memorandum by Frank Duff.
39. *Ibid*.
40. F. Duff (1961) *Miracles*, p. 63.
41. *Ibid*, pp. 25–35. 130–137, 183, 187, 249.
42. DDA, Lay Organisations Section, Box 1, *The Work at 76 Harcourt Street*, Undated memorandum by Frank Duff. Emphases added.
43. T. O'Flynn (1981) *As I Knew Him*, pp. 34–35.
44. G.A. Boyd (2006) *Hospitals, Spectacle and Vice*, p. 191.
45. J. Smith (2007) *Ireland's Magdalen Laundries and the Nation's Architecture of Containment* (South Bend, IN: University of Notre Dame Press) pp. 46–47. Smith says that the 'architecture of containment' allowed 'the decolonizing nation-state to confine aberrant citizens, rendering invisible women and children who fell foul of society's moral proscriptions. In this way, I argue, the state regulated its national imaginary; it promoted a national identity that privileged Catholic morality and valorised the correlation between marriage and motherhood while at the same time effacing nonconforming citizens who were institutionally confined.'
46. M. Luddy (2007) *Prostitution*, p. 195.
47. D. Ferriter (2009) *Occasions of Sin* p. 150; M. Luddy (2007) *Prostitution*, pp. 215–217. There were also strong suspicions that Monto held a number of safe houses for anti-Treaty Irregulars, and this may have been a further reason for the state's desire for clearance.
48. UCDA, de Valera Papers, P150/2047, *Mr. De Valera's Introductory Speech at the Opening of the Ard Fheis of Fianna Fáil*, 24 November 1926.

49. UCDA, de Valera Papers, P150/2048, *Statement by Eamon de Valera, T.D., at 2nd Annual Ard Fheis of Fianna Fail, as President of that Organization.*
50. J.J. Lee (1973) *The Modernisation of Irish Society* (Dublin: Gill and Macmillan) p. 14.
51. Timothy McMahon, in his otherwise impressive study of the Gaelic League, falls into a trap of presenting these anxieties uncritically, as accurate depictions of a drunken Irish reality, rather than products of broader nationalist ideologies. T. McMahon (2008) *Grand Opportunity: The Gaelic Revival and Irish Society, 1893–1910* (Syracuse NY: Syracuse University Press) pp. 132–133.
52. 'Mr. Horgan is chairman of the Cork Harbour Board and one of the coroners for the county. He was a member of the Council of the C.T.S. [Catholic Truth Society]. A member of the national directory of the U.I.L., he was a strong supporter of the Irish Party in the pre-war electoral struggles in Cork City.' NAI TAOIS/3/S4251 A, Press Cutting, *Irish Independent*, 1 February 1925.
53. NAI TAOIS 90/75/508, Intoxicating Liquor Commission, Minutes of Evidence, 23 March 1925.
54. NAI TAOIS 90/75/508, Intoxicating Liquor Commission, Minutes of Evidence, 4 May 1925.
55. *Intoxicating Liquor Commission Report* (Dublin: The Stationery Office, 28 August 1925).
56. *Ibid.* Emphases added.
57. Military Archives BMH CD 250/4/15, Rev W.P. Hackett, S.J., *Character and Citizenship* (Cumann Léigheachtaí an Phobail [Republican Lecture Group], 1921).
58. NAI 90/75/509, Intoxicating Liquor Commission: Minutes of Evidence, List of Witnesses.
59. NAI TAOIS 90/75/508, Intoxicating Liquor Commission, Minutes of Evidence, 18 May 1925.
60. NAI TAOIS/3/S 5319, Intoxicating Liquor Act, 1927, Copy of Statement & Memorandum of Suggestions Submitted to the Minister of Justice from the Licensed Trade of the Saorstat, 1926.
61. NAI TAOIS/3/S 5319, Intoxicating Liquor Act, 1927, Resolution passed by Licenced Grocers Association, County Kerry Branch, 19 February 1927; NAI TAOIS/3/S 5319, Intoxicating Liquor Act, 1927, Telegram from Clonakilty Licenced Vintners Association to President Cosgrave, 11 February 1927. See also, NAI TAOIS/3/S 5319, Intoxicating Liquor Act, 1927, Resolution passed by the Licensed Traders of Urlingford and district, 8 February 1927; NAI TAOIS/3/S 5319, Intoxicating Liquor Act, 1927, Letter from Licenced Grocers &

Vintners' Protection Association, Castlebar Branch to President Cosgrave.
62. NAI TAOIS/3/S 5319, Intoxicating Liquor Act, 1927, Resolution passed by Killarney Urban District Council, 15 February 1927.
63. NAI TAOIS/3/S 5319, Intoxicating Liquor Act, 1927, Letter from Irish Association for the Prevention of Intemperance, 11 February 1927; NAI TAOIS/3/S 5319, Intoxicating Liquor Act, 1927, Resolution of the Urlingford and Greane Branches of the Pioneer Total Abstinence Association, 15 February 1927; NAI TAOIS/3/S 5319, Intoxicating Liquor Act, 1927, Letter from Cork Women's Christian Temperance Association, to the President, 23 February 1927; NAI TAOIS/3/S 5319, Intoxicating Liquor Act, 1927, Resolution of the Free State Branch of The World Women's Christian Temperance Union, 8 February, 1927.
64. See, for example: I. Tyrell (1991) *Woman's World/Woman's Empire: The Woman's Christian Temperance Union in International Perspective, 1800–1930* (Chapel Hill NC: University of North Carolina Press); C. Mattingly (1998) *Well-Tempered Women: Nineteenth-Century Temperance Rhetoric* (Carbondale, IL: Southern Illinois University Press).
65. D. Ferriter (1999) *A Nation of Extremes: The Pioneers in Twentieth-Century Ireland* (Dublin: Irish Academic Press) p. 97.
66. T. Inglis (1998) *Moral Monopoly: The Rise and Fall of the Catholic Church in Modern Ireland*, 2nd edn (Dublin: UCD Press) p. 170.
67. This was the apposite phrase used in Peter Lennon's 1967 documentary, *The Rocky Road to Dublin*.
68. *Report of the Committee on Evil Literature* (Dublin: Stationery Office, 28 December 1926).
69. *Ibid.*
70. R.S. Devane (n.d. [c. 1925]) *Indecent Literature: Some Legal Remedies* (Dublin: Browne and Nolan). Reprinted from *Irish Ecclesiastical Record*, February 1925.
71. 'The Committee on Evil Literature: Some Notes of Evidence' in R.S. Devane (n.d.) *Evil Literature: Some Suggestions* (Dublin: Browne and Nolan). Much of this is reprinted from *Irish Ecclesiastical Record*, Vol. 28 (July–December 1926).
72. IJA, Censorship Judgements (1924–1968), ADMN12/13 (1), Note to Fr. Nicholas Tomkin, 28 November 1924.
73. Catholic Truth Society (1926) *The Problem of Undesirable Printed Matter: Suggested Remedies. Evidence of the Catholic Truth Society of Ireland Presented to Departmental Committee of Enquiry, 1926* (Dublin: Catholic Truth Society).

74. See, for example, NAI TAOIS/S 2325, 'Ropers Row' Complaint from Catholic Truth Society, Letter From F. O'Reilly, Secretary, Catholic Truth Society, to President Cosgrave, 25 October 1929, in which the Society threatened to publish their correspondence with the Government, to embarrass Cosgrave, if their demands to censor *Roper's Row*, an obscure novel that supposedly advocated contraception, were not met.
75. NAI JUS 7/2/2, Testimony of Charles Eason to the Committee on Evil Literature, 26 May 1926.
76. 'Report of the Committee on Evil Literature' (1926).
77. NAI TAOIS/S 5381, Censorship of Publications Act, 1929, Letter from Kevin O'Higgins, to each Member of the Executive Council, 16 March 1927.
78. Writers as diverse as William Faulkner, Upton Sinclair, Aldous Huxley, H.G. Wells, Maxim Gorki, W. Somerset Maugham, H.E. Bates, Colette, Hermann Hesse, Theodore Dreiser, Sinclair Lewis, Ernest Hemingway, John Dos Passos, Graham Greene, Sholem Asch, Seán O'Faoláin, Liam O'Flaherty and Kate O'Brien, for example, are all listed on the 1938 edition. *Register of Prohibited Publications* (Dublin: Stationery Office, 1938).
79. DDA, Archbishop Byrne Papers, Box 467, Department of Justice Files, *Rough Notes made by the Minister for Justice after an interview on the 1st December 1932, between the Bishop of Limerick, the Bishop of Ossory, the Bishop of Thasos and the Minister.* These notes can also be found here: NAI JUS H247/41B, Criminal Law Amendment Committee (1932–1933).
80. NAI 2004/32/105, Report of the Committee on the Criminal Law Amendment Acts (1880–85) and Juvenile Prostitution.
81. NAI JUS 90/4/1, Criminal Law Amendment Committee (1930) Minute Book.
82. NAI 2004/32/105, Report of the Committee on the Criminal Law Amendment Acts (1880–85) and Juvenile Prostitution.
83. NAI JUS 90/4/1, Criminal Law Amendment Committee (1930) Minute Book. See also NAI JUS 90/4/13, Memo of Evidence of Rev. R.S. Devane, S.J. These are 'Heads of Evidence', rough notes based on Devane's evidence. Under the heading Preventive Work, Devane spoke of 'Unmarried Mother; Mentally Defectives; Girls out of Control; Dance Halls'.
84. M. Finnane (2001) 'The Carrigan Committee of 1930–31 and the "Moral Condition of the Saorstát." ' *Irish Historical Studies*, Vol 32, No.128, p. 531.
85. F. McGarry (2007 *Eoin O'Duffy: A Self-Made Hero* (Oxford: Oxford University Press) pp. 150–162 and *passim*.

86. NAI JUS H247/41A, Evidence Submitted to Criminal Law Amendment Committee by Eoin O'Duffy. Unlike other witnesses, who presented written evidence before appearing for one day before the Committee, O'Duffy's evidence stretched over two days, 30 October and 6 November 1930. See NAI JUS 90/4/2, Criminal Law Amendment Committee, List of Witnesses. Maxine Leeds Craig has described the prevalence of quite comparable attitudes in North America: 'While the athlete is a masculine ideal, the man who dances professionally risks being perceived as the perfect example of a type of failed masculinity.' M. Leeds Craig (2014) *Sorry I Don't Dance: Why Men Refuse to Move* (Oxford: Oxford University Press) p. 8.
87. NAI JUS H247/41A, Evidence Submitted to Criminal Law Amendment Committee by Eoin O'Duffy.
88. No. 23 of the 24 suggestions, crossed out, presumably by O'Duffy, was 'That no license should be granted in respect of halls in remote Districts where there would be difficulty of supervision.'
89. NAI JUS H247/41A, Evidence Submitted to Criminal Law Amendment Committee by Eoin O'Duffy.
90. These last words, according to an addendum by John J. Hannon, S.J., were intended to deal with the fact that some drugs used commonly as contraceptives had other non-contraceptive uses. Thus Hannon reiterated that 'the Report does not make exception for the sale of contraceptives as such in any circumstances.' [underlining in pen in NAI copy of report]. But it was this loophole that would allow the legal veneer to be maintained about a prohibition on contraception whilst many forms of contraception remained legally available in Ireland.
91. NAI 2004/32/105, Report of the Committee on the Criminal Law Amendment Acts (1880-85) and Juvenile Prostitution.
92. NAI TAOIS/S 5998, Memorandum from the Secretary at the Department Justice to the Members of the Executive Council, 2 December 1931.
93. NAI TAOIS/S 5998, Strictly Confidential Memorandum from the Minister for Justice to the Members of the Executive Council, 28 October 1932.
94. J.M. Smith (2007)*Magdalen Laundries*, pp. 6-7. Smith also points out that with a general election looming, W.T. Cosgrave probably wanted to avoid contentious debates.
95. NAI JUS H247/41B, Criminal Law Amendment Committee (1932–1933), Rough Notes made by the Minister for Justice after an interview on the 1st December, 1932, between the Bishop of Limerick, the Bishop of Ossory, the Bishop of Thasos and the Minister; NAI JUS H247/41B, Criminal Law Amendment Committee (1932–1933), Letter from

M.J. Browne, Maynooth College, to James Geoghegan, 13 November 1932. While the bishops opposed publication, Rev. Browne was ambiguous: 'Certainly the publication of the report would not create a good impression. It would lead many to say, as the Departmental report suggests, that the influence of religion has failed in this country. They would be partly right. Religion has failed to neutralise the aphrodisiac influence of cinema, drama and literature on a great number of young people ... It [the report] will rejoice our enemies, I admit; but the more I consider it the more I see the need of wakening people up and the dangers of suppression.'

96. NAI 2002/32/105, Letter from Conor Cruise O'Brien, Minister for Posts and Telegraphs, to Patrick Cooney, Minister for Justice, 19 December 1973; NAI 2002/32/105, Letter from Patrick Cooney, Minister for Justice to Conor Cruise O'Brien, Minister for Posts and Telegraphs, January 1974.
97. NAI 2002/32/105, Letter from Patrick Cooney, Minister for Justice to Sen. John S. Horgan, Glenageary, Dublin, October 1974. Indeed, the report has still not been published and only one copy of the Carrigan Report is available in the National Archives of Ireland, with a suitably blank cover.
98. In Eamon de Valera's famous 1943 St Patrick's Day speech, he supposedly spoke of his ideal Ireland as one of 'comely maidens dancing at the crossroads.' H. Wulff (2009) *Dancing at the Crossroads: Memory and Mobility in Ireland* (New York: Berghahn Books) *passim*. Notwithstanding the fact that this specific phrase did not appear in this speech, it has come to be seen as symbolising his pastoral (and highly gendered) vision of the Irish nation.
99. NAI TAOIS/S 5998, Committee of Enquiry 1930-31, 'Criminal Law Amendment Acts', Letter from Secretary, Dept. of Justice, to Secretary, Executive Council, 24 March 1933.
100. NAI TAOIS/3/S6574, To Each Member of the Executive Council, Memorandum from the Department of Justice, 13 June 1934.
101. Criminal Law Amendment Act, 1935: Number 6 of 1935.
102. NAI TAOIS/3/S6574, Memorandum from the Department of Justice to each Member of the Executive Council,, 10 November 1933. Emphases added.
103. D. Ferriter (2009) *Occasions of Sin*, pp. 364–365.
104. Ibid., p. 367.
105. NAI 90/98/39, Memorandum from the Leas-Choimisinéir [Deputy Commissioner] of the Garda Síochána, n.d. [Probably December 1938]. Indeed, the report went so far as to allege that the restrictions on public dancing in some areas caused young people to travel longer distances to

areas where public dancing was more freely available: 'Such dancers are less sensitive to public opinion as to their conduct in the areas in which they are not known and in the absence of such a restraining influence excesses are likely to occur.'

106. One article by Devane, *The Dance Hall: A National and Moral Menace*, was censored by the Jesuits' authority for the 'province' of Ireland, since it was felt that the earlier draft included language 'more indelicate or suggestive than need be', particularly in its descriptions of dances. IJA, Censorship Judgements (1924-1968), ADMN12/15 (2), *Judicium Censorum Provinciae Hiberniae*, 29 December 1930.

107. R.S. Devane. 'The Dance Hall.' *The Irish Ecclesiastical Record*, Vol. 37 (January–June 1931) 170–194. Devane also supplied copies of this article to the members of the Carrigan Committee, along with a contemporaneous article, also from the *Irish Ecclesiastical Record*, on 'The Legal Protection of Girls'. NAI JUS 90/4/13, Memo of Evidence of Rev. R.S. Devane, S.J.

108. Public Dance Halls Act, 1935. Number 2 of 1935. Intriguingly, though, it was explicitly stipulated that none of these regulations would apply to dances 'managed or conducted under the authority of the Minister for Defence or of the Commissioner of the Gárda [sic] Síochána.'

109. For a representative example, see C. Hug (1999) *The Politics of Sexual Morality in Ireland* (London: Palgrave Macmillan), which primarily explains post-1922 Irish sexual politics as the result of Catholic theology. Similar post-Catholic/Celtic Tiger-era narratives of the Church as the overriding bulwark against modernity appear in T. Garvin (2005) *Preventing the Future: Why Was Ireland So Poor For So Long?* (Dublin: Gill and Macmillan) and J.S. Donnelly (2005) 'Opposing the "Modern World": The Cult of the Virgin Mary in Ireland, 1965-85.' *Éire-Ireland*, Volume 40, Nos. 1&2, 183–245. For an opposing view, see: A. Beatty (2013) 'Irish Modernity and the Politics of Contraception, 1979-1993.' *New Hibernia Review*, Vol. 17, No. 3, 100–118.

110. T. Inglis (2008) *Global Ireland: Same Difference* (New York: Routledge).

111. Sikata Banerjee has shown how debates about Irish whiteness can still be observed even as late as the early twenty-first century. S. Banerjee (2012) *Muscular Nationalism: Gender, Violence and Empire in India and Ireland* (New York: NYU Press) pp. 151–161.

112. P. Carroll-Burke (2000) *Colonial Discipline: The Making of the Irish Convict System* (Dublin: Four Courts Press) pp. 87–94.

113. T. Inglis (1998) *Moral Monopoly*, pp. 77–78.

114. M. Curtis (2010) *A Challenge to Democracy: Militant Catholicism in Modern Ireland* (Dublin: The History Press) p. 11.

115. Ibid., p. 41.

116. M. Shilo (2010) 'Kolot Nashim be-devar sheviun migdari u-tovet ha-umma ba-maavik al zicut ha-bachira ba-yishuv' [Women's Voices Regarding Gender Equality and the National Interest in the Struggle for the Right to Vote in the Yishuv] in E. Katvan, Eyal; M. Shilo; R. Halperin-Kaddari, eds. *Chuka Achat u-Mishpat echad la-Ish ve-la-Isha: Nashim, Zechuiot u-Mishpat bi-Tekufat ha-Mandat* [One Rule for a Man and one Law for a Woman: Women, Rights and Law in the British Mandate Period] (Ramat Gan: Bar-Ilan University Press) pp. 222–223.
117. Ibid., p. 223.
118. B. Margalit Stern (2006) 'Who's the Fairest of Them All? Women, Womanhood, and Ethnicity in Zionist Eretz Israel.' *Nashim: A Journal of Jewish Women's Studies and Gender Issues*, Vol. 11, 142–163. The 'beauty queens' in these events were usually Yemeni Jewish women rather than Ashkenazi women. As Margalit Stern argues, this was also about control of 'oriental' Jews and about incorporating them into the Zionist project (albeit at a subservient level).
119. N. Berkovitch (1997) 'Motherhood as a National Mission: The Construction of Womanhood in the Legal Discourse of Israel'. *Women's Studies International Forum*, Vol. 20, Nos. 5–6, 605–619; B. Kimmerling (2001) *Israeliness*, pp. 177–178. Kimmerling draws heavily on Berkovitch's essay in his analysis of this issue.
120. S. Fogiel-Bijaoui (1992) 'From Revolution to Motherhood: The Case of Women in the Kibbutz, 1910-1948' in D.S. Bernstein, ed. *Pioneers and Homemakers: Jewish Women in Pre-State Israel* (Albany: State University of New York Press) pp. 211–233.
121. J. Portugese (1998) *Fertility Policy in Israel: The Politics of Religion, Gender and Nation* (London: Praeger) p. 14. For an interesting comparative view, see: R.A. Kanaaneh (2002) *Birthing the Nation: Strategies of Palestinian Women in Israel* (Berkeley CA: University of California Press).
122. B. Kimmerling (2001) *Israeliness*, p. 179. Emphases in original. See also: D. Izraeli. 'Gendering Military Service in the Israeli Defence Forces' in M. Semyonov, N. Lewin-Epstein, eds. *Stratification in Israel: Class, Ethnicity, and Gender* (London: Transaction Publishers) pp. 281–311.
123. N. Abdo (2011) *Women in Israel: Race, Gender and Citizenship* (London: Zed Books) pp. 8–53.
124. O. Rozin (2011) *Rise of the Individual*, pp. 28–29.
125. Ibid., pp. 172–173.
126. B. Kimmerling (2001) '*Israeliness*' pp. 95–96. Rozin talks of the 'notoriously intrusive bureaucracy' in 1950s Israel. O. Rozin (2011) *Rise of the Individual*, xiv.
127. D.S. Bernstein (1987) *The Struggle for Equality: Urban Women Workers in Pre-State Israeli Society* (New York: Praeger); D.S. Bernstein (1992)

'Human Being or Housewife: The Status of Women in the Jewish Working Class Family in Palestine of the 1920s and 1930s' in D.S. Bernstein, ed. *'Pioneers and Homemakers'*, pp. 235–259.

128. The 'religious' differences between Ireland and Israel are perhaps deceptive. Israel also avoided a separation of religion and state, and many civil issues of obvious relevance to gender equality, remained under religious jurisdiction. In both cases, marriage and divorce, for instance, remained subject to religious edict, and this has served to reinforce women's status as 'bearers of the collective'. R. Halperin-Kaddari, Y. Yadgar (2010) 'Between Universal Feminism and Particular Nationalism: Politics, Religion, and Gender (In)Equality in Israel.' *Third World Quarterly*, Vol. 31, No. 6, 905–920.

129. J.M. Smith (2007) *'Magdalen Laundries'*, p. 3 and *passim*; See also: K. Conrad (2004) *Locked in the Family Cell: Gender, Sexuality and Political Agency in Irish National Discourse* (Madison WI: University of Wisconsin Press); B. Gray, L.Ryan (1998) 'The Politics of Irish Identity and the Interconnections between Feminism, Nationhood and Colonialism' in R. Roach Pierson, N. Chaudhuri, eds. *Nation, Empire, Colony: Historicizing Gender and Race* (Bloomington IN: Indiana University Press) pp. 121–138.

CHAPTER 8

Conclusions

The British had withdrawn. The Capital was in a fever of excitement and change. New classes were forming, blacksmiths and clerks filling the highest offices in the turn of an hour. Some who had worried how their next loaf or day might come were attending ceremonial functions. There was a brand new tricolour to wave high; a language of their own to learn; new anthems of faith and fatherland to beat on the drum of the multitude; but most of all, unseen and savage behind these floral screens, was the struggle for the numbered seats of power.[1]

THE IRISH RACE OLYMPIC

With the war over, it was time for a celebration. In 1922, the Irish Free State began to plan a major spectacle, the Tailteann Games, billed as 'The Irish Race Olympic'. It did not bode well, though, that the planned 1922 Games had to be cancelled due to threats of Republican violence.[2] Rescheduled to 1924, the Games were held every four years until 1932, when they ran afoul of government parsimony and Fianna Fáil hostility towards a Treatyite event.[3] While the *Northern Whig*, a solidly unionist newspaper, may have dismissed the 1924 Games as being nothing but 'An Anti-British Meeting',[4] in actuality they were an expression of the prevailing ideology of the new Free State, an ideology that stretched back at least to the 1880s. Indeed, most of the themes that this book has sought to

© The Editor(s) (if applicable) and The Author(s) 2016
A. Beatty, *Masculinity and Power in Irish Nationalism, 1884–1938*, Genders and Sexualities in History,
DOI 10.1057/978-1-137-44101-0_8

understand were present in these events. As well as signifying the power of the new state, the Games expressed a redeemed ancient Irish past, the reviving of a supposedly ancient, but in reality invented, festival said to have been inaugurated in 632 BC by the eponymous Tailte, 'a wise and much loved' Queen.[5] The Games' chief organiser, J.J. Walsh, echoed a common claim that the Tailteann Games had survived throughout antiquity, only to be ended by the Anglo-Norman invasion.[6] The 'revival' of these Games thus marked a return to a time when the nation was not under English control. This athletic form of time travel was suitable for 'the new historical days in Ireland'[7] after 1922.

The return to this ancient time was also a return to Europe, because 'Before the rise of either the Greek or Roman Powers the Tailteann games were a recurring festival on the plains of Royal Meath, then a province of an independent Ireland'.[8] The Irish were the original Europeans and these Games were surely proof of that. They had once been celebrated 'throughout all Celtica' (which is to say, all of Europe) and 'probably throughout Aryan Asia' also.[9] As a sporting event, muscular images of bodily resurgence were also to the fore (See Fig. 8.1). The Games show-

Fig. 8.1 *Dressing Up As Ancient Irish Men*, Tailteann Games, 1924
Source: NLI INDH524

cased 'the Athletic prowess of the whole Irish race ... proving to the world by their concerted athletic activities that the strength and purpose of the old days are still a dominant characteristic of the Irish people.'[10] The Games were held up as embodying the nation's regained sovereignty: 'The Saxon holds us slaves no more'[11] and, as a Thomas Davis poem used for the opening ceremony of the 1924 Games observed, self-sacrificial Irish men were again in control of an Ireland coded as female:

She is a rich and rare land,	Could beauty ever guard her,
Oh, she's a fresh and fair land	And virtue still reward her,
She is a dear and rare land	No foe would cross her border
This native land of mine;	No friend within it pine.
No men than her's [*sic*] are braver	Oh, she's a fresh and fair land,
Her women's hearts ne'er waver	Oh, she's a true and rare land,
I'd freely die to save her,	Yes, she's a rare and fair land,
And think my lot divine.	This native land of mine.[12]

Just as we saw in Chaps. 4 and 5, such visions of a spatially reclaimed Ireland regularly intertwined with idealised perceptions of the Irish language. In the programme for the same 1924 Games there appeared 'Dán Moladh na Gaedhilge' [A Poem in Praise of the Irish Language]:

Most beautiful in print is the Irish Language ...
    It is a great truth of our land
    That there is no language in the world as beautiful as it ...
    It is the language of the great Kings
    And of the Masters of Brave Ireland ...
    If there were Irish Kings still ruling
    Ruling their Kingdoms far and wide
    How sweet Irish would be to them ...
    Praising the King and his great deeds
    Their noble ancestry, strong warriors
    And Ancient Lands of Heroic Ireland

['*Sí 'n teanga Gaedhilge 's greanta cló ...*
  'Sir fíor go mór a h-áitreabh
  Níl teanga 'ar domhan dá bréághthachth í ...
  Is seanacus na riogh-fhlaith mór
  Is saoithe cróda cláirluirc ...
  Da mbéidheadh ríghthe Éireann fó

> 'Na suidhe san righeacht i gcéim 's i gcróin
> Ba bhinn siollaidhe na Gaedhilge leo...
> Ag moladh 'n ríogh 's ag sár-mhaith-ghníomh
> 'Sa shinsir uaisle tréana groidhe
> Sí gcríochaibh Fodla 'n ársacht.]¹³

The Irish language clearly remained a key element of this project of national masculine revival. It was a linguistic link to a heroic, pre-invasion, Irish past. This poem also points to the curious manner in which royalist ideas survived within Irish republicanism. Tellingly, the medal for the Games, a bust of the head of Queen Tailte designed by the nationalist sculptor Oliver Sheppard, bears a suspicious resemblance to a medal of Queen Victoria that still survives in Sheppard's archives.¹⁴

In general, the Tailteann Games were a means of showcasing how much Ireland had improved as a nation: 'With each recurring Aonach [holding of the games], the Motherland gives additional proof of her increasing development and progress along physical and cultural lines and this should be to you, as it is to us, a source of that satisfaction which pride of race dictates.'¹⁵ And as with so much else in Irish nationalism before and after 1922, women did take part in the Tailteann Games, but in a secondary role. To have done otherwise would have undermined an image of resurgent Irish men disproving accusations of national weakness by expressing their male strength in public spaces.

This book has sought to understand how and why masculine anxieties, of the kind so demonstratively on display in the Tailteann Games, became such important concerns for Irish nationalists. I have argued that Irish nationalism can be understood not simply as a movement for some kind of national liberation, but also as a quasi-postcolonial movement for expressing a deeply felt desire for male power. This, I've endeavoured to show, was something Irish nationalism shared with Zionism. And I have tried to show how both of these strands, nationalism and masculinity, were, and are, inorganic constructs. They are emotive ideas requiring continuous building and rebuilding. This is a necessary point to make, given that so much of the historiography on Irish nationalism starts from the presumption that the 'nation' is a natural form of political organisation, with the 'nation-state' its obvious and unquestioned *telos*.

Additionally, the Tailteann Games highlight the problem of seeing 1916 or 1922 as points of rupture in Irish history. These Games drew on a masculinist discourse that had long been to the fore in Irish nationalist thought, a discourse that was present in the work of various nationalist groups as well as the Gaelic League and the Gaelic Athletic Association. As early as 1884, when announcing his support for the GAA, Michael Davitt had called for 'the revival of the Taltine [*sic*] games'.[16] Plus, these Games highlight how this discourse would have a long half-life across twentieth century Ireland. The quote above from John McGahern, in the epigraph to this chapter, sums up a common view that there was a rupture in Ireland circa 1922. Along with a newfound state sovereignty, the Irish middle classes had come of age. In reality, of course, classes do not form overnight. The bourgeoisie, like the Nation, emerge in decades-long processes.[17] The use of such overly neat terms as 'revolution' and 'counter-revolution', words that suggest clean breaks with the past, elide this more messy reality. As this work has suggested, it is time for a new temporal schema for Irish history, one less wedded to notions of 'nation' or 'state'.

Irish history-writing tends to swing between two paradigms: republicanism and revisionism. Republicanism is frequently populist, sometimes bordering on hagiography in its views of Irish 'heroes', whilst conversely affording much emphasis to the negative effects of British rule in Ireland. Republican history-writing rarely receives more than short shrift in the Irish academy. Revisionism, on the other hand, tends to be more emotionally detached in tone and almost hyper-empirical in methodology. Revisionism has little time for nationalist mythologies and yet is often more understanding of British concerns. It remains the dominant methodology of academic history-writing in Ireland. This book is neither republican nor revisionist, but remains sympathetic to *certain* aspects of both. Revisionism's healthy disrespect for nationalist myth-making has clearly been an improvement on that which came before it. Similarly, republicanism's focus on the unequal power relations between Irish nationalists and the British imperial state, and the effects this has had on Irish identity, are a welcome antidote to revisionism's apparent inability to factor British imperialism into its equations.[18]

There are clearly serious ideological and methodological differences between these two approaches to Ireland's past. Yet there is one point where, both ontologically and epistemologically, both paradigms are in close harmony; the centrality of the 'nation'. Both understand Irish history in terms of this category, and both uncritically accept its objective reality. The scholar of nationalism John Hutchinson and the British imperial historian Stephen Howe have each labelled revisionist historians 'methodological nationalists', for the manner in which they avoid comparative analyses and shy away from questioning the historicity and ontological reality of the Irish 'nation'.[19] For most Irish historians, whether republican or revisionist, the nation exists, has always existed (or at least, for revisionists has existed for a very long time) and Irish politics is understood in terms of the nation, either as a movement towards or away from national liberation or as a battle between those who wish to achieve national ends through only peaceful means against those who are willing to resort to violence.

Kerby Miller's bitingly accurate comment that 'much revisionist history—once innovative and stimulating—has become tediously predictable'[20] could be applied in differing measures to republican history writing. Equally, John Regan's criticism of the micro-histories and local studies favoured by mainstream Irish historians points to revisionism's obvious cul-de-sac: 'In these approaches—local, personal, intimate—the greater political forces at play—abstract, impersonal, universal—too easily can go overlooked... Rather than liberating us this approach may be limiting, even voyeuristic ... It also marginalises ideology as a motivational factor.'[21] Additionally, revisionists have, in the main, avoided comparative postcolonial approaches, perhaps for fear that it would provide fodder (after 1969) for the Provisional IRA's claim to be an anti-colonial army.

In his recent collection of historiographical essays, *Myth and the Irish State*, John Regan offers a challenging set of arguments as to why Irish revisionist history writing has shied away from certain themes and questions. He argues that Irish academic historians, since the outbreak of violence in Northern Ireland in the late 1960s, have produced works that 'reinforce southern nationalist mythologies' and 'after 1969 some historians superimposed the ideological battles of the contemporary Northern Ireland conflict on to their conceptualization of the earlier revolutionary period, demonstrably on to the southern civil war of 1922–3.'[22] Regan's views are, themselves, not without their problems. He tends to speak of revisionist historians in monolithic terms, his tone can border on the polemical, and, in general, his work has often remained trapped in the same positivist mould that, in my opinion, is revisionism's original sin. None of this, however, should detract from the cogency of his observations. It is quite reasonable to say that many Irish historians have viewed the past through the prism of Ireland's violent present(s).

It was with such sideswipes in mind that this book sought to move away from more conventional analyses of Irish high politics, in favour of analysing a previously understudied element in Irish nationalism, masculinity.

Not only was this intended to highlight a new and innovative approach to Irish nationalism (hopefully answering Miller's charge that Irish academic history-writing has become tedious), it was also intended to show the political work this masculinist ideology did for Irish nationalism. Where Miller and Regan have rightly drawn attention to the problems inhering in Irish historiography's supposedly objective and non-ideological methodology and predominant focus on micro-histories, this work has taken a macro-historical approach (with an attempt to study nationalist culture *tout court* across almost 60 years of history) and foregrounds ideology. Thus I have sought to show how, in parallel to masculinity, national identity was also continuously constructed and reconstructed between 1884 and 1938. More than that, this book has sought to achieve all this via a comparative analysis that to revisionists might appear odd and to republicans would probably be politically dubious. Comparing Irish nationalism to Zionism, however, has allowed me to pose a set of questions about race and whiteness and about how Irish nationalism was strongly comparable to another European minority nationalist ideology. Where revisionists and republicans both continue to understand the past through prisms of the 'nation' and the 'state', I conclude that it is well past time for Irish historians to experiment with some new explanatory categories; categories such as 'class', 'capitalist development', 'the construction of whiteness' or 'the construction of masculinity', categories which can provide a refreshingly different perspective on Irish history.

Notes

1. J. McGahern (1963/1983) *The Barracks* (London: Faber & Faber) p. 28.
2. Military Archives BMH CD 250/6/16, *Why Republicans Boycott Aonach Tailteann*, undated handbill (1922?); despite their cancellation, a programme had been drawn up for the 1922 Games. Copies survive at: NLI PIA 1-20, *Tailteann Games: Irish Race Olympic, Dublin, 6–13 August 1922* and NAI TAOIS/S 1592.
3. On the Games' troubled finances, see: NAI TAOIS/ S 8970, Aonach Tailteann 1928, Memorandum Relative To Financing of Tailteann Games, 1928; for the accusation that Fianna Fáil intentionally scuppered the Games in 1932, see the autobiography of the Games' chief organiser: J.J. Walsh (1944) *Recollections of a Rebel* (Tralee: The Kerryman) pp. 78–79.
4. CCA U335/2, Papers of J.J. Walsh, Tailteann Games Newspaper Cuttings, *Northern Whig*, 19 August 1924.

5. GAA Archives, GAA/Prog/1887—GAA/Prog/1944, *Aonach Tailteann Clar Cuimhneachan* [Tailteann Games Commemorative Programme], 29 June–1 July 1932.
6. J.J. Walsh (1944) *Recollections of a Rebel*, p. 76.
7. NLI PIA 1-20, 'Aonach Tailteann/Irish Race Olympic,' 1922. See also, GAA Archives, GAA/Prog/1887—GAA/Prog/1944, *Aonach Tailteann Clar Cuimhneachan* [Tailteann Games Commemorative Programme], 29 June–1 July 1932, which claims that 'from 632 BC until the eve of the Norman invasion, almost without interruption, the Gaels of Eire assembled around Queen Tailte's tomb on the first week of August. The king presided over the assembly. It was a symbol of national unity.'
8. NLI PIA 1-20, 'Aonach Tailteann/Irish Race Olympic', 1922.
9. J.J. Walsh, quoted in CCA U335/2, Papers of J.J. Walsh, Tailteann Games Newspaper Cuttings, *Daily Chronicle*, 13 August 1924. Indeed, Walsh later claimed the Greek Olympics were a copy of their Irish predecessor. J.J. Walsh (1944) *Recollections of a Rebel*, p. 76.
10. NLI PIA 1-20, Aonach Tailteann/Irish Race Olympic, 1922.
11. From *Bright Sun! Before Whose Glorious Ray*, the song for the opening ceremony of the 1924 Games, described as an 'Irish war song'. GAA Archives, GAA/Prog/1887—GAA/Prog/1944, *Tailteann Games Programme*, 2–3 August 1924.
12. '*My Land/Mo Tir*', GAA Archives, GAA/Prog/1887—GAA/Prog/1944, *Tailteann Games Programme*, 2–3 August 1924. That this poem was written by Thomas Davis was not mentioned in the programme, which merely stated that the musical arrangement was by Brendan J. Rogers and that Douglas Hyde had written the Irish-language translation.
13. GAA.Prog.1887 to GAA.Prog.1944, Tailteann Games Programme 2–3 August 1924.
14. Queen Victoria Medal, 1856, IE/NIVAL/OS/06, Oliver Sheppard Collection, National Irish Visual Arts Library, Dublin. Accessed 2013; Tailteann Games Medal, 1922, IE/NIVAL/OS/02, Oliver Sheppard Collection, National Irish Visual Arts Library, Dublin. Accessed 2013; Tailteann Games Medal, n.d., IE/NIVAL/OS/06, Oliver Sheppard Collection, National Irish Visual Arts Library, Dublin. Accessed 2013.
15. GAA Archives, GAA/Prog/1887—GAA/Prog/1944, *Aonach Tailteann Clar Cuimhneachan* [Tailteann Games Commemorative Programme], 29 June–1 July 1932.
16. *The Gaelic Athletic Association for the Preservation and Cultivation of our National Pastimes* (1887) 2nd edn (Dublin: A & E Cahill).
17. Showing, however, how perceptive a commentator he was, elsewhere in *The Barracks* McGahern notes that in the 1960s, when the book is set, 'There's a new class growing up in this country that won't be shamed out

of doing things because they haven't come out of big houses.' J. McGahern (1963/1983) *The Barracks*, pp. 208–209, the latter quote presumably being McGahern's nod at recognising how slow such class formation can actually be.
18. Kerby Miller has summed up revisionist methodologies thusly: 'Purportedly blessed with unbiased, "value-free" perspectives and armed with new "scientific" methodologies, revisionists have claimed to write "objective" history.' K. Miller (2008) *Ireland and Irish-America: Culture, Class, and Transatlantic Migration* (Dublin: Field Day) p. 370. That revisionism is anything but 'objective' is Miller's central conclusion (and one I strongly agree with).
19. J. Hutchinson (1996) 'Irish Nationalism' in G. Boyce and A. O'Day, eds. *The Making of Modern Irish History: Revisionism and the Revisionist Controversy.* (London: Routledge).
20. K. Miller (2008) *Ireland and Irish-America*, p. 371.
21. J.M. Regan (2013) *Myth and the Irish State* (Dublin: Irish Academic Press) pp. 210–211.
22. Ibid., pp. 73, 169. Regan also talks of revisionism as being part of 'the Irish power-structure', Ibid., p. 278.

Bibliography

Archival Sources

Central Archives for the History of the Jewish People (CAHJP)
- Papers of Judah Leb Magnes

Central Zionist Archives (CZA)
- Arieh Rafaeli (Tsentsiper) Collection
- General Collection
- Posters Collection
- Printed Matter Collection

Cork City and County Archives (CCCA)
- Terence MacSwiney Papers
- J.J. Walsh Papers

Dublin Diocesan Archives (DDA)
- Archbishop Byrne Papers
- Lay Organisations Section

Gaelic Athletic Association Archives (GAA)
- Programmes Collection

Garda Síochána Archives
- *Aonach an Gharda* [Garda Festival] *Souvenir Programme*, 14–16 July 1926

Irish Jesuit Archives (IJA)
- Censorship Judgements (1924–1968)

Military Archives
- Bureau of Military History: Contemporary Documents (BMH CD)

National Archives of Ireland (NAI)
- Files of the Department of Justice
- Files of the Department of the Taoiseach
- Files of the Committee on the Criminal Law Amendment Acts

National Irish Visual Arts Library (NIVAL)
- Oliver Sheppard Collection

National Library of Ireland (NLI)

- Shane Leslie Papers	- Pearse Papers
- John L. Burke Papers	- Ephemera Collection (EPH)
- Bulmer Hobson Papers	- Douglas Hyde Additional Papers
- Irish Large Books collection (ILB)	- Irish Books collection (IR)
- Librarian's Office collection (LO)	- Piaras Béaslaí Papers
- *Seán* T. Ó Ceallaigh Papers	- Thomas MacDonagh Family Papers
- Eoin O'Duffy Papers	- Uncatalogued Ephemera Collections
- Papers of Douglas Hyde relating to the Gaelic League	

National University of Ireland-Galway (NUIG)
- Stephen Barrett Papers
- Michael Cusack Papers

University College Dublin Archives (UCDA)

- De Valera Papers	- Eoin MacNeill Papers
- Archives of the Fianna Fáil Party	- Patrick McGilligan Papers
- Sean MacEntee Papers	- Mary MacSwiney Papers
- Terence MacSwiney Papers	- Kevin O'Higgins Papers

Government Publications

Intoxicating Liquor Commission Report (Dublin: The Stationery Office, 28 August 1925).

Official Standing Orders and Regulations for the Government and Guidance of the Dublin Metropolitan Police, as Approved by His Excellency the Lord Lieutenant (Dublin: Her Majesty's Stationery Office, 1889).

Orders and Regulations for the Instruction and Control of the Garda Síochána. As Approved by the Minister for Justice (Dublin: The Stationery Office, 1928).

Register of Prohibited Publications (Dublin: Stationery Office, 1938).

Report with Appendices of the Inter-Departmental Committee of Inquiry Regarding Venereal Disease (Dublin: The Stationery Office, 1926).

Report of the Committee on Evil Literature (Dublin: Stationery Office, 28 December 1926).

Register of Prohibited Publications (Dublin: Stationery Office, 1938).

Standing Rules and Regulations for the Government and Guidance of the Royal Irish Constabulary, Sixth Edition, as Approved by his Excellency the Lord Lieutenant (Dublin: His Majesty's Stationery Office, 1911).

Newspapers

Bean na hÉireann	*Clare Champion*
Fianna	*Fianna Fáil/The Irish Army: A Journal for Militant Ireland*
Garda Review/Iris an Ghárda	*Guth an Ghárda*
Ha-Aretz	*Irisleabhar na Gaedhilge*
Irish Ecclesiastical Record	*Irish Freedom*
Irish Volunteer	*An t-Oglách: The Official Organ of the Irish Volunteers*

Published Primary Sources

Barry, Tom. *Guerrilla Days in Ireland* (Dublin: Irish Press, 1949).
Barton, Brian, ed. *From Behind a Closed Door: Secret Court Martial Records of the 1916 Easter Rising* (Belfast: Blackstaff Press, 2002).
Breen, Dan. *My Fight for Irish Freedom* (Dublin, Talbot Press, 1924).
– *My Fight for Irish Freedom* (Tralee, Anvil Press, 1964) 2nd Edition.
Catholic Truth Society. *The Problem of Undesirable Printed Matter: Suggested Remedies. Evidence of the Catholic Truth Society of Ireland Presented to Departmental Committee of Enquiry, 1926* (Dublin: Catholic Truth Society, 1926).
Clarke, Kathleen, Helen Litton, ed. *Revolutionary Woman: Kathleen Clarke, 1878–1972: An Autobiography* (Dublin: The O'Brien Press, 1991).
De Valera, Eamon. *India and Ireland* (New York: Friends of Freedom for India, 1920).
De Valera, Eamon, Maurice Moynihan, ed. *Speeches and Statements by Eamon De Valera: 1917–73* (Dublin: Gill and Macmillan, 1980).
– *National Discipline and Majority Rule: Three Speeches by Eamon de Valera*, Fianna Fail Pamphlet No. 1, 1936.
Dershowitz, Alan. *The Case for Israel* (New York: John Wiley & Sons, 2003).
Devane, R.S. *Indecent Literature: Some Legal Remedies* (Dublin: Browne and Nolan, n.d. [1925]).
– *Evil Literature: Some Suggestions* (Dublin: Browne and Nolan, n.d.).
Devoy, John. *Recollections of an Irish Rebel* (Shannon: Irish University Press, 1969).
Duff, Frank, Denis McAuliffe, ed. *Miracles on Tap* (New York: Montfort Publications, 1961).
Firtel, Hilde. *A Man For Our Time: Frank Duff and The Legion of Mary* (Cork: Mercier Press, 1985).
Griffith, Arthur. *How Ireland Has 'Prospered' Under English Rule, and The Slave Mind* (New York: Irish Progressive League, n.d.).

- *Sinn Féin Pamphlets No. 3: England's Colossal Robbery of Ireland, The Final Relations of the Two Countries since the Union. Extract from Mr. Arthur Griffith's Speech, made at No. 11, Lower O'Connell St., Dublin, on 22nd Oct., 1906* (Dublin: National Council, n.d.).
- *To Re-Build the Nation*, undated pamphlet (circa 1919).
- *Arguments for the Treaty*, undated pamphlet (circa 1922).

Gwynn, Denis. *The Life and Death of Roger Casement* (London: J. Cape, 1930).

The Handbook for Irish Volunteers: Simple Lectures on Military Subjects (Dublin: M.H. Gill, 1914).

Hertzberg, Arthur, ed. *The Zionist Idea: A Historical Analysis and Reader* (New York: Atheneum, 1973).

Herzl, Theodor. *The Jewish State: An Attempt at a Modern Solution of the Jewish Question* (New York: American Zionist Emergency Council, 1946).

Higgins, T.A. *The Rise of the Irish National Volunteer Movement* (United Irish League, 1914).

Hobson, Bulmer. *Defensive Warfare: A Handbook for Irish Nationalists* (Belfast: The West Belfast Branch of Sinn Féin, 1909).
- *The Flowing Tide*, Pamphlet reprint of an article from *Irish Freedom* (Belfast: Freedom Club Leaflets No. 1, n.d.).

Joyce, James. *Ulysses* (New York: Random House, 1986).

Lewis, Sinclair. *It Can't Happen Here* (New York: The Sun Dial Press, 1935).

MacSwiney, Terence. *Principles of Freedom* (New York: E.P.Dutton, 1921).

McGahern, John. *The Barracks* (London: Faber & Faber, 1963/1983).

McLoughlin, Michael, ed. *Great Irish Speeches of the Twentieth Century* (Dublin: Poolbeg Press, 1996).

Moran, D.P. *The Philosophy of Irish-Ireland* (Dublin: James Duffy & Co., 1905).
- *Tom O'Kelly* (Dublin: Cahill & Co., 1905).

Moran, James, ed. *Four Irish Rebel Plays* (Dublin: Irish Academic Press, 2007).

Na gCopaleen, Myles. *An Béal Bocht, nó An Milleánach: Drochscéal ar an Drochshaol Curtha in Eager le Myles na gCopaleen* [The Poor Mouth, or The Millenarian: A Terrible Tale of the Terrible Life edited by Myles na gCopaleen] (Cork: Mercier Press, 1999).

Ní Dhubhghall, C. Maire. *Women in Ancient and Modern Ireland* (Dublin: The Kenny Press, 1917).

Ní Dubhsláine, Máire. *A Chailíní, Èistigidh! nó [Oh Girls, Listen! or] For Girls Only* (Dublin: Craobh na hAiséirghe, 1942?).

Nolan, M.J. *The Increase in Insanity in Ireland and Its Causes* (Dublin: Fannin & Co, 1906).

O'Donnell, Peadar. *For or Against the Ranchers? Irish Working Farmers in the Economic War* (n.d. circa 1932).
- *There Will Be Another Day* (Dublin: Dolmen Press, 1963).

O'Flynn, Thomas. *Frank Duff: As I Knew Him* (Dublin: Praedicanda Publications, 1981).

O'Brien, Flann; Patrick C. Power, trans. *The Poor Mouth: A Bad Story about the Hard Life* (Normal IL: Dalkey Archive Press/Illinois State University, 1996).
O'Brien, William; Desmond Ryan, eds. *Devoy's Post Bag: Volume II, 1880–1928* (Dublin: C.J. Fallon, 1953).
O'Donovan Rossa, Margaret. *My Father and My Mother Were Irish* (New York: Devid-Adair, 1939).
O'Hegarty, P.S. *A Short Memoir of Terence MacSwiney* (Dublin: Talbot Press, 1922).
– *The Victory of Sinn Féin: How and It Won It, And How It Used It* (Dublin: Talbot Press, 1924).
O'Higgins, Kevin. *The Catholic Layman in Public Life* (Dublin: Catholic Truth Society, n.d.).
O'Malley, Ernie. *On Another Man's Wounds* (London: Rich & Cowan, 1936).
– *The Singing Flame* (Dublin: Anvil Books, 1978).
– *Raids and Rallies* (Cork: Mercier, 2011).
The O'Rahilly. *Secret History of the Volunteers: Tracts for the Times, No.3.* (Dublin: Irish Publicity League, 1915) 3rd Edition.
Ó Sándair, Cathal. *Tusa agus an Ghaedhilg [You and the Irish Language]: A Word to the Worker*, Paimpléid Reatha Uimhir 12 [Pamphlet Series Number 12] (Dublin: Glún na Buaidhe, n.d.).
Oz, Amos. *Sipur al Ahava ve-Choshekh* [A Tale of Love and Darkness] (Jerusalem: Keter Publishing, 2002).
Pearse, P.H. *Three Lectures on Gaelic Topics* (Dublin: M.H. Gill, 1898).
– *Collected Works of P.H. Pearse* (Dublin: Phoenix, 1917) 2 Vols.
– *Political Writings and Speeches* (Dublin: Talbot Press, 1966).
Pearse, P.H., Desmond Ryan, ed. *The Story of a Success, Being a Record of St. Enda's College, September 1908 to Easter, 1916* (Dublin: Maunsel, 1917).
Pearse, P.H., Séamus Ó Buachalla, ed. *The Letters of P.H. Pearse* (London: Colin Smythe, 1980).
Ratosh, Yonatan, *Kitav Al Ha-Noar Ha-Ivri* [Epistle to the Hebrew Youth], n.d.
Skinnider, Margaret. *Doing My Bit for Ireland* (New York: The Century Co., 1917).
Stopford Green, Alice. *The Irish Republican Army* (American Association for the Recognition of the Irish Republic, n.d.).
Trotsky, Leon. *My Life: An Attempt at an Autobiography* (New York: Pathfinder Press, 1970).
Walsh, J.J. *Recollections of a Rebel* (Tralee: The Kerryman, 1944).

Cumann Léigheachtaí an Phobail [Republican Lecture Society] Pamphlets

Hackett, Rev. W.P. Character and Citizenship (Cumann Léigheachtaí an Phobail, 1921).
O hAodha, R. *Hygiene* (Cumann Léigheachtaí an Phobail, 1921).

Gaelic Athletic Association Publications

Constitution and rules of games of Gaelic Athletic Association (Dublin: Alley & Co., n.d. [1885?]).

The Gaelic Athletic Association for the Preservation and Cultivation of our National Pastimes, 2nd Edition (Dublin: A&E Cahill, 1887).

Gaelic Athletic Year Book, 1926: A Complete Compendium of Irish Athletic Records (Dublin: The Gaelic Press, 1926).

The Gaelic Athletic Annual, 1927–28 (Kilkenny: Kilkenny Journal, 1927).

Gaelic League Publications

A Gaelic League Catechism (Gaelic League of London, n.d.).

Butler, Mary. *Irishwomen and the Home Language* (Gaelic League Pamphlets, No. 6, n.d. [circa 1900])

Forde, Patrick. *The Irish Language Movement: Its Philosophy* (Gaelic League Pamphlets, No. 21, 1900).

Hyde, Douglas. *The Irish Language and Irish Intermediate Education, III: Dr. Hyde's Evidence* (Gaelic League Pamphlets, No. 13).

Kavanagh, P.F. *Ireland's Defence: Her Language* (Gaelic League Pamphlets, No. 23, 1901).

O'Conor-Eccles, Charlotte. *Simple Advice: To be followed by all who desire the good of Ireland, and especially by Gaelic Leaguers* (1905) 2nd Edition.

O'Hickey, Michael. *Irish in the Schools* (Gaelic League Pamphlets, No. 3, 1900).

Films

The Rocky Road to Dublin (Peter Lennon, dir., 1967).

Reference Works

Dictionary of Irish Biography (Cambridge: Cambridge University Press, 2009).

Online Sources

Brennan, Cathal. 'The Curious Career of Herbert Moore Pim.' www.theirishstory.com, date accessed 22 July 2013.

Irish Election Literature. http://irishelectionliterature.wordpress.com, date accessed 4 June 2013.

Secondary Sources

Abdo, Nahla. *Women in Israel: Race, Gender and Citizenship* (London: Zed Books, 2011).
Allen, Kieran. *Fianna Fáil and Irish Labour, 1926 to the Present* (London: Pluto Press, 1997).
Allen, Theodore W. *The Invention of the White Race, Volume One: Racial Oppression and Social Control* (London: Verso, 2012) 2nd Edition.
Almog, Oz; Haim Watzman, trans. *The Sabra: The Creation of the New Jew* (Berkeley, CA: University of California Press, 2000).
Anderson, Benedict. *Imagined Communities: Reflections on the Origin and Spread of Nationalism* (London: Verso, 2006) 2nd Edition.
Anderson, Perry. *The Indian Ideology* (London: Verso, 2013)
Anderson, Malcolm; Eberhard Bort, eds. *The Irish Border: History, Politics, Culture* (Liverpool: Liverpool University Press, 1999).
Attias, Jean-Christophe; Esther Benbassa; Susan Emanuel, trans. *Israel, the Impossible Land* (Stanford: Stanford University Press, 2003).
Augusteijn, Joost. *Patrick Pearse: The Making of a Revolutionary* (London: Palgrave MacMillan, 2010).
– ed. *The Irish Revolution, 1913–23* (London: Palgrave Macmillan, 2002).
Banerjee, Sikata. *Muscular Nationalism: Gender, Violence and Empire in India and Ireland* (New York: NYU Press, 2012).
Beatty, Aidan. 'Irish Modernity and the Politics of Contraception, 1979–1993.' *New Hibernia Review*, Vol. 17, No. 3 (Autumn, 2013) 100–118.
Ben-Israel Kidron, Hedva. 'Zionism and European Nationalisms: Comparative Aspects.' *Israel Studies*, Vol. 8, No. 1 (Spring, 2003) 91–104.
Berkovitch, Nitza. 'Motherhood as a National Mission: The Construction of Womanhood in the Legal Discourse of Israel'. *Women's Studies International Forum*, Vol. 20, Nos. 5–6 (1997) 605–19.
Bernstein, Deborah S. *The Struggle for Equality: Urban Women Workers in Pre-State Israeli Society* (New York: Praeger, 1987).
– ed. *Pioneers and Homemakers: Jewish Women in Pre-State Israel* (Albany: State University of New York Press, 1992).
Benvenisiti, Meron; Maxine Kaufman-Lacusta, trans. *Sacred Landscape: The Buried History of the Holy Land since 1948* (Berkeley CA: University of California Press, 2000).
Bederman, Gail. *Manliness and Civilization: A Cultural History of Race and Gender in the United States, 1880–1917* (Chicago: University of Chicago Press, 1995).
Ben-Ari, Eyal; Yoram Bilu, eds. *Grasping Land: Space and Place in Contemporary Israeli Discourse and Experience* (Albany NY: State University of New York, 1997).

Biale, David. *Power and Powerlessness in Jewish History* (New York: Schocken Books, 1987).
– *Eros and the Jews: From Biblical Israel to Contemporary America* (Berkeley CA: University of California Press, 1997).
Bornstein, George. *The Colors of Zion: Blacks, Jews, and Irish from 1845 to 1945* (Cambridge MA: Harvard University Press, 2011).
Bourke, Joanna. *Dismembering the Male: Men's Bodies, Britain and the Great War* (Chicago IL: University of Chicago Press, 1996).
Boyarin, Daniel. *Unheroic Conduct: The Rise of Heterosexuality and the Invention of the Jewish Man* (Berkeley CA: University of California Press, 1997).
Boyarin, Jonathan, ed. *Remapping Memory: The Politics of TimeSpace* (Minneapolis, MN: University of Minnesota, 1994).
Boyce, George; Alan O'Day, eds. *The Making of Modern Irish History: Revisionism and the Revisionist Controversy* (London: Routledge, 1996).
Boyd, Gary A. *Dublin, 1745–1922: Hospitals, Spectacle and Vice* (Dublin: Four Courts Press, 2006).
Brady, Conor. *Guardians of the Peace* (London: Prendeville Publishing, 2000).
Breines, Paul. *Tough Jews: Political Fantasies and the Moral Dilemma of American Jewry* (New York: Basic Books, 1990).
Brenner, Michael; Gideon Reuveni, eds. *Emancipation Through Muscles: Jews and Sports in Europe* (Lincoln, NE: University of Nebraska Press, 2006).
Bristow, Joseph. *Empire Boys: Adventures in a Man's World* (London: Harper Collins, 1991).
Brodkin, Karen. *How Jews Became White Folks, and What That Says About Race in America* (New Brunswick NJ: Rutgers University Press, 1994).
Carroll-Burke, Patrick. *Colonial Discipline: The Making of the Irish Convict System* (Dublin: Four Courts Press, 2000).
Carter, Julian B. *The Heart of Whiteness: Normal Sexuality and Race in America, 1880–1940* (Durham NC: Duke University Press, 2007).
Chang, Ha-Joon. *Kicking Away the Ladder: Development Strategy in Historical Perspective* (London: Anthem Press, 2002).
Chatterjee, Partha. *The Nation and Its Fragments: Colonial and Postcolonial Histories* (Princeton NJ: Princeton University Press, 1993).
Chaver, Yael. *What Must Be Forgotten: The Survival of Yiddish in Zionist Palestine* (Syracuse, NY: Syracuse University Press, 2004).
Cleary, Joe. *Literature, Partition and the Nation State: Culture and Conflict in Ireland, Israel and Palestine* (Cambridge: Cambridge University Press, 2002).
Coakley, Maurice. *Ireland in the World Order: A History of Uneven Development* (London: Pluto Press, 2012).
Cohen, Jeremy. *Living Letters of the Law: Ideas of the Jew in Medieval Christianity* (Berkeley CA: University of California Press, 1999).
– *Sanctifying the Name of God: Jewish Martyrs and Jewish Memories of the First Crusade* (Philadelphia, PA: University of Pennsylvania Press, 2006).

Collins, Tony. *Sport in Capitalist Society: A Short History* (New York: Routledge, 2013).
Conforti, Yitzhak. 'Searching for a Homeland: The Territorial Dimension in the Zionist Movement and the Boundaries of Jewish Nationalism.' *Studies in Ethnicitiy and Nationalism*, Vol. 14, No. 1 (2014) 36–54.
Conrad, Kathryn. *Locked in the Family Cell: Gender, Sexuality and Political Agency in Irish National Discourse* (Madison WI: University of Wisconsin Press, 2004).
Conway, Vicky. *Policing Twentieth Century Ireland: A History of An Garda Síochána* (London: Routledge, 2014).
Coogan, Tim Pat. *Eamon de Valera: The Man Who Was Ireland* (New York: Harper Collins, 1993).
Cronin, Mike; Mark Duncan; Paul Rouse. *The GAA: A People's History* (Cork: The Collins Press, 2009).
Cronin, Mike; William Murphy; Paul Rouse, eds. *The Gaelic Athletic Association, 1884–2009* (Dublin: Irish Academic Press, 2009).
Cronin, Mike; John M. Regan, eds. *Ireland: The Politics of Independence* (London: Palgrave Macmillan, 2000).
Curtis, Maurice. *A Challenge to Democracy: Militant Catholicism in Modern Ireland* (Dublin: The History Press, 2010).
Daly, Mary E. *Industrial Development and Irish National Identity, 1922–1939* (Syracuse NY: Syracuse University Press, 1992).
– *The First Department: A History of the Department of Agriculture* (Dublin: Institute of Public Administration, 2002).
Deane, Seamus. *Civilians and Barbarians* (Belfast: Field Day, 1983).
Dekel, Mikhal. *The Universal Jew: Masculinity, Modernity, and the Zionist Moment* (Evanston, IL: Northwestern University Press, 2010).
De Nie, Michael. *The Eternal Paddy: Irish Identity and the British Press, 1798–1882* (Madison, WI: University of Wisconsin Press, 2004).
Donnelly, James S.. 'Opposing the "Modern World": The Cult of the Virgin Mary in Ireland, 1965–85.' *Éire-Ireland*, Volume 40, Nos. 1&2 (Spring/Summer, 2005) 183–245.
Dooley, Terence. *'The Land for the People': The Land Question in Independent Ireland* (Dublin: UCD Press, 2004)
Douglas, R.M.. *Architects of the Resurrection: Ailtirí na hAiséirghe and the Fascist 'New Order' in Ireland* (Manchester: Manchester University Press, 2009).
– 'Not So Different After All: Political Anti-Semitism in Independent Ireland and Continental Europe in Comparative Perspective.' Paper presented at a conference on *Irish and Jewish Identities: Links and Parallels*, University of Chicago, 22 February 2011.
Dudley Edwards, Ruth. *Patrick Pearse: The Triumph of Failure* (Dublin: Irish Academic Press, 2006) 2nd Edition.

Dunphy, Richard. *The Making of Fianna Fáil Power in Ireland, 1923–1948* (Oxford: Oxford University Press, 1995).

Elliot, Marianne. *Robert Emmet: The Making of a Legend* (London: Profile Books, 2003).

English, Richard. *Radicals and the Republic: Socialist Republicanism in the Irish Free State, 1925–1937* (Oxford: Clarendon Press, 1994).

Evans, Bryce. *Seán Lemass: Democratic Dictator* (Cork: The Collins Press, 2011).

Eyal, Gil. *The Disenchantment of the Orient: Expertise in Arab Affairs and the Israeli State* (Stanford, CA: Stanford University Press, 2006).

Farquharson, Diane; Sean Farrell, eds. *Shadows of the Gunmen: Violence and Culture in Modern Ireland* (Cork: Cork University Press, 2007).

Farrell Moran, Seán. *Patrick Pearse and the Politics of Redemption: The Mind of the Easter Rising, 1916* (Washington DC: Catholic University of America Press, 1994).

Feeney, Brian. *Sinn Féin: One Hundred Turbulent Years* (Dublin: O'Brien Press, 2002).

Feige, Michael. *Settling in the Hearts: Jewish Fundamentalism in the Occupied Territories* (Detroit: Wayne State University Press, 2009).

Felsenstein, Frank. *Anti-Semitic Stereotypes: A Paradigm of Otherness in English Popular Culture, 1660–1830* (Baltimore MD: Johns Hopkins University Press, 1995).

Ferriter, Diarmaid. *A Nation of Extremes: The Pioneers in Twentieth-Century Ireland* (Dublin: Irish Academic Press, 1999).

– *Occasions of Sin: Sex and Society in Modern Ireland* (London: Profile Books, 2009).

Finnane, Mark. 'The Carrigan Committee of 1930–31 and the "Moral Condition of the Saorstát."' *Irish Historical Studies*, Vol. 32, No. 128 (November, 2001).

Fitzpatrick, David. *Politics and Irish Life, 1913–1921: Provincial Experience of War and Revolution* (Dublin: Gill and Macmillan, 1998) 2nd Edition.

Foster, R.F. *Modern Ireland: 1600–1972* (London: Penguin, 1989).

Frye Jacobsen, Matthew. *Special Sorrows: The Diasporic Imagination of Irish, Polish, and Jewish Immigrants* (Cambridge MA: Harvard University Press, 1995).

Garrigan Mattar, Sinead. *Primitivism, Science, and the Irish Revival* (Oxford: Clarendon Press, 2004).

Garvin, Tom. *Preventing the Future: Why Was Ireland So Poor For So Long?* (Dublin: Gill and Macmillan, 2005).

Geller, Jay. *The Other Jewish Question: Identifying the Jew and Making Sense of Modernity* (New York: Fordham University Press, 2011).

Gilman, Sander. *Jewish Self-Hatred: Anti-Semitism and the Secret Language of the Jews* (Baltimore, MD: Johns Hopkins University Press, 1986).

– *The Jew's Body* (New York: Routledge, 1991).

Gluzman, Michael. *HaGuf HaTzioni: Le'umiyut, Migdar u-Miniyut ba-Sifrut ha-Ivrit ha-Chadashah* [The Zionist Body: Nationalism, Gender and Sexuality in Modern Hebrew Literature] (Tel Aviv: Ha-Kibbutz Ha-Meuchad, 2007).

Goldstein, Eric. *The Price of Whiteness: Jews, Race, and American Identity* (Princeton, NJ: Princeton University Press, 2006).

Greenspoon, Leonard J., ed. *Jews in the Gym: Judaism, Sports, and Athletics* (West Lafayette IN: Purdue University Press, 2012).

Gupta, Charu. *Sexuality, Obscenity, and Community: Women, Muslims, and the Hindu Public in Colonial India* (New York: Palgrave, 2001).

Halperin-Kaddari, Ruth; Yaacov, Yadgar. 'Between Universal Feminism and Particular Nationalism: Politics, Religion, and Gender (In)Equality in Israel.' *Third World Quarterly*, Vol. 31, No. 6 (2010) 905–920.

Harrowitz, Nancy; Barbara Hyams, eds. *Jews and Gender: Responses to Otto Weininger* (Philadelphia, PA: Temple University Press, 1994).

Harshav, Benjamin. *Language in Time of Revolution* (Berkeley CA: University of California Press, 1993).

Harvey, David. *Spaces of Hope* (Berkeley CA: University of California Press, 2000).

Hay, Marnie. *Bulmer Hobson and the Nationalist Movement in Twentieth-Century Ireland* (Manchester: Manchester University Press, 2009).

Havrelock, Rachel. *River Jordan: The Mythology of a Dividing Line* (Chicago: University of Chicago Press, 2011).

Higate, Paul R., ed. *Military Masculinities: Identity and the State* (Westport, CT: Praeger, 2003).

Hobsbawm, Eric. *Nations and Nationalism Since 1780: Programme, Myth, Reality* (Cambridge: Canto/Cambridge University Press, 1991).

Hobsbawm, Eric; Terence Ranger, eds. *The Invention of Tradition* (Cambridge: Cambridge University Press, 2012) 2nd Edition.

Horkheimer, Max. Theodor Adorno; Gunzelin Schmid Noerr, ed.; Edmund Jephcott, trans. *Dialectic of Enlightenment: Philosophical Fragments* (Stanford CA: Stanford University Press, 2002).

Howe, Stephen. *Ireland and Empire: Colonial Legacies in Irish History and Culture* (Oxford: Oxford University Press, 2000).

Hug, Chrystel. *The Politics of Sexual Morality in Ireland* (London: Palgrave-Macmillan, 1999).

Ignatiev, Noel. *How the Irish Became White* (New York: Routledge, 2008)

Inglis, Tom. *Moral Monopoly: The Rise and Fall of the Catholic Church in Modern Ireland* (Dublin: UCD Press, 1998) 2nd Edition.

– *Global Ireland: Same Difference* (New York: Routledge, 2008).

Kanaaneh, Rhoda Ann. *Birthing the Nation: Strategies of Palestinian Women in Israel* (Berkeley CA: University of California Press, 2002).

Kamel Kawar, Widad; Tania Nasir. 'The Traditional Palestinian Costume.' *Journal of Palestine Studies*, Vol.10, No. 1 (Autumn, 1980) 118–129.

Kane, Anne. *Constructing Irish National Identity: Discourse and Ritual During the Land War* (New York: Palgrave Macmillan, 2011).

Katvan, Eyal; Margalit Shilo; Ruth Halperin-Kaddari, eds. *Chuka Achat u-Mishpat echad la-Ish ve-la-Isha: Nashim, Zechuiot u-Mishpat bi-Tekufat ha-Mandat* [One Rule for a Man and One Law for a Woman: Women, Rights and Law in the British Mandate Period] (Ramat Gan: Bar-Ilan University Press, 2010).

Kemp, Adriana. 'Ha-Gvul Ke-Pnei Yanos: Merchav ve-Toda'ah Le'umit Be-Yisrael' [The Border as a Janus Face: Space and National Consciousness in Israel]. *Teoria u-Vikoret* [Theory and Criticism]. Vol. 16 (2000) 13–42.

Kennedy, Finola. *Frank Duff: A Life Story* (London: Continuum, 2011).

Kiberd, Declan. *Idir Dhá Chultúr* [Between Two Cultures] (Dublin: Coiscéim, 1993).

– *Inventing Ireland: The Literature of the Modern Nation* (Cambridge MA: Harvard University Press, 1996).

– *Irish Classics* (Cambridge MA: Harvard University Press, 2001).

– *Ulysses and Us: The Art of Everyday Life in Joyce's Masterpiece* (New York: W.W. Norton, 2009).

Kimmerling, Baruch. *Zionism and Territory: The Socio-Territorial Dimensions of Zionist Politics* (Berkeley, CA: University of California Press/Institute of International Studies, 1983).

– *The Invention and Decline of Israeliness: State, Society and the Military* (Berkeley, CA: University of California Press, 2001).

– *Clash of Identities: Explorations in Israeli and Palestinian Societies* (New York: Columbia University Press, 2008).

Knirck, Jason. 'A Cult of No Personality: W.T. Cosgrave and the Election of 1933.' *Éire-Ireland*, Volume 47, Nos. 3&4 (Fall/Winter, 2012) 64–90.

Kostick, Conor. *Revolution in Ireland: Popular Militancy, 1917–1923* (Cork: Cork University Press, 2009) 2nd Edition.

Kugelmass, Jack, ed. *Jews, Sports and the Rites of Citizenship* (Urbana IL: University of Illinois Press, 2007).

Laffan, Michael. *The Partition of Ireland: 1911–1925* (Dundalk: Dundalgan Press/Dublin Historical Association, 1983).

– *The Resurrection of Ireland: The Sinn Féin Party, 1916–1923* (Cambridge: Cambridge University Press, 1999).

Lainer-Vos, Dan. *Sinews of the Nation: Constructing Irish and Zionist Bonds in the United States* (Cambridge: Polity Press, 2013).

Landes Joan D., ed. *Feminism, the Public and the Private* (Oxford: Oxford University Press, 1998).

Lee, J.J. *The Modernisation of Irish Society* (Dublin: Gill and Macmillan, 1973).

Lee J.J.; Gearóid Ó Tuathaigh. *The Age of de Valera* (Dublin: Ward River Press/Radio Telefís Éireann, 1982).

Lee, Marti D.; Ed Madden, eds. *Irish Studies: Geographies and Genders* (Cambridge: Cambridge Scholars Publishing, 2008).
Leeds Craig, Maxine. *Sorry I Don't Dance: Why Men Refuse to Move* (Oxford: Oxford University Press, 2014).
Lloyd, David. *Anomalous States: Irish Writing and the Post-Colonial Moment* (Durham, NC: Duke University Press, 1993).
Losurdo, Domenico; Gregory Elliot, trans. *Liberalism: A Counter-History* (London: Verso, 2011).
Luddy, Maria. *Prostitution and Irish Society, 1800–1940* (Cambridge: Cambridge University Press, 2007).
Mac Giolla Chríost, Diarmait. *Jailtacht: The Irish Language, Symbolic Power and Political Violence in Northern Ireland, 1972–2008* (Cardiff: University of Wales Press/Gwasg Prifysgol Cymru, 2012).
Maher, John. *Slouching Towards Jerusalem: Reactive Nationalism in the Irish, Israeli and Palestinian Novel, 1985–2005* (Dublin: Irish Academic Press, 2012).
Mandle, W.F. *The Gaelic Athletic Association and Irish Nationalist Politics, 1884–1924* (Dublin: Gill and Macmillan, 1987).
Manela, Erez. *The Wilsonian Moment: Self-Determination and the International Origins of Anticolonial Nationalism* (Oxford: Oxford University Press, 2007).
Margalit Stern, Bat-Sheva. 'Who's the Fairest of Them All? Women, Womanhood, and Ethnicity in Zionist Eretz Israel.' *Nashim: A Journal of Jewish Women's Studies & Gender Issues*, Vol. 11 (Spring, 2006) 142–163.
Masalha, Nur. *The Bible and Zionism: Invented Traditions, Archaeology and Post-Colonialism in Israel-Palestine* (London: Zed Books, 2007).
Massad, Joseph. *Desiring Arabs* (Chicago: University of Chicago Press, 2007).
Mathews, P.J. *Revival: The Abbey Theatre, Sinn Féin, The Gaelic League and the Co-Operative Movement* (Cork: Cork University Press, 2003).
Mattingly, Carol. *Well-Tempered Women: Nineteenth-Century Temperance Rhetoric* (Carbondale, IL: Southern Illinois University Press, 1998).
Maume, Patrick. *The Long Gestation: Irish Nationalist Life, 1891–1918* (New York: St. Martin's Press, 1999).
McCabe, Conor. *Sins of the Father: Tracing the Decisions that Shaped the Irish Economy* (Dublin: The History Press Ireland, 2011).
McClintock, Anne. 'Family Feuds: Gender, Nationalism and the Family.' *Feminist Review*, No. 44 (Summer, 1993) 61–80.
McCormack, W.J. *Roger Casement in Death: Or, Haunting the Free State* (Dublin: UCD Press, 2003).
McDevitt, Patrick F. *May The Best Man Win: Sport, Masculinity, and Nationalism in Great Britain and the Empire, 1880–1935* (New York: Palgrave Macmillan, 2004).
McGarry, Fearghal. *Eoin O'Duffy: A Self-Made Hero* (Oxford: Oxford University Press, 2007).
– *The Rising, Ireland: Easter 1916* (Oxford: Oxford University Press, 2010).

McGaughey, Jane. *Ulster's Men: Protestant Unionist Masculinities and Militarization in the North of Ireland, 1912–1923* (Montreal: McGill-Queen's University Press, 2012).

McKibben, Sarah. *Endangered Masculinities in Irish Poetry, 1540–1780* (Dublin: UCD Press, 2010).

McMahon, Timothy. *Grand Opportunity: The Gaelic Revival and Irish Society, 1893–1910* (Syracuse NY: Syracuse University Press, 2008).

Meehan, Ciara. *The Cosgrave Party: A History of Cumann na nGaedheal, 1923–33* (Dublin: Royal Irish Academy, 2010)

Mendelsohn, Ezra. *Class Struggle in the Pale: The Formative Years of the Jewish Worker' Movement in Tsarist Russia* (Cambridge: Cambridge University Press, 1970).

– ed. *Jews and the Sporting Life: Studies in Contemporary Jewry, An Annual, XXIII* (Oxford: Oxford University Press, 2008).

Memmi, Albert. *The Colonizer and the Colonized* (Boston: Beacon Press, 1991).

Miller, Kerby. *Ireland and Irish-America: Culture, Class, and Transatlantic Migration* (Dublin: Field Day, 2008).

Mitchell, Timothy. *Colonising Egypt* (Berkeley CA: University of California Press, 1988).

Moran, James. *Staging the Easter Rising: 1916 as Theatre* (Cork: Cork University Press, 2005).

Mort, Frank. *Capital Affairs: London and the Making of the Permissive Society* (New Haven, CT: Yale University Press, 2010).

Mosse, George. *Toward the Final Solution: A History of European Racism* (New York: Harper & Row, 1978).

– *Nationalism and Sexuality: Respectability and Abnormal Sexuality in Modern Europe* (New York: Howard Fertig, 1985).

– *Fallen Soldiers: Reshaping the Memory of the World Wars* (Oxford: Oxford University Press, 1990).

– *The Image of Man: The Creation of Modern Masculinity* (Oxford: Oxford University Press, 1996).

Murphy, Brian. *Patrick Pearse and the Lost Republican Ideal* (Dublin: James Duffy, 1991).

Myers, David N. *Re-Inventing the Jewish Past: European Jewish Intellectuals and the Zionist Return to History* (Oxford: Oxford University Press, 1995).

Najmabadi, Afsaneh. *Women with Mustaches and Men without Beards: Gender and Sexual Anxieties of Iranian Modernity* (Berkeley CA: California University Press, 2005).

Nic Congáil, Ríona. *Úna Ní Fhaircheallaigh agus an Fhís Útóipeach Ghaelach* [Úna Ní Fhaircheallaigh and the Gaelic Utopian Vision] (Dublin: Arlen House, 2010).

- '"Looking on for Centuries from the Sideline": Gaelic Feminism and the Rise of Camogie.' *Éire-Ireland*, Volume 48, Nos. 1 & 2 (Spring/Summer 2013) 168–190.
Nirenberg, David. *Anti-Judaism: The Western Tradition* (New York: W.W. Norton, 2013).
Novick, Ben. *Conceiving Revolution: Nationalist Propaganda During The First World War* (Dublin: Four Courts Press, 2001).
Ó Broin, León. *Frank Duff: A Biography* (Dublin: Gill and Macmillan, 1982).
Ó Conchubhair, Brian. *Fin de Siècle na Gaeilge: Darwin, An Athbheochan agus Smaointearacht na hEorpa* [Irish Language *Fin de Siècle*: Darwin, the Gaelic Revival and European Intellectual Thought] (Indreabhán: Cló Iar-Chonnachta, 2009).
Ó Gráda, Cormac. *Ireland Before and After the Famine: Explorations in Economic History, 1800–1925* (Manchester, Manchester University Press, 1993) 2nd Edition.
 – *Ireland: A New Economic History, 1780–1939* (Oxford: Oxford University Press, 1994).
 – *A Rocky Road: The Irish Economy since the 1920s* (Manchester: Manchester University Press, 1997).
Ó Laoire, Muiris. *Athbheochan na hEabhraise: Ceacht don Ghaeilge?* [The Hebrew Revival: A Lesson for the Irish Language?] (Dublin: An Clóchomhar, 1999).
O'Hearn, Denis. *The Atlantic Economy: Britain, the US and Ireland* (Manchester: Manchester University Press, 2001).
O'Sullivan, Donal J. *The Depot: A History of the Garda Síochána Depot at the Phoenix Park, Dublin* (No Place of Publication: Navillus Publishing, 2007).
Pašeta, Senia. *Before the Revolution: Nationalism, Social Change and Ireland's Catholic Elite, 1879–1922* (Cork: Cork University Press, 1999).
Penslar, Derek. *Zionism and Technocracy: The Engineering of Jewish Settlement in Palestine, 1870–1918* (Bloomington, IN: Indiana University Press, 1991).
 – *Shylock's Children: Economics and Jewish Identity in Modern Europe* (Berkeley CA: University of California Press, 2001).
 – *Jews and the Military: A History* (Princeton, NJ: Princeton University Press, 2013).
Piterberg, Gabriel. *The Returns of Zionism: Myths, Politics and Scholarship in Israel* (London: Verso, 2008)
Pomeranz, Kenneth. *The Great Divergence: China, Europe, and the Making of the Modern World Economy* (Princeton, NJ: Princeton University Press, 2000).
Porat, Dan A. 'Between Nation and Land in Zionist Teaching of Jewish History, 1920-1954'. *Journal of Israeli History*, Vol. 27, No. 2 (2008) 253–268.
Portugese, Jacqueline. *Fertility Policy in Israel: The Politics of Religion, Gender and Nation* (London: Praeger, 1998).

Poulantzas, Nicos; Patrick Camiller, trans. *State, Power, Socialism* (London: New Left Books, 1978).
Presner, Todd Samuel. *Muscular Judaism: The Jewish Body and the Politics of Regeneration* (London: Routledge, 2007).
Rabinovitch, Lara; Shiri Goren, eds. *Choosing Yiddish: New Frontiers of Language and Culture* (Detroit: Wayne State University Press, 2013).
Regan, John M. *The Irish Counter-Revolution, 1921–1936: Treatyite Politics and Settlement in Independent Ireland* (Dublin: Gill and Macmillan, 1999).
— *Myth and the Irish State* (Dublin: Irish Academic Press, 2013).
Reuveni, Gideon; Sarah Wobick-Segev, eds. *The Economy in Jewish History: New Perspectives On The Interrelationship Between Ethnicity and Economic Life* (New York: Berghahn Books, 2010).
Reynolds, Paige. *Modernism, Drama, and the Audience for Irish Spectacle* (Cambridge: Cambridge University Press, 2007).
Roach Pierson, Ruth; Nupur Chaudhuri, eds. *Nation, Empire, Colony: Historicizing Gender and Race* (Bloomington, IN: Indiana University Press, 1998).
Roediger, David R. *The Wages of Whiteness: Race and the Making of the American Working Class* (London: Verso, 1991).
Rozin, Orit. *The Rise of the Individual in 1950s Israel: A Challenge to Collectivism* (Waltham, MA: Brandeis University Press, 2011).
Ryan, Louise. *Gender, Identity and the Irish Press, 1922–1937: Embodying the Nation* (New York: Edwin Mellen, 2002).
Ryan, Louise; Margaret Ward, eds. *Irish Women and Nationalism: Soldiers, New Women and Wicked Hags* (Dublin: Irish Academic Press, 2003).
Saposnik, Arieh. *Becoming Hebrew: The Creation of a Jewish National Culture in Ottoman Palestine* (Oxford: Oxford University Press, 2008).
Seidman, Naomi. *A Marriage Made in Heaven: The Sexual Politics of Hebrew and Yiddish* (Berkeley, CA: University of California Press, 1997).
Segev, Tom, *1949: The First Israelis* (New York: The Free Press, 1986).
Semyonov, Moshe; Noah Lewin-Epstein, eds. *Stratification in Israel: Class, Ethnicity, and Gender* (London: Transaction Publishers, 2004).
Sengoopta, Chandak. *Otto Weininger: Sex, Sciences and Self in Imperial Vienna* (Chicago: University of Chicago Press, 2000).
Shafir, Gershon. *Land, Labor and the Origins of the Israeli-Palestinian Conflict, 1881–1914* (Berkeley CA: University of California Press, 1996).
Shapira, Anita. *Cherev ha-Yonah: ha-Tzyonutve-ha-Ko'ach, 1881–1948* [The Dove's Sword: Zionism and Force, 1881–1948]. (Tel Aviv: Am Oved, 1992).
— William Templer, trans. *Land and Power: The Zionist Resort to Force, 1881–1948* (Stanford CA: Stanford University Press, 1999).
Sisson, Elaine. *Pearse's Patriots: St. Enda's and the Cult of Boyhood* (Cork: Cork University Press, 2004).
Smith, James M. *Ireland's Magdalen Laundries and The Nation's Architecture of Containment* (South Bend, IN: University of Notre Dame Press, 2007).

Smith, Neil. *Uneven Development: Nature, Capital, and the Production of Space* (Athens GA: University of Georgia Press, 2008) 3rd Edition.
Stanislawski, Michael. *Zionism and the Fin de Siècle: Cosmopolitanism and Nationalism from Nordau to Jabotinsky* (Berkeley, CA: University of California Press, 2001).
Sufian, Sandra M. *Healing the Land and the Nation: Malaria and the Zionist Project in Palestine, 1920–1947* (Chicago: University of Chicago Press, 2007).
Tosh, John. *A Man's Place: Masculinity and the Middle-Class Home in Victorian England* (New Haven, CT: Yale University Press, 1999).
Toury, Gideon 'The Hebraization of Surnames as a Motive in Hebrew Literature.' *Actes du XVIe Congrès international des sciences onomastiques Québec, Université Laval, 16–22 août 1987* (Québec: Presses de l'Université Laval, 1990) 545–555.
Trachtenberg, Joshua. *Jewish Magic and Superstition: A Study in Folk Religion* (New York: Behrman's Jewish Book House, 1939).
Trevor-Roper, Hugh. *The Invention of Scotland: Myth and History* (New Haven, CT: Yale University Press, 2009).
Tyrell, Ian. *Woman's World/Woman's Empire: The Woman's Christian Temperance Union in International Perspective, 1800–1930* (Chapel Hill NC: University of North Carolina Press, 1991).
Valente, Joseph. *The Myth of Manliness in Irish National Culture, 1882–1922* (Urbana IL: University of Illinois Press, 2011).
Wallerstein, Immanuel. *The Modern World-System I: Capitalist Agriculture and the Rise of the European World-Economy in the Sixteenth Century* (Berkeley CA: University of California Press, 2011) 2nd Edition.
    – *The Modern World-System III: The Second Era of Great Expansion of the Capitalist World-Economy, 1730s–1840s* (Berkeley CA: University of California Press, 2011) 2nd Edition.
Ward, Margaret. *Unmanageable Revolutionaries: Women and Irish Nationalism* (London: Pluto Press, 1983).
Weber, Eugen. *Peasants into Frenchmen: The Modernization of Rural France, 1870–1914* (Stanford CA: Stanford University Press, 1976).
Whelan, Yvonne 'Monuments, Power and Contested space: the Iconography of Sackville Street (O'Connell Street) before Independence (1922). *Irish Geography*, Vol. 34, No.1 (2001) 11–33.
Whyte, J.H. *Church and State in Modern Ireland, 1923–1970* (Dublin: Gill and Macmillan, 1971).
Wills, Clair. *That Neutral Island: A Cultural History of Ireland During World War II* (London: Faber & Faber, 2008).
Winter, Alison. *Mesmerized: Powers of Mind in Victorian Britain* (Chicago: University of Chicago Press, 1998).
Wulff, Helena. *Dancing at the Crossroads: Memory and Mobility in Ireland* (New York: Berghahn Books, 2009)

Zertal, Idith, Akiva Eldar. *Lords of the Land: The War over Israel's Settlements in the Occupied Territories, 1967–2007* (New York: Nation Books, 2007).

Zerubavel, Yael. *Recovered Roots: Collective Memory and the Making of Israeli National Tradition* (Chicago: University of Chicago Press, 1995).

Zuckermann, Ghil'ad. 'Af Achad Lo Medaber Ivrit' [Nobody at All Speaks Hebrew]. *NRG-Ma'ariv*, 25 December 2008.

INDEX[1]

A

Acton, John Dalberg, Lord, 35
African-Americans, 8
Aiken, Frank, 163, 164
Ailtirí na hAiséríghe [Architects of the Resurrection], 140
Algeria, 192
Anglo-Irish Treaty
  accusations about opponents of, 3
  accusations about supporters of, 3
An t-Óglách [The Youthful Volunteer], 43, 56n130
Antrim, 62
Arabic language, 96
Armagh, 23, 38, 46n18
Army Comrades Association. *See* Blueshirts
Ashe, Thomas, 31
Australia, 96

B

Baluchistan, 99
Barry, Tom, 36–7, 53n85, 80, 106
Basque language, 130
Béarlachais [Hiberno-English], 12, 127, 128, 139
Béaslaí, Piaras [Percy Frederick Beazley], 135
Beirut, 96
Ben-Gurion, David [David Grün]
  views on Hebrew and Yiddish of, 135, 139
Bennett, G.C., 166
Benvenisti, Meron, 96
Ben-Yehuda, Ben-Tsiyon [Itamar Ben-Avi], 135–6
Ben-Yehuda, Eliezer [Eliezer Yitzhak Perlman], 135
Betar, 47n30, 76, 77
Bialik, Chaim Nachman, 102, 139

[1] Note: Page numbers followed by "n" refers to end notes.

Blueshirts, The, 168, 169
Blythe, Ernest
  as Minister for Local Government, 64–6, 161
Breen, Dan
  My Fight For Irish Freedom (1924), 22, 45n3, 45n4
Brenner, Yosef Chaim, 139
Brian Boru, 21, 23, 45n3
Brighid, 126, 144n29
Brixton Prison, 28, 49n47
Brugha, Cathal, 151n103, 196
Butler, Mary, 132, 145n49

C

Callan MacArdle, Thomas, 199, 202
Camogie, 79
Canaanite Movement, 139
Canada, 96, 183n90, x
Carlow, 35
Carrigan, William, 204
Carrigan Committee, The, 204–7, 218n84, 221n107
Casement, Roger, 28, 46n11
Castleknock, 97
Catholic Truth Society, 201, 202, 216n52, 217n73, 218n74
Ceannt, Áine, 126, 144n30
Childers, Erskine, 43
Christian Science Monitor, 105, 117n77
Churchill, Winston, 135
Civil War, Irish, 190
Claddagh, The, 97
Claidheamh Soluis, An [The Sword of Light], 124, 144n24, 145n37, 145n47
Clann na Talmhan [Family of the Land], 174, 184n105
Clare, 21, 46n22, 183
Clonsilla, 97

Collins, Michael, 71, 104, 105, 116n73, 135
Committee on Evil Literature, The, 200, 202, 217n71, 218n76
Commonwealth Conference, 172, 183n90
Congo Free State, 106–7
Conradh na Gaeilge (*see* Gaelic League)
Conservative Party (Britain), 2
Contraceptives, 203, 207, 208, 219n90
Cork, city, 111, 216n52
Cork, county, 98
Cork Gaol, 30
Cork Women's Christian Temperance Association, 199
Cormac Mac Airt, 98
Cosgrave, W.T.
  and Fine Gael, 166, 168, 170
  hostility towards women of, 191
  leadership of *Cumann na nGaedheal* of, 166, 168, 170
  as Minister for Local Government, 191
Costello, Evelyn, 197
Council of the Church of Ireland Temperance Society, 197
Craig, James, 219n86
Craoibhín Aoibhinn, An (*see* Hyde, Douglas)
Criminal Law Amendment Act (1935), 203, 204, 207, 218n80, 218n82, 219n91, 220n99, 220n101. *See also* Carrigan Committee
Cruise O'Brien, Conor, 207, 220n96
Cumann Camógaíochta, An [The Camogie Association], 79, 80
Cumann na mBan [The Women's Organisation]
  relationship with male nationalist groups, 80
Cumann na nGaedhael [The Organisation of the Irish]

conservative economic policies of, 160
membership structure of, 42
and 1932 "Red Scare"`, 165–9
Cusack, Michael
as basis for *The Citizen*, 60
and Gaelic Athletic Association, 60, 78
Cyprus, 99, 110

D

Dáil Éireann, 21
Dalcassians, 22, 46n12
Darwinism, 127
Davis, Thomas, 62, 123, 227, 232n12
Davitt, Michael, 7, 61, 229
De Coubertin, Pierre, Baron, 79
Dempsey, James, 200
De Roiste, Liam, 36, 53n84, 104
De Valera, Eamon
East Clare by-election 1917, and, 22, 39, 163
and *Fianna Fáil*, 155, 162, 163, 165, 166, 169–71, 175, 176, 184n98
Hispanic origins of, 166
views on Anglo-Irish Treaty of, 155
views on partition of, 7, 105
views on Ulster Protestants of, 105
as a woman, 25
Devane, Richard, 201, 205, 208
Devoy, John, 91
Dillon, John, 23, 24
Disraeli, Benjamin, 36
Donovan, Robert, 200
Dracula (1897), 8
Dublin, city
international reputation of, 192
urban geography of, 193
Dublin Castle, 23, 46n15
Dublin Hurling Club, 61, 84

Dubnow, Simon, 102
Dubnow, Vladimir (Ze'ev), 102
Duff, Frank, 191–3, 195, 197, 205, 207, 214n18, 214n22, 215n37, 215n38, 215n42
Duff, John, 197

E

Eason, Charles, 202, 218n75
Easter Rising
as blood sacrifice, 26
as theatre, 99
Economic History of the Land of Erin, The (1932), 153–6
Economic War, The, 108, 155, 165, 168–75
Ellis, Havelock, 203
Emmet, Robert, 42
Encyclopaedia Britannica, 192
Engels, Friedrich, 8
England, English
Irish nationalist views of, 36
Ennis, 170, 192
Eoghan Roe [Owen Roe O'Neill], 31
Essex, 99

F

Fáinne an Lae [Dawning of the Day], 124, 138, 144n23
Fairfax, Thomas, Lord, 99
Famine, The, 7, 43, 62, 127, 166, 169–71, 183n98
Fanon, Frantz, 64
Fianna Fáil [Soldiers of Irish Destiny]
accusations of communism against, 165, 167
agrarian politics of, 155–7, 159, 160, 162–5
conservatism of, 175

as heirs of Sinn Féin economic policy, 162, 163
Fine Gael [Tribe of the Irish]
  activities during Economic War of, 168, 169, 175
  fascist elements in, 168
  origins of, 166
Fionn Mac Cumhaill, 97
Fitzgerald, Desmond, 41
Fitzgerald, Edward, Lord, 24
Flanagan, John, Rev., 197
Forde, Patrick, 125
Freeman's Journal, 124, 143n22
Free Masons, 153

G

Gaeilge. *See* Irish Language
Gaelic Athletic Association, The, 12, 60, 83n8–10, 84n13, 84n17, 84n23, 84n25, 229
Gaelic Football, 62
Gaelic League, The
  annual gathering *[Oireachtas]* of, 133, 134
  Branch of the Five Provinces *[Craobh na gCúig Cúigí]* of, 136
  educational work of, 98, 123
  Seachtain na Gaeilge [Irish language week], 128
  and traditional Irish clothing, 133
Gaelic Union, The, 124
Gallagher, Frank [Prionnsias Ó Gallchobhair], 106
Galway, city, 96
Galway, county, 97
Garda Síochána, An [Guardians of the Peace]
  and anti-leftist activity, 165
  attitudes towards women of, 77, 78
  masculinist ideology of, 9
  publications of, 87n65

and raid on "Monto", 191
and regulation of public dancing, 208
General Post Office (GPO), Dublin, 100, 180n44
Geoghegan, James, 203, 207, 208, 220n95
Glasnevin Cemetery, 91–3, 112n8, 112n16
Glún na Buaidhe [The Victorious Generation], 140, 151n105
Granuaile, 23
Great War. *See* World War One
Greenberg, Uri Tzvi, 135
Griffith, Arthur
  "self-hatred" of, 37
  views of Anglo-Irish Treaty, 107
Grossman, David, 138
Gwynn, Denis, 28, 49n37, 49n38

H

Hannon, John, Rev., 204, 219n90
Ha-Shachar [The Dawn], 137
Ha-Shomer Ha-Tzair [The Young Guard], 102
Haskalah [Jewish Enlightenment], 157
Hebrew language
  compared to Yiddish, 135, 136, 138–41
  Hebrew names, 135, 147n67
Herzl, Theodor
  The Jews State [1896], 110
  views on national space of, 101, 110
Heuston, Séan, 189
Hobson, Bulmer, 36, 49n38, 53n82, 53n83
Hogan, Seán, 22
Hope, Jimmy, 106
Horgan, John J., 197, 207
Hotel, Restaurant and Catering Association of Ireland, 198–9

INDEX   261

Hungarian language, 139
Hurling, 61, 62, 65, 79, 83n1, 84n11
Hyde, Douglas *[An Craoibhín Aoibhinn]*
  and Irish names, 136
  views on Irish language of, 128

I
India, 16n17, 52n80, 99, 188
Inginidhe na hEireann [The Daughters of Ireland], 190
Ingoldsby, Patrick [Pádraic Mac Giolla Iosa], 137
Inter-Departmental Committee of Inquiry Regarding Venereal Disease (1926), 193, 215n33
Intoxicating Liquors Act (1927), 196
Intoxicating Liquors Commission (1925), 196
Ireland, Irish
  alcohol and, 196
  ancient Irish, idealised, 12
  colonial status of, 127
  compared to Czechoslovaks, 40
  compared to English, 4, 12, 37, 97, 103, 107, 135
  economic links with Great Britain of, 160, 171
  historiography of, 228, 231
  as original Europeans, 226
  racial identity of, 12, 107
  slavery, claims of, 14, 37, 166
Irish Assocation for the Prevention of Intemperance, 199, 217n63
Irish Brewers Associaton, 198
Irish Citizen Army, 92, 100
Irish Ecclesiastical Record, 201, 217n70, 217n71, 221n107
Irish Freedom, 27, 52n75, 63–5, 67, 79, 85n31, 85n33, 85n35, 89n98, 101, 213n11

Irish Free State
  "architecture of containment" of, 195
  censorship in, 200, 202, 203, 212
  economics of, 190, 197, 198
  gender politics of, 190
  religion in, 188
Irish Language
  as European language, 139
  gender ideology of, 121–3, 140–2
  revival of, 123, 124, 131, 136
Irish Nationalism
  and prostitution, 192, 198, 204, 205, 207, 212
  role of women in, 190
  and "self-hatred" of, 11, 33–40, 51n69, 52n71, 52n72, 159
  "strong farmer" ideal of, 155–7, 169, 176
Irish Parliamentary Party (IPP), 2, 22–4, 38, 39, 130, 163
Irish Republican Army (IRA), 36–8, 43, 48n34, 53n93, 68, 72, 163, 164, 167, 182n68, 230
Irish Republican Brotherhood (IRB), 46n22, 46n23, 48n32, 62, 64, 91, 121
Irish Tourists Association, 199
Irish Vigilance Association, 204
Irish Volunteers, 2, 12, 48n32, 56n130, 64, 66, 67, 85n36, 85n45, 86n46, 89n114, 92, 112n8
Irisleabhar na Gaedhilge [The Gaelic Journal], 124, 143n20, 143n21
Israel, Land of. *See* Palestine
Israel, State of
  Israeli Defence Forces, 222n122
  Israeli Ministry of Education and Culture, 139
  status of women in, 77

J

Jabotinsky, Ze'ev [Vladimir], 7, 76, 77, 102, 110
Jalowicz, Herman, 74
Jamaica, 99
Jerusalem, 13, 96
Jesuits, 201, 204, 205, 221n106
Jews
  and claims of degeneration of, 34
  and exile, dispersion of, 35
  and racial identity of, 6
Johnson, Thomas, 161, 171, 183n90
Joyce, James, 11, 60, 83n6, 83n8, 191, 201, 242
Joy McCracken, Henry, 106

K

Kane, R.R., Rev., 137
Kashmir, 111
Kennedy, H.B., Rev., 204
Kent, 99
Kenya, 96
Kerry, 63, 199
Ketav Al Ha-Noar Ha-Ivri [Epistle to the Hebrew Youth], 139, 150n101
Kilkenny, 199
Kingsley, Charles, 5
Kitchener, Herbert Horatio, 96
Klausner, Joseph, 141, 152n109
Kosovo, 111

L

Labour Party (Ireland), 171
Labour Party (Israel), 212
Land War, The, 155, 157, 169
Lane-Poole, Stanley, 130
Lawrence, T.E., 96
Legion of Mary, The, 191, 196, 214n18

Lemass, Séan, 162, 167, 174, 175, 184n107
Lennon, Peter, 213n1, 217n67
Leo XIII, Pope, 202
Leslie, Shane, 133, 135
Lessing, Theodor, 33
Lewes Jail, 31
Lewis, Sinclair, 24, 218n78
Liberal Party (Britain), 2
Licenced Grocers and Vintners Association, 198
Lloyd George, David, 2, 28, 49n44
Loughrea, 61
Lynch, Patrick, 22, 24

M

MacCurtain, Tomás, 31
MacDonagh, Thomas
  fradulent last speech of, 32
  and Irish Volunteers, 66, 92
  and O'Donovan Rossa funeral, 92, 112n9, 112n10, 112n14, 112n15
MacEntee, Séan, 172–3, 184n107
MacMurrough, Dermot, 42
MacNeill, Eoin, 126, 144n30, 144n31, 149n82
MacSwiney, Mary
  and Eamon de Valera, 29, 30, 190
MacSwiney, Terence
  death of, 28
  and O'Donovan Rossa funeral, 94
  Principles of Freedom (1921), 34, 52n75, 111n1
Maebh, 126, 144n29
Magnes, Judah Leb, 109, 118n101
Malta, 99
Markievicz, Constance
  gendered representation of, 41, 81
  propaganda art by, 41
Martyrdom

and nationalism, 13, 31, 32, 77
and religion, 33
Marx, Karl, 51n70
Masada, 26
Mauritius, 99
Maynooth, 125
McCarron, E.P., 191
McCartan, Patrick, 38, 46n18, 54n97
McElligot, J.J., 197
McGahern, John, 214n18, 229, 231n1, 233n17
McGilligan, Patrick, 161, 167
Meir, Golda [Goldie Myerson], 135
Mellows, Liam, 106
Mexico, 166, 167
Meyer, Kuno, 130
Milton, John, 128
Mitchel, John, 106
Monroe, Henry, 106
Monto [Montgomery Street, Dublin], 191–6, 198, 201, 210, 215n47
Moore Pim, Herbert, 38, 54n95
Morrin, Francis J., 204
Moylan, Seán, 175
Mulcahy, Richard, 41, 167
Murphy, James, 197

N
Na gCopaleen, Myles, 149n81
Napper Tandy, 62, 84n17
National Society for the Prevention of Cruelty to Children, 204
National Volunteers, 67, 93
Negev Naming Committee, 96
Newfoundland, 99
Ní Bhriain, Neilí [Nelly O'Brien], 136, 149n78
Ní Chinnéide, Máire, 79
Ní Dhonnchadha, Cáit, 79
Ní Dhubhghaill, C. Maire [Crissie M. Doyle], 126, 144n29

Ní Fhaircheallaigh, Una [Agnes Farrelly]
and Gaelic League, 98, 137, 148n73
support for camogie of, 79
Nordau, Max
and *Muskeljudentum*, 74–6, 102
Northern Whig, 225, 232n4

O
O'Carroll, V., 204
O'Connell, Thomas, 200
O'Connell Street [Sackville Street], 100, 102n9, 180n44
O'Connor, Batt, 42
O'Connor, T.P., 28, 38
Ó Donnchadha, Tadhg, 79
O'Donnell, Hugh Roe, 106
O'Donnell, Peadar, 164–5, 173–4, 181n54, 181n57, 181n58
O'Donnell, Thomas, 170
O'Donovan Rossa, Jeremiah
funeral of, 12, 91, 92, 94, 112n8, 112n9
O'Duffy, Eoin
and An Garda Síochána, 9, 68, 69
and Blueshirts, 71, 168
and Carrigan Committee, 204–6
hostility towards public dancing of, 207
views on Irish masculinity, 10, 64
O'Duffy, Sean, 79
O'Farrell, J.T., 197
O'Flanagan, Michael, 38
O'Flynn, Thomas, 195, 214n20, 215n30, 215n43
O'Hegarty, P.S.
hostility towards women of, 41
The Victory of Sinn Féin, 40, 189, 213n8

writings on Terence MacSwiney, 30, 49n43
O'Hickey, Michael, 125, 130, 144n25, 145n43
O'Higgins, Brian (Brian O hUiginn), 28, 49n41, 79, 89n98, 140, 151n103
O'Higgins, Kevin
  and Committee on Evil Literature, 202
  views on de Valera of, 166
O'Kelly, Sean T. [Seán T. Ó Ceallaigh], 172, 183n93
O'Malley, Ernie
O'Malley, Grace. *See* Granuaile
O'Neill, John, 197
Orr, William, 106
Oz, Amos [Amos Klausner], 152n109

P

Palestine
  tiyul [tour] of, 95
Palestine Exploration Fund, 96
Palestinians, 76, 110, 146n59, 159, 211
Parnell, Charles Stewart, 11, 24
Partition, 3, 7, 13, 14n4, 105–11, 118, 118n102
Pearse, Patrick
  and Easter Rising, 11, 31
  and Irish Volunteers, 67
  The Murder Machine, 122–3
  and O'Donovan Rossa funeral, 91, 93, 94, 113n19
  prose writings of, 31, 125
  speculation over sexuality of, 9
  and St. Enda's College, 83n1
  and traditional Irish clothing, 133, 134
Philadelphia, 47n31, 51n69, 123
Philistines, 110, 119n110

Phoblacht, An [The Republic], 164
Pinsker, Leo
  Auto-Emancipation, 34–6, 52n74, 109, 118n105
  views on national space of, 110
Pioneer Total Abstinence Association, 199, 200, 217n63
Plunkett, George
  electoral propaganda of, 39
Plunkett, Joseph, 31
Poland, 87n67, 135
Polish language, 139
Postcolonialism, vii, 10, 127–31
Poulantzas, Nicos, 173, 184n98
Power, Jane, 204
Public Dance Halls Act (1935), 207–9, 221n108
Punch, 53n93

R

Rathcool, 97
Ratosh, Yonatan, 139–40, 150n101
Redmond, John, 2, 24, 39, 66–7
Register of Prohibited Publications, 203, 218n78
Renan, Ernest, 14
Revisionist Historiography, 229–230
Rhodesia, 96
Romanian language, 139
Royal Irish Constabulary
  as precursor to Garda Síochána, 71, 86n57

S

Sarajevo, 96
Sarsfield, Patrick, 22
Shakespeare, William, 128
Sharret, Moshe [Moshe Shertok], 135
Sholonsky, Avraham, 139
Shortt, Edward, 29, 49n44

Shylock, antisemitic stereotype of, 159
Sierra Leone, 99
Simon Bar Kochba, 26, 74
Sinai Peninsula, 110
Sinn Féin [Newspaper], 36, 40, 63, 84n26
Sinn Féin [Political Party]
　masculine image of, 21–6
Skinnider, Margaret, 39, 54n107
Smolenskin, Peretz, 138
Society for the Preservation of the Irish Language, 124
Soloheadbeg, 21, 45n2
Somerville Lindsay, Thomas, 197
South Africa, 68, 107
Spain, 167
Spenser, Edmund, 98
St. Vincent de Paul Society, 204
Stern, Avraham, 7
Stevenson, J. Sinclair, 200
Stoker, Bram, 8
Stopes, Marie, 203
Stopford-Green, Alice, 37, 38, 53n93
St Patrick's College, 125
Suffragettes, 190, 210

T
Tara, 62, 98
Tchernichovsky, Shaul, 95, 114n29
Tennyson, Alfred, Lord, 128
The O'Rahilly, 67, 85n41
Thomas, J.H., 171, 183n90
Thrift, William, 200
Traynor, Oscar, 55n117, 117n83, 169, 182n82
Treacy, Seán, 22, 100
Trench, Cesca Chenevix [Sadhbh Trinseach], 128, 130
Trumpeldor, Joseph
　"martyrdom" of, 77

U
Uganda, 110
Ulster, 105, 106, 108, 111
Ulysses, 60, 83n6, 201
United Kingdom, 87n62, 94, 99

V
Venereal Disease, 192, 193

W
Wall Street Crash, The, 161
Walsh, J.J.
　resignation from *Cumann na nGaedheal of*, 161
　and Tailteann Games, 226, 231n3, 232n4
War News, 100, 115n49
War of Independence, Irish, 21, 103
Weber, Max, 187
Weininger, Otto, 33, 51n69
Welsh language, 130
West Bank, The, 110
Wexford, 67
William III [William of Orange], 22, 173
Wilson, Richard, 197
Wolfe Tone, Theobald, 23, 24, 43, 46n11, 62, 81, 84n17, 88n91, 89n112, 113n16, 180n42
Wordsworth, William, 128
World Women's Christian Temperance Union, 199, 217n63

Y
Yeshurun, Avot [Yechiel Perlmutter], 135, 147n72

Z

Zionism
- *chalutzim* [pioneers] of, 23
- and creation of "new Jew", 26, 59, 138, 157, 211, 212
- hostility to Diaspora Jews of, 33, 113n27
- and *kibbutz* movement, 159, 176
- language politics of, 13, 138
- and "productivization", 157
- role of women in, 157, 211
- "sabra" ideal of, 156, 157, 159, 160
- and self-hatred, 34, 159
- and sports, 82

Zion Mule Corps, 32

The manufacturer's authorised representative in the EU is Springer Nature Customer Service Centre GmbH, Europaplatz 3, 69115 Heidelberg, Germany. If you have any concerns regarding our products, please contact ProductSafety@springernature.com

Printed and bound by CPI Group (UK) Ltd, Croydon, CR0 4YY

23/03/2026

02076682-0006